LECTURES

TO

PROFESSING CHRISTIANS.

DELIVERED

IN THE CITY OF NEW YORK,

IN THE YEARS 1836 AND 1837.

BY CHARLES G. FINNEY.

FROM NOTES BY THE EDITOR OF THE NEW-YORK EVANGELIST.

REVISED BY THE AUTHOR.

NEW YORK:

JOHN S. TAYLOR, BRICK CHURCH CHAPEL,

OPPOSITE THE CITY HALL.

1837.

Entered according to act of Congress, in the year 1837, by
CHARLES G. FINNEY & JOSHUA LEAVITT,
In the Clerk's Office of the District Court for the Southern District of New York.

CONTENTS.

	PAGE
PREFACE	7
LECTURE I - Self Deceivers.	9
LECTURE II - False Professors.	18
LECTURE III - Doubtful Actions Are Sinful.	29
LECTURE IV - Reproof, a Christian Duty.	47
LECTURE V - True Saints.	60
LECTURE VI - Legal Religion.	71
LECTURE VII - Religion of Public Opinion.	84
LECTURE VIII - Conformity to the World.	100
LECTURE IX - True and False Repentance.	121
LECTURE X - Dishonesty in Small Matters Inconsistent With Honesty in Any thing.	137
LECTURE XI - Bound to Know Your True Character.	149

1837

LECTURE I - True and False Conversions.	166
LECTURE II - True Submission.	183
LECTURE III - Selfishness Not True Religion.	197
LECTURE IV - Religion of the Law and Gospel.	212
LECTURE V - Justification By Faith.	222

LECTURE VI - Sanctification By Faith.	241
LECTURE VII - Legal Experience.	251
LECTURE VIII - Christian Perfection.	266
LECTURE IX - Christian Perfection.	285
LECTURE X - The Way of Salvation.	300
LECTURE XI - The Necessity of Divine Teaching.	312
LECTURE XII - Love is the Whole of Religion.	328
LECTURE XIII - Rest of the Saints.	342
LECTURE XIV - Christ the Husband of the Church.	355

REVIVAL AND HOLINESS THEOLOGY IN AMERICA
AN ALETHEA IN HEART REPRODUCTION
IN THE SERIES OF
THE COMPLETE WORKS OF CHARLES G. FINNEY.
Lecture Notes on Theology.
Skeletons of a Course of Theological Lectures.
Lectures on Systematic Theology I & II.
Lectures on Revivals of Religion, The Complete Restored Text.
The Way of Salvation.
Sermons on Gospel Themes.
Sermons on Important Subjects.
Lectures to Professing Christians.
How to Experience the Higher Life.
How to Pray to God.
The Right Way to "Train up a Child."
The Character, Claims and Practical Workings of Freemasonry.
Knowing and Loving God.
The Love of God for a Sinning World.
The Dreadful Results of Sin.
The Complete Sermon Collection.
The Memoirs of Charles G. Finney.
Letters on Revival and other Matters.
Treasured Memories of Charles G. Finney by his Associates, Students, and Oberlin Friends.

LECTURES TO

PROFESSING CHRISTIANS

REPUBLISHED BY THE EDITOR.
RICK FRIEDRICH OF ALETHEA IN HEART MINISTRIES,
PO BOX 127 Charlotte MI 48813
http://truthinheart.com
(208) 304-2954
JUNE 2001.

Finney, Charles, 1792-1875.
Lectures to Professing Christians.

ISBN 1-932370-12-9

Second Alethea In Heart edition published in 2001.

MANUFACTURED IN THE UNITED STATES OF AMERICA

PREFACE.

As these Lectures occupied from an hour and a quarter to an hour and three quarters in the delivery, it will be seen by their length, as here given, that the reporter took down but little more than a full skeleton of them. I have made but very slight alterations and additions in revising them, for the following reasons:

1. Their publication was determined on too late, so that I had very little time.

2. My ill health and multiplied duties forbade.

3. To have enlarged them much would have swelled the volume beyond the contemplated size.

4. From experience I have learned that the conversational and condensed style in which they were reported, is more interesting and edifying to common readers, than a more elevated and less laconic style.

I have, therefore, left them as they were reported, with a few verbal and trifling alterations.

The author of the Lectures has no claim to literary merit; and, if he knows his own heart, has no desire that the Lectures should be anything else than *useful*.

I have reason to believe that, *upon the whole*, they will be as much so in their present as under any other form I could give them, circumstanced as I am.

As my friends wish to have them in a volume, they must take them as they are.

C. G. FINNEY

New York, 16th March 1837.

LECTURE I.

SELF DECEIVERS.

TEXT:— "But be ye doers of the word, and not hearers only, deceiving your own selves." James— 1:22

There are two extremes in religion, equally false and equally fatal. And there are two classes of hypocrites that occupy these two extremes. The first class make religion consist altogether in the belief of certain abstract doctrines, or what they call faith, and lay little or no stress on good works. The other class make religion to consist altogether in good works, (I mean dead works,) and lay little or no stress on faith in Jesus Christ, but hope for salvation by their own deeds. The Jews belonged generally to the last mentioned class. Their religious teachers taught them that they would be saved by obedience to the ceremonial law. And therefore, when Paul began to preach, he seems to have attacked more especially this error of the Jews. He was determined to carry the main question, that men are justified by faith in Jesus Christ, in opposition to the doctrine of the Scribes and Pharisees, that salvation is by obedience to the law. And he pressed this point so earnestly, in his preaching and in his epistles, that he carried it, and settled the faith of the church in the great doctrine of justification by faith. And then certain individuals in the church laid hold of this doctrine and carried it to the opposite extreme, and maintained that men are saved by faith altogether, irrespective of works of any kind. They overlooked the plain principle, that genuine faith always *results* in good works, and is itself a good work.

I said that these two extremes, that which makes religion consist altogether in outward works and that which makes it consist altogether in faith, are equally false and equally fatal. Those who make religion consist altogether in good works, overlook the fact that works themselves are not acceptable to God, unless they proceed from faith. For without faith it is impossible to please Him. And those who make religion consist altogether in faith, overlook the fact, that true faith always works by love, and invariably produces the works of love.

They are equally fatal, because, on the one hand, without faith they cannot be pardoned or justified; and on the other, without sanctification they cannot be fitted either for the employments or enjoyments of Heaven. Let a sinner turn from his sins altogether, and suppose his works to be as perfect as he thinks them to be, and yet he could not be pardoned, without faith in the atonement of Jesus Christ. And so if any one supposed he could be justified by faith while his works were evil, he ought to know that without sanctification his faith is but dead and cannot even be the instrument of his justification.

It appears that the apostle James designed in this epistle to put this matter upon the right ground, and show exactly where the truth lay, and to explain the necessity and the reason of the necessity of both faith and good works. This epistle is a very practical one, and it meets full in the face all the great practical questions of the day, and decides them.

Doctrines in religion are of two classes, those which refer to God, and those which refer to human practice. Many confine their idea of religious doctrines to the former class. They think nothing is properly called doctrine but what respects God, His attributes, mode of existence, decrees, and so on.—When I gave notice that I should commence a course of PRACTICAL LECTURES, I hope you did not understand me to mean that the lectures would not be doctrinal, or would have no doctrine in them. My design is to preach, if the Lord will, a course of lectures on *practical doctrines*.

The doctrine which I propose to consider tonight is this.

THAT PROFESSOR OF RELIGION WHO DOES NOT PRACTICE WHAT HE ADMITS TO BE TRUE, IS SELF-DECEIVED.

There are two classes of hypocrites among professors of religion —those that deceive others and those that deceive themselves. One class of hypocrites are those that, under a specious outside of morality and show of religion, cover up the enmity of their hearts against God, and lead others to think they are very pious people. Thus the Pharisees obtained the reputation of being remarkably pious, by their outside show of religion, their alms and their long prayers. The other class is that referred to in the text, who do not deceive others but themselves. These are orthodox in sentiment but loose in practice. They seem to suppose religion to consist in a parcel of *notions*, without regard to practice, and thus deceive themselves to think they are good Christians while destitute of true holiness. They are hearers of the word but not doers. They love orthodox preaching, and take great pleasure in hearing the abstract doctrines of religion exhibited, and perhaps have flights of imagination and glowing feelings in view of the character and government of God, but they are not careful to practice the precepts of God's word, nor are they pleased with the preaching of those doctrines which relate to human practice.

Perhaps there are some present tonight of both these classes of hypocrites. Now, mark: I am not going to preach tonight to those of you who, by great strictness of morals and outside show of religion, deceive others. I address now those of you who do not practice what you know to be true—who are hearers and not doers. Perhaps I had better say, to secure attention, that it is highly probable there are a number here now, of this character. I do not know your names, but I wish you to understand that if you are of that character, you are the persons I am speaking to, just as if I called out your names. I mean you. You hear the word and believe it in theory, while you deny it in practice. I say to you that YOU DECEIVE YOURSELVES. The text proves it. Here you have an express "Thus saith the Lord" for it, that all such characters are self-deceivers. I might quote a number of other passages of scripture, that are to the point, and there leave it. But I wish to call your attention to some other considerations, besides the direct scripture testimony.

In the first place, you *do not truly believe the word*. You hear it, and admit it to be true, but you do not truly believe it. And here let me say, that persons are themselves liable to deception on this point. Not that their consciousness deceives them, but they do not understand what it is that consciousness testifies. Two things are indispensable to evangelical or saving faith. The first is intellectual conviction of the truth of a thing. And here I do not mean merely the abstract truth of it, but in its bearing on you. The truth, in its relation to you, or its bearing on your conduct, must be received intellectually. And then true faith includes a corresponding state of heart. This always enters into the essence of true faith. When a man's understanding is convinced, and he admits the truth *in its relation to himself*, then there must be a hearty approbation of it in its bearing or relation to himself. Both these states of mind are indispensable to true faith. Intellectual conviction of the truth is not saving faith. But intellectual conviction, when accompanied with a corresponding state of the affections, is saving faith. Hence it follows that where there is true saving faith, there is always corresponding conduct. The conduct always follows the real faith. Just as certain as the will controls the conduct, men will act as they believe. Suppose I say to a man, Do you believe this? "Yes, I believe it." What does he mean? A mere intellectual conviction? He may have that, and yet not have faith.

A man may even feel an approbation of an abstract truth. *This* is what many persons suppose to be faith, the approbation which they feel for the character and government of God, and for the plan of salvation, when viewed abstractedly. Many persons, when they hear an eloquent sermon on the attributes or government of God, are set all in a glow at the sublimity and excellency displayed, when they have not a particle of true faith. I have heard of an infidel who would be moved even to ecstasy at such themes. The rational mind is so constituted that it naturally and necessarily approves of truth when viewed abstractedly. The wickedest devils in hell love it, if they can see it without its relation to themselves. If they could see the gospel without any relation that interferes with their own selfishness, they would not only see it to be true, but would heartily approve it. All hell, if they could view God in His absolute existence, without any relation to themselves, would heartily approve of His character. The reason why wicked men and devils hate God, is because they see Him in a relation to themselves. Their hearts rise up in rebellion, because they see Him opposed to their selfishness.

Here is the source of a grand delusion among men in regard to religion. They see it to be true, and they really rejoice in contemplating it: they do not enter into its relations to themselves, and so they love to hear such preaching, and say they are fed by it. But MARK:—They go away and do not practice! See that man. He is sick, and his feelings are tender. In view of Christ as a kind and tender Savior, his heart melts, and he feels strong emotions of approbation towards Jesus Christ. Why? For the very same reasons that he would feel strong emotions towards the hero of a romance. But he does not obey Christ. He never practices one thing out of obedience to Christ, but just views Him abstractedly, and is delighted with His glorious and lovely character, while he himself remains in the gall of bitterness. Thus it is apparent that your faith must be an efficient faith, such as regulates your practice and produces good works, or it is not the faith of the gospel, it is no real faith at all.

Again: It is further manifest that you are deceiving yourselves, because all true religion *consists in obedience*. And, therefore, however much you may approve of Christianity, you have no religion unless you obey it. In saying that all religion *consists* in obedience, I do not mean *outward* obedience. But faith itself, true faith, *works by love*, and produces corresponding action. There is no real obedience but the obedience of the heart: *love* is the fulfilling of the law; and religion consists in the obedience of the heart, with a corresponding course of life. The man, therefore, who hears the truth, and approves it, and does not practice it, deceiveth himself. He is like the man beholding his natural face in a glass; for he beholdeth himself, and goeth his way, and straightway forgetteth what manner of a man he was.

Again: That state of mind which you mistake for religion, an intellectual conviction of truth, and approval of it in the abstract, so far from being evidence that you are pious, is as common to the wicked as to the good, whenever they can be brought to look at it abstractedly. This is the reason why it is often so difficult to convince sinners that they are opposed to God and His truth. Men are so constituted that they do approve of virtue, and do admire the character and government of God, and would approve and admire every truth in the Bible, if they could view it abstractedly, and without any relation to themselves. And when they sit under preaching that holds up the truth in such a way, that it has not much of a practical bearing on themselves, they may sit for years and never consider that *they* are opposed to God and His government.

And I am more and more persuaded, that great multitudes are to be found in all our congregations, where the abstract doctrines of the gospel are much preached, who like the preaching and like to hear about God, and all these things, and yet are unconverted. And no doubt multitudes of them get into the churches, because they love orthodox preaching, when after all it is manifest that they are not doers of the word. And here is the difficulty: they have not had that searching preaching that made them see the truth in its bearing on themselves. And now they are in the church, whenever the truth is preached in its practical relation to them, they show the enmity of their hearts unchanged, by rising up in opposition to the truth.

They took it for granted that they were Christians, and so joined the church, because they could hear sound doctrinal preaching and approve of it, or because they read the Bible and approved of it. If their faith be not so practical as to influence their conduct, if they do not view the truth in its relation to their own practice, their faith does not affect them so much as the FAITH OF THE DEVIL.

REMARKS.

1. Great injury has been done by false representations regarding the wickedness of real Christians.

A celebrated preacher, not long since, is said to have given this definition of a Christian—"A little grace and a great deal of devil." I utterly deny this definition. It is false and ruinous. A great deal is said that makes an impression that real Christians are the wickedest beings on the face of the earth. It is true that when they do sin, they incur great guilt. For a Christian to sin is highly criminal. And it is also true that enlightened Christians see in their sins great wickedness. When they compare their obligations with their lives, they are greatly humbled, and express their humility in very strong language. But it is not true that they *are* as bad as the devil, or anywhere in the neighborhood of it. This is perfectly demonstrable. When they do sin, their sins have great aggravation, and appear extremely wicked in the sight of God. But to suppose that men are real Christians while they live in the service of the devil, and have little of even the appearance of religion, is a sentiment that is not only false but of very dangerous tendency. It is calculated to encourage all that class of hypocrites who are Antinomians, and to encourage backsliders, as well as to do a great injury to the cause of Christ in the estimation of scorners. The truth is, those who do not obey God are not Christians. The contrary doctrine is ruinous to the churches, by filling them up with multitudes whose claim to piety depends on their adoption of certain notions, while they never heartily intended to *obey* the requirements of the gospel in their lives.

2. Those who are so much more zealous for doctrines than for practice, and who lay much more stress on that class of doctrines which relate to God than on that class which relate to their own conduct, are *Antinomians.*

There are many who will receive that class of the doctrines of the Bible that relate to God, and approve and love them, who have not a particle of religion. Those who are never "fed," as they call it, on any preaching but that of certain abstract points of doctrine, are Antinomians. They are the very persons against whom the apostle James wrote this epistle. They make religion to consist in a set of notions, while they do not lead holy lives.

3. That class of professors of religion, who never like to hear about God or His attributes, or mode of existence, the Trinity,

decrees, election, and the like, but lay all stress on religious practice to the exclusion of religious doctrine, are *Pharisees.*

They make great pretensions to outward piety, and perhaps to inward flights of emotion of a certain poetical cast, while they will not receive the great truths that relate to God, but deny the fundamental doctrines of the gospel.

4. The proper end and tendency of all right doctrine, when truly believed, is to produce correct practice.

Wherever you find a man's practice heretical, you may be sure his belief is heretical too. The faith that he holds in his heart is just as heretical as his life. He may not be heretical in his *notions and theories.* He may be right there, even on the very points where he is heretical in his practice. But he does not *really* believe it.

For illustration: See that careless sinner, there, grasping wealth and rushing headlong in the search for riches. Does that man truly believe he is ever going to die? Perhaps you will say, he knows he must die. But I say, that while he is in this attitude, he does not actually believe he is ever going to die. It is not before his thoughts at all. It is therefore impossible that he should believe it in his utter thoughtlessness. You ask him if he expects ever to die, and he will reply, "O, yes, I know I must die, all men are mortal." As soon as he turns his thoughts to it, he assents to the truth. And if you could fasten the conviction on his mind till he is really and permanently impressed with it, he would infallibly change his conduct, and live for another world instead of this. It is just so in religion; whatever a man really believes, is just as certain to control his practice as that the will governs the conduct.

5. The church has for a long time acted too much on an Antinomial policy.

She has been sticklish for the more *abstract* doctrines, and left the more *practical* too much out of view. She has laid greater stress on orthodoxy in those doctrines that are not practical, than in those that are practical. Look at the creeds of the church, and see how they all lay the main stress on those doctrines that have little relation to our practice. A man may be the greatest heretic on points of practice, provided he is not openly profane and vicious, and yet maintain a good standing in the church, whether his life corresponds with the gospel or not. Is not this monstrous? And hence we see, that when it is attempted to purify the church in regard to practical errors, she cannot bear it.—Why else is it that so much excitement is produced by attempting to clear the church from participation in the sins of intemperance, and Sabbath-breaking, and slavery? Why is it so difficult to induce the church to do anything effectual for the conversion of the world? O, when shall the church be purified or the world converted? Not till it is a settled point, that heresy in practice is the proof of heresy in belief. Not while a man may deny the whole gospel in his practice every day, and yet maintain his standing in the church as a good Christian.

6. See how a minister may be deceived in regard to the state of his congregation.

He preaches a good deal on the abstract doctrines, that do not immediately relate to practice, and his people say they are fed, and rejoice in it, and he thinks they are growing in grace, when in fact it is no certain sign that there is any religion among them. It is manifest that this is not certain evidence. But if when he preaches practical doctrines, his people show that they love the truth in its relation to themselves, and show it by practicing it, then they give evidence of real love to the truth.

If a minister finds that his people love abstract doctrinal preaching, but that when he comes to press the practical doctrines they rebel, he may be sure that if they have any religion it is in a low state; and if he finds on fair trial that he cannot bring them up to it, so as to receive practical doctrine, he may be satisfied they have not a particle of religion, but are a mere company of Antinomians, who think they can go to heaven on a dead faith in abstract orthodoxy.

8. See what a vast multitude of professors of religion there are, who are deceiving themselves.

Many suppose they are Christians from the emotions they feel in view of truth, when in fact what they receive is truth presented to their minds in such a way that they do not see its bearing on themselves. If you bring the truth so to bear upon *them*, as to destroy their pride and cut them off from their worldliness, such professors resist it. Look abroad upon the church. See what a multitude of orthodox churches and orthodox Christians live and feed upon the abstract doctrines of religion from year to year. Then look further at their lives and see how little influence their professed belief has upon their practice. Have they saving faith? It cannot be. I do not mean to say that none of these church members are pious, but I do say that those who do not adopt in practice what they admit in theory—who are hearers of the word but not doers, deceive themselves.

Inquire now how many of you really believe the truths you hear preached. I have proposed to preach a course of *practical* lectures. I do not mean that I shall preach lectures that have no doctrine in them. That is not preaching at all. But what I desire is to see whether you will, as a church, do what you believe to be true. If I do not succeed in convincing you that any doctrine I may maintain is really true, that is another affair. That is reason enough why you should not do it. But if I do succeed in proving from the scriptures and convincing your understanding that it is true, and yet you do not practice it, I shall then have the evidence before my own eyes what your character is, and no longer deceive myself with the idea that this is a Christian church.

Are you conscious that the gospel is producing a practical effect upon you, according to your advancement in knowledge? Is it weaning you from the world? Do you find this to be your experience, that when you receive any practical truth into your minds you love it, and love to feel its application to yourself, and take pleasure in practicing it? If you are not growing in grace, becoming more and more holy, YIELDING YOURSELVES UP to the influence of the gospel, you are deceiving yourselves.—How is it now with you who are elders of this church? How is it with you who are heads of families—all of you? When you hear a sermon, do you seize hold of it and take it home to you, and practice it; or do you receive it in your minds, and approve of it and never practice it? Woe to that man who admits the truth, and yet turns away and does not practice it, like the man beholding his natural face in a glass turning away and forgetting what manner of man he was.

LECTURE II.

FALSE PROFESSORS.

"They feared the Lord, and served their own gods" 2 Kings xvii. 33.

When the ten tribes of Israel were carried away captives by the king of Assyria, their places were supplied with strangers of different idolatrous nations, who knew nothing of the religion of the Jews. Very soon, the wild beasts increased in the country, and the lions destroyed multitudes of the people, and they thought it was because they did not know the god of that country, and had therefore ignorantly transgressed his religion, and offended him, and he had sent the lions among them as a punishment. So they applied to the king, who told them to get one of the priests of the Israelites to teach them the manner of the god of the land. They took this advice, and obtained one of the priests to come to Bethel and teach them the religious ceremonies and modes of worship that had been practiced there. And he taught them to fear Jehovah, as the god of that country. But still, they did not receive Him as the only God. They feared Him; that is, they feared His anger and His judgments, and to avert these they performed the prescribed rites. But they *served* their own gods. They kept up their idolatrous worship, and this was what they loved and preferred, though they felt obliged to pay some reverence to Jehovah, as the god of that country. There are still multitudes of persons, professing to fear God, and perhaps possessing a certain kind of fear of the Lord, who nevertheless *serve* their own gods—they have other things to which their hearts are supremely devoted, and other objects in which they mainly put their trust.

There are, as you know, two kinds of fear. There is that fear of the Lord, which is the beginning of wisdom, which is founded in love. There is also a slavish fear, which is a mere dread of evil and is purely selfish. This is the kind of fear which is possessed by those people spoken of in the text. They were afraid Jehovah would send His judgments upon them, if they did not perform certain rites and this was the motive they had for paying Him worship. Those who have this fear are supremely selfish, and while they profess to reverence Jehovah, have other gods whom they love and serve.

There are several classes of persons to whom this is applicable, and my object tonight is to describe some of them, in such a way that those of you here, who possess this character, may know yourselves, and may see how it is that your neighbors know you and understand your real characters.

To *serve* a person is to be obedient to the will and devoted to the interests of that individual. It is not properly called serving, where only certain acts are performed, without entering into the service of the person, but to serve is to make it a business to do the will and promote the interest of the person. To serve God is to make religion the main business of life. It is to devote one's self, heart, life, powers, time, influence, and all, to promote the interests of God, to build up the kingdom of God, and to advance the glory of God. Who are they who, while they profess to fear the Lord, serve their own gods?

I answer, *First,* All those of you, who have not *heartily and practically renounced the ownership of your possessions,* and given them up to God.

It is self-evident that if you have not done this, you are not serving God. Suppose a gentleman were to employ a clerk to take care of his store, and suppose the clerk were to continue to attend to his own business, and when asked to do what is necessary for his employer, who pays him his wages, he should reply, "I really have so much business of my own to attend to, that I have no time to do these things;" would not everybody cry out against such a servant, and say he was not serving his employer at all, his time is not his own, it is paid for, and he but served himself? So where a man has not renounced the ownership of himself, not only in thought, but practically, he has not taken the first lesson in religion. He is not serving the Lord, but serving his own gods.

2. That man who does not make the *business in which he is engaged a part of his religion,* does not serve God.

You hear a man say sometimes, I am so much engaged all day in the world, or in worldly business, that I have not time to serve God. He thinks he serves God a little while in the morning, and then attends to his worldly business. That man, you may rely upon it, left his religion where he said his prayers. He is not serving God. It is a mere burlesque for him to pretend to serve God. He is willing, perhaps, to give God the time before breakfast, before he gets ready to go to his own business, but as soon as that is over, away he goes to his own work. He fears the Lord, perhaps, enough to go through with his prayers night and morning, but he serves his own gods.—That man's religion is the laughing-stock of hell! He prays very devoutly, and then, instead of engaging in his business for God, he is serving himself. No doubt the idols are well satisfied with the arrangement, but God is wholly displeased.

3. But, again: Those of you are serving your own gods, who devote to Jehovah that which costs you little or nothing.

There are many who make religion consist in certain acts of piety that do not interfere with their selfishness. You pray in the morning in your family, because you can do it then very conveniently, but do not suffer the service of Jehovah to interfere with the service of your own god's, or to stand in the way of your getting rich, or enjoying the world. The gods you serve make no complaint of being slighted or neglected for the service of Jehovah.

4. All that class are serving your own gods, who suppose that the six days of the week belong to yourselves and that the Sabbath only is God's day.

There are multitudes who suppose that the week is man's time, and the Sabbath only God's, and that they have a right to do their own work during the week, and to serve themselves, and promote their own interests, if they will only keep the Sabbath strictly and serve God on the Sabbath. For instance: A celebrated preacher, in illustrating the wickedness of breaking the Sabbath, used this illustration: "Suppose a man having seven dollars in his pocket should meet a beggar in great distress, and give him six dollars, keeping only one for himself, and the beggar, seeing that he retained one dollar, should turn and rob him of that; would not every heart despise his baseness?" You see it embodies this idea—that it is very ungrateful to break the Sabbath, since God has given to men six days for *their own*, to serve themselves, and only reserved the Sabbath to Himself, and to rob God of the seventh day is base ingratitude.

You that do this do not serve God at all. If you are selfish during the week, you are selfish altogether. To suppose you had any real piety would imply that you were converted every Sabbath and unconverted every Monday. If a man would serve himself all the week and really posses religion on the Sabbath, he requires to be converted for it. But is this the idea of the Sabbath, that it is a day to serve God in, exclusive of other days? Is God in need of your Services on the Sabbath to keep His work along? God requires all your services as much on the six days as on the Sabbath, only He has appropriated the Sabbath to peculiar duties, and required its observance as a day of rest from bodily toil and from those fatiguing cares and labors that concern the present world. But because God uses means in accomplishing His purposes, and men have bodies as well as souls, and the gospel is to be spread and sustained by the things of this world, therefore God requires you to work all the six days at your secular employments. But it is all for His service, as much as the worship of the Sabbath. The Sabbath is no more given for the service of God than Monday. You have no more right to serve yourselves on Monday than you have on the Sabbath. If any of you have thus considered the matter, and imagined that the six days of the week are your own time, it shows that you are supremely selfish. I beg of you not to consider that in prayer and on the Sabbath you are serving God at all, if the rest of the time you are considered as serving yourself. You have never known the radical principle of serving the Lord.

5. Those are serving themselves, or their own gods, who will not make any sacrifices of personal ease and comfort in religion.

For instance—There are multitudes who object to Free Churches on this ground, that they require a sacrifice of personal gratification. They talk like this: "We wish to sit with our families;" or, "We want our seats cushioned," or, "We always like to sit in the same place." They admit that Free Churches are necessary, in order to make the gospel accessible to the thousands who are going to hell in this city. But they cannot make these little sacrifices, to throw open the doors of God's house to this great mass of impenitent sinners.

These little things often indicate most clearly the state of men's hearts. Suppose your servant were to say, "I can't do this," or "I can't do that," because it interferes with his personal ease and comfort. He cannot do this because he likes to sit on a cushion and work. Or he cannot do that because it would separate him from his family an hour and a half. What! is that doing service? When a man enters into service, he gives up his ease and comfort, for the interest and at the will of his employer. Is it true that any man is supremely devoted to the service of God, when he shows that his own ease and comfort are dearer than the kingdom of Jesus Christ, and that he would sooner sacrifice the salvation of sinners than sit on a hard seat, or be separated from his family an hour or two?

6. Those are serving their own gods, who give their time and money to God's service, when they do give, grudgingly, by constraint, and not of a ready mind and with a cheerful heart.

What would you think of your servant, if you had to dun or drive him all the time to do anything for your interest? Would you not say he was an eye-servant? How many people there are who, when they do anything on account of religion, do it grudgingly. If they do anything, it comes hard. If you go to one of these characters, and want his time or his money, for any religious object, it is difficult to get him engaged. It seems to go across the grain, and is not easy or natural. It is plain he does not consider the interests of Christ's kingdom the same with his own. He may make a show of fearing the Lord, but he *serves* some other gods of his own.

7. Those who are always ready to ask how little they may do for religion, rather than *how much they may do*, are serving their own gods.

There are multitudes of persons who seem always to ask how little they can get along with in what they do for God. You hear such a man making up his account of profits and loss—"So much made this year—then so much it costs for charity—so much obliged to give for religion." (OBLIGED to give for the interests of religion!)—"and so much lost by fire, and so much by bad debts," and so on. Is that man serving God? It is a simple matter of fact, that you have never set your hearts on the object of promoting religion in the world. If you had, you would ask, How much *can* I do for this object and for that?—Cannot I do so much—or so MUCH—or SO MUCH?

8. They who are laying up wealth for their own families, to elevate and aggrandize them, are serving gods of their own, and not Jehovah.

Those who are thus aiming to elevate their own families into a different sphere, by laying up wealth for them, show that they have some other object to live for than bringing this world under the authority of Jesus Christ. They have other gods to serve. They may pretend to fear the Lord, but they *serve* their own gods.

9. Those who are making it their object to accumulate so much property that they can retire from business and live at ease, are serving their own gods.

There are many persons who profess to be the servants of God, but are eagerly engaged in gathering property, and calculating to retire to their country seat by-and-by, and live at their ease. What do you mean? Has God given you a right to a perpetual Sabbath, as soon as you have made so much money? Did God tell you, when you professed to enter His service, to work hard so many years, and then you might have a perpetual holiday? Did He promise to excuse you after that from making the most of your time and talents, and let you live at ease the rest of your days? If your thoughts are set upon this notion, I tell you, you are not serving God, but your own selfishness and sloth.

10. Those persons are serving their own gods, who, would sooner gratify their appetites than deny themselves things that are unnecessary, or even hurtful, for the sake of doing good.

You find persons who greatly love things that do them no good, and others even form an artificial appetite for a thing positively loathsome, and after it they will go, and no arguments will prevail upon them to abandon it for the sake of doing good. Are such persons *absorbed* in the service of God? Certainly not. Will they sacrifice their lives for the kingdom of God? Why, you cannot make them even give up a quid of TOBACCO, a *weed* that is injurious to health and loathsome to society, they cannot give it up, were it to save a soul from death!

Who does not see that selfishness predominates in such persons? It shows the astonishing strength of selfishness. You often see the strength of selfishness showing itself in some such little thing more than in things that are greater. The real state of a man's mind stands out, that self-gratification is the law of his life, so strong that it will not give place, even in a trifle, to those great interests, for which he ought to be willing to lay down his life.

11. Those persons who are most readily moved to action by appeals to their own selfish interests, show that they are serving their own gods.

You see what motive influences such a man. Suppose I wish to get him to subscribe for building a church, what must I urge? Why, I must show how it will improve the value of his property, or advance his party, or gratify his selfishness in some other way. If he is more excited by these motives, than he is by a desire to save perishing souls and advance the kingdom of Christ, you see that he has never given himself up to serve the Lord. He is still serving himself. He is more influenced by his selfish interests than by all those benevolent principles on which all religion turns. The character of a true servant of God is right opposite to this.

Take the case of two servants, one devoted to his master's interests, and the other having no conscience or concern but to secure his wages. Go to one, and he throws into the shade all personal considerations, and enlists with heart and soul in achieving the object. The other will not act unless you present some selfish motive, unless you say, Do so, and I will raise your wages, or set you up in business, or the like. Is there not a radical difference between these two servants? Is not this an illustration of what actually takes place in our churches? Propose a plan of doing good that will cost nothing, and they will all go for it. But propose a plan which is going to affect their personal interest, to cost money, or take up time, in a busy season, and you will see they begin to divide. Some hesitate, some doubt, some raise objections, and some resolutely refuse. Some enlist at once, because they see it will do great good. Others stand back till you devise some way to excite their selfishness in its favor. What causes the difference? Some of them are serving their own gods.

12. Those are of this character, who are more interested in other subjects than in religion.

If you find them more ready to talk on other subjects, more easily excited by them, more awake to learn the news, they are serving their own gods. What multitudes are more excited by the bank question, or the question about war, or about the fire, or anything of a worldly nature, than about revivals, missions, or anything connected with the interests of religion. You find them all engaged about politics or speculation, but if you bring up the subject of religion, ah, they are afraid of excitement, and talk about animal feeling, showing that religion is not the subject that is nearest their hearts. A man is always most easily excited on that subject that lies nearest his heart.—Bring that up, and he is interested. When you can talk early and late about the news and other worldly topics, and when you cannot possibly be interested in the subject of religion, you know that your heart is not in it, and if you pretend to be a servant of God, you are a hypocrite.

13. When persons are more jealous for their own fame than for God's glory, it shows that they live for themselves, and serve their own gods.

You see a man more vexed or grieved by what is said against him than against God, whom does he serve? Who is his God, himself or Jehovah? There is a minister thrown into a fever because somebody has said a word derogatory to his scholarship, or his dignity, or his infallibility, while he is as cool as ice at all the indignities thrown upon the blessed God. Is that man a follower of Paul, willing to be considered a fool for the cause of Christ? Did that man ever take the first lesson in religion? If he had, he would rejoice to have his name cast out as evil for the cause of religion. No, he is not serving God, he is serving his own gods.

14. Those are serving their own gods, who are not making the salvation of souls the great and leading object of their lives.

The end of all religious institutions, that which gives value to them all, is the salvation of sinners. The end for which Christ lives, and for which He has left His church in the world, is the salvation of sinners. This is the business which God sets His servants about, and if any man is not doing this, as his business, as the leading and main object of his life, he is not serving Jehovah, he is serving his own gods.

15. Those who are doing but little for God, or who bring but little to pass for God, cannot properly be said to serve Him.

Suppose you ask a professed servant of God. "What are you doing for God? Are you bringing anything to pass? Are you instrumental in the conversion of any sinners? Are you making impressions in favor of religion, or helping forward the cause of Christ?" He replies, "Why, I do not know, I have a hope; I sometimes think I do love God, but I do not know as I am doing any thing in particular at present." Is that man serving God? Or is he serving his own gods? "I talk to sinners some times," he says, "but they do not seem to feel much." Then YOU DON'T FEEL. If your heart is not in it, no wonder you cannot make sinners feel. Whereas, if you do your duty, with your heart in the work, sinners cannot help feeling.

16. Those who seek for happiness in religion, rather than for usefulness, are serving their own gods.

Their religion is entirely selfish. They want to *enjoy* religion, and are all the while inquiring how they can get happy frames of mind, and how they can be pleasurably excited in religious exercises. And they will go only to such meetings, and sit only under such preaching, as will make them happy; never asking the question whether that is the way to do the most good or not. Now, suppose your servant should do so, and be constantly contriving how to enjoy himself, and if he thought he could be most happy in the parlor, stretched on the sofa, with a pillow of down under his head, and another servant to fan him, refusing to do the work which you set him about, and which your interest urgently requires; instead of manifesting a desire to work for you, and a solicitude for your interest, and a willingness to lay himself out with all his powers in your service, he wants only to be happy! It is just so with those professed servants of Jehovah, who want to do nothing but sit on their handsome cushion, and have the minister *feed* them. Instead of seeking how to do good, they are only seeking to be happy. Their daily prayer is not, like that of the converted Saul of Tarsus, "Lord, what wilt thou have me to do?" but, "Lord, tell me how I can be happy." Is that the spirit of Jesus Christ? No, he said, "I delight to DO THY WILL, O God." Is that the spirit of the apostle Paul? No, he threw off his upper garments at once, and made his arms bare for the field of LABOR.

17. Those who make their own salvation their supreme object in religion, are serving their own gods.

There are multitudes in the church, who show by their conduct, and even avow in their language, that their leading object is to secure their own salvation, and their grand determination is to get their own souls planted on the firm battlements of the heavenly Jerusalem, and walk the golden fields of Canaan above. If the Bible is not in error all such characters will go to hell. Their religion is pure selfishness. And "he that will save his life shall loose it, and he that will loose his life for my sake, shall save it."

REMARKS.

1. See why so little is accomplished in the world for Jesus Christ.

It is because there are so few that do anything for it.—It is because Jesus Christ has so few real servants in the world. How many professors do you suppose there are in this church, or in your whole acquaintance, that are really at work for God, and making a business of religion, and *laying themselves out* to advance the kingdom of Christ? The reason why religion advances no faster is, that there are so few to advance it, and so many to hinder it. You see a parcel of people at a fire, trying to get out the goods of a store. Some are determined to get out the goods, but the rest are not engaged about it, and they divert their attention by talking about other things, or positively hinder them by finding fault with their way of doing it, or by holding them back. So it is in the church. Those who are desirous of doing the work are greatly hindered by the backwardness, the cavils, and the positive resistance of the rest.

2. See why so few Christians have the spirit of prayer.

How can they have the spirit of prayer? What should God give them the spirit of prayer for? Suppose a man engaged in his worldly schemes, and that God should give that man the spirit of *prayer*. Of course he would pray for that which lies nearest his heart; that is, for success in his worldly schemes, to serve his own gods with. Will God give him the spirit of prayer for such purpose?—Never. Let him go to his own gods for a spirit of prayer, but let him not expect Jehovah to bestow the spirit of prayer, while he is serving his own gods.

3. You see that there are a multitude of professors of religion that have not begun to be religious yet.

Said a man to one of them, Do you feel that your property and your business are all God's, and do you hold and manage them for God? "O, no," said he, "I have not got so far as that yet." Not got so far as that! That man had been a professor of religion for years, and yet had not got so far as to consider his property, and business, and all that he had as belonging to God! No doubt he was serving his own gods. For I insist upon it, that this is the very beginning of religion. What is conversion, but turning from the service of the world to the *service* of God? And yet this man had not found out that he was God's servant. And he seemed to think he was getting a great way in religion, to feel that all he had was the Lord's.

4. It is great dishonesty for persons to profess to serve the Lord, and yet in reality serve themselves.

You, who are performing religious duties from selfish motives, are in reality trying to make God your servant. If your own interest be the supreme object, all your religious services are only desires to induce God to promote your interests. Why do you pray, or keep the Sabbath, or give your property for religious objects? You answer, "for the sake of promoting my own salvation." Indeed! Not to glorify God, but to get to heaven! Don't you think the devil would do all that, if he thought he could gain his end by it—and be a devil still? The highest style of selfishness must be to get God, with all His attributes, enlisted in the service of your mighty self!

And now, my hearers, where are you all? Are you serving Jehovah, or are you serving your own gods? How have you been doing these six months that I have been absent? Have you done anything for God? Have you been living as servants of God? Is Satan's kingdom weakened by what you have done? Could you say now, "Come with me, and I will show you this and that sinner converted, or this and that backslider reclaimed, or this and that weak saint strengthened and aided?" Could you bring living witnesses of what you have done in the service of God? Or would your answer be, "I have been to meeting regularly on the Sabbath, and heard a great deal of good preaching, and I have generally attended the prayer meetings, and we had some precious meetings, and I have prayed in my family, and twice or thrice a day in my closet, and read the Bible." And in all that you have been merely passive, as to anything done for God. You have feared the Lord, and served your own gods.

"Yes, but I have sold so many goods, and made so much money, of which I intend to give a tenth to the missionary cause."

Who hath required this at your hand, instead of saving souls? Going to send the gospel to the heathen, and letting sinners right under your own eyes go down to hell. Be not deceived. If you loved souls, if you were engaged to serve God, you would think of souls here, and do the work of God here. What should we think of a missionary going to the heathen, who had never said a word to sinners around him at home? Does he love souls? There is burlesque in the idea of sending such a man to the heathen. The man that will do nothing at home, is not fit to go to the heathen. And he that pretends to be getting money for missions while he will not try to save sinners here, is an outrageous hypocrite.

LECTURE III.

DOUBTFUL ACTIONS ARE SINFUL.

Text:—"He that doubteth is damned if he eat, because he eateth not of faith: for whatsoever is not of faith is sin."—Romans xiv. 23.

It was a custom among the idolatrous heathen to offer the bodies of slain beasts in sacrifice, a part of every beast that was offered belonged to the priest. The priests used to send their portion to market to sell, and it was sold in the shambles as any other meat. The Christian Jews that were scattered everywhere, were very particular as to what meats they ate, so as not even to run the least danger of violating the Mosaic law, and they raised doubts and created disputes and difficulties among the churches. This was one of the subjects about which the church of Corinth was divided and agitated, until they finally wrote to the apostle Paul for directions. A part of the First Epistle to the Corinthians was doubtless written as a reply to such inquiries. It seems there were some who carried their scruples so far that they thought it not proper to eat any meat, for if they went to market for it they were continually in danger of buying that which was offered to idols.—Others thought it made no difference, they had a right to eat meat, and they would buy it in the market as they found it, and give themselves no trouble about the matter. To quell the dispute, they wrote to Paul, and in the 8th chapter he takes up the subject and discusses it in full.

Now, as touching things offered unto idols, we know that we all have knowledge. Knowledge puffeth up, but charity edifieth. And if any man think that he knoweth anything, he knoweth nothing yet as he ought to know. But if any man love God, the same is known of him. As concerning therefore the eating of those things that are offered in sacrifice unto idols, we know that an idol is nothing in the world, and that there is none other God but one. For though there be that are called gods, whether in heaven or in earth, (as there be gods many, and lords many;) but to us there is but one God, the Father, of whom are all things, and we in Him; and one Lord Jesus Christ, by whom are all things, and we by Him. Howbeit there is not in every man that knowledge; for some with conscience of the idol unto this hour eat it as a thing offered unto an idol; and their conscience, being weak, is defiled.

"His conscience is defiled," that is, he regards it as a meat offered to an idol, and is really practicing idolatry. The eating of meat is a matter of total indifference, in itself.

But meat commendeth us not to God; for neither if we eat are we the better; neither if we eat not, are we the worse.—But take heed lest by any means this liberty of yours become a stumbling block to them that are weak. For if any man see thee, which hast knowledge, sit at meat in the idol's temple, shall not the conscience of him which is weak be emboldened to eat those things offered to idols; and through thy knowledge shall the weak brother perish for whom Christ died?

Although they might have a sufficient knowledge on the subject to know that an idol is nothing, and cannot make any change in the meat itself, yet if they should be seen eating meat that was known to have been offered to an idol, those who were weak might be emboldened by it to eat the sacrifices as such, or as an act of worship to the idol, supposing all the while that they were but following the example of their more enlightened brethren.

But when ye sin so against the brethren, and wound their weak conscience, ye sin against Christ. Wherefore, if meat make my brother to offend, I will eat no more flesh while the world standeth, lest I make my brother to offend.

This is his benevolent conclusion, that he would rather forego the use of flesh altogether than be the occasion of drawing a weak brother away into idolatry. For, in fact, to sin so against a weak brother is to sin against Christ.

In writing to the Romans he takes up the same subject,—the same dispute had existed there. After laying down some general maxims and principles, he gives this rule:

Him that is weak in faith receive ye, but not to doubtful disputations. For one believeth that he may eat all things; another who is weak, eateth herbs.

There were some among them who chose to live entirely on vegetables, rather than run the risk of buying in the shambles flesh which had been offered in sacrifice to idols. Others ate their flesh as usual, buying what was offered in market, asking no questions for conscience' sake. Those who lived on vegetables charged the others with idolatry. And those that ate flesh accused the others of superstition and weakness. This was wrong.

Let not him that eateth, despise him that eateth not; and let not him which eateth not, judge him that eateth; for God hath received him. Who art thou that judgest another man's servant? to his own master he standeth or falleth: yea, he shall be holden up: for God is able to make him stand.

There was also a controversy about observing the Jewish festival days and holy days. A part supposed that God required this, and therefore they observed them. The others neglected them because they supposed God did not require the observance.

One man esteemeth one day above another; another esteemeth every day alike. Let every man be fully persuaded in his own mind. He that regardeth the day, regardeth it unto the Lord: and he that regardeth not the day, to the Lord he doth not regard it. He that eateth, eateth to the Lord, for he giveth God thanks; and he that eateth not, to the Lord he eateth not, and giveth God thanks. For none of us liveth to himself, and no man dieth to himself. For whether we live, we live unto the Lord: and whether we die, we die unto the Lord: whether we live therefore, or die, we are the Lord's. For to this end Christ both died, and rose, and revived, that he might be Lord both of the dead and living. But why dost thou judge thy brother? or why dost thou set at naught thy brother? for we shall all stand before the judgment-seat of Christ. For as it is written, As I live, saith the Lord, every knee shall bow to me, and every tongue shall confess to God. So then every one of us shall give account of himself to God. Let us not therefore, judge one another any more: but judge this rather, that no man put a stumbling-block, or an occasion to fall in his brother's way.

Now mark what he says.

But if thy brother be grieved with thy meat, now walkest thou not charitably: destroy not him with thy meat, for whom Christ died.

That is, I know that the distinction of meats into clean and unclean, is not binding under Christ, but to him that believes in the distinction, it is a crime to eat indiscriminately, because he does what he believes to be contrary to the commands of God. "All things indeed are pure, but it is evil to him that eateth with offense." Every man should be fully persuaded in his own mind, that what he is doing is right. If a man eat of meats called unclean, not being clear in his mind that it was right, he offended God.

It is good neither to eat flesh, nor to drink wine, nor *any thing* whereby thy brother stumbleth, or is offended, or is made weak.

This is a very useful hint to those wine-bibbers and beer guzzlers, who think the cause of temperance is going to be ruined by giving up wine and beer, when it is notorious, to every person of the least observation, that these things are the greatest hindrance to the cause all over the country.

Hast thou faith? have it to thyself before God. Happy is he that condemneth not himself in *that thing* which he alloweth. And he that doubteth is damned if he eat, because *he eateth* not of faith: for whatsoever is not of faith is sin.

The word rendered *damned* means *condemned*, or adjudged guilty of breaking the law of God. If a man doubts whether it is lawful to do a thing, and while in that state of doubt he does it, he displeases God, he breaks the law and is condemned whether the thing be in itself right or wrong. I have been thus particular in explaining the text in its connection with the context, because I wished fully to satisfy your minds of the correctness of the principle laid down.

That if a man does that of which he doubts the lawfulness, he sins, and is condemned for it in the sight of God.

Whether it is lawful itself, is not the question. If he doubts its lawfulness, it is wrong in him.

There is one exception which ought to be noticed here,—And that is, where a man as honestly and fully doubts the lawfulness of omitting to do it as he does the lawfulness of doing it. President Edwards meets this exactly in his 39th resolution.

"Resolved, never to do any thing that I so much question the lawfulness of, as that I intend, at the same time, to consider and examine afterwards, whether it be lawful or not: except I as much question the lawfulness of the omission."

A man may have equal doubts whether he is bound to do a thing or not to do it. Then all that can be said is, that he must act according to the best light he can get. But where he doubts the lawfulness of the act, but has no cause to doubt the lawfulness of the omission, and yet does it, he sins and is condemned before God, and must repent or be damned. In further examination of the subject, I propose,

I. To show some reasons why a man is criminal for doing that of which he doubts the lawfulness.

II. To show its application to a number of specific cases.

III. Offer a few inferences and remarks, as time may allow.

I. I am to show some reasons for the correctness of the principle laid down in the text—that if a man does that of which he doubts the lawfulness, he is condemned.

1. One reason why an individual is condemned if he does that of which he doubts the lawfulness, is—That if God so far enlightens his mind as to make him doubt the lawfulness of an act, he is bound to stop there and examine the question and settle it to his satisfaction.

To illustrate this: suppose your child is desirous of doing a certain thing, or suppose he is invited by his companions to go somewhere, and he doubts whether you would be willing, do you not see that it is his duty to ask you? If one of his schoolmates invites him home, and he doubts whether you would like it, and yet goes, is not this palpably wrong?

Or suppose a man cast away on a desolate island, where he finds no human being, and he takes up his abode in a solitary cave, considering himself as all alone and destitute of friends or relief or hope; but every morning he finds a supply of nutritious and wholesome food prepared for him, and set by the mouth of his cave, sufficient for his wants that day. What is his duty? Do you say, he does not know that there is a being on the island, and therefore he is not under obligations to any one? Does not gratitude, on the other hand, require him to search and find out his unseen friend, and thank him for his kindness? He cannot say, "I doubt whether there is any being here, and therefore will do nothing but eat my allowance and take my ease, and care for nothing." His not searching for his benefactor would of itself convict him of as desperate wickedness of heart, as if he knew who it was, and refused to return thanks for the favors received.

Or suppose an Atheist opens his eyes on this blessed light of heaven, and breathes this air sending health and vigor through his frame. Here is evidence enough of the being of God to set him on the inquiry after that great being who provides all these means of life and happiness. And if he does not inquire for further light, if he does not care, if he sets his heart against God, he shows that he has the heart as well as the intellect of an Atheist. He has, to say the least, evidence that there *may be* a God. What then is his business? Plainly, it is to set himself honestly, and with a most child-like and reverent spirit, to inquire after Him and pay Him reverence. If, when he has so much light as to doubt whether there may not be a God, he still goes around as if there were none, and does not inquire for truth and obey it, he shows that his heart is wrong, and that it says let there be no God.

There is a Deist, and here a Book claiming to be a revelation from God. Many good men have believed it to be so. The evidences are such as to have perfectly satisfied the most acute and upright minds of its truth. The evidences, both external and internal are of great weight. To say there are *no* evidences is itself enough to bring any man's soundness of mind into question, or his honesty. There is, to say the least, that can be said, sufficient evidence to create a doubt whether it is a fable and an imposture. This is in fact but a small part, but we will take it on this ground. Now is it his duty to reject it? No Deist pretends that he can be so fully persuaded in his own mind, as to be free from all doubt. All he dares to attempt is to raise cavils and create doubts on the other side. Here, then, it is his duty to stop, and not oppose the Bible, until he can prove without a doubt, that it is not from God.

So with the Unitarian. Granting (what is by no means true) that the evidence in the Bible is not sufficient to remove all doubts that Jesus Christ is God; yet it affords evidence enough to raise a doubt on the other side, he has no right to reject the doctrine as untrue, but is bound humbly to search the scriptures and satisfy himself. Now, no intelligent and honest man can say that the scriptures afford *no evidence* of the divinity of Christ. They do afford evidence which has convinced and fully satisfied thousands of the acutest minds, and who have before been opposed to the doctrine. No man can reject the doctrine without a doubt, because here is evidence that it *may be* true. And if it may be true, and there is reason to doubt, if it is not true, then he *rejects* it at his peril.

Then the Universalist. Where is one who can say he has not so much as a doubt whether there is not a hell, where sinners go after death into endless torment. He is bound to stop and inquire, and search the scriptures. It is not enough for him to say he does not believe in a hell. It may be there is, and if he rejects it, and goes on reckless of the truth whether there is or not, that itself makes him a rebel against God. He doubts whether there is not a hell which he ought to avoid, and yet acts as if he was certain and had no doubts. He is condemned. I once knew a physician who was a Universalist, and who has gone to eternity to try the reality of his speculations. He once told me that he had strong doubts of the truth of Universalism, and had mentioned his doubts to his minister, who confessed that he, too, doubted its truth, and he did not believe there was a Universalist in the world who did not.

2. For a man to do a thing when he doubts whether it is lawful shows that he is selfish, and has other objects besides doing the will of God.

It shows that he wants to do it to gratify himself. He doubts whether God will approve of it, and yet he does it. Is he not a rebel? If he honestly wished to serve God, when he doubted he would stop and inquire and examine until he was satisfied. But to go forward while he is in doubt, shows that he is selfish and wicked, and is willing to do it whether God is pleased or not, and that he wants to do it, whether it is right or wrong. He does it because he wants to do it, and not *because it is right.*

3. To act thus is an impeachment of the divine goodness.

He assumes it as uncertain whether God has given a sufficient revelation of His will, so that he *might* know his duty if he would. He virtually says that the path of duty is left so doubtful that he must decide at a venture.

4. It indicates slothfulness and stupidity of mind.

It shows that he had rather act wrong than use the necessary diligence to learn and know the path of duty. It shows that he is either negligent or dishonest in his inquiries.

5. It manifests a reckless spirit.

It shows a want of conscience, an indifference to right, a setting aside of the authority of God, a disposition not to do God's will, and not to care whether He is pleased or displeased, a desperate recklessness and headlong temper, that is the height of wickedness.

The principle then, which is so clearly laid down in the text and context, and also in the chapter which I read from Corinthians, is fully sustained by examination—That for a man to do a thing, when he doubts the lawfulness of it, is sin, for which he is condemned before God, and must repent or be damned.

II. I am now to show the *application of this principle* to a variety of particular cases in human life. But,

First—I will mention some cases where a person *may be equally in doubt* with respect to the lawfulness of a thing, whether he is bound to do it or not to do it.

Take the subject of *Wine at the Communion Table.*

Since the Temperance Reformation has brought up the question about the use of wine, and various wines have been analyzed and the quantity of alcohol they contain has been disclosed, and the difficulty shown of getting wines in this country that are not highly alcoholic, it has been seriously doubted by some whether it is right to use such wines as we can get here in celebrating the Lord's supper. Some are strong in the belief that wine is an essential part of the ordinance, and that we ought to use the best wine we can get, and there leave the matter. Others say that we ought not to use alcoholic or intoxicating wine at all, and that as wine is not in their view essential to the ordinance, it is better to use some other drink.—Both these classes are undoubtedly equally conscientious, and desirous to do what they have most reason to believe is agreeable to the will of God. And others, again, are in doubt on the matter. I can easily conceive that some conscientious persons may be very seriously in doubt which way to act. They are doubtful whether it is right to use alcoholic wine, and are doubtful whether it is right to use any other drink in the sacrament. Here is a case that comes under President Edwards' rule, "where it is doubtful in my mind, whether I ought to do it or not to do it," and which men must decide according to the best light they can get, honestly and with a single desire to know and do what is most pleasing to God.

I do not intend to discuss this question, of the use of wine at the communion, nor is this the proper place for a full examination of the subject. I introduced it now merely for the purpose of illustration. But since it is before us, I will make two or three remarks.

(1.) I have never apprehended so much evil as some do, from the use of common wine at the communion. I have not felt alarmed at the danger or evil of taking a sip of wine, a teaspoonful or so, once a month, or once in two months, or three months. I do not believe that the *disease* of intemperance (and intemperance, you know, is in reality a disease of the body) will be either created or continued by so slight a cause. Nor do I believe it is going to injure the Temperance cause so much as some have supposed. And therefore, where a person uses wine as we have been accustomed to do, and is fully persuaded in his own mind, he does not sin.

(2.) On the other hand, I do not think that the use of wine is any way essential to the ordinance. Very much has been said and written and printed on the subject, which has darkened counsel by words without knowledge. To my mind there are stronger reasons than I have anywhere seen exhibited, for supposing that wine is not essential to this ordinance. Great pains have been taken to prove that our Savior used wine that was unfermented, when he instituted the supper, and which therefore contained no alcohol. Indeed, this has been the point chiefly in debate. But in fact it seems just as irrelevant as it would to discuss the question, whether He used wheat or oaten bread, or whether it was leavened or unleavened. Why do we not hear *this* question vehemently discussed? Because all regard it as unessential.

In order to settle this question about the wine, we should ask what is *the meaning* of the ordinance of the supper.—What did our Savior design to do? It was to take the two staple articles for the support of life, *food* and *drink*, and use them to represent the necessity and virtue of the atonement.

It is plain that Christ had that view of it, for it corresponds with what He says, "My flesh is *meat* indeed, and thy blood is *drink* indeed." So He poured out water in the temple, and said, "If any man thirst, let him come unto me and drink."—He is called the "Bread of life." Thus it was customary to show the value of Christ's sufferings by *food* and *drink*. Why did He take bread instead of some other article of food? Those who know the history and usages of that country will see that he chose that article of food which was in most common use among the people. When I was in Malta, it seemed as if a great part of the people lived on bread alone. They would go in crowds to the market-place, and buy each a piece of coarse bread, and stand and eat it. Thus the most common and the most universally wholesome article of diet is chosen by Christ to represent His flesh. Then why did He take *wine* to drink? For the same reason; wine is the common drink of the people, especially at their meals, in all those countries. It is sold there for about a cent a bottle, wine being cheaper than small beer is here. In Sicily I was informed that wine was sold for five cents a gallon, and I do not know but it was about as cheap as water. And you will observe that the Lord's supper was first observed at the close of the feast of the passover, at which the Jews always used wine. The meaning of the Savior in this ordinance, then, is this:—As *food* and *drink* are essential to the life of the body, so His body and blood, or His atonement, are essential to the life of the soul. For myself, I am fully convinced that wine is not essential to the communion, and I should not hesitate to give water to any individual that conscientiously preferred it. Let it be the common food and drink of the country, the support of life to the body, and it answers the end of the institution. If I was a missionary among the Esquimaux Indians, where they live on dried seal's flesh and snow-water, I would administer the supper in those substances. It would convey to their minds the idea that they cannot live without Christ.

I say, then, that if an individual is fully persuaded in his own mind, he does not sin in giving up the use of wine. Let this church be fully persuaded in their own minds, and I shall have no scruple to do either way. If they will substitute any other wholesome drink, that is in common use, instead of the wine. And at the same time I have no objection myself against going on in the old way.

Now, don't lose sight of the great principle that is under discussion. It is this: where a man doubts honestly, whether it is lawful to do a thing, and doubts equally, on the other hand, whether it is lawful to omit doing it, he must pray over the matter, and search the scriptures, and get the best light he can on the subject, and then act. And when he does this, he is by no means to be judged or censured by others for the course he takes. "Who art thou that judgest another man's servant?" And no man is authorized to make his own conscience the rule of his neighbor's conduct.

A similar case is where a minister is so situated that it is necessary for him to go a distance on the Sabbath to preach, as where he preaches to two congregations, and the like. Here he may honestly doubt what is his duty, on both hands. If he goes, he appears to strangers to disregard the Sabbath. If he does not go, the people will have no preaching. The direction is, let him search the scriptures, and get the best light he can, make it a subject of prayer, weigh it thoroughly, and act according to his best judgment.

So in the case of a Sabbath-school teacher. He may live at a distance from the school, and be obliged to travel to it on the Sabbath, or they will have no school. And he may honestly doubt which is his duty, to remain in his own church on the Sabbath, or to travel there, five, eight, or ten miles, to a destitute neighborhood, to keep up the Sabbath school. Here he must decide for himself, according to the best light he can get. And let no man set himself up to judge over a humble and conscientious disciple of the Lord Jesus.

You see that in all these cases it is understood and is plain, that the design is to honor God, and the sole ground of doubt is, which course will really honor Him. Paul says, in reference to all laws of this kind, "He that regardeth the day, regardeth it unto the Lord; and he that regardeth not the day, to the Lord he doth not regard it." The design is to do right, and the doubt is as to the means of doing it in the best manner.

Secondly—I will mention some cases, where the *design is* wrong, where the object is to gratify self, and the individual has doubts whether he may do it lawfully. I shall refer to cases concerning which there is a difference of opinion—to acts of which the least that can be said is that a man must *have doubts* of their being lawful.

1. Take, for instance, *the making or vending of alcoholic drinks.*

After all that has been said on this subject, and all the light that has been thrown upon the question, is there a man living in this land who can say he sees no reason *to doubt* the lawfulness of this business. To say the least that can be said, there can be no honest mind but must be brought to doubt it. We suppose, indeed, that there is no honest mind but must know it is unlawful and criminal. But take the most charitable supposition possible for the distiller or the vender, and suppose he is not fully convinced of its unlawfulness. We say he must, at least, *doubt* its lawfulness. What is he to do then? Is he to shut his eyes to the light, and go on, regardless of truth so long as he can keep from seeing it? No. He may cavil and raise objections, as much as he pleases, but *he knows* that he has doubts, about the lawfulness of his business. And if he doubts, and still persists in doing it, without taking the trouble to examine and see what is right, he is just as sure to be damned as if he went on in the face of knowledge. You hear these men say, "Why, I am not fully persuaded in my own mind, that the Bible forbids making or vending ardent spirits." Well, suppose you are not fully convinced, suppose all your possible and conceivable objections and cavils are not removed, what then? You know you have doubts about its lawfulness. And it is not necessary to take such ground to convict you of doing wrong. If you doubt its lawfulness, and yet persist in doing it, you are in the way to hell.

2. So where an individual is engaged in an employment that requires him to break the Sabbath.

As for instance, attending on a Post-office that is opened on the Sabbath, or a Turnpike gate, or in a Steamboat, or any other employment that is not a work of necessity. There are always some things that must be done on the Sabbath, they are works of absolute necessity or of mercy.

But suppose a case in which the labor is not necessary, as in the transportation of the U.S. Mail on the Sabbath, or the like. The least that can be said, the lowest ground that can be taken by charity itself, without turning fool, is that the lawfulness of such employment is doubtful. And if they persist in doing it, they sin, and are on the way to hell. God has sent out the penalty of His law against them, and if they do not repent they must be damned.

3. Owning stocks in steamboat and railroad companies, in stages, canal boats, &c. that break the Sabbath.

Can any such owner truly say he does not doubt the lawfulness of such an investment of capital? Can charity stoop lower than to say that man must strongly doubt whether such labor is a work of necessity or mercy? It is not necessary in the case to demonstrate that it is unlawful, though that can be done fully, but only to show so much light as to create a doubt of its lawfulness. Then if he persists in doing it, with that doubt unsatisfied, he is condemned—and lost.

4. The same remarks will apply to all sorts of lottery gambling. He doubts.

5. Take the case of those indulgences of appetite, which are subject of controversy, and which to say the least, are of doubtful right.

(1.) The drinking of wine, and beer, and other fermented intoxicating liquors. In the present aspect of the temperance cause, is it not questionable at least, whether making use of these drinks is not transgressing the rule laid down by the apostle, "It is good neither to eat flesh nor drink wine, nor anything whereby thy brother stumbleth, or is offended, or made weak." No man can make me believe he has no doubts of the lawfulness of doing it. There is no certain proof of its lawfulness, and there is strong proof of its unlawfulness, and every man who does it while he doubts the lawfulness, is condemned, and if he persists, is damned.

If there is any sophistry in all this, I should like to know it, for I do not wish to deceive others nor to be deceived myself. But I am entirely deceived if this is not a simple, direct, and necessary inference from the sentiment of the text.

(2.) *Tobacco.* Can any man pretend that he has no doubt that it is agreeable to the will of God for him to use tobacco? No man can pretend that he doubts the lawfulness of his *omission* of these things. Does any man living think that he is *bound* in duty to make use of wine, or strong beer, or tobacco, as a luxury? No. The doubt is all on one side. What shall we say then, of that man who doubts the lawfulness of it, and still fills his face with the poisonous weed? He is condemned.

(3.) I might refer to tea and coffee. It is known generally, that these substances are not nutritious at all, and that nearly eight millions of dollars are spent annually for them in this country. Now, will any man pretend that he does not doubt the lawfulness of spending all this money for that which is of no use, and which are WELL KNOWN, to all who have examined the subject, to be positively injurious, intolerable to weak stomachs, and as much as the strongest can dispose of? And all this while the various benevolent societies of the age are loudly calling for HELP to send the gospel abroad and save a world from hell! To think of the church alone spending millions upon their tea tables, is there no doubt here?

6. Apply this principle to *various amusements*.

(1.) *The Theatre.* There are vast multitudes of professors of religion who attend the theater. And they contend that the Bible nowhere forbids it. Now mark.—What Christian professor ever went to a theater and did not doubt whether he was doing what is lawful. I by no means admit that it is a point which is only doubtful. I suppose it is a very plain case, and can be shown to be, that it is unlawful. But I am now only meeting those of you, if there are any here, who go to the theater, and are trying to cover up yourselves in the refuge that the Bible nowhere expressly forbids it.

(2.) *Parties of Pleasure*, where they go and eat and drink to surfeiting. Is there no reason to doubt whether that is such a use of time and money as God requires? Look at the starving poor, and consider the effect of this gaiety and extravagance, and see if you will ever go to another such party, or make one, without doubting its lawfulness. Where can you find a man, or a woman, that will go so far as to say they have no doubt? Probably there is not one honest mind who will say this. And if you doubt, and still do it, you are condemned.

You see that this principle touches a whole class of things, about which there is a controversy, and where people attempt to parry off by saying it is not worse than to do so and so, and thus get away from the condemning sentence of God's law. But in fact, if there is a doubt, it is their duty to abstain.

(3.) Take the case of balls, of novel reading, and other methods of wasting time. Is this God's way to spend your lives? Can you say you have no doubt of it?

7. Making calls on the Sabbath. People will make a call, and then make an apology about it. "I did not know as it was quite right, but I thought I would venture it." He is a Sabbath-breaker in heart, at all events, because he doubts.

8. Compliance with worldly customs at new-year's day.—Then the ladies are all at home, and the gentlemen are running all about town to call on them, and the ladies make their great preparations, and treat them with their cake, and their wine, and punch, enough to poison them *almost to* death, and all together are bowing down to the goddess of fashion. Is there a lady here that does not doubt the lawfulness of all this? I say it can be demonstrated to be wicked, but I only ask the ladies of this city. Is it NOT DOUBTFUL whether this is all lawful? I should call in question the sanity of the man or woman that had no doubt of the lawfulness of such a custom, in the midst of such prevailing intemperance as exists in this city.—Who among you will practice it again? Practice it if you dare—at the peril of your soul. If you do that which is merely doubtful, God frowns and condemns, and His voice must be regarded.

I know people try to excuse the matter, and say it is well to have a day appropriated to such calls, when every lady is at home and every gentleman freed from business, and all that. And all that is very well. But when it is seen to be so abused, and to produce so much evil, I ask every Christian here, if you can help doubting its lawfulness? And if it is doubtful, it comes under the rule: "If meat make my brother to offend," if keeping new-year's leads to so much gluttony, and drunkenness, and wickedness, does it not bring the lawfulness of it into doubt? Yes, that is the least that can be said, and they who doubt and yet do it, sin against God.

9. Compliance with the extravagant fashions of the day.

Christian lady! have you never doubted, do you not now doubt, whether it is lawful for you to copy these fashions, brought from foreign countries, and from places which it were a shame even to name in this assembly? Have you no doubt about it? And if you doubt and do it, you are condemned, and must repent of your sin, or you will be lost forever.

10. Intermarriages of Christians with impenitent sinners.

This answer always comes up. "But after all you say, it is not *certain* that these marriages are not lawful." Supposing it be so, yet does not the Bible and the nature of the case make it, at least, doubtful whether they are right? It can be demonstrated, indeed, to be unlawful. But suppose it could not be reduced to demonstration. What Christian ever did it and did not doubt whether it was lawful? And he that doubteth is condemned. See that Christian man or woman that is about forming such a connection—doubting all the way whether it is right—trying to pray down conscience under the pretext of praying for light, praying all round your duty, and yet pressing on—TAKE CARE—you know you doubt the lawfulness of what you propose, and REMEMBER that he that doubteth is damned.

Thus you see, my hearers, that here is a principle that will stand by you when you attempt to rebuke sin, and the power of society is employed to face you down and put you on the defensive, to bring absolute proof of the sinfulness of a cherished practice. Remember *the burden of* PROOF *does not lie on you*, to show beyond a doubt the absolute unlawfulness of the thing. If you can show sufficient reason to question its lawfulness, and to create a valid doubt whether it is according to the will of God, you shift the burden of proof to the other side. And unless they can remove the doubt, and show that there is no room for doubt, they have no right to continue and if they do, they sin against God.

REMARKS.

1. The knowledge of duty is not indispensable to moral obligation, but the possession of the means of knowledge is sufficient to make a person responsible.

If a man has the means of knowing whether it is right or wrong, he is bound to use the means, and is bound to inquire and ascertain, at his peril.

2. If those are condemned, and adjudged worthy of damnation, who do that of which they doubt the lawfulness, what shall we say of the multitudes who are doing continually that which they know and confess to be wrong?

Woe to that man who practices that which he condemns.—And "happy is he that condemneth not himself in that thing which he alloweth."

3. *Hypocrites* often attempt to shelter themselves behind their doubts to get clear of their duty.

The hypocrite is unwilling to be enlightened, he don't wish to know the truth, because he don't wish to obey the Lord, and so he hides behind his doubts, and turns away his eye from the light, and will not look or examine to see what his duty is, and in this way he tries to shield himself from responsibility. But God will drag them out from behind this refuge of lies, by the principle laid down in the text, that their very doubts condemn them.

Many will not be enlightened on the subject of *temperance*, and still persist in drinking or selling rum, because they are not *fully convinced* it is wrong. And they will not read a tract or a paper, nor attend a temperance meeting, for fear they shall be convinced. Many are resolved to indulge in the use of wine and strong beer, and they will not listen to anything calculated to convince them of the wrong. It shows that they are determined to indulge in sin, and they hope to hide behind their doubts. What better evidence could they give that they are hypocrites?

Who in all these United States can say, that he has no doubt of the lawfulness of slavery? Yet the great body of the people will not hear anything on the subject, and they go into a passion if you name it, and it is even seriously proposed, both at the north and at the south, to pass laws forbidding inquiry and discussion on the subject. Now, suppose these laws should be passed, for the purpose of enabling the nation to shelter itself behind its doubts whether slavery is a sin, that ought to be abolished immediately—will that help the matter? Not at all. If they continue to hold their fellow men as property, in slavery, while they doubt its lawfulness, they are condemned before God, and we may be sure their sin will find them out, and God will let them KNOW how He regards it.

It is amazing to see the foolishness of people on this subject—as if by refusing to get clear of their doubts they could get clear of their sin. Think of the people of the south; Christians, and even ministers refusing to read a paper on the subject of slavery, and perhaps sending it back with abusive or threatening words. Threatening—for what? For reasoning with them about their duty.—It can be demonstrated absolutely, that slavery is unlawful, and ought to be repented of and given up like any other sin. But suppose they only doubt the lawfulness of slavery, and do not mean to be enlightened, they are condemned of God. Let them know that they cannot put this thing down, they cannot clear themselves of it; so long as they doubt its lawfulness they cannot hold men in slavery without sin, and that they do doubt its lawfulness is demonstrated by this opposition to discussion.

We may suppose a case, and perhaps there may be some such in the southern country, where a man doubts the lawfulness of holding slaves and equally doubts the lawfulness of emancipating them in their present state of ignorance and dependence. In that case he comes under Pres. Edward's rule, and it is his duty, not to fly in a passion with those who would call his attention to it, not to send back newspapers and refuse to read, but to inquire on all hands for light, and examine the question honestly in the light of the word of God, till his doubts are cleared up. The least he can do is to set himself with all his power to educate them and train them to take care of themselves as fast and as thoroughly as possible, and to put them in a state where they can be set at liberty.

5. It is manifest there is but very little conscience in the church.

See what multitudes are persisting to do what they strongly doubt the lawfulness of.

6. There is still less love to God than there is conscience.

It cannot be pretended that love to God is the cause of all this following of fashions, this practicing indulgences, and other things of which people doubt the lawfulness.—They do not persist in these things because they love God so well. No, no, but they persist in it because they wish to do it, to gratify themselves, and they had rather run the risk of doing wrong than to have their doubts cleared up. It is because they have so little love for God, so little care for the honor of God.

7. Do not say, in your prayers, "O Lord, if I have sinned in this thing, O Lord, forgive me the sin."

If you have done that of which you doubted the lawfulness, you have sinned, whether the thing itself be right or wrong. And you must repent, and ask forgiveness.

And now, let me ask you all who are here present, are you convinced that to do what you doubt the lawfulness of, is sin? If you are, I have one more question to ask you. Will you from this time relinquish every thing of which you doubt the lawfulness? Every amusement, every indulgence, every practice, every pursuit? Will you do it, or will you stand before the solemn judgment seat of Jesus Christ, condemned? If you will not relinquish these things, you show that you are an impenitent sinner, and do not *intend* to obey God, and if you do not repent, you bring down upon your head God's condemnation and wrath for ever.

LECTURE IV.

REPROOF A CHRISTIAN DUTY.

TEXT:—"Thou shalt in any wise rebuke thy neighbor, and not suffer sin upon him."

Leviticus xix.17.

The whole verse reads thus: "Thou shalt not hate thy brother in thy heart: thou shalt in any wise rebuke thy neighbor, and not suffer sin upon him." In the margin, as those of you who have Bibles with marginal notes can see, the last words of the verse are rendered, "that thou bear not sin for him." And this, I am satisfied, is the correct translation. The idea is this:
THAT MEN ARE BOUND TO REPROVE THEIR NEIGHBORS FOR SIN, LEST THEY BECOME PARTAKERS WITH THEM, OR ACCESSORY TO THEIR SIN.

In speaking from these words I design to pursue the following order:
I. To show the reasons for the rule laid down by God in the text.
II. Show to whom the rule is applicable.
III. Mention several exceptions which God has made to the rule, or classes of persons who are not to be reproved for their sins.
IV. The manner of performing this duty.
V. Several specific applications of the principles established.

I. I am to show the reasons for the rule.
1. Love to God plainly requires this.
If we really love God, we shall of course feel bound to reprove those that hate and abuse Him and break His commands. If I love the government of the country, should I not reprove and rebuke a man who should abuse or revile the government? If a child loves his parents, will he not of course reprove a man that abuses his parents in his hearing?
2. Love to the universe will lead to the same thing.
If a man loves the universe, if he is actuated by universal benevolence, he knows that sin is inconsistent with the highest good of the universe, and that it is calculated to injure and ruin the whole if not counteracted; that its direct tendency is to overthrow the order and destroy the happiness of the universe. And therefore,

if he sees this doing, his benevolence will lead him to reprove and oppose it.

3. Love to the community in which you live, is another reason.

Not only love to the universe at large, but love to the particular people with which you are connected should lead you to reprove sin. Sin is a reproach to any people, and whoever commits it goes to produce a state of society that is injurious to every thing good. His example has a tendency to corrupt society, to destroy its peace and to introduce disorder and ruin, and it is the duty of every one who loves the community to resist and reprove it.

4. Love to your neighbor demands it.

Neighbor, here, means anybody that sins within the reach of your influence; not only in your presence, but in your neighborhood, if your influence can reach him, or in your nation, or in the world. If he sins he injures himself, and therefore if we love him we shall reprove his sins. Love to the intemperate induces us to warn him of the consequences of his course. Suppose we see our neighbor exposed to a temporal calamity, say his house on fire. True love will induce us to warn him and not to leave him to perish in the flames. Especially if we saw him inclined to persist in his course, and stay in the burning house, we should expostulate earnestly with him, and not suffer him to destroy himself, if we could possibly prevent it. Much more should we warn him of the consequences of sin, and reprove him, and strive to turn him, before he destroys himself.

5. It is cruel to omit it.

If you see your neighbor sin, and you pass by and neglect to reprove him, it is just as cruel as if you should see his house on fire, and pass by and not warn him of it. Why not? If he is in the house, and the house burns, he will lose his life. If he sins and remains in sin, he will go to hell. Is it not cruel to let him go unwarned to hell? Some seem to consider it not cruel to let a neighbor go on in sin till the wrath of God comes on him to the uttermost. Their feelings are so tender that they cannot wound him by telling him of his sin and his danger. No doubt, the tender mercies of the wicked are cruel. Instead of warning their neighbor of the consequences of sin, they actually encourage him in it.

6. To refuse to do it is rebellion against God.

For any one to see rebellion and not to reprove it or lift his hand to oppose it, is itself rebellion. It would be counted rebellion by the laws of the land. The man who should know of a treasonable plot, and did not disclose it or endeavor to defeat it, would be held an accessory, and condemned as such by law. So if a man sees rebellion breaking out against God, and does not oppose it or make efforts to suppress it, he is himself a rebel.

7. If you do not reprove your neighbors for their sin, you are chargeable with their death.

God holds us chargeable with the death of those whom we suffer to go on in sin without reproof, and it is right He should. If we see them sin, and make no opposition, and give no reproof, we consent to it, and countenance them in it. If you see a man preparing to kill his neighbor, and stand still and do nothing to prevent it, you consent, and are justly chargeable as accessory; in the eye of God and in the eye of law, you are justly chargeable with the same sin. So if you see a man committing any iniquity, and do nothing to resist it, you are guilty with him. His blood will be upon his own head, but at whose hand will God require it? What says God respecting a watchman? "Son of man, I have set thee a watchman unto the house of Israel; therefore thou shalt hear the word at my mouth, and warn them from me. When I say unto the wicked, O wicked man, thou shalt surely die; if thou dost not speak to warn the wicked from his way, that wicked man shall die in his iniquity, but his blood will I require at thy hand." This is true of all men. If you suffer a neighbor, who is within reach of your influence, to pass on in sin unwarned, he will die in his iniquity, but his blood shall be required at your hand.

8. Your silence encourages him in sin.

He is authorized to infer from your silence that you approve his sin, or, at least, that you do not care for it. Especially if he knows you as a professor of religion. It is an old maxim that *silence is consent.* Sinners do regard your silence as a virtual sanction of what they do.

9. By reproving your neighbor who sins, you may save him.

What multitudes have been reformed by timely reproof. Most of those who are saved, are saved by somebody's rebuking them for their sins and urging them to repentance. You may be instrumental in saving any man, if you speak to him and reprove him and pray for him, as you ought. How many instances there are, where a single reproof has been to the transgressor like the barbed arrow in his soul, that rankled, and rankled, the poison whereof drank up his spirits, until he submitted to God. I have known instances where even a look of reproof has done the work.

10. If you do not save the individual reproved, your reproof may save somebody else that may be acquainted with the fact.

Such cases have often occurred, where the transgressor has not been reclaimed, but others have been deterred from following his example by the rebukes directed to him.—Who can doubt that, if professors of religion were faithful in this duty, men would fear encountering their reproofs, and that fear would deter them from such conduct, and multitudes who now go on unblushing and unawed, would pause and think, and be reclaimed and saved? Will you, with such an argument for faithfulness before you, let sinners go on unrebuked till they stumble into hell?

11. God expressly requires it.

The language of the text is, in the original, exceedingly strong. The word is repeated, which is the way in which the Hebrew expresses a superlative, so as to leave no doubt on the mind, not the least uncertainty as to the duty, nor any excuse for not doing it. There is not a stronger command of God in the Bible than this. God has given it the greatest strength of language that He can. "Thou shalt *in any wise* rebuke him,"—that is, without any excuse, "and not bear his sin," not be accessory to his ruin. It is a maxim of law, that if a man knows of a murder about to be committed and does not use means to prevent it, he shall be held accessory before the fact. If he knows of murder which has been done, and does not endeavor to bring the criminal to justice, he is accessory after the fact. So by the law of God, if you do not endeavor to bring a known transgressor to repentance, you are implicated in the guilt of his crime, and are held responsible at the throne of God.

12. If you do it in a right manner, you will keep a conscience void of offense in regard to your neighbor, whatever may be his end.

And you cannot do this without being faithful in the reproof of sin. A man does not live conscientiously, towards God or man, unless he is in the habit of reproving transgressors who are within his influence. This is one grand reason why there is so little conscience in the church. In what respect are professors of religion so much in the habit of resisting their consciences, as in regard to the duty of reproving sin? Here is one of the strongest commands in the Bible, and yet multitudes do not pay any attention to it at all. Can they have a clear conscience? They may just as well pretend to have a clear conscience, and get drunk every day. No man keeps the law of God, or keeps his conscience clear, who sees sin and does not reprove it. He has additional guilt, who knows of sin and does not reprove it. He breaks two commandments. First, he becomes accessory to the transgression of his neighbor, and then he disobeys an express requirement by refusing to reprove his neighbor.

13. Unless you reprove men for their sins, you are not prepared to meet them in judgment.

Are you prepared to meet your children in the judgment, if you have not reproved nor chastised them, nor watched over their morals? "Certainly not," you say.—But why? "Because God has made it my duty to do this, and He holds me responsible for it." Very well. Then take the case of any other man that sins under your eye, or within reach of your influence, and goes down to hell, and you have never reproved him. Are you not responsible? Oh, how many are now groaning in hell, that you have seen commit sin, and have never reproved, and now they are pouring curses on your head because you never warned them. And how can you meet them in judgment?

14. Unless you do this, you are not prepared to meet God.

How many there are, who profess to love God, and yet never so much as pretend to obey this command. Are such people prepared to meet God? When He says, "Thou shalt *in any wise* rebuke thy neighbor"—that is, without any excuse.

II. To whom is this command addressed?

Manifestly, to all men that have neighbors. It was addressed to all the people of Israel, and through them to all who are under the government of God—to high and low, rich and poor, young and old, male and female, and every individual who is under the government of God or bound to obey His commands.

III. Some exceptions to the universal application of this law.

He that made the law has a right to admit of exceptions. And the rule is binding in all cases, unless they come within the exceptions. There are some exceptions to the rule before us, laid down in the Bible.

1. God says, "Rebuke not a scorner, lest he hate thee."

There is a state of mind, where a person is known to be a scorner, a despiser of religion, a hater of God, and has no regard to His law, and not to be influenced by any fear or care for God, why should you reprove him? It will only provoke a quarrel, without any good resulting to any body. Therefore God makes such a character an exception to the rule.

2. Jesus Christ says, "Cast not your pearls before swine, lest they trample them under their feet, and turn again and rend you."

Whatever else this passage means, it appears to me to mean this, that sometimes men are in such a state of mind that to talk to them about religion would be at once irrational and dangerous, like casting pearls before swine. They have such a contempt for religion, and such a stupid, sensual, swinish heart, that they will trample all your reproofs under their feet, and turn upon you in anger besides. It is lawful to let such men go on; and your not meddling with them will be greater wisdom than to attack them. But great charity should be used, not to suppose those of your neighbors to be swine, who do not deserve it, and who might be benefited by suitable reproof.

3. Men who are in a settled state of self-righteousness, it is best to let alone.

Christ said of the Scribes and Pharisees, "*Let them alone*, they be blind leaders of the blind." That is, they were so full of pride and conceit, so satisfied of their own wisdom and goodness, that they cannot be reached by any reproof, and it seems best to let them alone; for if you begin to reprove them, you might as well face a north-wester as to think of making an impression on them. They will face you down, and are so full of arguments and cavils and bullyings, that you gain nothing.

IV. The manner in which this duty is to be performed.

1. It should be done always in the name of the Lord.

It is important when you reprove your neighbor for sin, always to make him feel it is not a personal controversy with you, not a matter of selfishness on your part, or claiming any right of superiority, or to lord it over him, but that you reprove him in the name of the Lord, for the honor of God, because he has broken His law. If, by your manner, you in any way make the impression on his mind, that it is a personal controversy, or done for any private motive with you, he will invariably rise up against you, and resist, and perhaps retort upon you. But if you make the impression on his mind that it is done in the name of God, and bring him right up before God as an offender, he will find it exceedingly difficult to get away from you without at least confessing that he is wrong.

2. It should always be done with great solemnity.

Above all things, do not make him think that it is just a little thing that you hint to him, but make him feel that it is for a sin against God you are reproving him, and that it is what in your view ought to be looked upon as an awful thing.

3. You should use more or less severity, according to the nature of the case, and the circumstances under which the sin was committed.

(1.) The relation of the parties.

Your relation to the person who has been guilty of sin, should be properly regarded.

If a child is going to reprove a parent, he should do it in a manner suited to the relation he stands in. If a man is going to reprove a magistrate, or if an individual is about to rebuke an elder, the apostle says it must be in that way, "entreat him as a father." This relation should enter deeply into the manner of administering reproof. The relation of parents and children, of husbands and wives, of brothers and sisters, should all be regarded. So the ages of the parties, their relative circumstances in life. For servants to reprove their masters in the same manner as their equals is improper. This direction should never be overlooked or forgotten, for if it is, the good effect of reproof will be all lost. BUT REMEMBER, that no relations in life, or relative circumstances of the parties, take away the obligation of this duty. Whatever be the relation, you are to reprove sin, and are bound to do it in the name of the Lord. Do it, not as if you were complaining or finding fault for a personal injury committed against yourself, but as a sin against God. Thus, when a child reproves a parent for sin, he is not to do it as if he was expostulating with him for any injury done to himself, but with an eye to the fact that the parent has sinned against God, and therefore, with all that plainness and faithfulness and pungency that sin calls for.

(2.) Reproof should be regulated by the knowledge which the offender has of his duty.

If the individual is ignorant, reproof should be more in the form of instruction, rather than of severe rebuke. How do you do with your little child? You instruct him and strive to enlighten his mind respecting his duty. You proceed, of course, very differently from what you would do with a hardened offender.

(3.) With reference also to the frequency of the offense.

You would reprove a first offense in a very different manner from what you would use towards a habitual transgressor. If a person is accustomed to sin, and knows that it is wrong, you use more severity. If it is the first time, perhaps a mere allusion to it may be sufficient to prevent a repetition.

(4.) So, also, you are to consider whether he has been frequently reproved for the sin.

If he has not only often committed the sin, but been often reproved, and yet has hardened his neck, there is the greater necessity for using sharpness. The hardening influence of former reproofs resisted, shows that no common expostulations will take hold. He needs to have the terrors of the Lord poured upon him like a storm of hail.

4. Always show that your temper is not ruffled.

Never manifest any displeasure at the transgressor, which he can possibly construe into personal displeasure at himself. It is often important to show your strong displeasure at what he is doing. Otherwise he will think you are not in earnest. Suppose you reprove a man for murder, in a manner not expressing any abhorrence of his crime. You would not expect to produce an effect. The manner should be suited to the nature of the crime, yet so as not to lead him to think you have any personal feeling. Here is the grand defect in the manner of reproving crime, both in the pulpit and out of it. For fear of giving offence, men do not express their abhorrence of the sin, and therefore transgressors are so seldom reclaimed.

5. Always reprove in the Spirit of God.

You should always have so much of the Holy Ghost with you, that when you reprove a man for sin, he will feel as if it come from God. I have known cases, where reproof from a Christian in that state cuts the transgressor to the heart, and stings like the arrow of the Almighty, and he cannot get rid of it till he repents.

6. There are many different ways of giving reproof so as to reach the individual reproved.

Sometimes it can be done best by sending a letter, especially if the person is at a distance. And there are cases where it can be done so, even in your own neighborhood. I knew an individual who chose this way of reprimanding a sea-captain for intemperance in crossing the Atlantic. The captain drank hard, especially in bad weather, and when his services were most wanted. The individual was in great agony, for the captain was not only intemperate, but when he drank, he was ill-natured, and endangered the lives of all on board. He made it a subject of prayer. It was a difficult case—he did not know how to approach the captain so as to make it probable he should do good and not hurt; for a captain at sea, you know, is a perfect despot, and has the most absolute power on earth. After a while he sat down and wrote a letter, and gave it to the captain with his own hand, in which he plainly and affectionately, but faithfully and most pointedly set forth his conduct, and the sin he was committing against God and man. He accompanied it with much prayer to God. The captain read it, and it completely cured him; he made an apology to the individual, and never drank another drop of anything stronger than coffee or tea on the whole passage.

7. Sometimes it is necessary to reprove sin by forming societies, and getting up newspapers, and forming a public sentiment against a particular sin, that shall be a continued and overwhelming rebuke. The Temperance societies, Moral Reform societies, Anti- Slavery societies, &c. are designed for this end.

V. I will mention now some of the cases in which these principles are applicable.

They are peculiarly applicable to those crimes which are calculated to undermine the institutions of society, and to exert a wide-spread influence. Such sins can only be held in check and put down by faithfulness in reproof.

1. Sabbath-breaking.

If Christians would universally mark transgressors, and rebuke them that trample on the Sabbath, they would do more to put a stop to Sabbath breaking than by all other means. If Christians were united in this, how long do you suppose it would be before this sin would be put down? If only a few were faithful, and constant, and persevering, they might do much. If only a few do it, and these only now and then, it might not have much effect. But I believe if all professors of religion were to do it, every grocery and grog shop, and oyster cellar and fruit stand would be shut up. At all events, they are bound to do it, whatever may be the results; and so long as they neglect their duty, they are chargeable before God with all the Sabbath breaking in the city. If all the churches and ecclesiastical bodies in the land were united to remonstrate with the government, and would continue to do it, firmly and in the name of the Lord, do you suppose that government would continue to violate the Sabbath with their mail? I tell you, no. The church can do this, I believe, in one year, if all were united throughout the country and could speak out fully, in the fear of God, and without any fear of man. No man, who ever expected to be elected to office again, would ever again advise the breaking of the Sabbath. But now, while the church is divided and not half in earnest, there are so few speak out that Congress despises them, and pays no attention. Thus it is that the church connive at Sabbath breaking, and they are without excuse, till they speak out and rebuke their rulers, in the name of Jehovah, for breaking His holy law.

2. Intemperance and rum-selling.

Suppose every man in this city that sells rum were continually subject to the rebukes which God requires—suppose every man that passed by were to reprove him for his sin, how long could he sell rum? If only the church were to do it, if that deacon and that elder would do it, and every Christian would follow him with rebukes in the name of the Lord for poisoning men to death with rum, he could not go on and do it. Such a strong and decided testimony would soon drive him from his trade of death. In self-defense, he would have to yield to the pressure of solemn rebuke.

3. Lewdness.

This is a wide-spreading evil, that ought to be universally rebuked.

It should be rebuked unsparingly, not only from the pulpit, but by the press, and in the street, till it is driven from its strong holds, and made to hide itself in the chambers of hell.

4. Slavery.

What! shall men be suffered to commit one of the most God-dishonoring and most heaven-daring sins on earth, and not be reproved? It is a sin against which all men should bear testimony, and lift up their voice like a trumpet, till this giant iniquity is banished from the land and from the world.

VI. I shall consider some of the difficulties which are sometimes raised in the way of the performance of this duty.

1. It is often asked, Is it a duty to reprove my neighbor when there is no prospect of doing any good?

I answer, it may be very essential to reprove sin in many cases where there is no prospect that the individual whom you reprove will be benefited. As in cases where your silence would be taken for connivance in his sin. Or where the very fact of his being reproved may prevent others from falling into the like crime. Where the offender comes properly under the description of a scorner or a swine, there God has made an exception, and you are not bound to reprove. But in other cases, duty is yours, consequences God's.

2. It is asked, Should I reprove strangers? Why not? Is not the stranger your neighbor? You are not to reprove a stranger in the same way that you would a familiar acquaintance, but the fact of his being a stranger is not a reason why he should not be reproved, if he breaks the command of God. If a man swears profanely, or breaks the Sabbath, in your presence, his being a stranger does not excuse you from the duty and the responsibility of administering reproof, or trying to bring him to repentance and save his soul.

3. It is asked, Should we reprove a person when he is drunk?

Generally not, for when a person is drunk he is deranged. There may be cases where it is proper, for the purpose of warning others. But so far as the drunkard himself is concerned, as a general rule, it is not expedient. Yet there are many cases, where reproof to a man even when drunk, has taken such a hold on his mind as to sober him and turn him from his beastly sin.

4. Shall we reprove great men, and those who are above us in society, and who may look down on us and on our reproofs with contempt?

That does not alter your duty. "Thou shalt *in any wise* rebuke thy neighbor, and not bear sin for him." You should bear in mind the relation in which he stands and treat him accordingly. But still, if he sins against God, it is your duty to reprove him, in an appropriate manner.

REMARKS.

1. Do not talk about people's sins, but go and reprove them.

It is very common to talk about people's sins behind their backs, but this is great wickedness. If you want to talk about any person's sins, go and talk to him about them, and try to get him to repent and forsake them. Do not go and talk to others against him behind his back, and leave him to go on in his sins, unwarned, to hell.

2. How few professors of religion are sufficiently conscientious to practice this duty.

I suppose there are thousands in this city, who never think of doing it. Yes; professors of religion live in habitual disobedience to this plain, and strongly-expressed command of God. And then they wonder why they do not have the spirit of prayer, and why there are not more revivals! Wonder!

3. See why so few persons enjoy religion.

They live in habitual neglect of this command, making excuses, when God has said there shall be no excuse. And how can they enjoy religion? What would the universe think of God, if he should grant the joys of religion to such unfaithful professors?

4. We see that the great mass of professors of religion have more regard to their own reputation than to the requirements of God.

The proof is, that sooner than run the risk of being called censorious, or of getting enemies by rebuking sin, they will let men go on in sin unrebuked, notwithstanding God says, "Thou shalt in any wise rebuke thy neighbor." But I shall offend him if I reprove his sin. In any wise rebuke him, says Jehovah. It shows that they have greater fear of men than of God. For fear of offending men, they run the risk of offending God. Yea, they absolutely disobey God, in one of His plainest and strongest commandments, rather than incur the displeasure of men by rebuking their sins.

5. No man has a right to say to us, when we reprove him for his sin, that it is none of our business to meddle with him.

How often do transgressors tell faithful reprovers, they had better mind their own business and not meddle with what does not concern them. And they are called meddlers and busybodies, for interfering in other people's concerns. At the south, they have got themselves into a great rage because we at the north are trying to convince them of the wickedness of slavery. And they say it is none of our business, that slavery is a matter peculiarly their own, and they will not suffer anybody else to interfere with them, and they require us to let them alone, and will not even allow us to talk about the subject. And they want our northern legislatures to pass laws forbidding us to rebuke our southern neighbors for their sin in holding men in slavery. God forbid that we should be silent. Jehovah Himself has commanded us to rebuke our neighbor in any wise, let the consequences be as they may. And we will rebuke them, though all hell should rise up against it.

Are we to hold our peace and be partakers in the sin of slavery, by connivance, as we have been? God forbid.—We will speak of it, and bear our testimony against it, and pray over it, and complain of it to God and man.—Heaven shall know, and the world shall know, and hell shall know, that we protest against the sin and will continue to rebuke it, till it is broken up. God Almighty says, "Thou shalt in any wise rebuke thy neighbor," and we must do it.

So the rum-dealer is all the while pleading, "It is none of your concern what I do, please to mind your own business and let me alone." But it is our business to reprove him when he dispenses his poison, and it is everybody's concern, and every man is bound to rebuke his crime till he gives it up and ceases to destroy the lives and souls of his neighbors.

6. We see the importance of consistency in religion.

If a man professes to love God, he ought to have consistency enough to reprove those that oppose God. If Christians were only consistent in this duty, many would be converted by it, a right public sentiment would be formed, and sin would be rebuked and forced to retire before the majesty of Christian rebuke. If Christians were not such cowards, and absolutely disobedient to this plain command of God, one thing would certainly come of it—either they would be murdered in the streets as martyrs, because men could not bear the intolerable presence of truth, or they would be speedily converted to God.

What shall we say then to such professors of religion? Afraid to reprove sinners! When God commands, not prepared to obey? How will they answer it to God?

Now, beloved, will you practice this duty? Will you reprove sin faithfully, so as not to bear sin for your neighbors? Will you make your whole life a testimony against sin? Will you clear your souls, or will you hold your peace and be weighed down with the guilt of all transgressors around you and within the sphere of your influence? God says, "Thou shalt in any wise rebuke thy neighbor, and not bear sin for him."

LECTURE V.

TRUE SAINTS.

TEXT:—"Who is on the Lord's side?"— Exodus xxxii. 26.

This question was addressed by Moses to the professed people of God, immediately after their great departure from God while Moses was in the Mount, when they went and worshiped a golden calf which had been cast for them by Aaron. After expostulating with the guilty nation, he called out, "Who is on the Lord's side?" It is not my intention to dwell on the history of this case particularly, but to come at once to the main design I have in view this evening, which is to show that there are
THREE CLASSES OF PROFESSING CHRISTIANS.
I. The true friends of God and man.

II. Those who are actuated by hope and fear, or in other words, by self-love, or by selfishness.

III. Those who are actuated by public opinion.

These three classes may be known by attending to the characteristic developments which show what is the leading design in their religion. It needs not be proved, that persons may set out in religion from very different motives, some from real love to religion, and some from other motives. The differences may be arranged in these three classes, and by attending to the development of their real design in becoming religious, you learn their characters. They all profess to be servants of God, and yet by observing the lives of many, it becomes manifest that instead of their being God's servants they are only trying to make God their servant. Their leading aim and object is to secure their own salvation, or some other advantage for themselves, through the medium of the favor of God. They are seeking to make God their friend, that they may make use of Him to serve their own turn.

I. There is a class of professed Christians who are the true friends of God and man.

If you attend to those things which develop the true design and aim, of their religion, you will see it to be such. They are truly and sincerely benevolent.

1. They will make it manifest that this is their character, by their carefulness in avoiding sin.

They will show that they hate it in themselves, and they hate it in others. They will not justify it in themselves, and they will not justify it in others. They will not seek to cover up or to excuse their own sins, neither will they try to cover up or to excuse the sins of others. In short, *they aim* at PERFECT HOLINESS. This course of conduct makes it evident that they are the true friends of God. I do not mean to say that every true friend of God is perfect, no more than I would say that every truly affectionate and obedient child is perfect, or never fails in duty to his parent. But if he is an affectionate and obedient child, his aim is to obey always, and if he fails in any respect, he by no means justifies it, or pleads for it, or aims to cover it up, but as soon as he comes to think of the matter, is dissatisfied with himself, and condemns his conduct.

So these persons who are the true friends of God and man, are ever ready to complain of themselves, and to blame and condemn themselves for what is wrong. But you never see them finding fault with God. You never hear them excusing themselves and throwing off the blame upon their Maker, by telling of their inability to obey God, or speaking as if God had required impossibilities of His creatures. They always speak as if they felt that what God has required is right and reasonable, and themselves only to blame for their disobedience.

2. They manifest a deep *abhorrence of the sins of other people.*

They do not cover up the sins of others, or plead for them and excuse them, or smooth them over by "perhaps" this, or "perhaps" that. You never hear them apologizing for sin. As they are indignant at sin in themselves, they are just as much so when they see it in others. They know its horrible nature, and abhor it always.

3. Another thing in which this spirit manifests itself, is *zeal for the honor and glory of God.*

They show the same ardor to promote God's honor and interest, that the true patriot does to promote the honor and interest of his country. If he greatly loves his country, its government and its interest, he sets his heart upon promoting its advancement and benefit. He is never so happy as when he is doing something for the honor and advancement of his country. So a child that truly loves his father, is never so happy as when he is advancing his father's honor and interest. And he never feels more indignant grief, than when he sees his father abused or injured. If he sees his father disobeyed or abused by those who ought to obey and love and honor him, his heart breaks forth with indignant grief.

There are multitudes of professing Christians, and even ministers, who are very zealous to defend their own character and their own honor. But this one class feel more engaged, and their hearts beat higher when defending or advancing God's honor. These are the true friends of God and man.

4. They show that they *sympathize with God* in His feelings towards man.

They have the same kind of friendship for souls that God feels. I do not mean that they feel in the same degree, but that they have the same kind of feelings. There is such a thing as loving the souls of men and hating their conduct too. There is such a thing as constitutional sympathy, which persons feel for those who are in distress. This is natural. You always feel this for a person in distress, unless you have some selfish reason for feeling malevolent. If you saw a murderer hung, you would feel compassion for him. The wicked have this natural sympathy for those that suffer.

There is another peculiar kind of sympathy which the real child of God feels and manifests towards sinners. It is a mingled feeling of abhorrence and compassion, of indignation against his sins, and pity for his person. It is possible to feel this deep abhorrence of sin mingled with deep compassion for souls capable of such endless happiness, and yet bound to eternal misery.

I will explain myself. There are two kinds of love.—One is the love of benevolence. This has no respect to the character of the person loved, but merely views the individual as exposed to suffering and misery. This God feels towards all men. The other kind includes esteem or approbation of character. God feels this only towards the righteous. He never feels *this* love towards sinners. He infinitely abhors them. He has an infinitely strong exercise of compassion and abhorrence at the same time. Christians have the same feelings, only not in the same degree, but they have them at the same time. Probably they never feel right unless they have both these feelings in exercise at the same time. The Christian does not feel as God feels towards individuals, nor feel according to the true character of the individuals, unless both these feelings exist in his mind at the same time. You see this by one striking characteristic. The Christian will rebuke most pointedly and frequently those for whom he feels the deepest compassion. Did you never see this? Did you never see a parent yearning with compassion over a child, and reprove him with tears, and yet with a pungency that would make the little offender quail under his rebuke. Jesus Christ often manifested strongly these two emotions. He wept over Jerusalem, and yet He tells the reason, in a manner that shows His burning indignation against their conduct. "O Jerusalem, thou that killest the prophets and stonest them that are sent unto thee!"—Ah! what a full view He had of their wickedness, at the moment that He wept with compassion for the doom that hung over them. It is just so with this class of Christians. You never find one of them addressing a sinner so as merely to make him weep because somebody is weeping for him. But his most tender appeals are accompanied with strong rebuke for sin.

I wish you to remember this point—that the true friend of God and man never takes the sinner's part, because he never acts through mere compassion. And at the same time, he is never seen to denounce the sinner, without at the same time manifesting compassion for his soul, and a strong desire to save him from death.

5. It is a prominent object with such Christians, in all their intercourse with men, to make them friends of God.

Whether they converse, or pray, or attend to the duties of life, it is their prominent object to recommend religion and to lead everybody to glorify God. It is very natural they should do this, if they are the true friends of God. A true friend of the government wishes everybody to be a friend of the government. A true and affectionate child wishes everybody to love and respect his father. And if any one is at enmity, it is his constant aim and effort to bring him to reconciliation. The same you would expect from a true friend of God, as a leading feature of his character, that he would make it a PROMINENT object of his life to reconcile sinners to God.

Now, mark me! If this is not the leading feature of your character, if it is not the absorbing topic of thought and effort to reconcile men to God, you have not the root of the matter in you. Whatever appearance of religion you may have, you lack the leading and fundamental characteristic of true piety. It wants the leading feature of the character and aims of Jesus Christ, and of His apostles and prophets. Look at them, and see how this feature stands out in strong and eternal relief, as the leading characteristic, the prominent design and object of their lives. Now let me ask you, what is the leading object of your life, as appears in your daily walk? Is it to bring all God's enemies to submit to Him? If not, away with your pretensions to religion. Whatever else you have, you have not the true love of God in you.

6. Where there are persons of this class, you will see them scrupulously avoid everything that in their estimation is calculated to defeat their great end.

They always wish to avoid everything calculated to prevent the salvation of souls, everything calculated to divert attention, or in any way to hinder the conversion of souls. It is not the natural question with them, when anything is proposed which is doubtful, to ask, "Is this something which God expressly forbids?" The first question that naturally suggests itself to their minds is, "What will be the bearing of this upon religion? Will it have a tendency to prevent the conversion of sinners, to hinder the progress of revivals, to roll back the wheels of salvation?" If so, they do not need the thunders of Sinai to be pealed in their ears, to forbid their doing it. If they see it contrary to the spirit of holiness, and contrary to the main object they have in view, that is enough.

Look at the temperance reformation for an illustration of this. Here let me say, that it was the influence of intemperance in hindering the conversion and salvation of sinners that first turned the attention of the benevolent men who commenced the reformation, to inquire on the subject. And the same class of persons are still carrying it on. Such men do not stand and cavil at every step of the way, and say, "Drinking rum is no where prohibited in the Bible and I do not feel bound to give it up." They find that it hinders the great object for which they live, and that is enough for them, they give it up of course. They avoid whatever they see would hinder revival, as a matter of course, just as a merchant would avoid anything that had a tendency to impair his credit, and defeat his object of making money by his business. Suppose a merchant was about to do something that you knew would injuriously affect his credit, and you go to him in the spirit of friendship and advise him not to do it, would he turn round and say, "Show me the passage where God has prohibited this in the Bible?" No. He don't ask you to show him any thing more than this, that it is inconsistent with his main design.

Mark this, all of you. A person who is strongly desirous of the conversion of sinners does not need an express prohibition to prevent his doing that which he sees is calculated to prevent this. There is no danger of his doing that which will defeat the very object of his life.

7. This class of professing Christians are always distressed, unless they see the work of converting sinners going on.

They call it a lamentable state of things in the church, if no sinners are converted. No matter what else is true, no matter how rich the congregation grows, nor how popular their minister, nor how many come to hear him, their panting hearts are uneasy unless they see the work of conversion actually going on. They see that all the rest is nothing without this—yea, that even the means of grace are doing more hurt than good, unless sinners are converted.

Such professors as these are a great trouble to those who are religious from other motives, and who therefore wish to keep all quiet and have everything go on regularly in the *good old way*. They are often called "uneasy spirits in the church." And mark it! if a church has a few such spirits in it, the minister will be made uneasy unless his preaching is such as to convert sinners. You sometimes hear of these men reproving the church, and pouring out their expostulations for living so cold and worldly, and the church reply, "O, we are doing well enough, do you not see how we flourish, it is only because you are always uneasy." When in fact their hearts are grieved and their souls in agony because sinners are not converted and souls are pressing down to hell.

8. You will see them when manifesting a spirit of prayer, praying not for themselves but for sinners.

If you know the habitual tenor of people's prayers, it will show which way the tide of their feelings sets. If a man is actuated in religion mainly by a desire to save himself, you will hear him praying chiefly for himself—that he may have his sins pardoned and *enjoy* much of the Spirit of God, and the like. But if he is truly the friend of God and man, you will find that the burden of his prayers is for the glory of God in the salvation of sinners, and he is never so copious and powerful in prayer, as when he gets upon his favorite topic—the conversion of sinners. Go into the prayer meeting where such Christians pray, and instead of seeing them all shut up in the nut shell of their own interests, spending their whole prayer upon themselves, and just closing with a flourish about the kingdom of Christ, you will hear them pouring out their souls in prayer for the salvation of sinners. I believe there have been cases of such Christians who were so much absorbed in their desires for the salvation of sinners, that for weeks together they did not even pray for their own salvation. Or if they pray for themselves at all, it is that they may be clothed with the Spirit of God, so that they can go out and be mighty through God in pulling souls out of the fire.

You that are here can tell how it is with your prayers, whether you feel most and pray most for yourself or for sinners. If you know nothing about the spirit of prayer for sinners, you are not the true friend of God and man. What! no heart to feel, when sinners are going to hell by your side! No sympathy with the Son of God, who gave His life to save sinners! Away with all such professions of religion. "If any man have not the Spirit of Christ, he is none of His." Don't tell me men are truly pious, when their prayers are droned over, as much a matter of form as when the poor Popish priest counts over his beads. Such a man deceives himself, if he talks about being the true friend of God and man.

9. These persons do not want to ask what are the things they are *required* to do for the conversion of sinners.

When anything is presented to them that promises success in converting sinners, they do not wait to be *commanded* to do it, on pains and penalties if they do not. They only want the evidence that it is calculated to advance the object on which their hearts are set, and they will engage in it with all their soul. The question is not with them all the while, "What am I expressly commanded to do?" but, "In what way can I do most for the salvation of souls, and the conversion of the world to God?" They do not wait for an express command in the Bible, before they will engage in the work of missions, or Sabbath schools, or any other enterprise that promises to save souls; but they are ready to every good word and work.

10. Another characteristic of such Christians is a disposition to *deny themselves to do good to others.*

God has established throughout all the universe the principle of *giving.* Even in the natural world, the rivers, the ocean, the clouds, all *give.* It is so throughout the whole kingdom of nature and of grace. This diffusive principle is everywhere recognized. This is the very spirit of Christ. He sought not to please himself, but to do good to others. He found His highest happiness in denying himself to do good to others. So it is with this class of persons, they are ever ready to deny themselves of enjoyments and comforts, and even of necessaries, when by so doing they can do more good to others.

11. They are continually devising *new means and new measures* for doing good.

This is what would be expected from their continual desire *to do good.* Instead of being satisfied with what does not succeed, they are continually devising new ways and means to effect their object. They are not like those persons who make themselves satisfied with doing what they *call* their DUTY. Where an individual is aiming mainly at his own salvation, he may think if he does his duty he is discharged from responsibility, and so he is satisfied—he thinks he has escaped from divine wrath and gained heaven for himself, by doing what God required him to do, and he cannot help it, whether sinners are saved or lost. But with the other class, it is not so much their object to gain heaven and avoid wrath, but their leading object is to save souls and to honor God. And if this object is not advanced, they are in pain. Such a man is the one whose soul is all the while devising liberal things, and trying new things, and if one fails, trying another and another, and cannot rest till he has found something that will succeed in the salvation of souls.

12. They always manifest great grief when they see the church asleep and doing nothing for the salvation of sinners.

They know the difficulty—the impossibility of doing anything considerable for the salvation of sinners while the church are asleep. Go into a church where the great mass are doing nothing for the conversion of sinners, and floating along on the current of the world, and you will find that the true friends of God and man are grieved at such a state of things. Those who have other objects in view in being religious, may think they are going on very well. They are not grieved when they see the professed people of God going after show and folly. But if there are any of this class, you will find them grieved and distressed at heart, because the church is in such a state.

13. They are grieved if they see reason to think their minister temporizes, or does not reprove the church pointedly and faithfully for their sins.

The other classes of professors are willing to be rocked to sleep, and willing their minister should preach smooth, flowery and eloquent sermons, and flattering sermons, with no point and no power. But these are not satisfied unless he preaches powerfully and pointedly, and boldly, and rebukes and entreats and exhorts, with all long-suffering and doctrine. Their souls are not fed, or edified, or satisfied with anything that does not take hold, and do the work for which the ministry was appointed by Jesus Christ.

14. This class of persons will always stand by a faithful minister, who preaches the truth boldly and pointedly.

No matter if the truth he preaches hits them, they like it, and say, Let the righteous smite me, and it shall be an excellent oil. When the truth is poured forth with power, their souls are fed, and grow strong in grace. They can pray for such a minister. They can weep in their closet, and pour out their souls in prayer for him, that he may have the Spirit of God always with him. While others scold and cavil at him and talk about his being extravagant, and all that, you will find Christians of this sort will stand by him, yea, and would go to the stake with him for the testimony of Jesus. And this they do for the best of all reasons—such preaching falls in with the great design for which these Christians live.

15. This sort of Christians are especially distressed when ministers preach sermons not adapted to convert sinners.

I mean when the sermon is not specially addressed to the church, to stir them up. Others may approve the sermon, and praise it, and tell what a great sermon it is, or how eloquent, or lucid or grand or sublime, but it does not suit *them* if it lacks this one characteristic —a tendency to convert sinners. You will find some people that are great sticklers for the doctrine of election, and they will not believe it is a gospel sermon unless it has the doctrine of election in it, but if the doctrine of election is in it they are suited whether it is adapted to convert sinners or not.—But where a man has his heart set on the conversion of sinners, if he hears a sermon not calculated to do this, he feels as if it lacked the *great thing* that constitutes a gospel sermon. But if they hear a sermon calculated to save souls, then they are fed, and their souls rejoice.

Hence you see the ground for the astonishing difference you often find in the judgment which people pass upon preaching. There is in fact no better test of character than this. It is easy to see who they are that are filled with the love of God and of souls, by the judgment which they pass upon preaching. The true friends of God and man, when they hear a sermon that is not particularly designed to probe and rouse the church and bring them to action, if it is not such as to bear down on sinners and does not tend to convert sinners, it is not the sermon for them.

16. You will always find this class of persons speaking in terms of dissatisfaction with themselves, that they do no more for the conversion of sinners.

However much they may really *do* for this object, it seems that the more they do the more they long to do. They are never satisfied. Instead of being satisfied with the present degree of their success, there is no end of their longing for the conversion of sinners. I recollect a good man, who used to pray till he was exhausted with praying for individuals and for places and for the world's conversion. Once when he was quite exhausted with praying, he exclaimed "Oh! my longing, aching heart! There is no such thing as satisfying my unutterable desires for the conversion of sinners. My soul breaketh for the longing that it hath." That man, though he had been useful beyond almost any other man of his age, yet he saw so much to do, and he so longed to see the work go forward and sinners saved, that his mortal frame could not sustain it. "I find," said he one day, "that I am dying for want of strength to do more to save the souls of men; Oh, how much I want strength, that I may save souls."

17. If you wish to move this class of persons, you must make use of motives drawn from their great and leading object.

If you wish to move them, you must hold up the situation of sinners, and show how they dishonor God, and you will find this will move their souls and set them on fire sooner than any appeal to their hopes and fears. Roll on them this great object. Show them how they can convert sinners, and their longing hearts beat and wrestle with God in prayer, and travail for souls, until they see them converted and Christ formed in them the hope of glory.

I might mention many other characteristics which belong to this class of professing Christians—the true friends of God and man, did time and strength permit. But I must stop here, and postpone the consideration of the other two classes till next Friday evening, if we are spared and the Lord permit.

Now, do you belong to this class, or not? I have mentioned certain great fundamental facts, which when they exist, indicate the true character of individuals, by showing what is their main design and object in life. You can tell whether this is your character. When I come upon the other part of the subject, I shall endeavor to describe those classes of professing Christians, whose religious zeal, prayers and efforts have another design, and show their character and how this design is carried out.

And now, beloved, I ask you before God, have you these characteristics of a child of God? Do you KNOW they belong to you? Can you say, "O Lord, thou knowest all things, thou knowest that I love thee, and that these are the features of my character!"

LECTURE VI.
LEGAL RELIGION.

TEXT:—"Who is on the Lord's side?"—Exodus xxxii. 26.

Last Friday evening, you will remember, that in discoursing from this text, I mentioned three classes of professors of religion; those who truly love God and man, those who are actuated solely by selfishness or at most by self-love in their religious duties, and those who are actuated only by a regard for public opinion. I also mentioned several characteristics of the first class, by which they may be known. This evening I intend to mention several characteristics of the second class,

THOSE PROFESSORS WHO ARE ACTUATED BY SELF-LOVE OR BY SELFISHNESS.

I design to show how their leading or main design in religion develops itself in their conduct. The conduct of men invariably shows what is their true and main design. A man's character is as his supreme object is. And if you can learn by his conduct what that leading object is, then you can know with certainty what his character is. And I suppose this may generally be known by us with great certainty, if we would candidly and thoroughly observe their conduct.

These three classes of professors agree in many things, and it would be impossible to discriminate between them by an observation of these things only. But there are certain things in which they differ, and by *close* observation the difference will be seen in their conduct, from which we infer a difference in their character. And those points in which they differ belong to the very fundamentals of religion.

I will now proceed to mention some of the characteristics of the second class; those who are actuated in religion by self-love, or by selfishness, in whom hope and fear are the main springs of all they do in religion. And the things that I shall mention are such as, when they are seen, make it evident that the individual is actuated by a supreme regard to his own good, and that the fear of evil, or the hope of advantage to himself; is the foundation of all his conduct.

1. They make religion a subordinate concern.

They show by their conduct that they do not regard religion as the principal business of life, but as subordinate to other things. They consider religion as something that ought to come in by the by, as something that ought to come in and find a place among other things, as a sort of Sabbath-day business, or something to be confined to the closet and the hour of family prayer and the Sabbath, and not as the grand business of life. They make a distinction between religious duty and business, and consider them as entirely separate concerns. Whereas, if they had right views of the matter, they would consider religion as the *only* business of life, and nothing else either lawful or worth pursuing, any further than as it promotes or subserves religion. If they had the right feeling, religion would characterize all that they do, and it would be manifest that every thing they do is an act of obedience to God, or an act of irreligion.

2. Their religious duties are performed as a task, and are not the result of the constraining love of God that burns within them.

Such a one does not delight in the exercise of religious affections, and as to communion with God, he knows nothing of it. He performs prayer as a task. He betakes himself to religious duties as sick persons take medicine, not because they love it, but because they hope to derive some benefit from it.

And here let me ask those who are present tonight, Do you *enjoy* religious exercises, or do you perform them because you hope to receive benefit by them? Be honest, now, and answer this question, just according to the truth, and see where you stand.

3. They manifestly possess a legal spirit, and not a gospel spirit.

They do rather what they are obliged to do, in religion, and not what they love to do. They have an eye to the commands of God, and yield obedience to His requirements, in performing religious duties, but do not engage in those things because they love them. They are always ready to inquire, in regard to duty, not so much how they can do good, as how they can be saved. There is just the difference between them, that there is between a convinced sinner and a true convert. The convinced sinner asks, "What *must* I do to be *saved?*" The true convert asks, "Lord, what *wilt thou have me to do?*" So this class of professors are constantly asking, "What *must* I do to get to heaven?" and not "What *can* I do to get other people there?" The principal object of such a professor of religion is not to save the world, but to save himself.

4. They are actuated by fear much more than by hope.

They perform their religious duties chiefly because they *dare not* omit them. They go to the communion, not because they love to meet Christ, or because they love to commune with their brethren, but because they dare not stay away. They fear the censures of the church, or they are afraid they shall be damned if they neglect it. They perform their closet duties not because they enjoy communion with God, but because they dare not neglect them. They have the spirit of slaves, and go about the service of God, as slaves go about the service of their master, feeling that they are obliged to do about so much, or be beaten with many stripes. So these professors feel as if they were obliged to have about so much religion, and perform about so many religious duties, or be lashed by conscience and lose their hopes. And therefore they *go through*, painfully and laboriously enough, with about so many religious duties in a year, and that they call religion!

5. Their religion is not only produced by the fear of disgrace or the fear of hell, but it is *mostly of a negative character.*

They satisfy themselves, mostly, with doing nothing that is very bad. Having no spiritual views, they regard the law of God chiefly as a system of prohibitions, just to guard men from certain sins, and not as a system of benevolence fulfilled by love. And so, if they are moral in their conduct, and tolerably serious and decent in their general deportment, and perform the required amount of religious exercises, this satisfies them. Their conscience harasses them, not so much about sins of omission as sins of commission. They make a distinction between neglecting to do what God positively requires, and doing what He positively forbids. The most you can say of them is, that they are not very bad. They seem to think little or nothing of being useful to the cause of Christ, so long as they cannot be convicted of any positive transgression.

6. This class of persons are more or less strict in religious duties, according to the light they have and the sharpness with which conscience pursues them.

Where they have enlightened minds and tender consciences, you often find them the most rigid of all professors. They tithe even to mint and annise. They are stiff even to moroseness. They are perfect pharisees, and carry everything to the greatest extremes, so far as outward strictness is concerned.

7. They are more or less miserable in proportion to the tenderness of their conscience.

With all their strictness, they cannot but be sensible that they are great sinners after all; and having no just sense of gospel justification, this leaves them very unhappy. And the more enlightened and tender their conscience, the more they are unhappy. Notwithstanding their strictness, they feel that they come short of their duty, and not having any gospel faith, nor any of that holy anointing of the Holy Spirit that brings peace to the soul, they are unsatisfied and uneasy and miserable.

Perhaps many of you have seen such persons. Perhaps some of you are such, and you never knew what it was to feel justified before God, through the blood of Jesus Christ, and you know nothing what it is to feel that Jesus Christ has accepted and owned you as His. You never felt in your minds what that is which is spoken of in this text, "There is now no *condemnation* to them that are in Christ Jesus, who walk not after the flesh, but after the Spirit." Does such language bring home any warm and practical idea to you, that it is a reality because you experience it in your soul? Or do you, after all, still feel condemned and guilty, and have no sense of pardoned sin and no experimental peace with God or confidence in Jesus Christ?

9. This class of persons are encouraged and cheered by reading the accounts of ancient saints who fell into great sins.

They feel wonderfully instructed and edified when they hear the sins of God's people set forth in a strong light.—Then they are comforted and their hopes are wonderfully strengthened. Instead of feeling humbled and distressed, and feeling that such conduct is so contrary to all religion that they could hardly believe they were saints if it had not been found in the Bible, and that they could not believe at all that persons who should do such things under the light of the Christian dispensation, could be saints, they feel gratified and strengthened and their hopes confirmed by all these things. I once knew a man, an elder too, brought before the session of a church for the crime of adultery, and he actually excused himself by this plea. He did not know, he said, why he should be expected to be better than David, the man after God's own heart.

10. They are always much better pleased, by how much the lower the standard of piety is held out from the pulpit.

If the minister adopts a low standard, and is ready charitably to hope that almost everybody is a Christian, they are pleased, and compliment him for his expansive charity, and praise him as such an excellent man, so charitable, &c. It is easy to see why this class of persons are pleased with such an exhibition of Christianity. It subserves their main design. It helps them to maintain what they call a "comfortable hope," notwithstanding they *do* so little for God. Right over against this, you will see, is the conduct of the man whose main design is to rid the world of SIN. He wants all men to be holy, and therefore he wants to have the true standard of holiness held up. He wants all men to be saved, but he knows they cannot be saved unless they are truly holy. And he would as soon think of Satan's going to heaven as of getting a man there by frittering away the Bible standard of holiness by "charity."

11. They are fond of having *comfortable* doctrines preached.

Such persons are apt to be fond of having the doctrine of saints' perseverance much dwelt on, and the doctrine of election. Often, they want nothing else but what they call the doctrines of grace. And if they can be preached in such an abstract way, as to afford them comfort without galling their consciences too much, then they are fed.

12. They love to have their minister preach sermons *to feed Christians.*

Their main object is not to save sinners, but to be saved themselves, and therefore they always choose a minister, not for his ability in preaching for the conversion of sinners, but for his talents in feeding the church with mere abstractions.

13. They lay great stress on having a *comfortable hope.*

You will hear them talking very solemnly about the importance of having a comfortable hope. If they can only enjoy their minds, they show very little solicitude whether anybody else around them is saved or not. If they can have only their fears silenced and their hopes cherished, they have religion enough to satisfy them.

Right over against this, you will find the true friends of God and man are thinking mainly of something else.—They are trying to pull sinners out of the fire, and do not spend their energy in sustaining a comfortable hope for themselves.

In their prayers, you will find the class I am now speaking of, are praying mainly that their evidences may be brightened, and that they may feel assured that they are going to heaven, and know that they are accepted of God. Their great object is to secure their hopes, and so they pray that their evidences may be brightened, instead of praying that their faith may be strengthened, and their souls full of the Holy Ghost to pull sinners out of the fire.

14. They live very much on their own frames of mind.

They lay great stress on the particular emotions which they have from time to time. If at any time they have some high-wrought feelings of a religious nature, they dwell on them, and make this evidence last a great while. One such season of excitement will prop up their hopes as long as they can distinctly call it up to remembrance. No matter if they are not doing any thing *now*, and are conscious they have no exercises of love to God now, they recollect the time when they had such and such feelings, and that answers to keep alive their hopes. If there has been a revival, and they mingled in its scenes until their imagination has been wrought up so that they could weep and pray and exhort with feeling, during the revival, that will last them a long time, and they will have a comfortable hope for years on the strength of it. Although, after the revival is over, they do nothing to promote religion, and their hearts are as hard as adamant, they have a very comfortable hope all the while, patiently waiting for a revival to come and give them another move.

Are any of you who are here now, propping yourselves up by your past frames and feelings, leaning on evidences, not from what you are *now doing* but something that you felt last year, or years ago? Let me tell you, that if you are thus living on past experience, you will find it will fail when you come to need it.

15. They pray almost exclusively for themselves.

If you could listen at the door of their closets, you would hear eight-tenths of all their petitions going up for themselves. It shows how they value their own salvation in comparison with the salvation of others. It is as eight to two. And if they pray in meetings, very often it will be just the same, and you would not suppose, from their prayers, that they knew there was a sinner on earth traveling the road to hell. They pray for themselves just as they do in the closet, only they couple the rest of the church with them so as to say *we*.

16. Such persons pray to be fitted for death much more than they pray to befitted to live a useful life.

They are more anxious to be prepared to die, than to be prepared to save sinners around them. If they ask for the Spirit of God, they want it to prepare them to die, more than as the Psalmist prayed, "Then will I teach transgressors thy way, and sinners shall be converted unto thee." How many of you are of this character? How many are there here, whose prayers are described exactly? An individual who made it his great absorbing object to do good and save sinners, would not be apt to think so much about when or where or how he shall die, as how he may do the most good while he lives. And as to his death, he leaves that all to God, and he is not afraid to heave it all with Him. He has long ago given his soul up to Him, and now the great question with him is not, When shall I die? but, How shall I live so as to honor God?

17. They are more afraid of punishment than they are of sin.

Precisely over against this, you will find the true friends of God and man more afraid of sin than of punishment.—It is not the question with them, "If I do this, shall I be punished?" or "If I do this, will God forgive me?" But the question is that which Joseph asked, "How can I do this great wickedness, and sin against God?" There was the spirit of a child of God, afraid of sin more than punishment, and so much afraid of sin that he had no thought of punishment.

This class of persons I am speaking of, often indulge in sin if they can persuade themselves that God will forgive them, or when they think they can repent of it afterwards. They often reason in this way: "Such a minister does this," or "Such an elder or professor does this, and why may not I do the same?" There was a member of this church had a class in the Sabbath school; but seeing that others did not take a class, the individual reasoned in this way: "Why should I do it any more than they?" and so gave up the class. There is the spirit of this whole description of professors—"Others get along without doing such and such things, and why should I trouble myself to be better than they?" It is not sin that they fear, but punishment. They sin, THEY KNOW, but they hope to escape the punishment. Who cannot see that this is contrary to the spirit of the true friends of God, whose absorbing object it is to get sin, and all sin, out of the world? Such persons are not half so much afraid of hell as they are of committing sin.

18. They feel and manifest greater anxiety about being saved themselves, than if all the world was going to hell.

Such a professor, if his hope begins to fail, wants to have everybody engaged, to pray for *him,* and make a great ado; and move all the church, when he never thinks of doing anything for the sinners around him, who are certainly on the road to hell. He shows that his mind is absorbed in himself, and that his main design is not to see how much good he can do.

19. They are more fond of receiving good than of doing good.

You may know such persons have not the spirit of the gospel. They have never entered into the spirit of Jesus Christ, when He said, "It is more blessed to give than to receive." A person actuated by true love to God and man, enjoys what he does to benefit others, far more than they do who receive good at his hand. He is really benevolent, and it is a gratification to him to show kindness, because his heart is set upon it, and when he can do it, a holy joy is shed over his mind, and he enjoys it exquisitely.

The other class are more eager to receive than to impart. They want to receive instruction more than to impart it. They want to receive comfort, but are never ready to deny themselves to give the comforts of the gospel to others. How directly contrary this is to the diffusive spirit of the gospel, any one can see at a glance. *That* spirit finds its supreme happiness in communicating happiness to others. But this class of persons want to lay everybody under contribution to impart happiness to themselves, instead of laying themselves out to bless others.

Who does not know these two classes of professors?—One always seeking out objects to do good to, the other always trying to gain good themselves. One anxious to communicate, the other to receive. One to do good, the other to get good. These two classes of characters are just as opposite as light and darkness.

20. If this class of professors are led to pray for the conversion and salvation of others, you may observe that they are actuated by the same kind of considerations as they are when they pray for themselves.

They are chiefly afraid of hell themselves, and when they are strongly convicted, they are afraid others will go there too. They are seeking happiness for themselves, and when self is not in the way, they seek the same for others. They pray for sinners, not because they have such a sense of the evil of sin which sinners are committing, as because they have such a sense of the terrors of hell to which sinners are going. It is not because sinners dishonor God that they want them converted, but because they are in danger. Their great object in praying is to secure the safety of those they pray for, as it is their great object in religion to secure their own safety. They pity themselves and they pity others. If there was no danger, they would have no motive to pray either for themselves or others.

The true friends of God and man feel compassion for sinners too, but they feel much more for the honor of God. They are more distressed to see God abused and dishonored than to see sinners go to hell. And if God must be forever dishonored or men go to hell—just as certainly as they love God supremely, they will decide that sinners shall sink to endless torments sooner than God fail of His due honor. And they manifest their true feelings in their prayers. You hear them praying for sinners as rebels against God, as guilty criminals deserving of eternal wrath, as the enemies of God and the universe; and while they are full of compassion for sinners, they feel also the enkindlings of holy indignation against them for their conduct towards the blessed God.

21. This class of professors I am speaking of are very apt to be distressed with doubts.

They are apt to talk a great deal about their doubts. This makes up a great part of their history, the detail of their doubts. The great thing with them being the enjoyment of a comfortable hope, as soon as they begin to doubt, it is all over with them, and so they make a great ado with their doubts, and then they are not prepared to do any thing for religion because they have these doubts. The true friends of God and man, being engaged in doing good, if the devil at any time suggests that they are going to hell, the first answer they think of is, "What if I should? only let me pull sinners out of the fire while I can." I suppose a real Christian may have doubts. But they are much less apt to have them, by how much the more they are fully bent on saving sinners. It will be very hard work for Satan to get a church who are fully engaged in the work to be much troubled with doubts. Their attention is not on that, but on something else and he cannot get the advantage over them.

22. They manifest great uneasiness at the increasing calls for self-denial to do good.

Said an individual, "What will this Temperance Reformation come to? At first they only went against ardent spirit, and I gave up that, and did very well without it. Then they called on us to give up wine, and now they are calling on us to give up our tea and coffee and tobacco, and where will it end?" This class of persons are in constant distress at being called on to give up so much. The good that is to be done does not enter into their thoughts, because they are all the while dwelling on what they have to give up.

It is easily seen why it is that these aggressive movements on the kingdom of darkness distress such persons. Their object never was to search out and banish from this world everything that is dishonorable to God or injurious to man. They never entered upon religion with the determination to clear out every such thing from the earth, as far as they had the power, and as fast as they were convinced that it was injurious to themselves or others, in soul or body. And therefore they are distressed by the movements of those who are truly engaged to search out and clear away every evil.

These persons are annoyed by the continually increasing calls to give for missions, Bibles, tracts, and the like. The time was, when if a rich man gave $25 a year to such things, he was thought to be doing pretty well. But now there are so many calls for subscriptions and contributions, that they are in torment all the time. "I don't like these contributions, I am opposed to having contributions taken up in the congregation, I think they do hurt." They feel specially sore at these agents. "I don't know about these beggars that are going about." They are obliged to keep giving all the time, in order to keep up their character, or to have any hope, but they are much distressed about it, and don't know what the world is coming to, things are in such a strange pass.

As you raise the general standard of living in the church, this class of professors have to come up too, lest their hopes should be shaken. And the common standard of professors has been raised already so much, that I have no doubt it costs this class of persons now four times as much of what they call religion, to keep up a hope, as it did twenty years ago. And what will become of them, if there are to be so many new movements and new measures, and so much done to save the world? The Lord help them, for they are in great distress!

23. When they are called upon to exercise self-denial for the sake of doing good, instead of being a pleasant thing, it gives them unmingled pain.

Such a one does not know any thing about enjoying self-denial. He cannot understand how self-denial is pleasant, or how anybody can take pleasure in it, or have joy of heart in denying himself for the sake of doing good to others. That he thinks is a height in religion which he has not attained to. Yet the true friend of God and man, whose heart is fully set to do good, never enjoys any money he expends so well as that which he gives to promote Christ's kingdom. If he is really pious, he knows that is the best disposition he can make of his money. Nay, he is sorry to be obliged to use money for anything else, when there are so many opportunities to do good with it.

I want you who are here to look at this. It is easy to see that if an individual has his heart very much set upon any thing, all the money he can save for that object is most pleasing to him, and the more he can save from other objects for this that his heart is set on, the better he is pleased. If an individual finds it hard for him to give money for religious objects, it is easy to see that his heart is not set on it. If it were, he would have given his money with joy. What would you think of a man who should set himself against giving money for the advancement of religion, and get up an excitement in the church about the missionary cause, and having so many calls for money, when he had never given five dollars? It would be absolute demonstration that his heart was not truly set on the cause of Christ. If it was, he would give his money for it, as free as water. And the more he could spare for it, the better he would be pleased.

24. This class of persons are not forward in promoting revivals.

This is not their great object. They always have to be dragged into the work. When a revival has begun, and gone on, and the excitement is great, then they come in and appear to be engaged in it. But you never see them taking the lead, or striking out ahead of the rest, and saying to the rest of the brethren, Come on, and let us do something for the Lord.

25. As a matter of fact, they do not convert sinners to God.

They may be instrumental of good, in various ways, and so may Satan be instrumental of good. But as a general thing, they do not pull sinners out of the fire. And the reason is, that this is not their great object. How is it with you? Do you absolutely succeed in converting sinners? Is there any one who will look to you as the instrument of his conversion? If you were truly engaged for this, you could not rest satisfied without doing it, and you would go about it so much in earnest, and with such agonizing prayer that you would do it.

26. They do not manifest much distress when they behold sin.

They do not rebuke it. They love to mingle in scenes where sin is committed. They love to be where they can hear vain conversation, and even to join in it. They love worldly company and worldly books. Their spirit is worldly. Instead of hating even the garment spotted with the flesh, they love to hang around the confines of sin, as if they had complacency in it.

27. They take but very little interest in published accounts or revivals, missions, &c.

If any of the missions are tried severely, they neither know nor feel it. If missions prosper, they never know it, they take no interest in it. Very likely they do not take any religious paper whatever. Or if they do, when they sit down to read it, if they come to a revival, they pass it over, to read the secular news, or the controversy, or something else. The other class, the true friends of God and man, on the contrary, love to learn the progress of revivals. They love to read a religious paper, and when they take it up, the first thing they do is to run their eye over it to find where there are revivals, and there they feast their souls and give glory to God. And so with missions, their heart goes forth with the missionaries, and when they hear that the Lord has poured forth His Spirit on a mission, they feel a glow of holy joy thrill through them.

28. They do not aim at any thing higher than a legal, painful, negative religion.

The love of Christ does not constrain them to a constant warfare against sin, and a constant watch to do all the good in their power. But what they do is done only because they think they must. And they maintain a kind of piety that is formal, heartless, worthless.

29. They come reluctantly into all the special movements of the church for doing good.

If a protracted meeting is proposed, you will generally find this class of persons hanging back, and making objections, and raising difficulties as long as they can. If any other special effort is proposed, they come reluctantly, and prefer the good old way. They feel sore at being obliged to add so much every year to their religion in order to maintain their hope.

30. They do not enjoy secret prayer.

They do not pray in their closets because they *love* to pray, but because they think it is their duty, and they dare not neglect it.

31. They do not enjoy the Bible

They do not read the Bible because it is sweet to their souls, sweeter than honey or the honey comb. They do not *enjoy* the reading, as a person enjoys the most exquisite delights. They read it because it is their duty to read it, and it would not do to profess to be a Christian and not read the Bible, but in fact they find it a dry book.

32. They do not enjoy prayer meetings.

Slight excuses keep them away. They never go unless they find it necessary for the sake of keeping up appearances, or to maintain their hope. And when they do go, instead of having their souls melted and fired with love, they are cold, listless, dull, and glad when it is over.

33. They are very much put to it to understand what is meant by disinterestedness.

To serve God because they love Him, and not for the sake of the reward, is what they do not understand.

34. Their thoughts are not anxiously fixed upon the question, When shall the world be converted to God?

Their hearts are not agonized with such thoughts as this, O, how long shall wickedness prevail? O, when shall this wretched world be rid of sin and death? O, when shall men cease to sin against God? They think much more of the question, When shall I die and go to heaven, and get rid of all my trials and cares?

But I find I am again obliged to omit the examination of the last class of professors till next Friday evening, when, with the leave of Providence, it will be attended to.

REMARKS.

1. I believe you will not think me extravagant, when I say that the religion I have described, appears to be the religion of a very large mass in the church.

To say the least, it is greatly to be feared that a *majority* of professing Christians are of this description. To say this is neither uncharitable nor censorious.

2. This religion is *radically defective.*

There is nothing of true Christianity in it. It differs as much from Christianity as much as the Pharisees differed from Christ— as much as gospel religion differs from legal religion.

Now, let me ask you, to which of these classes do you belong? Or are you in neither? It may be that because you are conscious you do not belong to the second class, you may think you belong to the first, when in fact you will find, when I come to describe the third class of professors, that is your true character.

How important it is that you know for a certainty what is your true character—whether you are actuated in religion by true love to God and man, or whether you are religious only out of regard to yourself. O, what a solemn thought, if this church, of which I have been the pastor, have never come to an intelligent decision of the question, whether they are the true friends of God and man or not. Do settle it, beloved. Now is the time. Settle this, and then go to work for God.

LECTURE VII.

RELIGION OF PUBLIC OPINION.

"For they loved the praise or men more than the praise or God."
John xii. 43.

These words were spoken of certain individuals who refused to confess that Jesus was the Christ, because He was extremely unpopular with the scribes and pharisees, and principal people of Jerusalem.

There is a plain distinction between *self-love*, or the simple desire of happiness, and *selfishness.* Self-love, the desire of happiness and dread of misery, is constitutional, it is a part of our frame as God made us and as He intended us to be; and its indulgence, within the limits of the law of God, is not sinful. Whenever it is indulged contrary to the law of God, it becomes sinful. When the desire of happiness or the dread of misery becomes the controlling principle, and we prefer our own gratification to some other greater interest, it becomes selfishness. When to avoid pain or procure happiness, we sacrifice other greater interests, we violate the great law of disinterested benevolence. It is no longer self-love, acting within lawful bounds, but selfishness.

In my last Friday evening Lecture, I described a class of professors of religion, who are moved to perform religious exercises by hope and fear. They are moved sometimes by self-love, and sometimes by selfishness. Their supreme object is not to glorify God, but to secure their own salvation. You will recollect that this class, and the class I had described before as the real friends of God, and man, agree in many things, and if you look only at the things in which they agree, you cannot distinguish between them. It is only by a close observation of those things in which they differ, that you can see that the main design of the latter class is not to glorify God, but to secure their own salvation. In that way we can see their supreme object developed, and see that when they do the same things, outwardly, which those do whose supreme object is to glorify God, they do them from entirely different motives, and consequently the acts themselves are, in the sight of God, of an entirely different character.

To-night, I design to point out the characteristics of the third class of professing Christians, who "love the praise of men more than the praise of God."

I would not be understood to imply that a *mere* regard for reputation has led this class to profess religion. Religion has always been too unpopular with the great mass of mankind to render it a general thing to become professing Christians from a mere regard to reputation. But I mean, that where it is not generally unpopular to become a professor of religion, and will not diminish popularity, but will increase it with many, a complex motive operates—the hope of securing happiness in a future world and that it may increase reputation here. And thus many are led to profess religion, when after all, on a close examination it will be seen that the *leading* object, which is prized beyond any thing else, is the good opinion of their fellow men. Sooner than forfeit this utterly, they would not profess religion. Their profession turns on this. And although they do profess to be sincere Christians, you may see by their conduct, on close examination, that they will do nothing that will forfeit this good opinion of men. They will not encounter the odium that they must, if they were to give themselves up to root sin out of the world.

Observe, that impenitent sinners are always influenced by one of two things, in all that they do that appears like religion. Either they do them out of regard to mere natural principles, as compassion or self-love—principles that are constitutional in them—or from selfishness. They are done either out of regard to their own reputation or happiness, or the gratification of some natural principle in them, that has no moral character; and not from the love of God in them. They love the praise of men more than the praise of God.

I will now mention several things by which you may detect the true character of the class of persons of whom I have been speaking; who make the praise of men their idol, notwithstanding they profess to love God supremely. And they are things by which you can detect your own true characters, if there are any present who properly belong to this class.

1. They do what the apostle Paul says certain persons did in his day, and for that reason they remained ignorant of the true doctrine; they "measure themselves by themselves, and compare themselves among themselves."

There are a vast many individuals, who, instead of making Jesus Christ their standard of comparison, and the Bible their rule of life, manifestly aim at no such thing. They show that they never seriously dreamed of making the BIBLE their standard. The great question with them is, whether they do about as many things in religion, and are about as pious as other people, or as the churches around them. Their object is to maintain a *respectable* profession of religion. Instead of seriously inquiring for themselves, what the Bible really requires, and asking how Jesus Christ would act in such and such cases, they are looking simply at the common run of professing Christians, and are satisfied with doing what is commendable in their estimation. They prove to a demonstration, that their object is not so much to do what the Bible lays down as duty, as to do what the great mass of professing Christians do—to do what is respectable, rather than what is RIGHT.

2. This class of persons do not trouble themselves about *elevating the standard* of piety around them.

They are not troubled at the fact, that the general standard of piety is so low in the church, that it is impossible to bring the great mass of sinners to repentance. They think the standard at the present time is high enough. Whatever be the standard at the time, it satisfies them. While the real friends of God and man are complaining of the church, because the standard of piety is so low, and trying to wake up the church to elevate the tone of religion, it all seems to this class of persons like censoriousness, and a meddlesome, uneasy disposition, and as denoting a bad spirit in them. Just as when Jesus Christ denounced the scribes and pharisees and leading professors of His day, they said, "He hath a devil." "Why, He is denouncing our doctors of divinity, and all our best men, and even dares to call the scribes and pharisees hypocrites, and He tells us that except our righteousness shall exceed theirs, we can in no case enter the kingdom of heaven. What a bad spirit He has!"

A large part of the church at the present day have the same spirit, and every effort to open the eyes of the church, and to make Christians see that they live so low, so worldly, so much like hypocrites, that it is impossible the work of the Lord should go on, only excites ill will and occasions reproach. "O," they say, "what a bad spirit he shows, so censorious, and so unkind, surely that is anything but the meek, and kind, and loving spirit of the Son of God." They forget how Jesus Christ poured out His anathemas, enough to make the hills of Judea shake, against those that had the reputation of being the most pious people in that day. Just as if Jesus Christ never said any thing severe to anybody, but just fawned over them, and soothed them into His kingdom. Who does not know that it was the hypocritical spirit exhibited by professors of religion, that roused His soul and moved His indignation, and called forth His burning torrents of denunciation. He was always complaining of the very people who were set up as patterns of piety, and called them hypocrites, and thundered over their heads the terrible words, "HOW CAN YE ESCAPE THE DAMNATION OF HELL!"

It is not wonderful, when so many love the praise of men more than the praise of God, that there should be excitement when the truth is told. They are very well satisfied with the standard of piety as it is, and think that while the people are doing so much for Sabbath schools, and missions, and tracts, that is doing pretty well, and they wonder what the man would have. Alas! alas! for their blindness! They do not seem to know that with all this, the lives of the generality of professing Christians are almost as different from the standard of Jesus Christ as light is from darkness.

3. They make a distinction between those requirements of God that are strongly enforced by public sentiment and those that are not thus guarded.

They are very scrupulous in observing such requirements as public sentiment distinctly favors, while they easily set at nought those which public sentiment does not enforce. You have illustrations, of this on every side. I might mention the Temperance Reformation. How many there are who yield to public sentiment in this matter what they never would yield to God or man. At first they waited to see how it would turn. They resisted giving up of ardent spirits. But when that became popular, and they found that they could do very well with other alcoholic stimulants, they gave it up. But they are determined to yield no further than public sentiment drives them. They show that it is not their object, in joining the Temperance Society, to CARRY OUT the reform, so as to slay the monster, Intemperance, but their object is to maintain a good character. They love the praise of men more than the praise of God.

See how many individuals there are, who keep the Sabbath, not because they love God, but because it is respectable. This is manifest, because they keep it while they are among their acquaintances, or where they are known. But when they get where they are not known, or where it will not be a public disgrace, you will find them traveling on the Sabbath.

All those sins that are reprobated by public opinion this class of persons abstain from, but they do other things just as bad which are not thus frowned on. They do those duties which are enforced by public opinion, but not those that are less enforced. They will not stay away from public worship on the Sabbath, because they could not maintain any reputation for religion at all if they did. But they neglect things that are just as peremptorily enjoined in the word of God. Where an individual habitually disobeys any command of God, he knowing it to be such, it is just as certain as his soul lives, that the obedience he appears to render, is not from a regard to God's authority, or love to God, but from other motives. He does not, in fact, obey any command of God. The Apostle has settled this question. " Whosoever," says he, " Shall keep the whole law and offend in one point is guilty of all," i. e. does not truly keep any one precept of the law. Obedience to God's commands implies an obedient state of the heart, and therefore nothing is obedience that does not imply a supreme regard to the authority of God. Now, if a man's heart is right, then whatever God enjoins he regards as of more importance than anything else. And if a man regards anything else of superior weight to God's authority, that is his idol. Whatever we supremely regard, that is our God—whether it be reputation, or comfort, or riches, or honor, or whatever it is that we regard supremely, that is the God of our hearts. Whatever a man's reason is for habitually neglecting anything he knows to be the command of God, or that he sees to be required to promote the kingdom of Christ, there is demonstration absolute that he regards that as supreme. There is nothing acceptable to God in any of his services. Rest assured, all his religion is the religion of public sentiment. If he neglects anything required by the law of God, because he can pass along in neglect, and public sentiment does not enjoin it, or if he does other things inconsistent with the law of God, merely because public opinion does require it, it is a simple matter of fact, that it is public sentiment to which he yields obedience, in all his conduct, and not a regard to the glory of God.

How is it with you, beloved? Do you habitually neglect any requirement of God, because it is not sustained and enforced by public sentiment? If you are a professor of religion, it is to be presumed you do not neglect any requirement *that is* strongly urged by public sentiment.—But, how is it with others? Do you not habitually neglect some duties? Do you not live in some practices reputable among men, that you know to be contrary to the law of God? If you do, it is demonstration absolute that you regard the opinions of men more than the judgment of God. Write down your name HYPOCRITE.

4. This class of professors are apt to indulge in some sins when they are away from home, that they would not commit at home.

Many a man who is temperate at home, when he gets to a distance, will toss off his glass of brandy and water at the table, or step up to the bar of a steamboat and call for liquor without shame, or if they are in Europe, they will go to the theater. When I was in the Mediterranean, at Messina, a gentleman one day asked me if I would go to the theater with him. "What! I go to the theater? A minister go to the theater?" Why, said he, you are away from home, and no one would know it. "But would not God know it?" It was plain that he thought, although I was a minister, I could go to the theater when I was away from home. No matter if God knew it, so long as men did not know it. And how should he get that idea, but by seeing ministers who would do just such things?

5. Another development of the character of these individuals is, that they indulge themselves in secret sin.

I am now speaking of something, by which you may know yourselves. If you allow yourselves in any sins secretly, when you can get along without having any human being know it, know that God sees it, and that He has already written down your name, HYPOCRITE. You are more afraid of disgrace in the eye of mortals, than of disgrace in the eye of God. If you loved God supremely, it would be a small thing to you that any and everybody else knew your sins, in comparison with having them known to God. If tempted to any such thing, you would exclaim, "What! shall I commit sin under the eye of God?"

6. They indulge in secret omissions of duty, which they would not dare to have known to others.

They may not practice any secret sins, or indulge in those secret pollutions that are spoken of, but they neglect those duties, that if they were known to neglect, it would be called disreputable to their Christian character. Such as secret prayer, for instance. They will go to the communion—yes, to the communion!—and appear to be very pious on the Sabbath, and yet, as to private piety, they know nothing of it. Their closet for prayer is unknown to God or man. It is easy to see that reputation is their idol. They dread to lose their reputation more than to offend God.

How is it with you? Is it a fact, that you habitually omit those secret duties, and are more careful to perform your public duties than private ones? Then what is your character? Do you need to be told? They loved the praise of men more than the praise of God.

7. The conscience of this class of persons seems to be formed on other principles than those of the gospel.

They seem to have a conscience in those things that are popular, and no conscience at all on those things that are not required by public sentiment. You may preach to them ever so plainly, their duty, and prove it ever so clearly, and even make them confess that it is their duty, and yet so long as public sentiment does not require it, and it is not a matter of reputation, they will continue on in the same way as before. Show them a "Thus saith the Lord," and make them see that their course is palpably inconsistent with Christian perfection, and contrary to the interests of the kingdom of Christ, and yet they will not alter. They make it manifest that it is not the requirement of God they regard, but the requirement of public opinion. They love the praise of men more than the praise of God.

8. This class of persons generally dread, very much, the thought of being considered fanatical.

They are ignorant, practically, of a first principle in religion, that ALL THE WORLD IS WRONG! That the public sentiment of the world is all against God, and that everyone who intends to serve God must in the first instance set his face against the public sentiment of the world. They are to take it for granted, that in a world of rebels, public sentiment is as certainly wrong as that there is a controversy with God. They have never had their eyes open to this fundamental truth, that the world is wrong, and that God's ways are directly over against their ways. Consequently, it is true, and always has been true, that "all that will live godly in Christ Jesus shall suffer persecution." They shall be called fanatical, superstitious, ultras, and the like. They always have been, and they always will be, as long as the world is wrong.

But this class of persons will never go further than is consistent with the opinions of worldly men. They say they must do this and that in order to have influence over such men. Right over against this is the course of the true friends of God and man. Their leading aim is to reverse the order of the world, and turn the world upside down, to bring all men to obey God, and all the opinions of men to conform to the word of God, and all the usages and institutions of the world to accord with the spirit of the gospel.

9. They are very intent on making friends on both sides.

They take the middle course always. They avoid the reputation of being righteous over-much, on the one hand, and on the other hand, of being lax or irreligious. It has been so for centuries, that a person could maintain a reputable profession of religion, without ever being called fanatical. And the standard is still so low, that probably the great mass of the Protestant churches are trying to occupy this middle ground. They mean to have friends on both sides. They are not set down as reprobates, on the one hand, nor as fanatics or bigots on the other. They are FASHIONABLE CHRISTIANS! They may be called fashionable Christians for two reasons. One is, that their style of religion is popular and fashionable; and the other is, that they generally follow worldly fashions. Their aim in religion is not to do anything that will disgust the world. No matter what God requires, they are determined to be so prudent as not to bring on them the censures of the world, nor offend the enemies of God. They have manifestly more regard to men than to God. And if they are ever so circumstanced that they must do that which will displease their friends and neighbors, or offend God, they will offend God. If public sentiment clashes with the commands of God, they will yield to public sentiment.

10. They will do more to gain the applause of men than to gain the applause of God.

This is evident from the fact, that they will yield obedience only to those requirements of God which are sustained by public opinion. Although they will not exercise self-denial to gain the applause of God, yet they will exercise great self-denial to gain the applause of men. The men that gave up ardent spirit, because public sentiment rendered it necessary, will give up wine also, whenever a public sentiment sufficiently powerful shall demand it. And not till then.

11. They are more anxious to know what are the opinions of men about them, than to know what is God's opinion of them.

If one of this class is a minister, and preaches a sermon, he is more anxious to know what the people thought of it, than to know what God thought of it. And if he makes any thing like a failure, the disgrace of it with men cuts him ten times more than the thought that he has dishonored God, or hindered the salvation of souls. Just so with an elder, or a member of the church, of this class.

If he prays in a meeting, or exhorts, he is more concerned to know what is thought of it than to know how God is pleased.

If such a one has some secret sin found out, he is vastly more distressed about it because he is disgraced than because God is dishonored. Or if he falls into open sin, when he comes to be met with it, he cares as much again about the disgrace as about the sin of it.

They are more anxious about their appearance in the eyes of the world, than in the eyes of God. Females of this character are vastly more anxious, when they go to church, how the body shall appear in the eyes of men than how the heart shall appear in the eyes of God. Such a one will be all the week engaged in getting everything in order, so as to make her person appear to advantage, and perhaps will not spend half an hour in her closet, to prepare her heart to appear before God in His courts. Everybody can see, at a glance, what this religion is, the moment it is held up to view. Nobody is at a loss to say what that man or that woman's name is. It is HYPOCRITE. They will go into the house of God, with their heart dark as midnight, while everything in their external appearance is comely and decent. They must appear well in the eyes of men, no matter how that part is, on which God fixes His eye. The heart may be dark and disordered and polluted, and they care not, so long as the eye or man detects no blemish.

12. They refuse to confess their sins, in the manner which the law of God requires, lest they should lose reputation among men.

If they are ever required to make confession of more than they think consistent with their reputation, they are more anxious how it will affect their character, than whether God is satisfied.

Search your hearts, you that have made confessions, and see which most affects your minds, the question what God thought of it or what men thought of it. Have you refused to confess what you knew God required, because it will hurt your reputation among men? Will not God judge your hearts? Only be honest now, and let it be answered.

13. They will yield to custom what they know to be injurious to the cause of religion, and to the welfare of mankind.

A striking instance of this is found in the manner of keeping new year's day. Who does not know that the customary manner of keeping new year's day, setting out their wine and their rich cake and costly entertainments, and spending the day as they do, is a waste of money, hurtful to health, and injurious to their own souls and to the interests of religion? And yet they do it. Shall we be told that persons who will do this, when they KNOW it is injurious, supremely love God? I care not who attempts to defend such a custom, it is wrong, and every Christian must know it to be so. And those who persist in it when they know better, demonstrate that a supreme regard to God is not their rule of life.

14. They will do things of doubtful character, or things the lawfulness of which they strongly doubt, in obedience to public sentiment.

You will recollect that on the evening of the first day of the year I took up this subject, and showed that those who do things of doubtful character, of the lawfulness of which they are not satisfied, are condemned for it in the sight of God.

15. They are often *ashamed* to do their duty, and *so much* ashamed that they will not do it.

Now when a person is so much ashamed to do what God requires as not to do it, it is plain that his own reputation is his idol. How many do you find who are ashamed to acknowledge Jesus Christ, ashamed to reprove sin, in high places or low places, and ashamed to speak out when religion is assailed. If they supremely regarded God, could they ever be *ashamed* of doing their duty? Suppose a man's wife was calumniated, would he be ashamed to defend his wife? By no means. If his children were abused, would he be ashamed to take their part? Not if he loved them, it would not be *shame* that would deter him from defending his wife or children. If a man was friendly to the administration of the government of his country, and heard it calumniated, would he be ashamed to defend it? He might not think it *expedient* to speak, for other reasons; but if he was a true friend to the government, he would not be *ashamed* to speak in its behalf, anywhere.

Now such persons as I am speaking of, will not take decided ground when they are among the enemies of truth, where they would be subject to reproach for doing it.—They are very bold for the truth when among its friends, and will make a great display of their courage. But when put to the trial, they will sell the Lord Jesus Christ, or deny Him before His enemies, and put Him to open shame, rather than rebuke wickedness or speak out in His cause among His enemies.

16. They are opposed to all encroachments on their self-indulgence, by advancing light on practical subjects.

They are much disturbed by every new proposal that draws on their purses, or breaks in upon their habitual self-indulgence. And you may talk as much, and preach as much in favor of it as you please, there is only one way to reach this kind of people, and that is by creating a new public sentiment. When you have brought over, by the power of benevolence and of conscience, a sufficient number in the community to create a public sentiment in its favor, then they will adopt your new proposals, and not before.

17. They are always distressed at what they call the *ultraism* of the day.

They are much afraid the ultraism of the present day will destroy the church. They say we are carrying things too far, and we shall produce a reaction. Take, for instance, the Temperance Reformation. The true friends of temperance now know, that alcohol is the same thing, wherever it is found, and that to save the world and banish intemperance, it is necessary to banish alcohol in all its forms. The *pinch* of the Temperance Reformation has never yet been decided. The mass of the community have never been called to any self-denial in the cause. The place where it will pinch is, when it comes to the question, whether men will exercise *self-denial* to crush the evil. If they may continue to drink wine and beer, it is no self-denial to give up ardent spirits. It is only changing the form in which alcohol is taken, and they can drink as freely as before. Many friends of the cause, when they saw what multitudes were rushing into it, were ready to shout a triumph. But the real question is not yet tried. And multitudes will never yield, until the friends of God and man can form a public sentiment so strong as to crush the character of every man who will not give it up. You will find many doctors of divinity and pillars of the church, who are able to drink their wine, that will stand their ground, and no command of God, no requirement of benevolence, no desire to save souls, no pity for bleeding humanity, will move such persons, until you can form a public sentiment so powerful as to force them to it, on penalty of loss of reputation. For they love the praise of men.

And it is a query now in my mind, a matter of solemn and anxious doubt, whether in the present low state of piety and decline of revivals of religion in the church, a public sentiment can be formed, so powerful as to do this. If not, we shall be driven back. The Temperance Reformation, like a dam of sand, will be swept away, the floodgates will be opened again, and the world will go reeling—down to hell. And yet thousands of professors of religion, who want to enjoy public respect and at time same time enjoy themselves in their own way, are crying out as if they were in distress at the ultraism of the times!

18. They are often opposed to men, and measures, and things, while they are unpopular and subject to reproach, and when they become popular, fall in with them.

Let an individual go through the churches in any section, and wake them up to a revival of religion, and while he is little known, these persons are not backward to speak against him. But let him go on, and gain influence, and they will fall in and commend him and profess to be his warmest friends. It was just so with Jesus Christ. Before His death, He had a certain degree of popularity.— Multitudes would follow him, as He went through the streets, and cry "Hosanna, Hosanna!" But observe, they never would follow Him an atom further than His popularity followed him. As soon as He was arrested as a criminal, they all turned round and began to cry, "Crucify him, crucify him!"

This class of persons, as they set with the tide one way, when a man is reproached, so they will set with the tide the other way, when he comes to be honored. There is only one exception. And that is, when they have become so far committed to the opposition, that they cannot come round without disgrace. And then they will be silent, until another opportunity comes up for letting out the burning fires that are rankling within them.

Very often a revival in a church, when it first begins, is opposed by certain members of the church. They do not like to have such things carried on, they are afraid there is too much animal excitement, and the like. But the work goes on, and by and by, they seem to fall in and go with the multitude. At length the revival is over, and the church grows cold again, and before long you will find this class of persons renewing their opposition to the work, and as the church declines they press their opposition, and perhaps, in the end, induce the church itself to take ground against the very revival which they had so much enjoyed. This is the very way in which individuals have acted in regard to revivals in this country. There are many such cases. They were awed by public sentiment and made to bow down to the revival, while it was in its power, but by and by, as the revival declines, they begin to let out the opposition that is in their hearts, and which was suppressed for a time because the revival was popular.

It has been just so in regard to the cause of missions, in a degree, and if anything should turn up, unfavorable to missions, so as to break the present power of public sentiment in their favor, you would find plenty of these fair weather supporters turning to the opposition.

19. If any measure is proposed to promote religion, they are very sensitive and scrupulous not to have anything done that is unpopular.

If they live in a city, they ask what will the other churches think of such a measure? And if it is likely to bring reproach on their church or their minister, in view of the ungodly, or in view of the other churches, they are distressed about it. No matter how much good it will do, or how many souls it will save, they do not want to have anything done to injure the respectability of their church.

20. This class of persons never aim at *forming* a public sentiment in favor of perfect godliness.

The true friends of God and man are always aiming at forming public sentiment, and correcting public sentiment on all points where it is wrong. They are set, with all their hearts, to search out all the evils in the world, and to reform the world, and drive out iniquity from the earth. The other class are always following public sentiment as it is, and feeling after the course of the tide, to go that way, shrinking back from everything that goes in the face of public sentiment. And they are ready to brand as imprudent, or rash, any man or anything, that goes to stem the tide of public sentiment and turn it the other way.

REMARKS.

1. It is easy for persons to take credit for their sins, and make themselves believe certain things are acts of piety, which are in fact only acts of hypocrisy.

They do the things that outwardly pertain to piety, and they give themselves credit for being pious, when their motives are all corrupt and hollow, and not one of them drawn from a supreme regard to God's authority. This is manifest from the fact that they do nothing except where God's requirements are backed up by public sentiment.—Unless you aim to do ALL your duty, and yield obedience *in every thing,* the piety for which you claim credit is mere hypocrisy, and is in fact sin against God.

2. There is a great deal more apparent piety in the church, than there is real piety.

3. There are many things which sinners suppose are good, but which are abominable in the sight of God.

4. But for the love of reputation and the fear of disgrace, how many there are in the church, who would break out into open apostacy.

How many are there here, who know you would break out into open vice, were it not for the restraints of public sentiment, the fear of disgrace, and the desire to gain the credit of virtue? Where a person is virtuous from a regard to the authority of God, whether public sentiment favor it or frown upon it, that is true piety. If otherwise, they have their reward. They do it for the sake of gaining credit in the eyes of men, and they gain it. But if they expect any favor at the hand or God, they will assuredly be disappointed. The only reward which HE will bestow upon such selfish hypocrites is, that they may be damned.

And now I wish to know how many of you will determine to do your duty, and all your duty, according to the will of God, let public sentiment be as it may? Who of you will agree to take the Bible for your rule, Jesus Christ for your pattern, and do what is RIGHT, in all cases, whatever man may say or think? Everyone that is not willing to take this ground must regard himself as a stranger to the grace of God. He is by no means in a state of justification. If he is not resolved upon doing what he knows to be right, let public sentiment be as it may, it is proof positive that he loves the praise of men more than the praise of God.

And let me say to the impenitent sinners present—You see what it is to be a Christian. It is to be governed by the authority or God *in all things,* and not by public sentiment, to live not by hopes and fears, but by supreme consecration of yourself unto God. You see that if you mean to be religious, you must count the cost. I will not flatter you. I will never try to coax you to become religious, by keeping back the truth. If you mean to be Christians, you must give yourselves wholly up to Christ. You cannot float along to heaven on the waves of public sentiment. I will not deceive you on this point.

Do you ask, sinner, what is to become of all these professors of religion, who are conformed to the world, and who love the praise of men more than the praise of God? I answer—They will go to hell, with you, and with all other hypocrites. Just as certain as that the friendship of the world is in enmity with God.

Wherefore, come out from among them, my people, and be ye separate, and I will receive you, saith the Lord, I will be a Father to you, and ye shall be my sons and daughters. And now, who will do it? In the church and among sinners, who will do it? Who? Who is on the Lord's side? Who is willing to say, "We will no longer go with the multitude to do evil, but are determined to do the will of God, in all things whatsoever, and let the world think or say of us as it may." As many of you as are now willing to do this, will signify it by rising in your places before the congregation, and will then kneel down, while prayer is offered, that God would accept and seal your solemn covenant to obey God henceforth in everything, through evil report and through good report.

LECTURE VIII.

CONFORMITY TO THE WORLD.

TEXT:—"Be not conformed to this world."—Romans xii. 2.

It will be recollected by some who are present, that sometime since I made use of this text in preaching in this place, but the object of this evening's discourse is so far different that it is not improper to employ the same text again. The following is the order in which I design to discuss the subject of
CONFORMITY TO THE WORLD

I. To show what is *not* meant by the command of the text.

II. Show *what is* meant by the command, "Be not conformed to this world."

III. To mention some of the reasons why this requirement is made upon all who will live a godly life.

IV. To answer some objections that are made to the principles laid down.

I. I am to show what is *not meant* by the requirement, "Be not conformed to this world."

I suppose it is not meant, that Christians should refuse to benefit by the useful arts, improvements and discoveries of the world. It is not only the privilege but the duty of the friends of God to avail themselves of these, and to use for God all the really useful arts and improvements that arise among mankind.

II. I am to show *what is* meant by the requirement.

It is meant that Christians are bound not to conform to the world in the three following things. I mention only these three, not because there are not many other things in which conformity to the world is forbidden, but because these three classes are all that I have time to examine tonight, and further, because these three are peculiarly necessary to be discussed at the present time. The three things are three departments of life, in which it is required that you be not conformed to this world. They are
BUSINESS—FASHION—POLITICS

In all these departments it is required that Christians should not do as the world do, they should neither receive the maxims, nor adopt the principles, nor follow the practices of the world.

III. I am to mention some reasons for the command, "Be not conformed to this world."

You are by no means to act on the same principles, nor from the same motives, nor pursue your object in the same manner that the world do, either in the pursuits of business, or of fashion, or of politics. I shall examine these several departments separate.

First.—Of business.

1. The first reason why you are not to be conformed to this world in business, is that the principle of the world is that of supreme selfishness. This is true universally, in the pursuit of business. The whole course of business in the world is governed and regulated by the maxims of supreme and unmixed selfishness. It is regulated without the least regard to the commands of God, or the glory of God, or the welfare of their fellow men. The maxims of business generally current among business men, and the habits and usages of business men, are all based upon supreme selfishness. Who does not know, that in making bargains, the business men of the world consult their own interest, and seek their own benefit, and not the benefit of those they deal with? Who has ever heard of a worldly man of business making bargains, and doing business for the benefit of those he dealt with? No, it is always for their own benefit. And are Christians to do so? They are required to act on the very opposite principle to this: "Let *no man seek his own*, but every man *another's* wealth." They are required to copy the example of Jesus Christ. Did He ever make bargains for His own advantage?—And may His followers adopt the principle of the world—a principle that contains in it the seeds of hell! If Christians are to do this, is it not the most visionary thing on earth to suppose the world is ever going to be converted to the gospel.

2. They are required not to conform to the world, because conformity to the world is totally *inconsistent with the love of God or man.*

The whole system recognizes only the love of self. Go through all the ranks of business men, from the man that sells candy on the sidewalk at the corner of the street, to the greatest wholesale merchant or importer in the United States, and you will find that one maxim runs through the whole—to buy as cheap as you can, and sell as dear as you can—to Look out for number one—and to do always, as far as the rules of honesty will allow, all that will advance your own interests, let what will become of the interest of others. Ungodly men will not deny that these are the maxims on which business is done in the world. The man who pursues this course is universally regarded as doing business on business principles. Now, are these maxims consistent with holiness, with the love of God or the love of man, with the spirit of the gospel or the example of Jesus Christ? Can a man conform to the world in these principles, and yet love God? Impossible! No two things can be more unlike. Then Christians are by no means to conform to the business maxims of the world.

3. These maxims, and the rules by which business is done in the world, are directly opposite to the gospel of Jesus Christ, and the spirit He exhibited, and the maxims He inculcated, and the rules which He enjoined that all His followers should obey, on pain of hell.

What was the spirit Jesus Christ exemplified on earth? It was the spirit of self-denial, of benevolence, of sacrificing Himself to do good to others. He exhibited the same spirit that God does, who enjoys His infinite happiness in going out of himself to gratify His benevolent heart in doing good to others. This is the religion of the gospel, to be like God, not only doing good, but enjoying it, joyfully going out of self to do good. This is the gospel maxim: "It is more blessed to give than to receive." And again, "Look not every man on his own things, but every man also on the things of others." What says the business man of the world? "Look out for number one." These very maxims were made by men who knew and cared no more for the gospel, than the heathen do. Why should Christians conform to such maxims as these?

4. To conform to the world in the pursuits of business is a flat contradiction of the engagements that Christians make when they enter the church.

What is the engagement that you make when you enter the church? Is it not, to renounce the world and live for God, and to be actuated by the Spirit of Jesus Christ, and to possess supreme love to God, and to renounce self, and to give yourself to glorify God, and do good to men? You profess not to love the world, its honors or its riches. Around the communion table, with your hand on the broken body of your Savior, you avouch these to be your principles, and pledge yourself to live by these maxims. And then what do you do? Go away, and follow maxims and rules gotten up by men, whose avowed principle is the love of the world, and whose avowed object is to get the world? Is this your way? Then, unless you repent, let me tell you, you will be damned. It is no more certain, that any infidel or any profligate wretch will go to hell, than that all such professing Christians will go there, who conform to the world. They have double guilt. They are sworn before God to a different course, and when they pursue the business principles of the world, they show that they are perjured wretches.

5. Conformity to the world is such a manifest contradiction of the principles of the gospel, that sinners, when they see it, do not and cannot understand from it the true nature and object of the gospel itself.

How can they understand that the object of the gospel is to raise men above the love of the world, and above the influence of the world, and place them on higher ground, to live on totally different principles? When they see professing Christians acting on the same principles with other men, how can they understand the true principles of the gospel, or know what it means by heavenly-mindedness, self-denial, benevolence, and so on?

6. It is this spirit of conformity to the world, that has already eaten out the love of God from the church.

Show me a young convert, while his heart is warm, and the love of God glows out from his lips. What does he care for the world? Call up his attention to it, point him to its riches, its pleasures or its honors, and try to engage him in their pursuit, and he loathes the thought. But let him now go into business, and do business on the principles of the world one year, and you no longer find the love of God glowing in his heart, and his religion has become the religion of conscience, dry, meager, uninfluential—anything but the glowing love of God, moving in him to acts of benevolence. I appeal to every man in this house, and if my voice was loud enough I would appeal to every professor of religion in this city, if it is not. And if anyone should say, "No, it is not so," I should regard it as proof that he *never* knew what it was to feel the glow of a convert's first love.

7. This conformity to the world in business is one of the greatest stumbling blocks in the way of the conversion of sinners.

What do wicked men think, when they see professing Christians, with such professions on their lips, and pretending to believe what the Bible teaches, and yet driving after the world, as eager as anybody, making the best bargains, and dealing as hard as the most worldly?—What do they think? I can tell you what they say. They say "I do not see but these Christians do just as the rest of us do, they act on the same principles, look out as sharp for number one, drive as hard bargains, and get as high interest as anybody." And it must be said that these are not things of which the world accuse Christians slanderously. It is a notorious fact that most of the members of the church pursue the world, so far as appears in the same spirit, by the same maxims, and to the same degree, that the ungodly do who maintain a character for uprightness and humanity. The world say, "Look at the church, I don't see as they are any better than I am; they go to the full length that I do after the world." If professing Christians act on the same principles with worldly men, as the Lord liveth, they shall have the same reward. They are set down in God's book of remembrance as black hypocrites, pretending to be the friends of God while they love the world. For whoso loveth the world is the enemy of God. They profess to be governed by principles directly opposite to the world, and if they do the same things with the world, they are hypocrites.

8. Another reason for the requirement, "Be not conformed to this world," is the immense, salutary and instantaneous influence it would have if everybody would do business on the principles of the gospel.

Just turn the tables over, and let Christians do business one year on gospel principles. It would shake the world. It would ring louder than thunder. Let the ungodly see professing Christians, in every bargain, consulting the good of the person they are trading with—seeking not their own wealth, but every man another's wealth—living above the world—setting no value on the world any farther than it can be a means of glorifying God—what do you think would be the effect? What effect *did it* have in Jerusalem, when the whole body of Christians gave up their business, and turned out *en masse* to pursue the salvation of the world? They were only a few ignorant fishermen, and a few humble women, but they turned the world upside down. Let the church live so now, and it would cover the world with confusion of face, and overwhelm them with convictions of sin. Only let them see the church living above the world, and doing business on gospel principles, seeking not their own interests but the interests of their fellow men, and infidelity would hide its head, heresy would be driven from church, and this charming, blessed spirit of love, would go over the world like the waves of the sea.

Secondly.—Of Fashions.

Why are Christians required not to follow the fashions of the world?

1. Because it is directly at war with the spirit of the gospel, and is *minding earthly things*.

What is minding earthly things, if it is not to follow the fashions of the world, that like a tide are continually setting to and fro, and fluctuating in their forms, and keeping the world continually changing? There are many men of large business in the world, and men of wealth, who think they care nothing for the fashions. They are occupied with something else, and they trust the fashions altogether with their tailor, taking it for granted that he will make all right. But mind, if he should make a garment unfashionable, you would see that they do care about the fashions, and they never would employ that tailor again. Still, at present their thoughts are not much on the fashions. They have a higher object in view. And they think it beneath the dignity of a minister to preach about fashions. They overlook the fact, that with the greater part of mankind fashion is everything. The greater part of the community are not rich, and never expect to be, but they look to the world to enable them to make a *respectable* appearance, and to bring up their families in a *respectable* manner; that is, to *follow the fashions*. Nine-tenths of the population never look at anything higher, than to do as the world does, or to follow the fashions. For this they strain every nerve. And this is what they set their hearts on, and what they live for.

The merchant and the rich man deceives himself, therefore, if he supposes that fashion is a little thing. The great body of the people *mind* this, their minds are set upon it, the thing which they look for in life is to have their dress, equipage, furniture, and so on, like other people, in the fashion, or *respectable* as they call it.

2. To conform to the world is contrary to *their profession*.

When people join the church, they profess to give up the spirit that gives rise to the fashions. They profess to renounce the pomps and vanities of the world, to repent of their pride, to follow the meek and lowly Savior, to live for God. And now, what do they do? You often see professors of religion go to the extreme of the fashion. Nothing will satisfy them that is not in the height of fashion. And a Christian female dress-maker, who is conscientiously opposed to the following of fashions, cannot get her bread. She cannot get employment even among professing Christian ladies, unless she follows the fashions in all their countless changes. God knows it is so, and they must give up their business if their conscience will not permit them to follow the changes of fashion.

3. This conformity is a broad and complete approval of the spirit of the world.

What is it that lies at the bottom of all this shifting scenery? What is the cause that produces all this gaudy show and dash, and display? It is the love of applause. And when Christians follow the changes of fashion, they pronounce all this innocent. All this waste of money and time and thought, all this feeding and cherishing of vanity and the love of applause, the church sets her seal to, when she conforms to the world.

4. Nay, further, another reason is, that following the fashions of the world, professing Christians show that they do in fact love the world.

They show it by their conduct, just as the ungodly show it by the same conduct. As they act alike they give evidence that they are actuated by one principle, the love of fashion.

5. When Christian professors do this, they show most clearly that they love the praise of men.

It is evident that they love admiration and flattery, just as sinners do. Is not this inconsistent with Christian principle, to go right into the very things that are set up by the pride and fashion and lust of the ungodly?

6. Conforming to the world in fashion, you show that you do not hold yourself accountable to God for the manner in which you lay out money.

You practically disown your stewardship of the wealth that is in your possession. By laying out money to gratify your own vanity and lust, you take off the keen edge of that truth, which ought to cut that sinner in two, who is living to himself. It is practically denying that the earth is the Lord's, with the cattle on a thousand hills, and all to be employed for His glory.

7. You show that reputation is your idol.

When the cry comes to your ears on every wind, from the ignorant and the lost of all nations, "Come over and help us, come over and help us," and every week brings some call to send the gospel, to send tracts and Bibles, and missionaries to those who are perishing for lack of knowledge, if you choose to expend money in following the fashions, it is demonstration that reputation is your idol.—Suppose now, for the sake of argument, that it is not prohibited in the word of God to follow the fashions, and that professing Christians, if they will, may *innocently* follow the fashions, (I deny that it is innocent, but suppose it were,) does not the fact that they do follow them when there are such calls for money, and time, and thought, and labor to save souls, prove conclusively that they do not love God nor the souls of men?

Take the case of a woman, whose husband is in slavery, and she is trying to raise money enough for his redemption. There she is, toiling and saving, rising up early and sitting up late, and eating the bread of carefulness, because her husband, the father of her children, the friend of her youth, is in slavery. Now go to that woman and tell her that it is innocent for her to follow the fashions, and dress and display like her neighbors—will she do it? Why not? She does not desire to do it. She will scarcely buy a pair of shoes for her feet, she grudges almost the bread she eats, so intent is she on her great object.

Now suppose a person loved God and the souls of men and the kingdom of Christ, does he need an express prohibition from God to prevent him from spending his money and his life in following the fashion? No, indeed, he will rather need a positive injunction to take what is needful for his own comfort and the support of his own life. Take the case of Timothy. Did he need a prohibition to prevent him from indulging in the use of wine? So far from it, he was so cautious that it required an express injunction from God to make him drink a little as a medicine. Although he was sick, he would not drink it till he had the word of God for it, he saw the evils of it so clearly. Now, show me a man or woman, I care not what their professions are, that follows the fashions of the world, and I will show you what spirit they are of.

Now, don't ask me why Abraham, and David, and Solomon, who were so rich, did not lay out their money in spreading the kingdom of God. Ah, tell me, did they enjoy the light that professors now enjoy? Did they even know so much as this, that the world can be converted, as Christians now see clearly that it can? But suppose it were as allowable in you as it was in Abraham or David to be rich, and to lay out the property you possess in display and pomp and fashion. Suppose it were perfectly innocent, who that loves the Lord Jesus Christ would wish to lay out money in fashion when they could lay it out to gratify the ALL-ABSORBING passion, to do good to the souls of men?

8. By conforming to the world in fashion, you show that you differ not at all from ungodly sinners.

Ungodly sinners say, "I don't see but that these Christian men and women love to follow the fashions as well as I do." Who does not know, that this leads many to infidelity.

9. By following the fashions you are tempting God to give you up to a worldly spirit.

There are many now that have followed the world, and followed the fashions, till God seems to have given them over to the devil for the destruction of the flesh. They have little or no religious feeling, no spirit of prayer, no zeal for the glory of God or the conversion of sinners, the Holy Spirit seems to have withdrawn from them.

10. You tempt the church to follow the fashions.

Where the principal members, the elders and leaders in the church, and their wives and families, are fashionable Christians, they drag the whole church along with them into the train of fashion, and every one apes them as far as they can, down to the lowest servant. Only let a rich Christian lady come out to the house of God in full fashion, and the whole church are set agog to follow as far as they can, and it is a chance if they do not run in debt to do it.

11. You tempt yourself to pride and folly and a worldly spirit.

Suppose a man that had been intemperate and was reformed, should go and surround himself with wine and brandy and every seductive liquor, keeping the provocatives of appetite always under his eye, and from time to time tasting a little; does he not tempt himself?— Now see that woman that has been brought up in the spirit of pride and show, and that has been reformed and professed to abandon them all. Let her keep all these trappings, and continue to follow the fashions, and pride will drag her backwards as sure as she lives. She tempts herself to sin and folly.

12. You are tempting the world.

You are setting the world into a more fierce and hot pursuit of these things. The very things that the world love, and that they are sure to have scruples about their being right, professing Christians fall in with and follow, and thus tempt the world to continue in the pursuit of what will destroy their souls in hell.

13. By following the fashions, you are tempting the devil to tempt you.

When you follow the fashions, you open your heart to him. You keep it for him, empty, swept, and garnished. Every woman that suffers herself to follow the fashions may rely upon it, she is helping Satan to tempt her to pride and sin.

14. You lay a great stumbling block before the greatest part of mankind.

There are a few persons who are pursuing greater objects than fashion. They are engaged in the scramble for political power, or they are eager for literary distinction, or they are striving for wealth. And they do not know that their hearts are set on fashion at all. They are following selfishness on a larger scale. But the great mass of the community are influenced mostly by these fluctuating fashions. To this class of persons it is a great and sore stumbling block, when they see professing Christians just as prompt and as eager to follow the changings of fashion as themselves. They see, and say, "What does their profession amount to, when they follow the fashions as much as anybody?" or, "Certainly it is right to follow the fashions, for see, the professing Christians do it as much as we."

15. Another reason why professing Christians are required not to be conformed to the world in fashion is, the great influence their disregarding fashion would have on the world.

If professing Christians would show their contempt for these things, and not pretend to follow them or regard them, how it would shame the world, and convince the world that *they* were living for another object, for God and for eternity! How irresistible it would be! What an overwhelming testimony in favor of our religion! Even the *apparent* renunciation of the world, by many orders of monks, has doubtless done more than anything else to put down the opposition to their religion, and give it currency and influence in the world. Now suppose all this was hearty and sincere, and coupled with all that is consistent and lovely in Christian character, and all that is zealous and bold in labors for the conversion of the world from sin to holiness. What an influence it would have! What thunders it would pour into the ears of the world, to wake them up to follow after God!

Thirdly.—In Politics.

I will show why professing Christians are required not to be conformed to the world in politics.

1. Because the politics of the world are perfectly dishonest.

Who does not know this? Who does not know that it is the proposed policy of every party to cover up the defects of their own candidate, and the good qualities of the opposing candidate? And is not this dishonest? Every party holds up its candidate as a piece of perfection, and then aims to ride him into office by any means, fair or foul. No man can be an honest man, that is committed to a party, to go with them, let them do what they may. And can a Christian do it, and keep a conscience void of offense?

2. To conform to the world in politics is to tempt God.

By falling in with the world in politics, Christians are guilty of setting up rulers over them by their own vote, who do not fear nor love God, and who set the law of God at defiance, break the Sabbath, and gamble, and commit adultery, and fight duels, and swear profanely, and leave the laws unexecuted at their pleasure, and that care not for the weal or woe of their country, so long as they can keep their office. I say Christians do this. For it is plain that where parties are divided, as they are in this country, there are Christians enough to turn the scale in any election. Now let Christians take the ground that they will not vote for a dishonest man, or a Sabbath breaker, or gambler, or whoremonger, or duelist, for any office, and no party could ever nominate such a character with any hope of success. But on the present system, where men will let the laws go unexecuted, and give full swing to mobs, or lynch-murders, or robbing the mails, or anything else, so they can run in their own candidate who will give them the offices, any man is a dishonest man that will do it, be he professor or non-professor. And can a Christian do this and be blameless?

3. By engaging with the world in politics, Christians grieve the Spirit of God.

Ask any Christian politician if he ever carried the Spirit of God with him into a political campaign? Never. I would by no means be understood to say that Christians should refuse to vote, and to exercise their lawful influence in public affairs. But they ought not to follow a party.

4. By following the present course of politics, you are contributing your aid to undermine all government and order in the land.

Who does not know that this great nation now rocks and reels, because the laws are broken and trampled under foot, and the executive power refuses or dare not act? Either the magistrate does not wish to put down disorder, or he temporizes and lets the devil rule. And so it is in all parts of the country, and all parties. And can a Christian be consistent with his profession, and vote for such men to office?

5. You lay a stumbling-block in the way of sinners.

What do sinners think, when they see professing Christians acting with them in their political measures, which they themselves know to be dishonest and corrupt? They say, "We understand what we are about, we are after office, we are determined to carry our party into power, we are pursuing our own interest; but these Christians profess to live for another and a higher end, and yet here they come, and join with us, as eager for the loaves and fishes as the rest of us." What greater stumbling-block can they have?

6. You prove to the ungodly that professing Christians are actuated by the same spirit with themselves.

Who can wonder that the world is incredulous as to the reality of religion? If they do not look for themselves into the scriptures, and there learn what religion is, if they are governed by the rules of evidence from what they see in the lives of professing Christians, they ought to be incredulous. They ought to infer, so far as this evidence goes, that professors of religion do not themselves believe in it. It is the fact. I doubt, myself, whether the great mass of professors believe the Bible.

7. They show, so far as their evidence can go, that there is no change of heart.

What is it? Is it going to the communion table once in a month or two, and sometimes to prayer meeting? In that a change of heart, when they are just as eager in the scramble for office as any others? The world must be fools to believe in a change of heart on such evidence.

8. Christians ought to cease from conformity to the world in politics, from the influence which such a course would have on the world.

Suppose Christians were to act perfectly conscientious and consistent in this matter, and to say, "We will not vote for any man to office, unless he fears God and will rule the people in righteousness." Ungodly men would not set men as candidates, who themselves set the laws at defiance. No. Every candidate would be obliged to show that he was prepared to act from higher motives, and that he would lay himself out to make the country prosperous, and to promote virtue, and to put down vice and oppression and disorder, and to do all he can to make the people happy and HOLY! It would shame the dishonest politicians, to show that the love of God and man is the motive that Christians have in view. And a blessed influence would go over the land like a wave.

IV. I am to answer some objections that are made against the principles here advanced.

1. *In regard to business.*

Objection. "If we do not transact business on the same principles on which ungodly men do it, we cannot compete with them, and all the business of the world will fall into the hands of the ungodly. If we pursue our business for the good of others, if we buy and sell on the principle of not seeking our own wealth, but the wealth of those we do business with, we cannot sustain a competition with worldly men, and they will get all the business."

Let them have it, then. You can support yourself by your industry in some humbler calling, and let worldly men do all the business.

Objection. "But then, how should we get money to spread the gospel?"

A holy church, that would act on the principles of the gospel, would spread the gospel faster than all the money that ever was in New York, or that ever will be. Give me a holy church, that would live above the world, and the work of salvation would roll on faster than with all the money in Christendom.

Objection. "But we must spend a great deal of money to bring forward an educated ministry."

Ah! if we had a *holy* ministry, it would be far more important than an educated ministry. If the ministry were holy enough, they would do without so much education. God forbid that I should undervalue an educated ministry. Let ministers be educated as well as they can, the more the better, if they are only holy enough. But it is all a farce to suppose that a literary ministry can convert the world. Let the ministry have the spirit of prayer, let the baptism of the Holy Ghost be upon them, and they will spread the gospel. Only let Christians live as they ought, and the church would shake the world. If Christians in New York would do it, the report would soon fill every ship that leaves the port, and waft the news on every wind, till the earth was full of excitement and inquiry, and conversions would multiply like the drops of morning dew.

Suppose you were to give up your business, and devote yourselves entirely to the work of extending the gospel. The church once did so, and you know what followed. When that little band in Jerusalem gave up their business and spent their time in the work of God, salvation spread like a wave. And, I believe, if the whole

Christian church were to turn right out, and convert the world, it would be done in a very short time.

And further, the fact is, that you would not be required to give up your business. If Christians would do business in the spirit of the gospel, they would soon engross the business of the world. Only let the world see, that if they go to a Christian to do business, he will not only deal honestly, but benevolently, that he will actually consult the interest of the person he deals with, as if it were his own interest, and who would deal with anybody else? What merchant would go to an ungodly man to trade, who he knew would try to get the advantage of him, and cheat him, while he knew that there were Christian merchants to deal with that would consult his interests as much as they do their own? Indeed, it is a known fact, that there are now Christian merchants in this city, who regulate the prices of the articles they deal in. Merchants come in from the country, and inquire around to see how they can buy goods, and they go to these men to know exactly what articles are worth at a fair price, and govern themselves accordingly.

The advantage, then, is all on one side. The church can make it for the interest of the ungodly to do business on right principles. The church can regulate the business of the world, and woe to them if they do not.

2. *In regard to fashion.*

Objection. "Is it best for Christians to be singular?"

Certainly, Christians are bound to be singular. They are called to be peculiar people, that is, a singular people, essentially different from the rest of mankind. To maintain that we are not to be singular, is the same as to maintain that we *are* to be conformed to the world. "Be not singular," that is, Be like the world. In other words, "Be ye conformed to the world." This is the direct opposite to the command in the text.

But the question now regards fashion, in dress, equipage, and so on. And here I will confess that I was formerly myself in error. I believed, and I taught, that the best way for Christians to pursue, was to dress so as not to be noticed, to follow the fashions and changes so as not to appear singular, and that nobody would be led to think of their being different from others in these particulars. But I have seen my error, and now wonder very much at my former blindness. It is your duty to dress so plain as to show to the world that you place no sort of reliance in the things of fashion, and set no value at all on them, but despise and neglect them altogether.

But unless you are singular, unless you separate yourselves from the fashions of the world, you show that you do value them. There is no way in which you can bear a proper testimony by your lives against the fashions of the world but by dressing plain. I do not mean that you should *study singularity*, but that you should consult *convenience and economy*, although it may be singular.

Objection. "But if we dress plain, the attention of people will be taken with it."

The reason of it is this, so few do it that it is a novelty, and everybody stares when they see a professing Christian so strict as to disregard the fashions. Let them all do it, and the only thing you show by it is that you are a Christian, and do not wish to be confounded with the ungodly. Would it not tell on the pride of the world, if all the Christians in it were united in bearing a practical testimony against its vain show.

Objection. "But in this way you carry religion too far away from the multitude. It is better not to set up an artificial distinction between the church and the world."

The direct reverse of this is true. The nearer you bring the church to the world, the more you annihilate the reasons that ought to stand out in view of the world, for their changing sides and coming over to the church. Unless you go right out from them, and show that you are not of them in any respect, and carry the church so far as to have a broad interval between saints and sinners, how can you make the ungodly feel that so great a change is necessary.

Objection. "But this change which is necessary is a change of heart."

True; but will not a change of heart produce a change of life?

Objection. "You will throw obstacles in the way of persons becoming Christians. Many respectable people will become disgusted with religion, and if they cannot be allowed to dress and be Christians, they will take to the world altogether."

This is just about as reasonable as it would be for a temperance man to think he must get drunk now and then, to avoid disgusting the intemperate, and to retain his influence over them. The truth is, that persons ought to know, and ought to see in the lives of professing Christians, that if they embrace religion, they must be weaned from the world, and must give up the love of the world, and its pride and show and folly, and live a holy life, in watchfulness and self-denial and active benevolence.

Objection. "Is it not better for us to disregard this altogether, and not pay any attention to such little things, and let them take their course; let the milliner and mantua-maker do as they please, and follow the usages of society in which we live, and the circle in which we move?"

Is this the way to show contempt for the fashions of the world? Do people ordinarily take this course of showing contempt for a thing, to practice it? Why, the way to show your abhorrence of ardent spirit is to drink it! And so the way to show your abhorrence of the world is to follow along in the customs and the fashions of the world! Precious reasoning, this.

Objection. "No matter how we dress, if our hearts are right?"

Your heart right! Then your heart may be right when your conduct is all wrong. Just as well might the profane swearer say, "No matter what words I speak, if my heart is right." No, your heart is not right, unless your conduct is right. What is outward conduct, but the acting out of the heart? If your heart was right, you would not wish to follow the fashions of the world.

Objection. "What is the standard of dress? I do not see the use of all your preaching, and laying down rules about plain dress, unless you give us a standard."

This is a mighty stumbling block with many. But to my mind the matter is extremely simple. The whole can be comprised in two simple rules. One is, Be sure in all your equipage, and dress and furniture to show that you have no fellowship with the designs and principles of those who are aiming to set off themselves, and to gain the applause of men. The other is, Let economy be first consulted, and then convenience. Follow Christian economy, that is, save all you can for Christ's service; and then let things be as convenient as Christian economy will admit.

Objection. "Would you have us to turn all Quakers, and put on their plain dress?"

Who does not know, that the plain dress of the Quakers has won for them the respect of all the thinking part of the ungodly in the community? Now, if they had coupled with this the zeal for God, and the weanedness from the world, and the contempt for riches, and the self-denying labor for the conversion of sinners to Christ, which the gospel enjoins, and the clear views of the plan of salvation which the gospel inculcates, they would long since have converted the world. And if all Christians would imitate them in their plain dress, (I do not mean the precise cut and fashion of their dress, but in a *plain* dress, throwing contempt upon the fashions of the world,) who can doubt that the conversion of the world would hasten on apace?

Objection. "Would you make us all Methodists?"

Who does not know that the Methodists, when they were noted for their plain dress, and for renouncing the fashions and show of the world, used to have power with God in prayer? And that they had the universal respect of the world as sincere Christians. And who does not know that since they have laid aside this peculiarity, and conformed to the world in dress and other things, and seemed to be trying to lift themselves up as a denomination, and gain influence with the world, they are losing the power of prayer? Would to God they had never thrown down this wall. It was one of the leading excellences of Wesley's system, to have his followers distinguished from others by a plain dress.

Objection. "We may be proud of a plain dress as well as of a fashionable dress. The Quakers are as proud as we are."

So may any good thing be abused. But that is no reason why it should not be used, if it can be shown to be good. I put it back to the objector; Is that any reason why a Christian female, who fears God and loves the souls of men, should neglect the means which may make an impression that she is separated from the world, and pour contempt on the fashions of the ungodly, in which they are dancing their way to hell?

Objection. "This is a small thing, and ought not to take up so much of a minister's time in the pulpit."

This is an objection often heard from worldly professors. But the minister that fears God will not be deterred by it. He will pursue the subject, until such professing Christians are cut off from their conformity to the world or cut off from the church. It is not merely the dress, as dress, but it is the conformity to the world in dress and fashion, that is the great stumbling-block in the way of sinners. How can the world be converted, while professing Christians are conformed to the world? What good will it do to give money to send the gospel to the heathen, when Christians live so at home? Well might the heathen ask, "What profit will it be to become Christians, when those who are Christians are pursuing the world with all the hot-haste of the ungodly?" The great thing necessary for the church is to break off from conformity to the world, and then they will have power with God in prayer, and the Holy Ghost will descend and bless their efforts, and the world will be converted.

Objection. "But if we dress so, we shall be called fanatics."

Whatever the ungodly may call you, fanatics, Methodists, or anything, you will be known as Christians, and in the secret consciences of men will be acknowledged as such. It is not in the power of unbelievers to pour contempt on a holy church, that are separated from the world. How was it with the early Christians? They lived separate from the world, and it made such an impression, that even infidel writers say of them, "These men win the hearts of the mass of the people, because they *give themselves up* to deeds of charity, and pour contempt on the world." Depend upon it, if Christians would live so now, the last effort of hell would soon be expended in vain to defeat the spread of the gospel. Wave after wave would flow abroad, till the highest mountain tops were covered with the waters of life.

3. *In regard to politics.*

Objection. "In this way, by acting on these principles, and refusing to unite with the world in politics, we could have no influence in government and national affairs."

I answer, first, It is so now. Christians, as such, have no influence. There is not a Christian principle adopted because it is Christian, or because it is according to the law of God.

I answer, secondly, If there is no other way for Christians to have an influence in the government, but by becoming conformed to the world in their habitual principles and parties, then let the ungodly take the government and manage it in their own way, and do you go and serve God.

I answer, thirdly, No such result will follow. Directly the reverse of this would be the fact. Only let it be known that Christian citizens will on no account assist bad men into office; only let it be known that the church will go only for men that will aim at the public good, and both parties will be sure to set up such men. And in this way, the church could legitimately exert an influence, by compelling all parties to bring forward only men who are worthy of an honest man's support.

Objection. "In this way the church and the world will be arrayed against each other."

The world is too selfish for this. You cannot make parties so. Such a line can never be a permanent division. For one year, the ungodly might unite against the church, and leave Christians in a small minority. But in the end, the others would form two parties, each courting the suffrages of Christians, by offering candidates such as Christians can conscientiously vote for.

REMARKS.

1. By non-conformity to the world, you may save much money for doing good.

In one year a greater fund might be saved by the church, than all that has ever been raised for the spread of the gospel.

2. By non-conformity to the world, a great deal of time may be saved for doing good, that is now consumed and wasted in following the fashions, and obeying the maxims, and joining in the pursuits of the world.

3. At the same time, Christians in this way would preserve their peace of conscience, would enjoy communion with God, would have the spirit of prayer, and would possess far greater usefulness.

Is it not time something was done? Is it not time that some church struck out a path, that should be not conformed to the world, but should be according to the example and Spirit of Christ?

You profess that you want to have sinners converted. But what avails it, if they sink right back again into conformity with the world? Brethren, I confess, I am filled with pain in view of the conduct of the church. Where are the proper results of the glorious revivals we have had? I believe they were genuine revivals of religion and outpourings of the Holy Ghost, that the church has enjoyed the last ten years. I believe the converts of the last ten years are among the best Christians in the land. Yet, after all, the great body of them are a disgrace to religion. Of what use would it be to have a thousand members added to the church, to be just such as are now in it? Would religion be any more honored by it, in the estimation of ungodly men? One holy church, that are really crucified to the world, and the world crucified to them, would do more to recommend Christianity, than all the churches in the country, living as they now do. O, if I had strength of body, to go through the churches again, instead of preaching to convert sinners, I would preach to bring up the churches to the gospel standard of holy living. Of what use is it to convert sinners, and make them such Christians as these? Of what use is it to try to convert sinners, and make them feel there is something in religion, and then when they go to trade with you, or meet you in the street, have you contradict it all, and tell them, by your conformity to the world, that there is nothing in it?

Where shall I look, where shall the Lord look for a church like the first church, that will come out from the world and be separate, and give themselves up to serve God? O, if this church would do so. But it is of little use to make Christians, if they are not better. Do not understand me as saying that the converts made in our revivals are spurious conversions. But they live so as to be a disgrace to religion. They are so stumbled by old professors that many of them do more hurt than good. The more there are of them, the more occasion infidelity seems to find for her jeers and scoffs.

Now do you believe, that God commands you not to be conformed to the world? Do you believe it? And DARE YOU obey it, let people say what they will about you? Dare you now separate yourselves from the world, and never again be controlled by its maxims, and never again copy its practices, and never again will be whiffled here and there by its fashions? I know a man that lives so, I can mention his name, he pays no attention to the customs of the world in this respect. And what is the result? Wherever that man goes, he leaves the impression behind that he is a Christian. O, if one church would do so, and would engage in it with all the energy that men of the world engage in their business, they would turn the world upside down. Will you do so? Will you break off from the world now, and enter into covenant with God, and declare that you will *dare* to be singular enough to be separate from the world, and from this time set your faces as a flint to obey God, let the world say what they will? Dare you do it? Will you do it?

LECTURE IX.

TRUE AND FALSE REPENTANCE.

TEXT:—"For godly sorrow worketh repentance into salvation, not to be repented of; but the sorrow of the world worketh death."
                                                            2 Corinthians vii. 10

In this chapter the apostle refers to another epistle, which he had formerly written to the church at Corinth, on a certain subject, in which they were greatly to blame. He speaks here of the effect that it had, in bringing them to true repentance. They sorrowed after a godly sort. This was the evidence that their repentance was genuine.

"For behold this self-same thing, that ye sorrowed after a godly sort, what carefulness it wrought in you, yea, what clearing of yourselves, yea, what indignation, yea, what fear, yea, what vehement desire, yea, what zeal, yea, what revenge! In all things ye have approved yourselves to be clear in this matter."

In the verse which I have taken for my text, he speaks of two kinds of sorrow for sin, one working repentance unto salvation, the other working death. He alludes to what is generally understood by two kinds of repentance. And this is the subject of discourse tonight.

TRUE AND FALSE REPENTANCE

In discoursing on the subject, I design to show
I. What true repentance is:
II. How it may be known:
III. What is false and spurious repentance:
IV. How it may be known:

It is high time professors of religion were taught to discriminate much more than they do in regard to the nature and character of various exercises on the subject of religion. Were it so, the church would not be so overrun with false and unprofitable professors. I have of late been frequently led to examine, over and over again, the reason why there is so much spurious religion, and I have sought to know what is the foundation of the difficulty. That multitudes suppose themselves to be religious, who are not so, unless the Bible is false—is notorious. Why is it that so many are deceived? Why do so many, who are yet impenitent sinners, get the idea that they have repented? The cause is doubtless a want of discriminating instruction respecting the foundation of religion, and especially a want of discrimination respecting true and false repentance.

I. I am to show what is true repentance.

It involves a change of opinion respecting the nature of sin, and this change of opinion followed by a corresponding change of feeling towards sin. Feeling is the result of thought. And when this change of opinion is such as to produce a corresponding change of feeling, if the opinion is right and the feeling corresponds, this is true repentance. It must be right opinion. The opinion now adopted might be such an opinion as God holds respecting sin. Godly sorrow, such as God requires, must spring from such views of sin as God holds.

First. There must be a change of opinion in regard to sin.

1. A change of opinion in regard to the nature of sin.

To one who truly repents, sin looks like a very different thing from what it does to him who has not repented. Instead of looking like a thing that is desirable or fascinating, it looks the very opposite, most odious and detestable, and he is astonished at himself, that he ever could have desired such a thing. Impenitent sinners may look at sin and see that it will ruin them, because God will punish them for it. But after all, it appears in itself desirable. They love it. They roll it under their tongue. If it could end in happiness, they never would think of abandoning it. But to the other it is different; he looks at his own conduct as perfectly hateful. He looks back upon it, and exclaims, "How hateful, how detestable, how worthy of hell, such and such a thing was in me."

2. A change of opinion of the character of sin as respects its relation to God.

Sinners do not see why God threatens sin with such terrible punishment. They love it so well themselves, that they cannot see why God should look at it in such a light as to think it worthy of everlasting punishment. When they are strongly convicted, they see it differently, and so far as opinion is concerned, they see it in the same light as a Christian does, and then they only want a corresponding change of feeling to become Christians. Many a sinner sees its relation to God to be such that it deserves eternal death, but his *heart* does not go with his opinions. This is the case with the devils and wicked spirits in hell. Mark, then; a change of opinion is indispensable to true repentance, and always precedes it.

The heart never goes out to God in true repentance without a previous change of opinion. There may be a change of opinion without repentance, but no genuine repentance without a change of opinion.

3. A change of opinion in regard to the tendencies of sin.

Before, the sinner thinks it utterly incredible that sin should have such tendencies as to deserve everlasting death. He may be fully changed, however, as to his *opinions* on this point without repentance, but it is impossible a man should truly repent without a change of opinion. He sees sin in its tendency, as ruinous to himself and everybody else, soul and body, for time and eternity, and at variance with all that is lovely and happy in the universe. He sees that sin is calculated in its tendencies to injure himself, and everybody else, and that there is no remedy but universal abstinence. The devil knows it to be so. And possibly there are some sinners now in this congregation who know it.

4. A change of opinion in regard to the desert of sin.

The word rendered repentance implies all this. It implies a change in the state of the mind including all this. The careless sinner has almost no right ideas, even so far as this life is concerned, respecting the desert of sin. Suppose he admits in theory that sin deserves eternal death, he does not believe it. If he believed it, it would be impossible for him to remain a careless sinner. He is deceived, if he supposes that he honestly holds such an opinion as that sin deserves the wrath of God forever. But the truly awakened and convicted sinner has no more doubt of this than he has of the existence of God. He sees clearly that sin must deserve everlasting punishment from God. He knows that this is a simple matter of fact.

Secondly. In true repentance there must be a corresponding change of feeling.

The change of feeling respects sin in all these particulars, its nature, its relations, its tendencies, and its deserts. The individual who truly repents, not only sees sin to be detestable and vile and worthy of abhorrence, but he really abhors it, and hates it in his heart. A person may see sin to be hurtful and abominable, while yet his heart loves it, and desires it, and clings to it. But when he truly repents, he most heartily abhors and renounces it.

In relation to God, he feels towards sin as it really is. And here is the source of those gushings of sorrow in which Christians sometimes break out, when contemplating sin. The Christian views it as to its nature, and simply feels abhorrence. But when he views it in relation to God, then he feels like weeping, the fountains of his sorrow gush forth, and he wants to get right down on his face and pour out a flood of tears over his sins.

Then as to the tendencies of sin, the individual who truly repents feels it as it is. When he views sin in its tendencies, it awakens a vehement desire to stop it, and to save people from their sins, and roll back the tide of death. It sets his heart on fire, and he goes to praying, and laboring, and pulling sinners out of the fire with all his might, to save them from the awful tendencies of sin. When the Christian sets his mind on this, he will bestir himself to make people give up their sins. Just as if he saw all the people taking poison which he knew would destroy them, and he lifts up his voice to warn them to BEWARE.

He feels right, as to the desert of sin. He has not only an intellectual conviction that sin deserves everlasting punishment, but he feels that it would be so right and so reasonable, and so just for God to condemn him to eternal death, that so far from finding fault with the sentence of the law that condemns him, he thinks it the wonder of heaven, a wonder of wonders, if God can forgive him. Instead of thinking it hard, or severe, or unkind in God, that incorrigible sinners are sent to hell, he is full of adoring wonder that he is not sent to hell himself, and that this whole guilty world has not long since been hurled down to endless burnings. It is the last thing in the world he would think to complain of, that all sinners are not saved, but O, it is a wonder of mercy that all the world is not damned. And when he thinks of such a sinner's being saved, he feels a sense of gratitude that he never knew anything of till he was a Christian.

II. I am to show what are the works or effects of genuine repentance.

I wish to show you what are the works of true repentance, and to make it so plain to your minds, that you can know infallibly whether you have repented or not.

1. If your repentance is genuine, there is in your mind a *conscious* change of views and feeling in regard to sin.

Of this you will be just as conscious as you ever were of a change of views and feelings on any other subject. Now, can you say this? *Do you* know, that on this point there has been a change in you, and that old things are done away and all things have become new?

2. Where repentance is genuine, the disposition to repeat sin is gone.

If you have truly repented, you do not now love sin; you do not now abstain from it through fear, and to avoid punishment, but because you hate it. How is this with you? Do you know that your disposition to commit sin is gone? Look at the sins you used to practice when you were impenitent. How do they appear to you? Do they look pleasant, and would you really love to practice them again if *you dared?*—If you do, if you have the disposition to sin left, you are only convicted. Your *opinions* of sin may be changed, but if the love of that sin remains, as your soul lives, you are still an impenitent sinner.

3. Genuine repentance worketh a reformation of conduct.

I take this to be the idea chiefly intended in the text, where it says "Godly sorrow worketh repentance." Godly sorrow produces a reformation of conduct. Otherwise it is a repetition of the same idea or saying, that repentance produces repentance. Whereas, I suppose the apostle was speaking of such a change of mind as produces a change of conduct, ending in salvation. Now, let me ask you, are you really reformed? Have you forsaken your sins? Or, are you practicing them still? If so, you are still a sinner. However you may have changed your mind, if it has not wrought a change of conduct, an actual reformation, it is not godly repentance, or such as God approves.

4. Repentance, when true and genuine, leads to confession and restitution.

The thief has not repented, while he keeps the money he stole. He may have conviction, but no repentance. If he had repentance, he would go and give back the money. If you have cheated anyone, and do not restore what you have taken unjustly; or if you have injured anyone, and do not set about it to undo the wrong you have done, as far as in you lies, you have not truly repented.

5. True repentance is a permanent change of character and conduct.

The text says it is repentance unto salvation, *not to be repented of.* What else does the apostle mean by that expression but this, that true repentance is a change so deep and fundamental that the man never changes back again? People often quote it as if it read repentance that does not *need* to be repented of. But that is not what he says. It is *not to be* repented of, or in other words, repentance that *will not* be repented of, so thorough that there is no going back. The love of sin is truly abandoned. The individual, who has truly repented, has so changed his views and feelings, that he will not change back again, or go back to the love of sin. Bear this in mind now, all of you, that the truly penitent sinner exercises feelings of which he never will repent. The text says it is "unto salvation." It goes right on, to the very rest of heaven. The very reason why it ends in salvation is because it is such as will not be repented of.

And here I cannot but remark, that you see why the doctrine of the Saints' Perseverance is true, and what it means. True repentance is such a thorough change of feelings, and the individual who exercises it comes so to abhor sin, that he will persevere of course, and not go and take back all his repentance and return to sin again.

III. I am to speak of false repentance.

False or spurious repentance is said to be worldly, the sorrow of the world, that is, it is sorrow for sin, arising from worldly considerations and motives connected with the present life, or at most, has respect to his *own happiness* in a future world, and has no regard to the true nature of sin.

1. It is not founded on such a change of opinion as I have specified to belong to true repentance.

The change is not on fundamental points. A person may see the evil consequences of sin in a worldly point of view, and it may fill him with consternation. He may see that it will greatly affect his character, or endanger his life; that if some of his concealed conduct should be found out, he would be disgraced, and this may fill him with fear and distress. It is very common for persons to have this kind of worldly sorrow, when some worldly consideration is at the bottom of it all.

2. False repentance is founded in selfishness.

It may be simply a strong feeling of regret, in the mind of the individual, that he has done as he has, because he sees the evil consequences of it to himself, because it makes him miserable, or exposes him to the wrath of God, or injures his family or his friends, or because it produces some injury to himself in time or in eternity. All this is pure selfishness. He may feel remorse of conscience—biting, consuming REMORSE—and no true repentance. It may extend to fear—deep and dreadful fear—of the wrath of God and the pains of hell, and yet be purely selfish, and all the while there may be no such thing as a hearty abhorrence of sin, and no feelings of the heart going out after the convictions of the understanding, in regard to the infinite evil of sin.

IV. I am to show how this false or spurious repentance may be known.

1. It leaves the feelings unchanged.

It leaves unbroken and unsubdued the disposition to sin in the heart. The feelings as to the nature of sin are not so changed, but that the individual still feels a desire for sin. He abstains from it, not from abhorrence of it, but from dread of the consequences of it.

2. It works death.

It leads to hypocritical concealment. The individual who has exercised true repentance is willing to have it known that he has repented, and willing to have it known that he was a sinner. He who has only false repentance, resorts to excuses and lying to cover his sins, and is ashamed of his repentance. When he is called to the anxious seat, he will cover up his sins by a thousand apologies and excuses, trying to smooth them over, and extenuate their enormity. If he speaks of his past conduct, he always does it in the softest and most favorable terms. You see a constant disposition to cover up his sin. This repentance leads to death. It makes him commit one sin to cover up another. Instead of that ingenuous, openhearted breaking forth of sensibility and frankness, you see a palavering, smooth-tongued, half-hearted mincing out of something that is intended to answer the purpose of a confession, and yet to confess nothing.

How is it with you? Are you ashamed to have any person talk with you about your sins? Then your sorrow is only a worldly sorrow, and worketh death. How often you see sinners getting out of the way to avoid conversation about their sins, and yet calling themselves anxious inquirers, and expecting to become Christians in that way. The same kind of sorrow is found in hell. No doubt all those wretched inhabitants of the pit wish to get away from the eye of God. No such sorrow is found among the saints in heaven. Their sorrow is open, ingenuous, full and hearty. Such sorrow is not inconsistent with true happiness. The saints are full of happiness, and yet full of deep and undisguised, and gushing sorrow for sin. But this worldly sorrow is ashamed of itself, is mean and miserable, and worketh death.

3. False repentance produces only a partial reformation of conduct.

The reformation that is produced by worldly sorrow extends only to those things of which the individual has been strongly convicted. The heart is not changed. You will see him avoid only those cardinal sins, about which he has been much exercised.

Observe that young convert. If he is deceived, you will find that there is only a partial change in his conduct. He is reformed in certain things, but there are many things which are wrong that he continues to practice. If you become intimately acquainted with him, instead of finding him tremblingly alive to sin everywhere, and quick to detect it in everything that is contrary to the spirit of the gospel, you will find him, perhaps, strict and quick-sighted in regard to certain things, but loose in his conduct and lax in his views on other points, and very far from manifesting a Christian spirit in regard to all sin.

4. Ordinarily, the reformation produced by false sorrow is temporary even in those things which are reformed.

The individual is continually relapsing into his old sins. The reason is, the *disposition* to sin is not gone, it is only checked and restrained by fear, and as soon as he has a hope and is in the church, and gets bolstered up so that his fears are allayed, you see him gradually wearing back, and presently returning to his old sins. This was the difficulty with the house of Israel, that made them so constantly return to their idolatry and other sins. They had only worldly sorrow. You see it now everywhere in the church. Individuals are reformed for a time, and taken into the church, and then relapse into their old sins. They love to call it getting cold in religion, and backsliding, and the like, but the truth is, they always loved sin, and when the occasion offered, they returned to it, as the sow that was washed to her wallowing in the mire, because she was always a sow.

I want you should understand this point thoroughly.—Here is the foundation of all those fits and starts in religion, that you see so much of. People are awakened, and convicted, and by and by they get to hope and settle down in false security, and then away they go. Perhaps, they may keep so far on their guard as not to be turned out of the church, but the foundations of sins are not broken up, and they return to their old ways. The woman that loved dress loves it still, and gradually returns to her ribands and gewgaws. The man who loved money loves it yet, and soon slides back into his old ways, and dives into business, and pursues the world as eagerly and devotedly as he did before he joined the church.

Go through all the departments of society, and if you find thorough conversions, you will find that their most besetting sins before conversion are farthest from them now. The real convert is least likely to fall into his old besetting sin, because he abhors it most. But if he is deceived and worldly minded, he is always tending back into the same sins. The woman that loves dress comes out again in all her glory, and dashes as she used to. The fountain of sin was not broken up. They have not purged out iniquity from their heart, but they regarded iniquity in their heart all the time.

5. It is a forced reformation.

The reformation produced by a false repentance is not only a partial reformation, and a temporary reformation, but it is also forced and constrained. The reformation of one who has true repentance is from the heart; he has no longer a disposition to sin. In him the Bible promise is fulfilled. He actually finds that "Wisdom's ways are ways of pleasantness, and all her paths are peace." He experiences that the Savior's yoke is easy and His burden is light. He has felt that God's commandments are not grievous but joyous. More to be desired are they than gold, yea, than much fine gold; sweeter also than honey and the honeycomb. But this spurious kind of repentance is very different: it is a legal repentance, the result of fear and not of love; a selfish repentance, anything but a free, voluntary, hearty change from sin to obedience. You will find, if there are any individuals here that have this kind of repentance, you are conscious that you do not abstain from sin by choice, because you hate it, but from other considerations. It is more through the forbiddings of conscience, or the fear you shall lose your soul, or lose your hope, or lose your character, than from abhorrence of sin or love to duty.

Such persons always need to be crowded up to do duty, with an express passage of scripture, or else they will apologize for sin, and evade duty, and think there is no great harm in doing as they do. The reason is, they love their sins, and if there is not some express command of God which they *dare not* fly in the face of, they will practice them. Not so with true repentance. If a thing seems contrary to the great law of love, the person who has true repentance will abhor it, and avoid it of course, whether he has an express command of God for it or not. Show me such a man and I tell you he don't need an express command to make him give up the drinking or making or vending of strong drink. He sees it is contrary to the great law of benevolence, and he truly abhors it, and would no more do it than he would blaspheme God, or steal, or commit any other abomination.

So the man that has true repentance does not need a "Thus saith the Lord," to keep him from oppressing his fellow men, because he would not do anything wrong. How certainly men would abhor anything of the kind, if they had truly repented of sin.

6. This spurious repentance leads to self-righteousness.

The individual who has this repentance may know that Jesus Christ is the only Savior of sinners, and may profess to believe on Him and to rely on Him alone for salvation, but after all, he is actually placing ten times more reliance on his reformation than on Jesus Christ for his salvation. And if he would watch his own heart, he might know it is so. He may say he expects salvation by Christ, but in fact he is dwelling more on his reformation, and his hope is founded more on that, than on the atonement of Christ, and he is really patching up a righteousness of his own.

7. It leads to false security.

The individual supposes the worldly sorrow he has had to be true repentance, and he trusts to it. It is a curious fact, that so far as I have been able to get at the state of mind of this class of persons, they seem to take it for granted that Christ will save them because they have had sorrow on account of their sins, although they are not conscious that they have ever felt any resting in Christ. They felt sorrow, and then they got relief and felt better, and now they expect to be saved by Christ, when their very consciousness will teach them that they have never felt a hearty reliance on Christ.

8. It hardens the heart.

The individual who has this kind of sorrow becomes harder in heart, in proportion to the number of times that he exercises such sorrow. If he has strong emotions of conviction, and his heart does not break up and flow out, the fountains of feeling are more and more dried up, and his heart more and more difficult to be reached. Take a real Christian, one who has truly repented, and everytime you bring the truth to bear upon him so as to break him down before God, he becomes more and more mellow, and more easily affected, and excited, and melted, and broken down under God's blessed word, so long as he lives—and to all eternity. His heart gets into the habit of going along with the convictions of his understanding, and he becomes as teachable and tractable as a little child.

Here is the grand distinction. Let churches, or individual members, who have only this worldly repentance, pass through a revival, and get waked up and bustle about, and then grow cold again. Let this be repeated and you find them more and more difficult to be roused, till by and by they become as hard as the nether mill-stone, and nothing can ever rally them to a revival again. Directly over against this are those churches and individuals who have true repentance. Let them go through successive revivals, and you find them growing more and more mellow and tender until they get to such a state, that if they hear the trumpet blow for a revival, they kindle and glow instantly and are ready for the work.

This distinction is as broad as between light and darkness. It is everywhere observable among the churches and church members. You see the principle illustrated in sinners, who after passing through repeated revivals, by and by will scoff and rail at all religion, and although the heavens hang with clouds of mercy over their heads, they heed it not but reject it. It is so in churches and members, if they have not true repentance, every fresh excitement hardens the heart and renders them more difficult to be reached by the truth.

9. It sears the conscience.

Such persons are liable at first to be thrown into distress, whenever the truth is flashed upon their mind. They may not have so much conviction as the real Christian. But the real Christian is filled with peace at the very time that his tears are flowing from conviction of sin. And each repeated season of conviction makes him more and more watchful, and tender, and careful, till his conscience becomes, like the apple of his eye, so tender that the very appearance of evil will offend it. But the other kind of sorrow, which does not lead to hearty renunciation of sin, leaves the heart harder than before, and by and by sears the conscience as with a hot iron. This sorrow worketh death.

10. It rejects Jesus Christ as the ground of hope.

Depending on reformation and sorrow, or anything else, it leads to no such reliance on Jesus Christ, that the love of Christ will *constrain* him to labor all his days for Christ.

11. It is transient and temporary.

This kind of repentance is sure to be repented of. By and by you will find such persons becoming ashamed of the deep feelings that they had. They do not want to speak of them, and if they talk of them it is always lightly and coldly. They perhaps bustled about in time of revival, and appeared as much engaged as anybody, and very likely were among the extremes in everything that was done. But now the revival is over, and you find them opposed to new measures, and changing back, and ashamed of their zeal. They in fact repent of their repentance.

Such persons, after they have joined the church, will be ashamed of having come to the anxious seat. When the height of the revival has gone by, they will begin to talk against being too enthusiastic, and the necessity of getting into a more sober and consistent way in religion. Here is the secret—they had a repentance of which they afterwards repented.

You sometimes find persons who profess to be converted in a revival, turning against the very measures, and means, and doctrines, by which they profess to have been converted. Not so with the true Christian. He is never ashamed of his repentance. The last thing he would ever think of being ashamed of, is the excitement of feeling he felt in a revival.

REMARKS

1. We learn from what has been said, one reason why there is so much spasmodic religion in the church.

They have mistaken conviction for conversion, the sorrow of the world for that godly sorrow that worketh repentance unto salvation, not to be repented of. I am convinced, after years of observation, that here is the true reason for the present deplorable state of the church all over the land.

2. We see why sinners under conviction feel as if it was a great cross to become Christians.

They think it a great trial to give up their ungodly companions, and to give up their sins. Whereas, if they had true repentance, they would not think it any cross to give up their sins. I recollect how I used to feel, when I first saw young persons becoming Christians and joining the church. I thought it was a good thing on the whole to have religion, because they would save their souls and get to heaven. But for the time, it seemed to be a very sorrowful thing. I never dreamed then, that these young people could be really happy now. I believe it is very common for persons, who know that religion is good on the whole, and good in the end, to think they cannot be happy in religion. This is all owing to a mistake respecting the true nature of repentance. They do not understand that true repentance leads to an abhorrence of those things that were formerly loved. Sinners do not see that when their young friends become true Christians, they feel an abhorrence for their balls and parties, and sinful amusements and follies, that the love for these things is crucified.

I once knew a young lady who was converted to God. Her father was a very proud worldly man. She used to be very fond of dress, and the dancing school, and balls. After she was converted, her father would force her to go to the dancing school. He used to go along with her, and force her to stand up and dance. She would go there and weep, and sometimes when she was standing up on the floor to dance, her feelings of abhorrence and sorrow would so come over her, that she would turn away and burst into tears. Here you see the cause of all that. She truly repented of these things, with a repentance not to be repented of. O, how many associations would such a scene recall to a Christian, what compassion for her former gay companions, what abhorrence of their giddy mirth, how she longed to be in the prayer-meeting, how could she be happy there? Such is the mistake which the impenitent, or those who have only worldly sorrow, fall into, in regard to the happiness of the real Christian.

3. Here you see what is the matter with those professing Christians who think it a cross to be very strict in religion.

Such persons are always apologizing for their sins, and pleading for certain practices, that are not consistent with strict religion. It shows that they love sin still, and will go as far as they dare in it. If they were true Christians, they would abhor it, and turn from it, and would feel it to be a cross to be dragged to it.

4. You see why some know nothing what it is to *enjoy* religion.

They are not cheerful and happy in religion. They are grieved because they have to break off from so many things they love, or because they have to give so much money. They are in the fire all the time. Instead of rejoicing in every opportunity of self-denial, and rejoicing in the plainest and most cutting exhibitions of truth, it is a great trial to them to be told their duty, when it crosses their inclinations and habits. The plain truth distresses them. Why? Because their hearts do not love to do duty. If they loved to do their duty, every ray of light that broke in upon their minds from heaven, pointing out their duty, would be welcomed, and make them more and more happy.

Whenever you see such persons, if they feel cramped and distressed because the truth presses them, if their hearts do not yield and go along with the truth, HYPOCRITE is the name of all such professors of religion. If you find that they are distressed like anxious sinners, and that the more you point out their sins the more they are distressed, be you sure, that they have never truly repented of their sins, nor given themselves up to be God's.

5. You see why many professed converts, who have had very deep exercises at the time of their conversion, afterwards apostatize.

They had deep convictions and great distress of mind, and afterwards they got relief and their joy was very great, and they were amazingly happy for a season. But by and by they decline, and then they apostatize. Some, who do not discriminate properly between true and false repentance, and who think there cannot be such *deep* exercises without divine power, call these cases of falling from grace. But the truth is, they went out from us because they were not of us. They never had that repentance that kills and annihilates the disposition to sin.

6. See why backsliders are so miserable.

Perhaps you will infer that I suppose all true Christians are perfect, from what I said about the disposition to sin being broken up and changed. But this does not follow. There is a radical difference between a backslidden Christian and a hypocrite who has gone back from his profession. The hypocrite loves the world, and *enjoys* sin when he returns to it. He may have some fears and some remorse, and some apprehension about the loss of character; but after all *he enjoys sin.* Not so with the backslidden Christian. He loses his first love, then he falls a prey to temptation, and so he goes into sin. But he does not love it; it is always bitter to him; he feels unhappy and away from home. He has indeed, at the time, no Spirit of God, no love of God in exercise to keep him from sin, but he does not love sin; he is unhappy in sin; he feels that he is a wretch. He is as different from the hypocrite as can be. Such an one, when he leaves the love of God, may be delivered over to Satan for a time, for the destruction of the flesh, that the Spirit may be saved; but he can never again *enjoy sin* as he used to, or delight himself as he once could in the pleasures of the world. Never again can he drink in iniquity like water. So long as he continues to wander, he is a wretch. If there is one such here tonight, you know it.

7. You see why convicted sinners are afraid to pledge themselves to give up their sins.

They tell you they dare not promise to do it, because they are afraid they shall not keep the promise. There you have the reason. *They love sin.* The drunkard knows that he loves rum, and though he may be constrained to keep his promise and abstain from it, yet his appetite still craves it. And so with the convicted sinner. He feels that he loves sin, that his hold on sin has never been broken off, and he dares not promise.

8. See why some professors of religion are so much opposed to pledges.

It is on the same principle. They love their sins so well, they know their hearts will plead for indulgence, and they are afraid to promise to give them up. Hence many who profess to think they are Christians, refuse to join the church. The secret reason is, they feel that their heart is still going after sin, and they dare not come under the obligations of the church-covenant. They do not want to be subject to the discipline of the church, in case they should sin. That man knows he is a hypocrite.

9. Those sinners who have worldly sorrow, can now see where the difficulty lies, and what is the reason they are not converted.

Their intellectual views of sin may be such, that if their hearts corresponded, they would be Christians. And perhaps they are thinking that this is true repentance. But if they were truly willing to give up sin, and all sin, they would not hesitate to pledge themselves to it, and to have all the world know that they had done it. If there are any such here, I ask you now to come forward, and take these seats. If you are willing to give up sin, you are willing to promise to do it, and willing to have it known that you have done it. But if you resist conviction, and when your understanding is enlightened to see what you ought to do, your heart still goeth forth after your sins, tremble, sinner, at the prospect before you. All your convictions will avail you nothing. They will only sink you deeper in hell for having resisted them.

If you are willing to give up your sins, you can signify it as I have named. But if you still love your sins, and want to retain them, you can keep your seats. And now, shall we go and tell God in prayer, that these sinners are unwilling to give up their sins, that though they are convinced they are wrong, they love their idols and after them they will go? The Lord have mercy on them, for they are in a fearful case.

LECTURE X.

DISHONESTY IN SMALL MATTERS INCONSISTENT WITH HONESTY IN ANYTHING.

"He that is unjust in the least is unjust also in much." Luke xvi. 10.

These words are a part of the parable of the unjust steward, or rather, a principle which our Lord lays down in connection with the parable. The words do not require that I should go into an explanation of the parable itself, as they make no part of the story which the Lord Jesus was relating. The *principle* involved or laid down, is what I have to do with to-night. In preaching from these words I design to illustrate the principle laid down which is this:

One who is dishonest in small matters, is not really honest in any thing.

The order which I shall pursue is the following:

I. I shall show what I do not mean by this principle.

II. Show what I do mean by it.

III. Prove the principle, that one who is dishonest in small matters is not really honest at all.

IV. Show by what principle those individuals are governed who, while they are dishonest in small things, appear to be honest, and even religious, in larger affairs.

V. Mention several instances where persons often manifest a want of principle in small matters.

I. I am to show what I do not mean by the principle, that one who is dishonest in small matters is not really honest in anything.

Answer. I do not mean that if a person is dishonest in small matters, and will take little advantages in dealing, it is therefore certain that in greater matters he will not deal openly and honorably according to the rules of business.

Or that it is certain, if a man will commit petty thefts and depredations, that he will commit highway robbery. There may be various reasons why a man who will commit such depredations will not go into more daring and outrageous crimes.

Or that if a man indulges unclean thoughts, it is certain he will commit adultery.

Or that if he indulges covetous desires, it is certain he will steal.

Or that if he indulges in ill-will towards anyone, he will commit murder.

Or that if he would enslave a fellow man, and deprive him of instruction and of all the rights of man, he will certainly commit other crimes of equal enormity.

Or that if he will defraud the government in little things, such as postage, or duties on little articles, he will rob the treasury.

II. I am to explain what I do mean by the principle laid down, that if a man is dishonest in little things, he is not really honest in any thing.

What I mean is, that if a man is dishonest in small matters, it shows that he is not governed *by principle* in anything. It is therefore certain that it is not real honesty of heart which leads him to act right in greater matters. He must have other motives than honesty of heart, if he appears to act honestly in larger things, while he acts dishonestly in small matters.

III. I am to prove the principle.

I am not going to take it for granted, although the Lord Jesus Christ expressly declares it. I design to mention several considerations in addition to the force of the text. I believe it is a general impression that a person may be honest in greater matters, and deserve the character of honesty, notwithstanding he is guilty of dishonesty in small matters.

1. If he was actuated by a supreme regard to the authority of God, and if this was the habitual state of his mind, such a state of mind would be quite as apt to manifest itself in smaller matters as in large. Nay, where the temptation is small, he would be more certain to act conscientiously than in greater matters, because there is less to induce him to act otherwise. What is honesty? If a man has no other motives for acting honestly than mere selfishness, the devil is as honest as he is; for I dare say he is honest with his fellow devils, as far as it is for his interest or *policy* to be so. Is that honesty? Certainly not. And, therefore, if a man does not act honestly from higher motives than this, he is not honest at all, and if he appears to be honest in certain important matters, he has other motives than a regard to the honor of God.

2. It is certain that, if an individual is dishonest in small matters, he is not actuated by love to God. If he was actuated by love to God, he would feel that dishonesty in small matters is just as inconsistent as in great. It is as real a violation of the law of God,

and one who truly loves God would no more act dishonestly in one than in the other.

3. It is certain that he is not actuated by real love to his neighbor, such as the law of God requires. If he loved his neighbor as himself, he would not defraud him in small things any more than in great. Nay, he might do it in great things, where the temptation to swerve from his integrity was powerful. But where the temptation is small, it cannot be that one who truly loves his neighbor would act dishonestly. See the case of Job. Job truly loved God, and you see how far he went, and what distress he endured, before he would say a word that even seemed disparaging or complaining of God. And when the temptation was overwhelming, and he could see no reason why he should be so afflicted, and his distress became intolerable, and his soul was all in darkness, and his wife set in and told him to curse God and die, he would not do it then, but said, "Thou speakest as one of the foolish women speaketh. What! shall we receive good at the hand of God, and shall we not receive evil?" Do you suppose Job would have swerved from his integrity in little things, or for small temptations? Never. He loved God. And if you find a man who truly loves his neighbor, you will not see him deceiving or defrauding his neighbor for trifling temptations.

IV. I am to examine some of the motives by which a person may be actuated, who is dishonest in little things, while he may appear to be honest in greater matters.

Our business here is to ascertain how this apparent discrepancy can consist with the declaration in the text. The Lord Jesus Christ has laid down the principle, that if a man is dishonest in small matters, he is not strictly honest at all. Now, here are facts, which to many appear to contradict this. We see many men that in small matters exhibit a great want of principle, and appear to be quite void of principle, while in larger things they appear to be honorable and even pious. This must be consistent, or Jesus Christ has affirmed a falsehood. That it is consistent with truth will be admitted, if we can show that their conduct in regard to larger matters can be accounted for on other principles than honesty of heart. If we can account for it on principles of mere selfishness, it will be admitted, that where a man is dishonest in small things, he is not really honest at all, however honestly he may act in regard to larger matters.

1. They may act honestly in larger matters for fear of disgrace.

They may know that certain small things are not likely to be mentioned in public, or to have a noise made about them, and so they may do such things, while the fear of disgrace deters them from doing the same things in regard to larger matters, because it will make a noise. What is this but one form of selfishness overbalancing another form? It is selfishness still, not honesty.

2. He may suppose it will injure his business, if he is guilty of dishonesty with men of business, and so he deals honestly in important matters, while in little things he is ready to take any advantage he can, that will not injure his business. Thus a man will take advantage of a seamstress, and pay her a few cents less than he knows it is really worth for making a garment, while the same individual, in buying a *bale* of goods, would not think of showing a disposition to cheat, because it would injure his business. In dealing with an abused and humble individual, he can gripe and screw out a few cents without fear of public disgrace, while he would not for any consideration do an act which would be publicly spoken of as disreputable and base.

3. Fear of human law may influence a man to act honestly in such things as are likely to be taken up, while in such small matters as the law is not likely to notice, he will defraud or take advantage.

4. The love of praise influences many to act honestly and honorably, and even piously, in matters that are likely to be noticed. Many a man will defraud a poor person out of a few cents in the price of labor, and then, in some great matter on public occasion, appear to act with great liberality. What is the reason, that individuals who habitually screw down their servants, seamstresses, and other poor people that they employ, to the lowest penny, and take all the advantage they can of such people, will then, if a severe winter comes, send out cart loads of fuel to the poor, or give hundreds of dollars to the committees? You see that it is for the love of praise, and not the love of God nor the love of man.

5. The fear of God. He may be afraid of the divine wrath, if he commits dishonest acts of importance, while he supposes God will overlook little things, and not notice it if he is dishonest in such small matters.

6. He may restrain his dishonest propensities from mere selfrighteousness, and act honestly in great things for the sake of bolstering up his own good opinion of himself, while in little things he will cheat and play the knave.

I said in the beginning, that I did not mean, that if a man would take advantages, he would certainly never act with apparent uprightness. It often comes to pass, that individuals who act with great meanness and dishonesty in small affairs, will act uprightly and honorably, on the ground that their character and interest are at stake. Many a man who among merchants is looked upon as an honorable dealer, is well known, by those who are more intimately acquainted with him, to be mean and knavish and overreaching in small matters, or in his dealings with more humble and more dependent individuals. It is plain that it is not real honesty of heart, which makes him act with apparent honesty in his more public transactions.

So I said, that if an individual will commit petty thefts, it is not certain he would commit highway robbery. He might have various reasons for abstaining, without having a particle too much honesty to rob on the highway, or to cut a purse out of your pocket in the crowd. The individual may not have courage enough to break out in highway robbery, or not skill enough, or nerve enough, or he may be afraid of the law, or afraid of disgrace, or other reasons.

An individual may indulge unclean thoughts, habitually, and yet never actually commit adultery. He may be restrained by fear, or want of opportunity, and not by principle. If he *indulges* unclean thoughts, he would certainly act uncleanly, if it were not for other reasons than purity of principle.

An individual may manifest a covetous spirit, and yet not steal. But he has the spirit that would lead him to steal, if not restrained by other reasons than honesty or principle.

A man may be angry, and yet his anger never break out in murder. But his hatred would lead him to do it, so far as principle is concerned. And if it is not done, it is for other reasons than true principle.

An individual may oppress his fellow man, enslave him, deprive him of instruction, and compel him to labor without compensation, for his own benefit, and yet not commit murder, or go to Africa to engage in the slave trade, because it would endanger his reputation or his life. But if he will do that which divests life of all that is desirable to gratify his own pride or promote his own interest, it cannot be principle, either of love to God or love to man, that keeps him from going any length, if his interest requires it. If a man, from regard to his own selfish interest, will take a course towards any human being which will deprive him of all that renders life desirable, it is easy to see that, so far as principle is concerned, there is nothing in the way of his doing it by violence on the coast of Africa, or taking life itself, when his interest requires it.

So an individual who will defraud the United States' treasury of eighteen cents in postage, has none too much principle to rob the treasury, if he had the same prospect of impunity. The same principle that allowed him to do the one, would allow him to do the other. And the same motive that led him to do the one, would lead him to do the other if he had an opportunity, and if it were not counteracted by some other motive equally selfish.

A man may, in like manner, be guilty of little misrepresentations, who would not dare to tell a downright LIE. Yet if he is guilty of coloring the truth, and misrepresenting facts, with a design to deceive, or to make facts appear otherwise than they really are, he is really lying, and the individual who will do this would manufacture ever so many lies, if it was for his interest, or were he not restrained by other reasons than a sacred regard to truth.

V. I will mention some instances, where persons are dishonest in small matters, while they appear to act honestly and even piously in regard to matters of greater importance.

1. We often find individuals manifesting a great want of principle in regard to the payment of small debts, while they are extremely careful and punctual in the payment of notes in the bank, and in all their commercial transactions.

For instance, there is a man takes a newspaper, the price is only a small sum, and the publisher cannot send a collector to every individual, so this man lets his subscription lie along perhaps for years, and perhaps never pays it. The same individual, if it had been a note at the bank, would have been punctual enough; and no pains would have been spared, rather than let the note run beyond the day. Why? Because, if he does not pay his note in the bank, it will be protested, and his credit will be injured, but the little debt of twenty shillings or five dollars will not be protested, and he knows it, and so he lets it go by, and the publisher has to be at the trouble and expense of sending for it, or go without his money. How manifest it is that this man does not pay his notes at the bank from honesty of principle, but purely from a regard to his own credit and interest.

2. I have before referred to the case of seamstresses. Suppose an individual employs women to sew for him, and for the sake of

underselling others in the same trade, he beats down these women below the just price of such work. It is manifest that the individual is not honest in any thing. If, for the sake of making more profits, or of underselling, he will beat down these women—suppose he is honorable and prompt in his public transactions—no thanks to him, it is not because he is honest in his heart, but because it is his interest to seem so.

3. Some manifest this want of principle by committing little petty thefts. If they live at a boarding house, where there are boarders, they will commit petty thefts, perhaps, for fuel in the cellar. An individual will not be at the expense of getting a little charcoal for himself, to kindle his fire in the morning, but gets along by pilfering from the stores laid in by others, a handful at a time. Now the individual that will do that, shows himself to be radically rotten at heart.

A case once came to my knowledge, of this kind. An individual was sitting in a room, where the gentleman had on the table for some purpose a tumbler of wine and a pitcher of water. The gentleman had occasion to go out of the room a moment, but accidentally left the door a-jar, and while he was out, looking back he saw this individual drink part of the wine in the tumbler, and then to conceal it, fill up the tumbler with water, and take his seat. Now, the individual who did that showed that he loved wine, and that he was none too good to steal, he showed that so far as principle was concerned, he would get drunk if he had the means, and steal if he had a chance; in fact, at heart, he was both a drunkard and a thief.

4. Individuals often manifest great dishonesty when they find articles that have been lost, especially articles of small value. One will find a penknife, perhaps, or a pencil case, and never make the least inquiry, even among those he has reason to believe were the losers. Now, the man that would find a penknife, and keep it without making inquiry, where there was any prospect of finding the owner, so far as principle is concerned, would keep a pocket-book full of bank notes, if he should find it and have an equal chance of concealment. And yet this same individual, if he should find a pocket book with five thousand dollars in it, would advertise it in the newspapers, and make a great noise, and profess to be wonderfully honest. But what is his motive? He knows that the five thousand dollars will be inquired after, and if he is discovered to have concealed it, he shall be ruined. Fine honesty, this!

5. Many individuals conceal little mistakes that are made in their favor, in reckoning, or in giving change. If an individual would keep still, say nothing, and let it pass, when such a mistake is made in his favor, it is manifest that nothing but a want of opportunity and impunity would prevent him from taking any advantage whatever, or overreaching to any extent.

6. *Frauds on the Post Office* are of the same class.

Who does not know that there is a great deal of dishonesty practiced here. Some seem to think there is no dishonesty in cheating the government out of a little postage. Postmasters will frank letters that they have no right to. Many will frank letters not only for their families but for their neighbors, all directly contrary to law, and a fraud upon the Post Office. The man that will do that is not honest. What would not such a man do, if he had the same prospect of impunity in other frauds, that he has in this?

7. *Smuggling* is a common form of petty dishonesty. How many a man will contrive to smuggle little articles in his trunk, when he comes home from England, that he knows ought to pay duty to the custom house, and he thinks but little of it, because the sum is so small, whereas, the smaller the sum, the more clearly the principle is developed. *Because* the temptation is so small, it shows how weak is the man's principle of honesty, that can be overcome by such a trifle. The man that would do this, if he had the same opportunity, would smuggle a cargo. If, for so little, he will lose sight of his integrity, and do a dishonest act, he is not too good to rob the treasury.

REMARKS.

1. The real state of a man's heart is often more manifested in smaller matters than in business of greater moment.

Men are often deceived here, and think their being honest in greater things will go to prove their honesty of heart, notwithstanding their knavishness in smaller things, and so they are sure to be on their guard in great things, while they are careless of little matters, and so act out their true character. They overlook the fact, that all their honesty in larger matters springs from a wrong principle, from a desire to *appear* honest, and not from a determination to *be* honest. They overlook their own petty frauds because they guard their more public manifestations of character, and then take it for granted that they are honest, while they are nothing but rottennes at heart. The man who will take advantage in little things, where he is not watched, is not actuated by principle. If you want to know your real character, watch your hearts, and see how your principles develop themselves in little things.

For instance, suppose you are an eye-servant. You are employed in the service of another, and you do not mind being idle at times, for a short time, in the absence of your employer. Or you slight your work when not under the eye of your employer, as you would if he was present. The man who will do this is totally dishonest, and not to be trusted in any thing, and very likely would take money from his employer's pocket book, if it were not for the fear of detection, or some other equally selfish motive. Such a person is not to be trusted at all, except in circumstances where it is his interest to be honest.

Mechanics that slight their work when it will not be seen or known by their employer, are rotten at heart, and not to be trusted at all, any farther than you can make it for their interest to be honest.

Persons who will knowingly misstate facts in conversation, would bear false witness in court under oath, if favored with opportunity and impunity. They never tell the truth at all because it is truth, or from the love of truth. Let no such man be trusted.

Those who are, are unchaste in conversation would be unchaste in conduct, if they had opportunity and impunity.—Spurn the man or woman who will be impure in speech, even among their own sex, they have no principle at all, and are not to be trusted *on the ground of their principles.* If persons are chaste from principle, they will no more indulge in unclean conversation than unclean actions. They will abhor even the garment spotted with the flesh.

2. The individual who will indulge in any one sin, does not abstain from any sin because it is sin.

If he hated sin, and was opposed to sin because it is sin, he would no more indulge in one sin than another. If a person goes to pick and choose among sins, avoiding some, and practicing others, it is certain that it is not because he regards the authority of God, or hates sin, that he abstains from any sin whatever.

3. Those individuals who will not abandon all intoxicating drinks for the purpose of promoting temperance, never gave up ardent spirits for the sake of promoting temperance.

It is manifest that they gave up ardent spirits from some other consideration than a regard to the temperance cause. If that had been their object, they would give up alcohol in all its forms, and when they find that there is alcohol in wine and beer and cider, they would give them up of course. Why not?

4. The man who, for the sake of gain, will sell rum, or intoxicating drinks, to his neighbor, and put a cup to his neighbor's mouth, and would thus consent to ruin him, soul and body, would consent to sell his neighbor into slavery to promote his own selfish interests, if he could do it with impunity. And if he did not rob and murder him for the sake of his money, it certainly would not be because the love of God or of man restrained him. If the love of self is so strong, that he will consent to do his neighbor the direct injury of selling him ardent spirits, nothing but selfishness under some other form, prevailing over the love of money, could prevent his selling men into slavery, robbing, or murdering them, to get their money. He might love his own reputation; he might fear the penalty of human law; he might fear the destruction of his own soul, so much as to restrain him from these acts of outrage and violence. But certainly it could not be the principle of love to God or man that would restrain him.

5. The individual who will enslave his fellow men for his own selfish objects, would enslave others, any or all, if his interest demanded, and if he had the same opportunity.

If a man will appropriate the rights of one, he would appropriate the rights of all men, if he could do it with impunity. The individual who will deprive a black man of his liberty, and enslave him, would make no scruple to enslave a white man, if circumstances were equally favorable. The man who contends that the black laborer of the south ought to be held in slavery, if he dared, would contend to have the white laborers of the north enslaved, and would urge the same kind of arguments, that the peace and order of society requires it, and laborers are so much better off when they have a master to take care of them. The famous Bible argument too, is as good in favor of white slaves as blacks, if you only had the *power* to carry it out. The man who *holds* his fellow man as property, would *take* his fellow man as property, if he could with impunity. The principle is the same in all. It is not principle that keeps men who holds slaves from kidnapping on the coast of Africa, or from making war to enslave the free laborers of the north.

6. The man that will not practice self-denial in little things to promote religion, would not endure persecution for the sake of promoting religion.

Those who will not deny their appetite would not endure the scourge and the stake. Perhaps, if persecution were to arise, some might endure it for the sake of the applause it would bring, or to show their spirit, and to face opposition. There is a natural spirit of obstinacy, which is often roused by opposition, that would go to the stake rather than yield a point. But it is easily seen, that it is not true love to the cause which prompts a man to endure opposition, if he will not endure self-denial in little things for the sake of the cause.

7. Little circumstances often discover the state of the heart.

The individual that we find delinquent in small matters, we of course infer would be much more so in larger affairs, if circumstances were equally favorable.

Where you find persons wearing little ornaments from vanity, set them down as rotten at heart. If they could, they would go all lengths in display, if they were not restrained by some other considerations than a regard to the authority of God and the honor of religion. You may see this every day in the streets. Men walking with their cloaks very carefully thrown over their shoulders so as to show the velvet, and women with their feathers tossing in the air—it is astonishing how many ways there are in which these little things show their pride and rottenness of heart.

You say these are little things. I know they are little things, and *because they are* little things, I mention them. It is because they are little things, that they show the character so clearly. If their pride was not deeply rooted, they would not show it in little things. If a man had it put in his power to live in a palace, with every thing corresponding, it would be no wonder if he should give way to the temptation. But when his vanity shows itself in little things, he gives full evidence that it has possession of his soul.

How important it is for you to see this, and to keep a watch over these little things, so as to see what you are, and to know your characters, as they appear in the sight of God.

How important to cultivate the strictest integrity, such as will carry itself out in small things as well as in large. There is something so beautiful, when you see an individual acting in little things with the same careful and conscientious uprightness as in matter of the greatest moment. Until professors of religion will cultivate this universal honesty, they will always be a reproach to religion.

Oh, how much would be gained, if professors of religion would evince that entire purity and honesty on all occasions and to all persons, and do what is just right, so as to commend religion to the ungodly. How often do sinners fix their eye on some petty delinquencies of professors of religion, and look with amazement at such things in persons who profess the fear of God. What an everlasting reproach to religion, that so many of its professors are guilty of these little, mean, paltry knaveries. The wicked have cause enough to see, that such professors cannot have any *principle* of honesty, and that such religion as they exhibit is good for nothing, and is not worth having.

Of what use is it for that woman to talk to her impenitent servant about religion, when her servant knows that she will not hesitate to overreach and screw down and cheat in petty things? Or for that merchant to talk to his clerks, who know that however honorable he may be in his greater and more public transactions, he is mean and knavish in little things? It is worse than useless.

LECTURE XI.

BOUND TO KNOW YOUR TRUE CHARACTER.

TEXT:—"Examine yourselves, whether ye be in the faith; prove your own selves"— 2 Corinthians xiii. 5.

In speaking from this text I design to pursue the following order:

I. Show what is intended by the requirement in the text.
II. The necessity of this requirement.
III. The practicability of the duty enjoined.
IV. Give some directions as to the manner of performing the duty.

I. I am to show what is intended by the requirement in the text, "Examine yourselves, whether ye be in the faith; prove your own selves."

It requires that we should understand our own hearts, that we should take the proper steps to make proof of our real characters, as they appear in the sight of God. It refers not to a trial or proof of our strength, or knowledge, but our moral character, that we should thoroughly test it, so as to understand it as it is. It implies that we should know how God regards us, and what He thinks of us, whether He considers us saints or sinners. It is nothing less than a positive command, that we should ascertain our own true character, and settle the question definitely for ourselves, whether we are saints or sinners, heirs of heaven or heirs of hell.

II. I am to show the necessity of this requirement.

1. It is indispensable to our own peace of mind, that we should prove and ascertain our true character, as it is in the sight of God.

The individual who is uncertain as to his real character, can have no such thing as settled peace of mind. He may have apathy, more or less complete and perfect, but apathy is very different from peace. And very few professors of religion, or persons who continue to hear the gospel, can have such apathy for any length of time, as to suppress all uneasy feelings, at being uncertain respecting their true character and destiny. I am not speaking of hypocrites, who have seared their consciences, or of scoffers who may be given up of

God. But in regard to others, it is strictly true that they must have this question settled in order to enjoy peace of mind.

2. It is essential to Christian Honesty.

A man who is not truly settled in his mind as to his own character is hardly honest in religion. If he makes a profession of religion when he does not honestly believe himself a saint, who does not know that that is not exactly honest? He is half a hypocrite, at heart. So when he prays, he is always in doubt whether his prayers are acceptable, as coming from a child of God.

3. A just knowledge of one's own character is indispensable to usefulness.

If a person has always to agitate this question in his mind, "Am I a Christian?"—if he has to be always anxiously looking at his own estate all the while, and doubtful how he stands, it must be a great hindrance to his usefulness. If when he speaks to sinners, he is uncertain whether he is not himself a sinner, he cannot exhort with that confidence and simplicity, that he could if he felt his own feet on a rock. It is a favorite idea with some people, that it is best for saints to be always in the dark, to keep them humble. Just as if it was calculated to make a child of God proud to know that *he is* a child of God. Whereas, one of the most weighty considerations in the universe to keep him from dishonoring God is, to know that he is a child of God. When a person is in an anxious state of mind, he can have but little faith, and his usefulness cannot be extensive till the question is settled.

III. The practicability of this requirement.

It is a favorite idea with some, that in this world the question never can be settled. It is amazing what a number of persons there are, that seem to make a virtue of their great doubts, which they always have, whether they are Christians. For hundreds of years it has been looked upon by many as a suspicious circumstance, if a professor of religion is not filled with doubts. It is considered as almost a certain sign, he knows nothing of his own heart. One of the universal questions put to candidates for admission has been, "Have you any doubts of your good estate?" And if the candidate answers, "O, yes, I have great doubts," that is all very well, and is taken as *evidence* that he is spiritual, and has a deep acquaintance with his own heart, and has a great deal of humility. But if he has no doubts, it is taken as evidence that he knows little of his own heart, and is most probably a hypocrite. Over against all this, I maintain that the duty enjoined in the text is a practicable duty, and that Christians can put themselves to such a proof, as to know their own selves, and have a satisfactory assurance of their real character.

1. This is evident from the command in the text, "Examine yourselves, whether ye be in the faith; prove your own selves." Will any one believe that God requires us to examine ourselves, and prove ourselves, and see what is our true character, when he knows it to be impossible for us ever *to learn* our true character?

2. We have the best possible medium of proof, to try ourselves, and prove our character, and that is our *consciousness.*

Consciousness gives the highest possible certainty as to the facts by which our characters are to be determined, and the great question is settled, What is our state before God? We may have, and ought to have, the same kind of evidence of our state before God as we have of our existence; and that is, consciousness. Nay, we cannot help *having* the evidence. Consciousness is continually testifying what are our states of mind, and it only needs for us to take notice of what consciousness testifies, and we can settle the question as certainly as we can our own existence.

3. God gives men such constant opportunities to act out what is in their hearts, that nothing but negligence can prevent their coming to a decision of the matter.

If men were shut up in dungeons, where they had no opportunity to act, and no chance of being influenced by circumstances, and no way to develop the state of their hearts, they would not be so much to blame for not knowing themselves. But God has placed them in the circumstances in which they are in this life on purpose, as He said to the children of Israel, to prove them, and to know what is in their hearts, and whether they will keep His commandments or no. The things around us must produce an impression on our minds, and lead us to feel and act in some way. And this affords opportunities of self-knowledge, when we see how we feel and how we are inclined to act in such diversified circumstances.

4. We are further qualified to trust our own true characters, by having a perfect rule to try them by.

The law of God is a true standard by which to try our characters. We know exactly what that is, and we have therefore an infallible and an invariable rule by which to judge of ourselves. We can bring all our feelings and actions to this rule, and compare them with this standard, and know exactly what is their true character in the sight of God, for God himself tries them by the same standard.

5. Our circumstances are such that nothing but dishonesty can possibly lead us to self-deception.

The individual who is self-deceived is not only careless and negligent, but decidedly dishonest, or he would not deceive himself. He must be to a great degree prejudiced by pride, and blinded by self-will, or he could not but know that he is not what he professes to be. The circumstances are so many and so various, that call forth the exercises of his mind, that it must be willful blindness that is deceived. If they never had any opportunities to act, or if circumstances did not call forth their feelings, they might be ignorant. A person who had never seen a beggar, might not be able to tell what were his true feelings towards beggars. But place him where he meets beggars every day, and he must be willfully blind or dishonest, if he does not know the temper of his heart towards a beggar.

IV. I will mention a few things as to the manner of performing this duty.

First. Negatively.

I. It is not done by waiting for evidence to come to us.

Many seem to wait, in a passive attitude, for the evidence to come to them, to decide whether they are Christians or not. They appear to be waiting for certain feelings to come to them. Perhaps they pray about it; perhaps they pray very earnestly, and then wait for the feelings to come which will afford them satisfactory evidence of their good estate. Many times they will not do anything in religion till they get this evidence, and they sit and wait, and wait, in vain expectation that the Spirit of God will come some time or other, and lift them out of this slough, while they remain thus passive and stupid. They may wait till doomsday and never get it in this way.

2. Not by any direct attempt to force the feelings into exercise which are to afford the evidence.

The human mind is so constituted, that it never will feel by trying to feel. You may try as hard as you please, to feel in a particular way. Your efforts to put forth feelings are totally unphilosophical and absurd. There is now nothing before the mind to produce emotion or feeling. Feeling is always awakened in the mind by the mind's being intensely fixed on some object calculated to awaken feeling. But when the mind is fixed, not upon the object, but on direct attempts to put forth feeling, this will not awaken feeling. It is impossible. The attention must be taken up with the object calculated to awaken feeling, or there will be no feeling. You may as well shut up your eyes and attempt to see, or go into a dark room. In a dark room there is no object to awaken the sense of sight, and you may EXERT yourself, and strain your eyes, and try to see, but you will see nothing. When the mind's attention is taken up with looking inward, and attempting to examine the nature of the present emotion, that emotion at once ceases to exist, because the attention is no longer fixed on the object that causes the emotion. I hold my hand before this lamp, it casts a shadow; but if I take the lamp away, there is no shadow; there must be light to produce a shadow. It is just so certain that if the mind is turned away from the object that awakens emotion, the emotion ceases to exist. The mind must be fixed on the object, not on the emotion, or there will be no emotion, and consequently no evidence.

3. You will never get evidence by spending time in mourning over the state of your heart.

Some people spend their time in nothing but complaining, "O, I don't feel, I can't feel, my heart is so hard." What are they doing? Nothing but mourning and crying because they don't feel. Perhaps they are trying to work themselves up into feeling! Just as philosophical as trying to fly. While they are mourning all the while, and thinking about their hard hearts, and doing nothing, they are the ridicule of the devil. Suppose a man should shut himself out from the fire and then go about complaining how cold he is, the very children would laugh at him. He must expect to freeze, if he will shut himself out from the means of warmth. And all his mourning and feeling bad will not help the matter.

Second. Positively. What must be done in this duty?

If you wish to test the true state of your heart with regard to any object, you must fix your attention on that object. If you wish to test the power or accuracy of sight, you must apply the faculty to the object, and then you will test the power and state of that faculty. You place yourself in the midst of objects, to test the state of your eyes, or in the midst of sounds, if you wish to test the perfectness of your ears. And the more you shut out other objects that excite the other senses, and the more strongly you fasten your minds on this one, the more perfectly you test the keenness of your vision, or the perfectness of your hearing. A multiplicity of objects is liable to distract the mind. When we attend to any object calculated to awaken feeling, it is impossible not to feel. The mind is so constituted that it cannot but feel. It is not necessary to stop and ask, "Do I feel?" Suppose you put your hand near the fire, do you need to stop and ask the question, "Do I really feel the sensation of warmth?" You know, of course, that you do feel. If you pass your hand rapidly by the lamp, the sensation may be so slight as not to be noticed, but is none the less real, and if you paid attention strictly enough, you would know it. Where the impression is slight, it requires an effort of attention to notice your own consciousness. So the passing feeling of the mind may be so slight as not to occupy your thoughts, and thus may escape your notice, but it is not the less real. But hold your hand in the lamp a minute, and the feeling will force itself upon your notice, whatever be your other occupations. If the mind is fixed on an object calculated to excite emotions of any kind, it is impossible not to feel those emotions in a degree; and if the mind is *intently* fixed, it is impossible not to feel the emotions in such a degree as to be conscious that they exist. These principles will show you how we are to come at the proof of our characters, and know the real state of our feelings towards any object. It is by fixing our attention on the object till our emotions are so excited that we become conscious what they are.

I will specify another thing that ought to be borne in mind. *Be sure the things on which your mind is fixed*, and on which you wish to test the state of your heart *are realities*.

There is a great deal of imaginary religion in the world, which the people who are the subjects of it mistake for real. They have high feelings, their minds are much excited, and the feeling corresponds with the object contemplated. But here is the source of the delusion—*the object is imaginary.* It is not that the feeling is false or imaginary. It is real feeling. It is not that the feeling does not correspond with the object before the mind. It corresponds perfectly. But the object is a fiction. The individual has formed a notion of God, or of Jesus Christ, or of salvation, that is altogether aside from the truth, and his feelings in view of these imaginations are such as they would be towards the true objects, if he had true religion, and so he is deluded. Here is undoubtedly a great source of the false hopes and professions in the world.

V. I will now specify a few things on which it is your duty to try the state of your minds.

1. *Sin*—not your own particular sins, but sin itself, as an outrage committed against God.

You need not suppose you will get at the true state of your hearts, merely by finding in your mind a strong feeling of disapprobation of sin. This belongs to the nature of an intelligent being, as such. All intelligent beings feel a disapprobation of sin, when viewed abstractly, and without reference to their own selfish gratification. The devil, no doubt, feels it. The devil no more feels approbation for sin, when viewed abstractly, than Gabriel. He blames sinners, and condemns their conduct, and whenever he has no selfish reason for being pleased at what they do, he abhors it. You will often find in the wicked on earth a strong abhorrence of sin. There is not a wicked man on earth, that would not condemn and abhor sin, in the abstract. The mind is so constituted, that sin is universally and naturally and necessarily abhorrent to right reason and to conscience. Every power of the mind revolts at sin. Man has pleasure in them that commit iniquity, only when he has some selfish reason for wishing them to commit it. No rational being approves of sin, as sin.

But there is a striking difference between the constitutional disapprobation of sin, as an abstract thing, and that hearty detestation and opposition that is founded on love to God. To illustrate this idea. It is one thing for that youth to feel that a certain act is wrong, and quite another thing to view it as an injury to his father. Here is something in addition to his former feeling. He has not only indignation against the act as wrong, but his love to his father produces a feeling of *grief* that is peculiar. So the individual who loves God feels not only a strong disapprobation of sin, as wrong, but a feeling of grief mingled with indignation when he views it as committed against God.

If, then, you want to know how you feel towards sin, how do you feel when you move round among sinners, and see them break God's law? When you hear them swear profanely, or see them break the Sabbath, or get drunk, how do you feel? Do you feel as the Psalmist did when he wrote, "I beheld the transgressors, and was *grieved*, because they kept not thy word?" So he says, "Rivers of waters run down mine eyes, because they keep not thy law." And again, "*Horror* hath taken hold upon me, because of the wicked that forsake thy law."

2. You ought to test the state of your hearts towards your own sins.

Look back on your past sins, call up your conduct in former times, and see whether you do cordially condemn it and loathe it, and feel as an affectionate child would feel, when he remembers how he has disobeyed or dishonored a beloved parent. It is one thing to feel a strong conviction that your former conduct was wicked. It is quite another thing to have this feeling attended with strong emotions of *grief,* because it was sin against God. Probably there are few Christians who have not looked back upon their former conduct towards their parents with deep emotion, and thought how a beloved father and an affectionate mother have been disobeyed and wronged; and who have not felt, in addition to a strong disapprobation of their conduct, a deep emotion of *grief,* that inclined to vent itself in weeping, and perhaps did gush forth in irrepressible tears. Now this is true repentance towards a parent. And repentance towards God is the same thing, and if genuine, it will correspond in degree to the intensity of attention with which the mind is fixed on the subject.

3. You want to test your feelings towards impenitent sinners.

Then go among them, and converse with them, on the subject of their souls, warn them, see what they say, and how they feel, and get at the real state of their hearts, and then you will know how you feel towards the impenitent. Do not shut yourself up in your closet and try to imagine an impenitent sinner. You may bring up a picture of the imagination that will affect your sympathies, and make you weep and pray. But go and bring your heart in contact with the living reality of a sinner, reason with him, exhort him, find out his cavils, his obstinacy, his insincerity, pray with him if you can. You cannot do this without waking up emotions in your mind, and if you are a Christian, it will wake up such mingled emotions of grief, compassion and indignation, as Jesus Christ feels, and as will leave you no room to doubt what is the state of your heart on this subject. Bring your mind in contact with sinners, and fix it there, and rely on it you will feel.

4. You want to prove the state of your mind towards God.

Fix your thoughts intently on God. And do not set yourselves down to imagine a God after your own foolish hearts, but take the Bible and learn there what is the true idea of God. Do not fancy a shape or appearance, or imagine how He looks, but fix your mind on the Bible description of how He feels and what He does, and what He says, and you cannot but feel. Here you will detect the real state of your heart. Nay, this *will constitute the real state of your heart,* which you cannot mistake.

5. Test your feelings toward Christ.

You are bound to know whether you love the Lord Jesus Christ or not. Run over the circumstances of His life, and see whether they appear as realities to your mind, His miracles, His sufferings, His lovely character, His death, His resurrection, His ascension, His intercession now at the right hand of the throne of God. Do you believe all these? Are they realities to your mind? What are your feelings in view of them? When you think of His willingness to save, His ability to save, His atoning death, His power, if these things are realities to you, you will have feelings, of which you will be conscious, and concerning which there will be no mistake.

6. What are your feelings towards the saints?

If you wish to test your heart on this point, whether you love the saints, do not let your thoughts run to the ends of the earth, but fix your mind on the saints by you, and see whether you love them, whether you desire their sanctification, whether you really long to have them grow in grace, whether you can bear them in your heart to the throne of grace in faith, and ask God to bestow blessings on them.

7. So in regard to revivals.

You wish to know what is the state of your feelings toward revivals, then read about them, think about them, fix your mind on them, and you cannot but have feelings that will evince the state of your heart. The same is true of the heathen, of the slaves, of drunkards, of the Bible, of any object of pious regard. The only way to know the state of your heart is to fix your mind on the reality of those things, till you feel so intensely that there is no mistaking the nature of your feelings.

Should you find a difficulty in attending to any of these objects sufficiently to produce feeling, it is owing to one of two reasons, either your mind is taken up with some other parts of religion, so as not to allow of such fixed attention to the specified object, or your thoughts wander with the fool's eyes, to the ends of the earth. The former is sometimes the case, and I have known some Christians to be very much distressed because they did not feel so intensely as they think they ought on some subjects. Their own sins, for instance. A person's mind may be so much taken up with anxiety and labor and prayer for sinners, that it requires an effort to think enough about his own soul to feel deeply, and when he goes on his knees to pray about his own sins, that sinner with whom he has been talking comes right up before his mind, and he can hardly pray for himself. It is not to be regarded as evidence against you, if the reason why you do not feel on one subject in religion is because your feelings are so engrossed about another, of equal importance. But if your thoughts run all over the world, and that is the reason you do not feel deeply enough to know what is your true character, if your mind will not come down to the Bible, and fix on *any* object of religious feeling, lay a strong hand on yourself, and fix your thoughts with a death-grasp, till you do feel. You can command your thoughts: God has put the control of your mind in your own hands. And in this way, you can control your own feelings, by turning your attention upon the object you wish to feel about. Bring yourself, then, powerfully and resolutely, to that point, and give it not over till you fasten your mind to the subject, and till the deep fountains of feeling break up in your mind, and you know what is the state of your heart, and understand your real character in the sight of God.

REMARKS.

1. Activity in religion is indispensable to self-examination.

An individual can never know what is the true state of his heart, unless he is active in the duties of religion. Shut up in his closet, he never can tell how he feels towards objects that are without, and he never can feel right towards them until he goes out and acts. How can he know his real feelings towards sinners, if he never brings his mind in contact with sinners? He goes into his closet, and his imagination may make him feel, but it is a deceitful feeling, because not produced by a reality. If you wish to test the reality of your feelings towards sinners, go out and warn sinners, and then the reality of your feelings will manifest itself.

2. Unless persons try their hearts by the reality of things, they are constantly subject to delusion, and are all the time managing to delude themselves.

Suppose an individual shut up in a cloister, shut out from the world of reality, and living in a world of imagination. He becomes a perfect creature of imagination. So it is in religion, with those who do not bring their mind in contact with realities. Such persons think they love mankind, and yet do them no good. They imagine they abhor sin, and yet do nothing to destroy it. How many persons deceive themselves, by an excitement of the imagination about *missions*, for instance; how common it is for persons to get up a great deal of feeling, and hold prayer meetings for missions, who really do nothing to save souls. Women will spend a whole day at a prayer meeting to pray for the conversion of the world, while their impenitent servant in the kitchen is not spoken to all day, and perhaps not in a month, to save her soul. People will get up a public meeting, and talk about feeling for the heathen, when they are making no direct efforts for sinners around them. This is all a fiction of the imagination. There is no reality in such a religion as that. If they had real love of God, and love of souls, and real piety, the pictures drawn by the imagination about the distant heathen would not create so much more feeling than the reality around them.

It will not do to say, it is because their attention is not turned towards sinners around them. They hear the profane oaths, and see the Sabbath breaking and other vices, as a naked reality before their eyes, everyday. And if these produce no feeling, it is in vain to pretend that they feel as God requires for sinners in heathen lands, or anywhere. Nay, take this very individual, now so full of feeling for the heathen, as he imagines, and place him *among the heathen*, transport him to the Friendly Islands, or elsewhere, away from the fictions of imagination, and in the midst of the cold and naked reality of heathenism, and all his deep feeling is gone. He may write letters home about the abominations of the heathen, and all that, but his feeling about their salvation is gone. You hear people talk so about the heathen, who have never converted a soul at home, rely upon it that is all imagination. If they do not promote revivals at home, where they understand the language, and where they have direct access to their neighbors, much less can they be depended on to promote the real work of religion on heathen ground. The churches ought to understand this, and keep it in mind in selecting men to go on foreign missions. They ought to know that if the naked reality at home does not excite a person to action, the devil would only laugh at a million such missionaries.

The same delusion often manifests itself in regard to *revivals*. There is an individual who is a great friend to revivals. But mark; they are always the revivals of former days, or of revivals in the abstract, or distant revivals, or revivals that are yet to come. But as to any present revival, he is always aloof and doubtful. He can read about the revivals in President Edward's day, or in Scotland, or Wales, and be greatly excited and delighted. He can pray, "O Lord, revive thy work, O Lord, let us have such revivals, let us have a pentecost season, when thousands shall be converted in a day." But get him into the reality of things, and he never happens to see a revival in which he can take any interest, or feel real complacency. He is friendly to the fictitious imaginings of his own mind, he can create a state of things that will excite his feelings, but no naked reality ever brings him out to cooperate in actually promoting a revival.

In the days of our Savior, the people said, and no doubt really believed, that they abhorred the doings of those who persecuted the prophets. They said, "If we had been in the days of our fathers, we would not have been partakers with them of the blood of the prophets." No doubt they wondered that people could be so wicked as to do such things. But they had never seen a prophet, they were moved simply by their imagination. And as soon the Lord Jesus Christ appeared, the greatest of prophets, on whom all the prophecies centered, they rejected Him, and finally put Him to death with as much cold-hearted cruelty as ever their fathers had killed a prophet. "Fill ye up," says our Savior, "the measure of your fathers, that upon you may come all the righteous blood shed upon the earth."

Mankind have always, in every age of the world, fallen in love with fictions of their own imagination, over which they have stumbled into hell. Look at the Universalist. He imagines a God that will save everybody, at any rate, and a heaven that will accommodate everybody; and then he loves the God he has made and the heaven he has imagined, and perhaps will even weep with love. His feelings are often deep, but they are all delusive, because excited by fiction and not by truth.

3. The more an individual goes out from himself, and makes things not belonging to himself the subject of thought, the more piety he will have, and the more evidence of his piety.

Religion consists in love, in feeling right and doing right, or doing good. If therefore you wish to have great piety, don't think of having it by cultivating it in a way which never caused piety to grow; that is, by retiring into a cloister and withdrawing from contact with mankind.—If the Lord Jesus Christ had supposed such circumstances to be favorable to piety, He would have directed them so. But He knew better. He has therefore appointed circumstances as they are, so that His people may have a thousand objects of benevolence, a thousand opportunities to do good. And if they go out of themselves and turn their hearts upon these things, they cannot fail to grow in piety, and to have their evidences increasing and satisfactory.

4. It is only in one department of self-examination that we can consistently shut ourselves up in the closet to perform the duty. That is when we want to look back and calmly examine the motives of our past conduct. In such cases it is often necessary to abstract our thoughts and keep out other things from our minds, to turn our minds back and look at things we have done and the motives by which we were actuated. To do this effectually it is often necessary to resort to retirement, and fasting, and prayer. Sometimes it is impossible to wake up a lively recollection of what we wish to examine, without calling in the laws of association to our aid. We attempt to call up past scenes, and all seems to be confusion and darkness, until we strike upon some associated idea, that gradually brings the whole fresh before us. Suppose I am to be called as a witness in court concerning a transaction, I can sometimes regain a lively recollection of what took place, only by going to the place, and then all the circumstances come up, as if but of yesterday. So we may find in regard to the re-examination of some part of our past history, that no shutting ourselves up will bring it back, no protracted meditation, or fasting, or prayer, till we throw ourselves into some circumstances that will wake up the associated ideas, and thus bring back the feelings we formerly had.

Suppose a minister wishes to look back and see how he felt, and the spirit with which he had preached years ago. He wishes to know how much real piety there was in his labors. He might get at a great deal in his closet on his knees, by the aid of the strong influences of the Spirit of God. But he will come at it much more effectually by going to the place, and preaching there again. The exact attitude in which his mind was before, may thus recur to him and stand in strong reality before his mind.

5. In examining yourselves, be careful to avoid expecting to find all the graces of the Christian in exercise in your mind at once.

This is contrary to the nature of mind. You ought to satisfy yourselves, if you find the exercises of your mind are right, *on the subject that is before* your mind. If you have *wrong* feelings at the time, that is another thing. But if you find that the emotions at the time are right, do not draw a wrong inference, because some other right emotion is not in present exercise. The mind is so constituted, that it can only have one train of emotions at a time.

6. From this subject you see why people often do not feel more than they do.

They are taking a course not calculated to produce feeling. They feel, but not on the right subjects. Mankind always feel on some subjects, and the reason why they do not feel deeply on religious subjects is, because their attention is not deeply fixed on these subjects.

7. You see the reason why there is such a strange diversity in the exercises of real Christians.

There are some Christians whose feelings, when they have any feeling, are always of the happy kind. There are others whose feelings are always of a sad and distressing kind. They are in almost constant agony for sinners. The reason is, that their thoughts are directed to different objects. One class are always thinking of the class of objects calculated to make them happy; the other are thinking of the state of the church, or the state of sinners, and weighed down as with a burden, as if they had a mountain on their shoulders. Both may be religious, both classes of feelings are right, in view of the objects at which they look. The apostle Paul had continual heaviness and sorrow of heart on account of his brethren. No doubt he felt right. The case of his brethren, who had rejected the Savior, was so much the object of his thoughts, the dreadful wrath that they had brought upon themselves, the doom that hung over them, was constantly before his mind, and how could he be otherwise than sad?

8. Observe the influence of these two classes of feelings in the usefulness of individuals.

Show me a very joyful and happy Christian, and he is not generally a *very* useful Christian. Generally, such are so taken up with enjoying the sweets of religion, that they *do* but little. You find a class of ministers, who preach a great deal on these subjects, and make their pious hearers very happy in religion, but such ministers are seldom instrumental in converting many sinners, however much they may have refreshed and edified and gratified saints. On the other hand you will find men who are habitually filled with deep agony of soul in view of the state of sinners, and these men will be largely instrumental in converting men. The reason is plain. Both preached the truth, both preached the gospel, in different proportions, and the feelings awakened correspond with the views they preached. The difference is, that one comforted the saints, the other converted sinners.

You may see a class of professors of religion who are always happy, and they are lovely companions, but they are very seldom engaged in pulling sinners out of the fire. You find others always full of agony for sinners, looking at their state, and longing to have souls converted. Instead of enjoying the antepast of heaven on earth, they are sympathizing with the Son of God when He was on earth, groaning in His spirit, and spending all night in prayer.

9. The real *revival* spirit is a spirit of agonizing desires and prayer for sinners.

10. You see how you may account for your own feelings at different times.

People often wonder why they feel as they do. The answer is plain. You feel so, because you think so. You direct your attention to those objects which are calculated to produce those feelings.

11. You see why some people's feelings are so changeable.

There are many whose feelings are always variable and unsteady. That is because their thoughts are unsteady. If they would fix their thoughts, they would regulate their feelings.

12. You see the way to beget any desired state of feeling in your own mind, and how to beget any desired state of feeling in others.

Place the thoughts on the subject that is calculated to produce those feelings, and confine them there, and the feelings will not fail to follow.

13. There are multitudes of pious persons who dishonor religion by their doubts.

They are perpetually talking about their doubts, and they take up a hasty conviction that they have no religion. Whereas, if instead of dwelling on their doubts they will fix their minds on other objects, on Christ for instance, or go out and seek sinners, and try to bring them to repentance, rely upon it, they will feel, and feel right, and feel so as to dissipate their doubts.

Remember, you are not to wait till you feel right before you do this. Perhaps some things that I said to this church have not been rightly understood. I said you could do nothing for God unless you felt right. Do not therefore infer, that you are to sit still and do nothing till you are satisfied that you do feel right. But place yourself in circumstances to make you feel right, and go to work. On one hand, to bustle about without any feeling is no way, and on the other hand, to shut yourself up in your closet and wait for feeling to come, is no way. Be sure to be always active. You never will feel right otherwise. And then keep your mind constantly under the influence of those objects that are calculated to create and keep alive Christian feelings.

1837

LECTURE I.

TRUE AND FALSE CONVERSION.

TEXT:—"Behold, all ye that kindle a fire, that compass yourselves about with sparks; walk in the light of your fire, and in the sparks that ye have kindled. This shall ye have of my hand; ye shall lie down in sorrow."—Isaiah l. 11.

It is evident, from the connection of these words in the chapter, that the prophet was addressing those who professed to be religious, and who flattered themselves that they were in a state of salvation, but in fact their hope was a fire of their own kindling, and sparks created by themselves. Before I proceed to discuss the subject, let me say, that as I have given notice that it was my intention to discuss the nature of true and false conversion, it will be of no use but to those who will be honest in applying it to themselves. If you mean to profit by the discourse, you must resolve to make a faithful application of it to yourselves—just as honest as if you thought you were now going to the solemn judgment. If you will do this, I may hope to be able to lead you to discover your true state, and if you are now deceived, direct you in the true path to salvation. If you will not do this, I shall preach in vain, and you will hear in vain.

I design to show the difference between true and false conversion, and shall take up the subject in the following order:

I. Show that the natural state of man is a state of pure selfishness.

II. Show that the character of the converted is that of benevolence.

III. That the New Birth consists in a change from selfishness to benevolence.

IV. Point out some things wherein saints and sinners, or true and spurious converts, may agree, and some things in which they differ. And,

V. Answer some objections that may be offered against the view I have taken, and conclude with some remarks.

I. I am to show that the natural state of man, or that in which all men are found before conversion, is pure, unmingled selfishness.

By which I mean, that they have no gospel benevolence. Selfishness is regarding one's own happiness supremely, and seeking one's own good because it is his own. He who is selfish places his own happiness above other interests of greater value; such as the glory of God and the good of the universe. That mankind, before conversion, are in this state, is evident from many considerations.

Every man knows that all other men are selfish. All the dealings of mankind are conducted on this principle. If any man overlooks this, and undertakes to deal with mankind as if they were not selfish, but were disinterested, he will be thought deranged.

II. In a converted state, the character is that of benevolence.

An individual who is converted is benevolent, and not supremely selfish. Benevolence is loving the happiness of others, or rather, choosing the happiness of others. Benevolence is a compound word, that properly signifies good willing, or choosing the happiness of others. This is God's state of mind. We are told that God is love; that is, He is benevolent. Benevolence comprises His whole character. All His moral attributes are only so many modifications of benevolence. An individual who is converted is in this respect like God. I do not mean to be understood, that no one is converted, unless he is purely and perfectly benevolent, as God is; but that the balance of his mind, his prevailing choice is benevolent. He sincerely seeks the good of others, for its own sake. And, by disinterested benevolence I do not mean, that a person who is disinterested feels no interest in his object of pursuit, but that he seeks the happiness of others for its own sake, and not for the sake of its reaction on himself, in promoting his own happiness. He chooses to do good because he rejoices in the happiness of others, and desires their happiness for its own sake. God is purely and disinterestedly benevolent. He does not make His creatures happy for the sake of thereby promoting His own happiness, but because He loves their happiness and chooses it for its own sake. Not that He does not feel happy in promoting the happiness of His creatures, but that He does not do it *for the sake* of His own gratification. The man who is disinterested feels happy in doing good. Otherwise doing good itself would not be virtue in him. In other words, if he did not love to do good, and enjoy doing good, it would not be virtue in him.

Benevolence is holiness. It is what the law of God requires: "Thou shalt love the Lord thy God, with all thy heart and soul and strength, and thy neighbor as thyself." Just as certainly as the converted man yields obedience to the law of God, and just as certainly as he is like God, he is benevolent. It is the leading feature of his character, that he is seeking the happiness of others, and not his own happiness, as his supreme end.

III. That true conversion is a change from a state of supreme selfishness to benevolence.

It is a change in the end of pursuit, and not a mere change in the means of attaining the end. It is not true that the converted and the unconverted differ only in the means they use, while both are aiming at the same end. It is not true that Gabriel and Satan are pursuing the same end, and both alike aiming at their own happiness, only pursuing a different way. Gabriel does not obey God for the sake of promoting his own happiness. A man may change his means, and yet have the same end, his own happiness. He may do good for the sake of the temporal benefit. He may not believe in religion, or in any eternity, and yet may see that doing good will be for his advantage in this world. Suppose, then, that his eyes are opened, and he sees the reality of eternity; and then he may take up religion as a means of happiness in eternity. Now, everyone can see that there is no virtue in this. It is the design that gives character to the act, not the means employed to effect the design. The true and the false convert differ in this. The true convert chooses, as the end of his pursuit, the glory of God and the good of His kingdom. This end he chooses for its own sake, because he views this as the greatest good, as a greater good than his own individual happiness. Not that he is indifferent to his own happiness, but he prefers God's glory, because it is a greater good. He looks on the happiness of every individual according to its real importance, as far as he is capable of valuing it, and he chooses the greatest good as his supreme object.

IV. Now I am to show some things in which true saints and deceived persons may agree, and some things in which they differ.

1. They may agree in leading a strictly moral life.

The difference is in their motives. The true saint leads a moral life from love to holiness; the deceived person from selfish considerations. He uses morality as a means to an end, to effect his own happiness. The true saint loves it as an end.

2. They may be equally prayerful, so far as the form of praying is concerned.

The difference is in their motives. The true saint loves to pray; the other prays because he hopes to derive some benefit to himself from praying. The true saint expects a benefit from praying, but that is not his leading motive. The other prays from no other motive.

3. They may be equally zealous in religion.

One may have great zeal, because his zeal is according to knowledge, and he sincerely desires and loves to promote religion, for its own sake. The other may show equal zeal, for the sake of having his own salvation more assured, and because he is afraid of going to hell if he does not work for the Lord, or to quiet his conscience, and not because he loves religion for its own sake.

4. They may be equally conscientious in the discharge of duty; the true convert because he loves to do duty, and the other because he dare not neglect it.

5. Both may pay equal regard to what is right; the true convert because he loves what is right, and the other because he knows he cannot be saved unless he does right. He is honest in his common business transactions, because it is the only way to secure his own interest. Verily, they have their reward. They get the reputation of being honest among men, but if they have no higher motive, they will have no reward from God.

6. They may agree in their desires, in many respects. They may agree in their desires to serve God; the true convert because he loves the service of God, and the deceived person for the reward, as the hired servant serves his master.

They may agree in their desires to be useful; the true convert desiring usefulness for its own sake, the deceived person because he knows that is the way to obtain the favor of God. And then in proportion as he is awakened to the importance of having God's favor, will be the intensity of his desires to be useful.

In desires for the conversion of souls; the true saint because it will glorify God; the deceived person to gain the favor of God. He will be actuated in this, just as he is in giving money. Who ever doubted that a person might give his money to the Bible Society, or the Missionary Society, from selfish motives alone, to procure happiness, or applause, or obtain the favor of God? He may just as well desire the conversion of souls, and labor to promote it, from motives purely selfish.

To glorify God; the true saint because he loves to see God glorified, and the deceived person because he knows that is the way to be saved. The true convert has his heart set on the glory of God, as his great end, and he desires to glorify God as an end, for its own sake. The other desires it as a means to *his* great end, the benefit of himself.

To repent. The true convert abhors sin on account of its hateful nature, because it dishonors God, and therefore he desires to repent of it. The other desires to repent, because he knows that unless he does repent he will be damned.

To believe in Jesus Christ. The true saint desires it to glorify God, and because he loves the truth for its own sake. The other desires to believe, that he may have a stronger hope of going to heaven.

To obey God. The true saint that he may increase in holiness; the false professor because he desires the rewards of obedience.

7. They may agree not only in their desires, but in their resolutions. They may both resolve to give up sin, and to obey God, and to lay themselves out in promoting religion, and building up the kingdom of Christ; and they may both resolve it with great strength of purpose, but with different motives.

8. They may also agree in their designs. They may both really design to glorify God, and to convert men, and to extend the kingdom of Christ, and to have the world converted; the true saint from love to God and holiness, and the other for the sake of securing his own happiness. One chooses it as an end, the other as a means to promote a selfish end.

They may both design to be truly holy; the true saint because he loves holiness, and the deceived person because he knows that he can be happy in no other way.

9. They may agree not only in their desires, and resolutions, and designs, but also in their affection towards many objects.

They may both love the Bible; the true saint because it is God's truth, and he delights in it, and feasts his soul on it; the other because he thinks it is in his own favor, and is the charter of his own hopes.

They may both love God; the one because he sees God's character to be supremely lovely and excellent in itself, and he loves it for its own sake; the other because he thinks God is his particular friend, that is going to make him happy for ever, and he connects the idea of God with his own interest.

They may both love Christ. The true convert loves His character; the deceived person thinks He will save *him* from hell, and give him eternal life, and why should he not love Him?

They may both love Christians: the true convert because he sees in them the image of Christ, and the deceived person because they belong to his own denomination, or because they are on his side, and he feels the same interest and the same hopes with them.

10. They may also agree in hating the same things. They may both hate infidelity, and oppose it strenuously—the true saint because it is opposed to God and holiness, and the deceived person because it injures an interest in which he is deeply concerned, and if true, destroys all his own hopes for eternity. So they may hate error; one because it is detestable in itself, and contrary to God—and the other because it is contrary to his views and opinions.

I recollect seeing in writing, some time ago, an attack on a minister for publishing certain opinions, "because," said the writer, "these sentiments would destroy all *my hopes* for eternity." A very good reason indeed! As good as a selfish being needs for opposing an opinion.

They may both hate sin; the true convert because it is odious to God, and the deceived person because it is injurious to himself. Cases have occurred, where an individual has hated his own sins, and yet not forsaken them. How often the drunkard, as he looks back at what he once was, and contrasts his present degradation with what he might have been, abhors his drink; not for its own sake, but because it has ruined him. And he still loves his cups, and continues to drink, though when he looks at their effects, he feels indignation.

They may be both opposed to sinners. The opposition of true saints is a benevolent opposition, viewing and abhorring their character and conduct, as calculated to subvert the kingdom of God. The other is opposed to sinners because they are opposed to the religion he has espoused, and because they are not on his side.

11. So they may both rejoice in the same things. Both may rejoice in the prosperity of Zion, and the conversion of souls; the true convert because he has his heart set on it, and loves it for its own sake, as the greatest good, and the deceived person because that particular thing in which he thinks he has such a great interest is advancing.

12. Both may mourn and feel distressed at the low state of religion in the church: the true convert because God is dishonored, and the deceived person because his own soul is not happy, or because religion is not in favor.

Both may love the society of the saints; the true convert because his soul enjoys their spiritual conversation, the other because he hopes to derive some advantage from their company. The first enjoys it because out of the abundance of the heart the mouth speaketh; the other because he loves to talk about the great interest he feels in religion, and the hope he has of going to heaven.

13. Both may love to attend religious meetings; the true saint because his heart delights in acts of worship, in prayer and praise, in hearing the word of God and in communion with God and His saints, and the other because he thinks a religious meeting a good place to prop up his hope. He may have a hundred reasons for loving them, and yet not at all for their own sake, or because he loves, in itself, the worship and the service of God.

14. Both may find pleasure in the duties of the closet. The true saint loves his closet, because he draws near to God, and finds delight in communion with God, where there are no embarrassments to keep him from going right to God and conversing. The deceived person finds a kind of satisfaction in it, because it is his duty to pray in secret, and he feels a self-righteous satisfaction in doing it. Nay, he may feel a certain pleasure in it, from a kind of excitement of the mind which he mistakes for communion with God.

15. They may both love the doctrines of grace; the true saint because they are so glorious to God, the other because he thinks them a guarantee of his own salvation.

16. They may both love the precept of God's law; the true saint because it is so excellent, so holy, and just, and good; the other because he thinks it will make him happy if he loves it, and he does it as a means of happiness.

Both may consent to the penalty of the law. The true saint consents to it in his own case, because he feels it to be just in itself for God to send him to hell. The deceived person because he thinks *he* is in no danger from it. He feels a respect for it, because he knows that it is right, and his conscience approves it, but he has never consented to it in his own case.

17. They may be equally liberal in giving to benevolent societies. None of you doubt that two men may give equal sums to a benevolent object, but from totally different motives. One gives to do good, and would be just as willing to give as now, if he knew that no other living person would give. The other gives for the

credit of it, or to quiet his conscience, or because he hopes to purchase the favor of God.

18. They may be equally self-denying in many things. Self-denial is not confined to true saints. Look at the sacrifices and self-denials of the Mohammedans, going on their pilgrimage to Mecca. Look at the heathen, throwing themselves under the car of Juggernaut. Look at the poor ignorant papists, going up and down over the sharp stones on their bare knees, till they stream with blood. A Protestant congregation will not contend that there is any religion in that. But is there not self-denial? The true saint denies himself, for the sake of doing more good to others. He is more set on this than on his own indulgence or his own interest. The deceived person may go equal lengths, but from purely selfish motives.

19. They may both be willing to suffer martyrdom. Read the lives of the martyrs, and you will have no doubt that some were willing to suffer, from a wrong idea of the rewards of martyrdom, and would rush upon their own destruction because they were persuaded it was the sure road to eternal life.

In all these cases, the motives of one class are directly over against the other. The difference lies in the choice of different *ends*. One chooses his own interest, the other chooses God's interest, as his chief end. For a person to pretend that both these classes are aiming at the same end, is to say that an impenitent sinner is just as benevolent as a real Christian; or that a Christian is not benevolent like God, but is only seeking his own happiness, and seeking it in religion rather than in the world.

And here is the proper place to answer an inquiry, which is often made: "If these two classes of persons may be alike in so many particulars, how are we to know our own real character, or to tell to which class we belong? We know that the heart is deceitful above all things, and desperately wicked, and how are we to know whether we love God and holiness for their own sake, or whether we are seeking the favor of God, and aiming at heaven for our own benefit?" I answer:

1. If we are truly benevolent, it will appear in our daily transactions. This character, if real, will show itself in our business, if anywhere. If selfishness rules our conduct there, as sure as God reigns we are truly selfish. If in our dealings with men we are selfish, we are so in our dealings with God. "For whoso loveth not his brother, whom he hath seen, how can he love God, whom he hath not seen?" Religion is not merely love to God, but love to man

also. And if our daily transactions show us to be selfish, we are unconverted; or else benevolence is not essential to religion, and a man can be religious without loving his neighbor as himself.

2. If you are disinterested in religion, religious duties will not be a task to you. You will not go about religion as the laboring man goes to his toil, for the sake of a living. The laboring man takes pleasure in his labor, but it is not for its own sake. He would not do it if he could help it. In its own nature it is a task, and if he takes any pleasure in it, it is for its anticipated results, the support and comfort of his family, or the increase of his property.

Precisely such is the state of some persons in regard to religion. They go to it as the sick man takes his medicine, because they desire its effects, and they know they must have it or perish. It is a task that they never would do for its own sake. Suppose men love labor, as a child loves play. They would do it all day long, and never be tired of doing it, without any other inducement than the pleasure they enjoy in doing it. So it is in religion, where it is loved for its own sake, there is no weariness in it.

3. If selfishness is the prevailing character of your religion, it will take sometimes one form and sometimes another. For instance: If it is a time of general coldness in the church, real converts will still enjoy their own secret communion with God, although there may not be so much doing to attract notice in public. But the deceived person will then invariably be found driving after the world. Now, let the true saints rise up, and make a noise, and speak their joys aloud, so that religion begins to be talked of again; and perhaps the deceived professor will soon begin to bustle about, and appear to be even more zealous than the true saint. He is impelled by his convictions, and not affections. When there is no public interest, he feels no conviction; but when the church awakes, he is convicted, and compelled to stir about, to keep his conscience quiet. It is only selfishness in another form.

4. If you are selfish, your enjoyment in religion will depend mainly on the strength of your hopes of heaven, and not on the exercise of your affections. Your enjoyments are not in the employments of religion themselves, but of a vastly different kind from those of the true saint. They are mostly from anticipating. When your evidences are renewed, and you feel very certain of going to heaven, then you enjoy religion a good deal. It depends on your hope, and not on your love for the *things* for which you hope. You hear persons tell of their having no enjoyment in religion when

they lose their hopes. The reason is plain. If they loved religion for its own sake, their enjoyment would not depend on their hope. A person who loves his employment is happy anywhere. And if you loved the employments of religion, you would be happy, if God should put you in hell, provided He would only let you employ yourself in religion. If you might pray and praise God, you would feel that you could be happy anywhere in the universe; for you would still be doing the things in which your happiness mainly consists. If the duties of religion are not the things in which you feel enjoyment, and if all your enjoyment depends on your hope, you have no true religion; it is all selfishness.

I do not say that true saints do not enjoy their hope. But that is not the great thing with them. They *think* very little about their own hopes. Their thoughts are employed about something else. The deceived person, on the contrary, is sensible that he does not enjoy the duties of religion; but only that the more he does, the more confident he is of heaven. He takes only such kind of enjoyment in it, as a man does who thinks that by great labor he shall have great wealth.

5. If you are selfish in religion, your enjoyments will be chiefly from anticipation. The true saint already enjoys the peace of God, and has heaven begun in his soul. He has not merely the prospect of it, but eternal life actually begun in him. He has that faith which is the very substance of things hoped for. Nay, he has the very feelings of heaven in him. He anticipates joys higher in degree, but the same in kind. He knows that he has heaven begun in him, and is not obliged to wait till he dies to taste the joys of eternal life. His enjoyment is in proportion to his holiness, and not in proportion to his hope.

6. Another difference by which it may be known whether you are selfish in religion, is this—that the deceived person has only a *purpose* of obedience, and the other has a *preference* of obedience. This is an important distinction, and I fear few persons make it. Multitudes have a purpose of obedience, who have no true preference of obedience. Preference is actual choice, or obedience of heart. You often hear individuals speak of their having had a purpose to do this or that act of obedience, but failed to do it. And they will tell you how difficult it is to execute their purpose. The true saint, on the other hand, really prefers, and in his heart chooses obedience, and therefore he finds it easy to obey. The one has a purpose to obey, like that which Paul had before he was converted,

as he tells us in the seventh chapter of Romans. He had a strong purpose of obedience, but did not obey, because his heart was not in it. The true convert prefers obedience for its own sake; he actually chooses it, and does it. The other purposes to be holy, because he knows that is the only way to be happy. The true saint chooses holiness for its own sake, and he is holy.

7. The true convert and the deceived person also differ in their faith. The true saint has a confidence in the general character of God, that leads him to unqualified submission to God. A great deal is said about the kinds of faith, but without much meaning. True confidence in the Lord's special promises, depends on confidence in God's general character. There are only two principles on which any government, human or divine, is obeyed, fear and confidence. No matter whether it is the government of a family, or a ship, or a nation, or a universe. All obedience springs from one of these two principles. In the one case, individuals obey from hope of reward and fear of the penalty. In the other, from that confidence in the character of the government, which works by love. One child obeys his parent from confidence in his parent. He has faith which works by love. The other yields an outward obedience from hope and fear. The true convert has this faith, or confidence in God, that leads him to obey God because he loves God. This is the obedience of faith. He has that confidence in God, that he submits himself wholly into the hands of God.

The other has only a partial faith, and only a partial submission. The devil has a partial faith. He believes and trembles. A person may believe that Christ came to save sinners, and on that ground may submit to Him, to be saved; while he does not submit wholly to Him, to be governed and disposed of. His submission is only on condition that he shall be saved. It is never with that unreserved confidence in God's whole character, that leads him to say, "Let thy will be done." He only submits to be saved. His religion is the religion of law. The other is gospel religion. One is selfish, the other benevolent. Here lies the true difference between the two classes. The religion of one is outward and hypocritical. The other is that of the heart, holy, and acceptable to God.

8. I will only mention one difference more. If your religion is selfish, you will rejoice particularly in the conversion of sinners, where your own agency is concerned in it, but will have very little satisfaction in it, where it is through the agency of others. The selfish person rejoices when he is active and successful in converting

sinners, because he thinks he shall have a great reward. But instead of delighting in it when done by others, he will be even envious. The true saint sincerely delights to have others useful, and rejoices when sinners are converted by the instrumentality of others as much as if it was his own. There are some who will take interest in a revival, only so far as themselves are connected with it, while it would seem they had rather sinners should remain unconverted, than that they should be saved by the instrumentality of an evangelist, or a minister of another denomination. The true spirit of a child of God is to say, "Send, Lord, by whom thou wilt send—only let souls be saved, and thy name glorified!"

V. I am to answer some objections which are made against this view of the subject.

Objection 1. "Am I not to have any regard to my own happiness?"

Answer. It is right to regard your own happiness according to its relative value. Put it in this scale, by the side of the glory of God and the good of the universe, and then decide, and give it the value which belongs to it. This is precisely what God does. And this is what He means, when He commands you to love your neighbor as yourself.

And again: You will in fact promote your own happiness, precisely in proportion as you leave it out of view. Your happiness will be in proportion to your disinterestedness. True happiness consists mainly in the gratification of virtuous desires. There may be pleasure in gratifying desires that are selfish, but it is not real happiness. But to be virtuous, your desires must be disinterested. Suppose a man meets a beggar in the street; there he sits on the curbstone, cold and hungry, without friends, and ready to perish. The man's feelings are touched, and he steps into a grocery near by, and buys him a loaf of bread. At once the countenance of the beggar lights up, and he looks unutterable gratitude. Now it is plain to see, that the gratification of the man in the act is precisely in proportion to the singleness of his motive. If he did it purely and solely out of benevolence, his gratification is complete in the act itself. But if he did it partly to have it known that he is a charitable and humane person, then his happiness is not complete until the deed is published to others. Suppose here is a sinner in his sins; he is very wicked and very wretched. Your compassion is moved, and you convert and save him. If your motive was to obtain honor among men and to secure the favor of God, you are not completely happy until the deed is told, and perhaps put in the newspaper. But if you wished purely to save a soul from death, then as soon as you see that done, your gratification is complete, and your joy is unmingled. So it is in all religious duties; your happiness is precisely in proportion as you are disinterested.

If you aim at doing good for its own sake, then you will be happy in proportion as you do good. But if you aim directly at your own happiness, and if you do good simply as a means of securing your own happiness, you will fail. You will be like the child pursuing his own shadow; he can never overtake it, because it always keeps just so far before him. Suppose in the case I have mentioned, you have no desire to relieve the beggar, but regard simply the applause of a certain individual. Then you will feel no pleasure at all in the relief of the beggar; but when that individual hears of it and commends it, then you are gratified. But you are not gratified in the thing itself. Or suppose you aim at the conversion of sinners; but if it is not love to sinners that leads you to do it, how can the conversion of sinners make you happy? It has no tendency to gratify the desire that prompted the effort. The truth is, God has so constituted the mind of man, that it must seek the happiness of others as its end, or it cannot be happy. Here is the true reason why all the world, seeking their own happiness and not the happiness of others, fail of their end. It is always just so far before them. If they would leave off seeking their own happiness, and lay themselves out to do good, they would be happy.

Objection 2. "Did not Christ regard the joy set before Him? And did not Moses also have respect unto the recompense of reward? And does not the Bible say we love God because He first loved us?"

Answer 1. It is true that Christ despised the shame and endured the cross, and had regard to the joy set before Him. But what was the joy set before Him? Not His own salvation, not His own happiness, but the great good He would do in the salvation of the world. He was perfectly happy in himself. But the happiness of others was what He aimed at. This was the joy set before Him. And that He obtained.

Answer 2. So Moses had respect to the recompense of reward. But was that his own comfort? Far from it. The recompense of reward was the salvation of the people of Israel. What did he say? When God proposed to destroy the nation, and make of *him* a great nation, had Moses been selfish he would have said, "That is right, Lord; be it unto thy servant according to thy word." But what does he say? Why, his heart was so set on the salvation of his people, and the glory of God, that he would not think of it for a moment, but said, "If thou wilt, forgive their sin; and if not, blot me, I pray thee, out of thy book, which thou hast written." And in another case, when God said He would destroy them, and make of Moses a greater and a mightier nation, Moses thought of God's glory, and said, "Then the Egyptians shall hear of it, and all the nations will say, Because the Lord was not able to bring this people into the land." He could not bear to think of having his own interest exalted at the expense of God's glory. It was really a greater reward, to his benevolent mind, to have God glorified, and the children of Israel saved, than any personal advantage whatever to himself could be.

Answer 3. Where it is said, "We love him because he first loved us" the language plainly bears two interpretations; either that His love to us has provided the way for our return and the influence that brought us to love Him, or that we love Him for His favor shown to ourselves.—That the latter is not the meaning is evident, because Jesus Christ has so expressly reprobated the principle, in His sermon on the mount: "If ye love them which love you, what thank have ye? Do not the publicans the same?" If we love God, not for His character but for His favors to us, Jesus Christ has written us reprobate.

Objection 3. "Does not the Bible offer happiness as the reward of virtue?"

Answer. The Bible speaks of happiness as the result of virtue, but nowhere declares virtue to consist in the pursuit of one's own happiness. The Bible is everywhere inconsistent with this, and represents virtue to consist in doing good to others. We can see by the philosophy of the mind, that it must be so. If a person desires the good of others, he will be happy in proportion as he gratifies that desire. Happiness is the result of virtue, but virtue does not consist in the direct pursuit of one's own happiness, but is wholly inconsistent with it.

Objection 4. "God aims at our happiness, and shall we be more benevolent than God? Should we not be like God? May we not aim at the same thing that God aims at? Should we not be seeking the same end that God seeks?"

Answer. This objection is specious, but futile and rotten. God is benevolent to others. He aims at the happiness of others, and at our happiness. And to be like Him, we must aim at, that is, delight in

His happiness and glory, and the honor and glory of the universe, according to their real value.

Objection 5. "Why does the Bible appeal continually to the hopes and fears of men, if a regard to our own happiness is not a proper motive to action?"

Answer 1. The Bible appeals to the constitutional susceptibilities of men, not to their selfishness. Man dreads harm, and it is not wrong to avoid it. We may have a due regard to our own happiness, according to its value.

Answer 2. And again; mankind are so besotted with sin, that God cannot get their attention to consider His true character, and the reasons for loving Him, unless He appeals to their hopes and fears. But when they are awakened, then He presents the gospel to them. When a minister has preached the terrors of the Lord till he has got his hearers alarmed and aroused, so that they will give attention, he has gone far enough in that line; and then he ought to spread out all the character of God before them, to engage their hearts to love Him for His own excellence.

Objection 6. "Do not the inspired writers say, Repent, and believe the gospel, and you shall be saved?"

Answer. Yes; but they require *true* repentance; that is, to forsake sin because it is hateful in itself. It is not true repentance, to forsake sin on condition of pardon, or to say, "I will be sorry for my sins, if you will forgive me." So they require true faith, and true submission; not conditional faith, or partial submission. This is what the Bible insists on. It says he shall be saved, but it must be disinterested repentance, and disinterested submission.

Objection 7. "Does not the gospel hold out pardon as a motive to submission."

Answer. This depends on the sense in which you must the term *motive*. If you mean that God spreads out before men His whole character, and the whole truth of the case, as reasons to engage the sinner's love and repentance, I say, Yes; His compassion, and willingness to pardon, are reasons for loving God, because they are a part of His glorious excellence, which we are bound to love. But if you mean by *motive* a condition, and that the sinner is to repent on condition he shall be pardoned, then I say, that the Bible no where holds out any such view of the matter. It never authorizes a sinner to say, "I will repent *if* you will forgive," and nowhere offers pardon as a motive to repentance, in such a sense as this.

With two short remarks I will close:

1. We see, from this subject, why it is that professors of religion have such different views of the nature of the gospel.

Some view it as a mere matter of accommodation to mankind, by which God is rendered less strict than He was under the law; so that they may be fashionable or worldly, and the gospel will come in and make up the deficiencies and save them. The other class view the gospel as a provision of divine benevolence, having for its main design to destroy sin and promote holiness; and that therefore so far from making it proper for them to be less holy than they ought to be under the law, its whole value consists in its power to make them holy.

II. We see why some people are so much more anxious to convert sinners, than to see the church sanctified and God glorified by the good works of His people.

Many feel a natural sympathy for sinners, and wish to have them saved from hell; and if that is gained, they have no farther concern. But true saints are most affected by sin as dishonoring God. And they are more distressed to see Christians sin, because it dishonors God more. Some people seem to care but little how the church live, if they can only see the work of conversion go forward. They are not anxious to have God honored. It shows that they are not actuated by the love of holiness, but by mere compassion for sinners.

In my next lecture, I propose to show to how persons whose religion is selfish may become truly religious.

LECTURE II.

TRUE SUBMISSION.

TEXT:—"Submit yourselves therefore to God."—James iv. 7.

The subject of this lecture is, "What Constitutes True Submission?"

Before I enter on the discussion of this subject, I wish to make two remarks, introductory to the main question.

1. The first remark is this: If any of you are deceived in regard to your hopes, and have built on a false foundation, the fundamental error in your case was your embracing what you thought was the gospel plan of salvation from selfish motives. Your selfish hearts were unbroken. This is the source of your delusion, if you are deceived. If your selfishness was subdued, you are not deceived in your hope. If it was not, all your religion is vain, and your hope is vain.

2. The other remark I wish to make is, that if any of you are deceived, and have a false hope, you are in the utmost danger of reviving your old hope, whenever you are awakened to consider your condition. It is a very common thing for such professors, after a season of anxiety and self-examination, to settle down again on the old foundation. The reason is, their habits of mind have become fixed in that channel, and therefore, by the laws of the mind it is difficult to break into a new course. It is indispensable, therefore, if you ever mean to get right, that you should see clearly that you have hitherto been wholly wrong, so that you need not multiply any more the kind of efforts that have deceived you heretofore.

Who does not know that there is a great deal of this kind of deception? How often will a great part of the church lie cold and dead, till a revival commences? Then you will see them bustling about, and they get engaged, as they call it, in religion, and renew their efforts and multiply their prayers for a season; and this is what they call getting revived. But it is only the same kind of religion that they had before. Such religion lasts no longer than the public excitement. As soon as the body of the church begin to diminish their efforts for the conversion of sinners, these individuals relapse into their former worldliness, and get as near to what they were before their supposed conversion, as their pride and their fear of the censures of the church will let them. When a revival comes again, they renew the same round; and so they live along by spasms, over and over again, revived and backslidden, revived and backslidden, alternately, as long as they live. The truth is, they were deluded at first, by a spurious conversion, in which selfishness never was broken down; and the more they multiply such kind of efforts, the more sure they are to be lost.

I will now enter upon the direct discussion of the subject, and endeavor to show you what true gospel submission is, in the following order, viz.:

I. I shall show what is not true submission.

II. Show what true submission is.

I. I am to show what true submission *is not*.

1. True submission to God is not indifference. No two things can be more unlike than indifference and true submission.

2. It does not consist in being willing to be sinful for the glory of God. Some have supposed that true submission included the idea of being willing to be sinful for the glory of God. But this is a mistake. To be willing to be sinful is itself a sinful state of mind. And to be willing to do anything for the glory of God, is to choose not to be sinful. The idea of being sinful for the glory of God is absurd.

3. It does not consist in a willingness to be punished?

If we were now in hell, true submission would require that we should be willing to be punished. Because then it would be certain that it was God's will we should be punished. So, if we were in a world where no provision was made for the redemption of sinners, and where our punishment was therefore inevitable, it would be our duty to be willing to be punished. If a man has committed murder, and there is no other way to secure the public interest but for him to be hung, it is his duty to be willing to be hung for the public good. But if there was any other way in which the murderer could make the public interest whole, it would not be his duty to be willing to be hung. So if we were in a world solely under law, where there was no plan of salvation, and no measure to secure the stability of government in the forgiveness of sinners, it would be the duty of every man to be willing to be punished. But as it is in this world, genuine submission does not imply a willingness to be punished. Because we know it is not the will of God that all shall be punished, but on the other hand, we know it is His will that all who truly repent and submit to God shall be saved.

II. I am to show what genuine submission *is*.

1. It consists in perfect acquiescence in all the providential dealings and dispensations of God; whether relating to ourselves, or to others, or to the universe. Some persons suppose they do acquiesce in the abstract, in the providential government of God. But yet, if you converse with them you see they will find fault with God's arrangements in many things. They wonder why God suffered Adam to sin? Or why He suffered sin to enter the universe at all? Or why He did this or that? Or why He made this or that thus or so? In all these cases, supposing we could assign no reason at all that would be satisfactory, true submission implies a perfect acquiescence in what ever he has suffered or done; and feeling that, so far as his providence is concerned, it is all right.

2. True submission implies acquiescence in the precept of God's moral law. The general precept of God's moral law is, "Thou shalt love the Lord thy God, with all thy heart, and with all thy mind, and with all thy soul, and with all thy strength, and thou shalt love thy neighbor as thyself." Perhaps some will say, "I do acquiesce in this precept, I feel that it is right, and I have no objection to this law." Here I want you to make the distinction carefully between a constitutional approbation of God's law, and actual submission to it. There is no mind but what naturally, and by its own common sense of what is right, approves of this law. There is not a devil in hell that does not approve of it. God has so constituted mind, that it is impossible to be a moral agent, and not approve His law. But this is not the acquiescence I am speaking of. A person may feel this approbation to so great a degree as to be even delighted without having true submission to it. There are two ideas included in genuine submission, to which I wish your particular attention.

(1.) The first idea is, that true acquiescence in God's moral law includes actual obedience. It is vain for a child to pretend a real acquiescence in his father's commands, unless he actually obeys them. It is in vain for a citizen to pretend an acquiescence in the laws of the land, unless he obeys the laws.

(2.) The main idea of submission is the yielding up of that which constitutes the great point in controversy. And that is this; that men have taken off their supreme affection from God and His kingdom, and set up self-interest as the paramount object of regard. Instead of laying themselves out in doing good, as God requires, they have adopted the maxim that "Charity begins at home." This is the very point in debate, between God and the sinner. The sinner aims at promoting his own interest, as his supreme object. Now, the first ideal implied in submission is the yielding up of this point. We must cease placing our own interest as supreme, and let the interests of God and His kingdom rise in our affections just as much above our own interests as their real value is greater. The man who does not do this is a rebel against God.

Suppose a civil ruler were to set himself to promote the general happiness of his nation; and should enact laws wisely adapted to this end, and should embark all his own resources in this object; and that he should then require every subject to do the same. Then suppose an individual should go and set up his own private interest in opposition to the general interest. He is a rebel against the government, and against all the interest which the government is set to promote. Then the first idea of submission, on the part of the rebel, is *giving up that point*, and falling in with the ruler and the obedient subjects in promoting the public good. Now, the law of God absolutely requires that you should make your own happiness subordinate to the glory of God and the good of the universe. And until you do this, you are the enemy of God and the universe, and a child of hell.

And the gospel requires the same as the law. It is astonishing, that many, within a few years, have maintained that it is right for a man to aim directly at his own salvation, and make his own happiness the great object of pursuit. But it is plain that God's law is different from this, and requires everyone to prize God's interest supremely. And the gospel requires the same with the law. Otherwise, Jesus Christ is the minister of sin, and came into the world to take up arms against God's government.

It is easy to show, from the Bible, that the gospel requires disinterested benevolence, or love to God and love to man, the same as the law. The first passage I shall quote is this, "Seek first the kingdom of God and his righteousness." What does that mean? Strange as it may seem, a writer has lately quoted this very text to prove that it is right to seek first our own salvation or our own happiness and to make that the leading object of pursuit. But that is not the meaning. It requires everyone to make the promotion of the kingdom of God his great object. I suppose it to enjoin the duty of aiming at being *holy*, and not at our *own happiness*. Happiness is connected with holiness, but it is not the *same thing*, and to such holiness or obedience to God, and to honor and glorify Him, is a very different thing from seeking supremely our own interests.

Another passage is, "Whether ye eat or drink, or whatsoever ye do, do all to the glory of God." Indeed! What? may we not eat and drink to please ourselves? No. We may not even gratify our natural appetite for food, but as subordinate to the glory of God. This is what the gospel requires, for the apostle wrote this to the Christian church.

Another passage is, "Look not on your own things, but every man on the things of another." But it is vain to attempt to quote all the passages that teach this. You may find, on almost every page of the Bible, some passage that means the same thing, requiring us not to seek our own good, but the benefit of others.

Our Savior says, "Whosoever will save his life shall lose it: and whosoever will lose his life shall save it." That is, If a man aims at his own interest, he shall lose his own interest; if he aims at saving his own soul, as his supreme object, he will lose his own soul; he must go out of himself, and make the good of others his supreme object, or he will be lost.

And again he says, "There is no man that hath left house, or brethren, or sisters, or father, or mother, or wife, or children, or lands, for my sake, and the gospel's, but he shall receive a hundred-fold now in this time, houses, and brethren, and sisters, and mothers, and children, and lands, with persecutions; and in the world to come, eternal life." Here some people may stumble, and say, There is a reward held out as a motive. But, mark! What are you to do? Forsake self for the sake of a reward to self? No; but to forsake self for the sake of Christ and His gospel; and the *consequence* will be as stated. Here is the important distinction.

In the 13th chapter of Corinthians Paul gives a full description of this disinterested love, or charity, without which a person is nothing in religion. It is remarkable how much he says a person may do, and yet be nothing. "Though I speak with the tongues of men and of angels, and have not charity, I am become as sounding brass, or a tinkling cymbal. And though, I have the gift of prophecy, and understand all mysteries, and all knowledge; and though I have all faith, so that I could remove mountains, and have not charity, I am nothing. And though I bestow all my goods to feed the poor, and though I give my body to be burned, and have not charity, it profiteth me nothing." But true gospel benevolence is of this character. "Charity suffereth long, and is kind; charity envieth not; charity vaunteth not itself, is not puffed up, doth not behave itself unseemly, seeketh not her own, is not easily provoked, thinketh no evil; rejoiceth not in iniquity, but rejoiceth in the truth; beareth all things, believeth all things, hopeth all things, endureth all things." She seeketh not her own. Mark that; it has no selfish end, but seeks the happiness of others as its great end. Without this kind of benevolence, we know there is not a particle of religion. You see, I might stand here all night quoting and explaining passages to the same point; showing that all pure religion consists in disinterested benevolence.

Before I go farther, I wish to mention several objections to this view, which may arise in your minds. I do this more particularly, because some of you may stumble right here, and after all get the idea that it is *right* to have our religion consist in aiming at our own salvation as our great object.

Objection l. "Why are the threatenings of the word of God given, if it is selfishness to be influenced by a fear of the wrath to come?"

Many answers may be given to this objection.

Answer 1. Man is so constituted that by the laws of his being he dreads pain. The scripture threatenings therefore answer many purposes. One is, to arrest the attention of the selfish mind, and lead it to examine the reasons there are for loving and obeying God. When the Holy Spirit thus gets the attention, then he rouses the sinner's conscience, and engages that to consider and decide on the reasonableness and duty of submitting to God.

Objection 2. "Since God has given us these susceptibilities to pleasure and pain, is it wrong to be influence by them?"

Answer. It is neither right nor wrong. These susceptibilities have no moral character. If I had time tonight, I might make all plain to you. In morals, there is a class of actions that come under the denomination of prudential considerations. For instance: Suppose you stand on a precipice, where, if you throw yourself down, you will infallibly break your neck. You are warned against it. Now, if you do not regard the warning, but throw yourself down, and destroy your life, that will be sin. But regarding it is no virtue. It is simply a prudential act. There is no virtue in avoiding danger, although it may often be sinful not to avoid it. It is sinful for men to brave the wrath of God. But to be afraid of hell is not holy, no more than the fear of breaking your neck down a precipice is holy. It is simply a dictate of the constitution.

Objection 3. "Does not the Bible make it our immediate duty to seek our own happiness?"

Answer. It is not sinful to seek our own happiness, according to its real value. On the contrary, it is a real duty to do so. And he that neglects to do this, commits sin. Another answer is, that although it is right to seek our own happiness, and the constitutional laws of the mind require us to regard our own happiness, still our constitution does not indicate that to pursue our own happiness as the chief good, is right. Suppose any one should argue, that because our constitution requires food, therefore it is right to seek food as the supreme good—would that be sound? Certainly not; for the Bible expressly forbids any such thing, and says—"Whether ye eat or drink, do all to the glory of God."

Objection 4. "Each one's happiness is put particularly in his own power; and if everyone should seek his own happiness, the happiness of the whole will be secured, to the greatest amount that is possible."

This objection is specious, but not sound. I deny the conclusion altogether. For,

(1.) The laws of the mind are such, that it is impossible for anyone to be happy while he makes his own happiness the supreme object. Happiness consists in the gratification of virtuous desires. But to be gratified, the thing must be obtained *that is desired.* To be happy, therefore, the desires that are gratified must be right, and therefore they must be disinterested desires. If your desires terminate on yourself; for instance—if you desire the conversion of sinners for the sake of promoting your own happiness, when sinners are converted it does not make you happy, because it is not the thing on which your desire terminated. The law of the mind, therefore, renders it impossible, if each individual pursues his own happiness, that he should ever obtain it. To be more definite. Two things are indispensable to true happiness. First, there must be virtuous desire. If the desire be not virtuous, conscience will remonstrate against it, and therefore a gratification would be attended with pain. Secondly, this desire must be gratified in the attainment of its object. The object must be desired for its own sake, or the gratification would not be complete, even should the object be attained. If the object is desired as a means to an end, the gratification would depend on obtaining the end by this means. But if the thing was desired as an end, or for its own sake, obtaining it would produce unmingled gratification. The mind must, therefore, desire not its own happiness, for in this way it can never be attained, but the desire must terminate on some other object which is desired for its own sake, the attainment of which would be a gratification, and thus result in happiness.

(2.) If each one pursues his own happiness, as his supreme end, the interests of different individuals will clash, and destroy the happiness of all. This is the very thing we see in the world. This is the reason of all the fraud, and violence, and oppression, and wickedness in earth and hell. It is because each one is pursuing his own interest, and their interests clash. The true way to secure our own happiness is, not to pursue that as an end, but to pursue another object, which, when obtained, will afford complete gratification—the glory of God and the good of the universe. The question is not, whether it is right to desire and pursue our own happiness at all, but whether it is right to make our own happiness our supreme end.

Objection 5. "Happiness consists in gratifying virtuous desire. Then the thing I aim at, is gratifying virtuous desire. Is not that aiming at my own happiness?"

Answer. The mind does not aim at gratifying the desire, but at accomplishing the thing desired. Suppose you see a beggar, as mentioned last week, and you give him a loaf of bread. You aim at relieving the beggar. That is the object desired, and when that is done, your desire is gratified, and you are happy. But if, in relieving the beggar, the object you aimed at was your own happiness, then relieving the beggar will not gratify the desire, and you render it impossible to gratify it.

Thus you see, that both the law and the gospel require disinterested benevolence, as the only condition on which man can be happy.

3. True submission implies acquiescence in the penalty of God's law.

I again advert to the distinction, which I have made before. We are not, in this world, simply under a government of naked law. This world is a province of Jehovah's empire, that stands in a peculiar relation to God's government. It has rebelled, and a new and special provision has been made, by which God offers us mercy. The conditions are, that we obey the precepts of the law, and submit to the justice of the penalty. It is a government of law, with the gospel appended to it. The gospel requires the same obedience with the law. It maintains the ill desert of sin, and requires the sinner's acquiescence, in the justice of the penalty. If the sinner were under mere law, it would require that he should submit to the infliction of the penalty. But man is not, and never has been, since the fall, under the government of mere law, but has always known, more or less clearly, that mercy is offered. It has, therefore, never been required, that men should be willing to be punished. In this respect it is, that gospel submission differs from legal submission. Under naked law, submission would consist in willingness to be punished. In this world, submission consists in acquiescence in the justice of the penalty, and regarding himself as *deserving* the eternal wrath of God.

4. True submission implies acquiescence in the sovereignty of God.

It is the duty of every sovereign to see that all his subjects submit to his government. And it is his duty to enact such laws, that every individual, if he obeys perfectly, will promote the public good, in the highest possible degree. And then, if any one refuses to obey, it is his duty to take that individual by force, and make him subserve the public interest in the best way that is possible with a rebellious subject. If he will not subserve the public good voluntarily, he should be made to do it involuntarily. The government must either hang him, or shut him up, or in some way make him an example of suffering; or if the public good admits of mercy, it may show mercy in such a way as will best subserve the general interest. Now God is a sovereign ruler, and the submission which He requires is just what He is bound to require. He would be neglecting His duty as a ruler, if He did not require it. And since you have refused to obey this requirement, you are now bound to throw yourself into His hands, for Him to dispose of you, for time and eternity, in the way that will most promote the interests of the universe. You have forfeited all claim to any portion in the happiness of the universe or the favor of God. And the thing which is now required of you is, that since you cannot render obedience for the past, you should acknowledge the justice of His law, and leave your future destiny entirely and unconditionally at His disposal, for time and for eternity. You must submit all you have and all you are to Him. You have justly forfeited all, and are bound to give up all at His bidding, in any way that He calls for them, to promote the interests of His kingdom.

5. Finally, it requires submission to the terms of the gospel. The terms of the gospel are—

(1.) Repentance, hearty sorrow for sin, justifying God and taking His part against yourself.

(2.) Faith, perfect trust and confidence towards God, such as leads you without hesitation to throw yourself, body and soul, and all you have and are, into His hand, to do with you as He thinks good.

(3.) Holiness, or disinterested benevolence.

(4.) To receive salvation as a mere matter of pure grace, to which you have no claim on the score of justice.

(5.) To receive Christ as your mediator and advocate, your atoning sacrifice, your ruler and teacher, and in all the offices in which He is presented to you in God's word. In short, you are to be wholly acquiescent in God's appointed way of salvation.

REMARKS.

I. You see why there are so many false hopes in the church.

The reason is, that so many persons embrace what they consider the gospel, without yielding obedience to the law. They look at the law with dread, and regard the gospel as a scheme to get away from the law. These tendencies have always been manifested among men. There is a certain class that hold to the gospel and reject the law; and another class that take the law and neglect the gospel. The Antinomians think to get rid of the law altogether. They suppose the gospel rule of life is different from the law; whereas, the truth is, that the rule of life is the same in both, and both require disinterested benevolence. Now, if a person thinks that, under the gospel, he may give up the glory of God as his supreme object, and instead of loving God with all his heart, and soul, and strength, may make his own salvation his supreme object, his hopes are false. He has embraced another gospel—which is no gospel at all.

II. The subject shows how we are to meet the common objection, that faith in Christ implies making our own salvation our object or motive.

Answer. What is faith? It is not believing that *you* shall be saved, but believing God's word concerning His Son. It is nowhere revealed that you shall be saved. He has revealed the fact that Jesus Christ came into the world to save sinners. What you call faith, is more properly hope. The confident expectation that you shall be saved is an *inference* from the act of faith; and an inference which you have a right to draw when you are conscious of obeying the law and believing the gospel. That is, when you exercise the feelings required in the law and gospel, you have a right to trust in Christ for your *own* salvation.

III. It is an error to suppose that despair of mercy is essential to true submission.

This is plain from the fact that, under the gospel, everybody knows it is the will of God that every soul shall be saved that will exercise disinterested benevolence. Suppose a man should come to me and ask, "What shall I do to be saved?" and I should tell him, "If you expect to be saved you must despair of being saved," what would he think? What inspired writer ever gave any such direction as this? No, the inspired answer is, "Love the Lord thy God with all thy heart," "Repent," "Believe the gospel," and so on. Is there any thing here that implies despair?

It is true that sinners sometimes do despair, before they obtain true peace. But what is the reason? It is not because despair is essential to true peace; but because of their ignorance, or of wrong instructions given to them, or misapprehension of the truth. Many anxious sinners despair because they get a false impression that they have sinned away their day of grace, or that they have committed the unpardonable sin, or that their sins are peculiarly aggravated, and the gospel provision does not reach them. Sometimes they despair for this reason—they know that there is mercy provided, and ready to be bestowed as soon as they will comply with the terms, but they find all their efforts at true submission vain. They find they are so proud and obstinate, that they cannot get their own consent to the terms of salvation. Perhaps most individuals who do submit, do in fact come to a point where they give up all as lost. But is that necessary? That is the question. Now, you see, it is nothing but their own wickedness drives them to despair. They are so unwilling to take hold of the mercy that is offered. Their despair, then, instead of being essential to true submission under the gospel, is inconsistent with it, and no man ever did embraced the gospel while in that state. It is horrid unbelief then, it is sin to despair; and to say it is essential to true submission, is saying that sin is essential to true submission.

IV. True submission is acquiescing in the whole government of God.

It is acquiescing in His Providential government, in His moral government, in the precept of His law, and in the penalty of His law, so that he is himself deserving of an exceeding great and eternal weight of damnation; and submission to the terms of salvation in the gospel. Under the gospel, it is no man's duty to be willing to be damned. It is wholly inconsistent with his duty to be willing to be damned. The man who submits to the naked law, and consents to be damned, is as much in rebellion as ever; for it is one of God's express requirements that he should obey the gospel.

V. To call on a sinner to be willing to be punished is a grand mistake, for several reasons.

It is to set aside the gospel, and place him under another government than that which exists. It sets before him a partial view of the character of God, to which he is required to submit. It keeps back the true motives to submission. It presents not the real and true God, but a different being. It is practicing a deception on him, by holding out the idea that God desires his damnation, and he must submit to it; for God has taken His solemn oath that He desires not the death of the wicked, but that he turn from his wickedness and live. It is a slander upon God, and charging God with perjury. Every man under the gospel, knows that God desires sinners to be saved, and it is impossible to hide the fact. The true ground on which salvation should be placed is, that he is not to seek his own salvation, but to seek the glory of God; not to hold out the idea that God desires or means he should go to hell.

What did the apostles tell sinners, when they inquired what they must do to be saved? What did Peter tell them at the Pentecost? What did Paul tell the jailer? To repent and forsake their selfishness, and believe the gospel. This is what men must do to be saved.

There is another difficulty in attempting to convert men in this way. It is attempting to convert them by the law, and setting aside the gospel. It is attempting to make them holy, without the appropriate influences to make them holy. Paul tried this way, thoroughly, and found it never would answer. In the 7th of Romans, he gives us the result in his own case. It drove him to confess that the law was holy and good, and he ought to obey it; and there it left him in distress, and crying, "The good that I would, I do not, but the evil that I would not, that I do." The law was not able to convert him, and he cries out, "O wretched man that I am! who shall deliver me from the body of this death?" Just here the love of God in sending his Son, Jesus Christ, is presented to his mind, and that did the work. In the next chapter he explains it; "What the law could not do in that it was weak through the flesh, God sending his own Son in the likeness of sinful flesh, and for sin, condemned sin in the flesh, that the righteousness of the law might be fulfilled in us, who walk not after the flesh but after the Spirit." The whole Bible testifies that it is only the influence of the gospel which can bring sinners to obey the law. The law will never do it. Shutting out from the soul that class of motives which cluster around it from the gospel, will never convert a sinner.

I know there may be some persons who suppose they were converted in this way, and that they have submitted to the law, absolutely, and without any influence from the gospel. But was it ever concealed from them for a moment, that Christ had died for sinners, and that if they should repent and believe, they should be saved? These motives must have had their influence, for all the time that they think they were looking at the naked law, they expected that if they believed they should be saved.

I suppose the error of attempting to convert men by the law, without the gospel, lies here; in the old Hopkinsion notion that men, in order to be saved must be willing to be damned. It sets aside the fact, that this world is, and since the fall always has been, under a dispensation of mercy. If we were under a government of mere law, true submission to God would require this. But men are not, in this sense, under the law, and never have been; for immediately after the fall, God revealed to Adam the intimations of mercy.

An objection arises here in the mind of some, which I will remove.

Objection. "Is not the offer of mercy, in the gospel, calculated to produce a selfish religion?"

Answer. The offer of mercy may be perverted, as every other good thing may be, and then it may give rise to a selfish religion. And God knew it would be so, when He revealed the gospel. But observe: Nothing is calculated to subdue the rebellious heart of man, but this very exhibition of the benevolence of God, in the offer of mercy.

There was a father who had a stubborn and rebellious son, and he tried long to subdue him by chastisement. He loved his son, and longed to have him virtuous and obedient. But the child seemed to harden his heart against his repeated efforts. At length the poor father was quite discouraged, and burst out into a flood of convulsive weeping—"My son! my son! what shall I do? Can I save you? I have done all that I could to save you; O! what can I do more?" The son had looked at the rod with a brow of brass, but when he saw the tears rolling down his father's furrowed cheeks and heard the convulsive sobs of anguish from his aged bosom, he too burst into tears, and cried out, "Whip me father! do whip me, as much as you please, but don't cry!" Now the father had found out the way to subdue that stubborn heart. Instead of holding over him nothing but the iron hand of law, he let out his soul before him; and what was the effect? To crush him into hypocritical submission? No, the rod did that. The gushing tears of his father's love broke him down at once to true submission to his father's will.

So it is with sinners. The sinner braves the wrath of Almighty God, and hardens himself to receive the heaviest bolt of Jehovah's thunder; but when he sees the LOVE of his Heavenly Father's heart, if there is anything that will make him abhor and execrate himself, that will do it, when he sees God manifested in the flesh, stooping to take human nature, hanging on the cross, and pouring out His soul in tears and bloody sweat and death. Is this calculated to make hypocrites? No, the sinner's heart melts, and he cries out, "O, do any thing else, and I can bear it; but the love of the blessed Jesus overwhelms me." This is the very nature of the mind, to be thus influenced. Instead, therefore, of being afraid of exhibiting the love of God to sinners, it is the only way to make them truly submissive and truly benevolent. The law may make hypocrites; but nothing but the gospel can draw out the soul in true love to God.

Next Thursday, evening I design to pursue the same subject farther.

LECTURE III.

SELFISHNESS NOT TRUE RELIGION.

TEXT:—"Seeketh not her own."—1. Cor. xiii. 5.

That is, Charity, or Christian love, seeketh not her own.

The proposition which I design to establish this evening, is the following:

THAT A SUPREME REGARD TO OUR OWN HAPPINESS IS INCONSISTENT WITH TRUE RELIGION.

This proposition is naturally the first in the series that I have been laboring to illustrate in the present lectures, and would have been the first to be discussed, had I been aware that it was seriously called in question by any considerable number of professed Christians. But I can honestly say, that when I commenced these lectures, I did not expect to meet any serious difficulty here; and therefore I took it in a great measure for granted, that selfishness is not religion. And hence, I passed over this point with but a slight attempt at proving it. But since, I learn that there are many professed Christians who maintain that a supreme regard to our own happiness is true religion, I think it necessary to examine the subject more carefully, and give you the arguments in favor of what I suppose to be the truth. In establishing my proposition, I wish to distinguish between things that differ; I shall therefore

I. Show what is not intended by the proposition, that a supreme regard to our own happiness is not religion.

II. Show what is meant by it. And

III. Attempt to prove it.

I. I am to explain what is not meant by the proposition.

1. The point in dispute is not, whether it is lawful to have any regard to our own happiness. On the contrary; it is admitted and maintained to be a part of our duty to have a *due* regard to our own happiness, according to its real value, in the scale with other interests. God has commanded us to love our neighbor as ourselves. This plainly makes it a duty to love ourselves or regard our own happiness, by the same rule that we regard that of others.

2. The proposition is not that we ought to have no regard to the promises and threatenings of God, as affecting ourselves. It is

plainly right to regard the promises of God and threatenings of evil, as affecting ourselves, according to the relative value of our own interests. But who does not see that a threatening against us is not so important as a threatening against a large number of individuals. Suppose a threatening of evil against yourself as an individual. This is plainly not so important as if it included your family. Then suppose it extend to the whole congregation, or to the state, or the whole nation, or the world. Here, it is easy to see, that the happiness of an individual, although great, ought not to be regarded as supreme.

I am a minister. Suppose God says to me, "If you do not do not your duty, you will be sent to hell." This is a great evil, and I ought to avoid it. But suppose Him to say, "If your people do not do their duty, they will all be sent to hell; but if you do your duty faithfully, you will probably save the whole congregation." Is it right for me to be as much influenced by the fear of evil to myself, as by the fear of having a whole congregation sent to hell? Plainly not.

3. The question is not whether our own eternal interests ought to be pursued in preference to our temporal interests. It is expressly maintained by myself, and so it is by the Bible, that we are bound to regard our eternal interests as altogether of more consequence than our temporal interests.

Thus, the Bible tells us "Labor not for the meat that perisheth, but for that which endureth unto everlasting life." This teaches that we are not to regard or value our temporal interests at all, in comparison with eternal life.

So, where our Savior says, "Lay not up for yourselves treasures on the earth, where moth and rust doth corrupt, and where thieves break through and steal; but lay up for yourselves treasures in heaven, where neither moth nor rust doth corrupt, and where thieves break not through nor steal." Here the same duty is enjoined, of preferring eternal to temporal interests.

There is another. When Christ sent out his disciples, two and two, to preach and to work miracles, they came back full of joy and exultation, because they found even the devils yielding to their power. "Lord, even the devils are subject to us." Jesus saith, "Rejoice not that the devils are subject to you; but rather rejoice in this, that your names are written in heaven." Here He teaches, that it is a greater good to have our names written in heaven, than to enjoy the greatest temporal power, even authority over devils themselves.

The Bible everywhere teaches, that eternal good is to be preferred in all our conduct to temporal good. But this is very different from maintaining that our own individual eternal interest is to be aimed at as the supreme object of regard.

4. The proposition is not, that hope and fear should not influence our conduct. All that is implied is, that when we are influenced by hope and fear, the things that are hoped or feared should be put into the scale according to their real value, in comparison with other interests.

5. The question is not, whether the persons did right, who are spoken of in the Bible, as having been at least in some degree influenced by hope and fear, or having respect unto the recompense of reward, or to the joy that was set before them. This is admitted. Noah was moved with fear and built the ark. But was it the fear of being drowned himself, or fear for his own personal safety that chiefly moved him? The Bible does not say it. He feared for the safety of his family; yea, more, he dreaded the destruction of the whole human race, with all the interests depending thereon.

Whenever it is said that good men were influenced by hope and fear, it is admitted. But in order to make it bear on this subject, it must be shown that this hope or fear respecting their own personal interest was the controlling motive. Now, this is no where affirmed in the Bible. It was right for them to be influenced by promises and threatenings. Otherwise, they could not obey the second part of the law: "Thou shalt love thy neighbor as *thyself*."

II. I am to show what is meant by the proposition, that a supreme regard to our own interest is inconsistent with true religion.

The question is, whether supreme regard to our own happiness is religion. It is, whether we are to fear our own damnation *more than* the damnation of all other men, and the dishonor of God thereby. And whether we are to aim at securing our own happiness *more than* the happiness of all other men, and the glory of God. And whether, if we do this, we act according to the requirements of the true religion, or inconsistent with true religion. This is the proper point of inquiry, and I wish you to bear it constantly in mind, and not to confound it with any of the other points that I have referred to.

III. For the proof of the proposition.

Before proceeding to the proof of the proposition, that a supreme regard to our own happiness is inconsistent with true religion, I will observe that all true religion consists in being like God; in acting on the same principles and grounds, and having the same feelings towards different objects. I suppose this will not be denied. Indeed, it cannot be, by any sane mind. I then observe, as the first proof of the proposition,

1. That a supreme regard to our own happiness is not according to the example of God; but is being totally unlike Him.

The Bible tells us that "God is love." That is, benevolence is the sum total of His character. All His other moral attributes, such as justice, mercy, and the like, are but modifications of this benevolence. His love is manifested in two forms. One is that of benevolence, good willing, or desiring the happiness of others. The other is complacency, or approving the character of others who are holy. God's benevolence regards all beings that are capable of happiness. This is universal. Towards all holy beings, He exercises the love of complacency.—In other words, God loves His neighbor as Himself. He regards the interests of all beings, according to their relative value, as much as His own. He seeks His own happiness, or glory, as the supreme good. But not because it is His own, but because *it is* the supreme good. The sum total of His happiness, as an infinite being, is infinitely greater than the sum total of the happiness of all other beings, or of any possible number of finite creatures.

Take a very familiar illustration. Here is a man that is kind to brutes. This man and his horse fall into the river. Now, does true benevolence require the man to drown himself in order to extricate his horse? No. It would be true disinterested benevolence in him, to save himself, and, if need be, leave his horse to perish; because his happiness is of so much greater value than that of the horse. You see this at a glance. But the difference between God and all created beings is infinitely greater than between a man and a horse, or between the highest angel and the meanest insect.

God, therefore, regards the happiness of all creatures precisely according to its real value. And unless we do the same, we are not like God. If we are like God, we must regard God's happiness and glory in the same light that He does; that is, as the supreme good, beyond everything else in the universe. And if we desire our own happiness more than God's happiness, we are infinitely unlike God.

2. To aim at our own happiness supremely is inconsistent with true religion, because it is contrary to the spirit of Christ.

We are told, that "if any man have not the spirit of Christ, he is none of his." And it is repeatedly said of Him as a man, that he sought not His own, that He sought not His own glory, and the like. What was He seeking? Was it His own personal salvation? No. Was it His own personal happiness? No. It was the glory of His Father, and the good of the universe, through the salvation of men. He came on an errand of pure benevolence, to benefit the kingdom of God, not to benefit Himself. This was "the joy that was set before him," for which "he endured the cross, despising the shame." It was the great good He could do by thus throwing Himself out to labor and suffer for the salvation of men.

3. To regard our own happiness as the supreme object of pursuit is contrary to the law of God.

I have mentioned this before, but recur to it again for the sake of making my present demonstration complete. The sum of that law is this—"Thou shalt love the Lord thy God, with all thy heart, and with all thy soul, and with all thy mind, and with all thy strength; and thou shalt love thy neighbor as thyself." This is the great thing required; benevolence towards God and man. The first thing is really to love the happiness and glory of God, above all other things, because it is so infinitely lovely and desirable, and is properly the supreme good. Some have objected that it was not our duty to seek the happiness of God, because His happiness is already secured. Suppose, now, that the king of England is perfectly independent of me, and has his happiness secured without me; does that make it any the less my duty to wish him well, to desire his happiness, and to rejoice in it? Because God is happy, in Himself, independent of His creatures, is that a reason why we should not love His happiness, and rejoice in it? Strange!

Again: We are bound by the terms of God's law to exercise complacency in God, because He is holy, infinitely holy.

Again: This law binds us to exercise *the same* good will, or benevolence, towards others that we do to ourselves; that is, to seek both their interests and our own, according to their relative value. Who of you is doing this? And we are bound to exercise the love of complacency toward those who are good and holy.

Thus we see that the sum of the law of God is to exercise benevolence towards God and all beings, according to their relative value, and complacency in all that are holy. Now I say, that to regard our own happiness supremely, or to seek it as our supreme end, is contrary to that law, to its letter and to its spirit. And,

4. It is as contrary to the gospel as it is to the law.

In the chapter from which the text is taken, the apostle begins—"Though I speak with the tongues of men and of angels, and have not charity, I am become as sounding brass, or a tinkling cymbal. And though I have the gift of prophecy, and understand all mysteries and all knowledge; and though I have all faith, so that I could remove mountains, and have not charity, I am nothing." Charity here means love. In the original it is the same word that is rendered love. "And though I bestow all my goods to feed the poor, and though I give my body to be burned, and have not charity, it profiteth me nothing."

Now mark! In no stronger language could he have expressed the idea that charity, or benevolence, is essential to true religion. See how he throws out his guards on every side, so that it is impossible to mistake his views. If a person has not true charity, he is nothing. He then proceeds and shows what are the characteristics of this true charity. "Charity suffereth long, and is kind; charity envieth not; charity vaunteth not itself, is not puffed up, doth not behave itself unseemly, seeketh not her own, is not easily provoked, thinketh no evil; rejoiceth not in iniquity, but rejoiceth in the truth; beareth all things, believeth all things, hopeth all things endureth all things." Here you see that one leading peculiarity of this love is that charity "seeketh not her own." Mark that! If this is true religion, and without it there is no religion, then one peculiarity of true religion is, that it "seeketh not her own."

Those of you who have Bibles with marginal references can follow out these references and find a multitude of passages that plainly teach the same thing. Recollect the passages I quoted in the last lecture. I will just refer to one of them—"Whosoever will save his life shall lose it." Here you see it laid down as an established principle of God's government, that if a person aims supremely at his own interest he will lose his own interest.

The same is taught in the tenth chapter of this epistle, verse 24: "Let no man seek his own, but every man another's wealth." If you look at the passage, you will see that word *wealth* is in italic letters, to show that it is a word added by the translators, that is not in the Greek. They might just as well have used the word happiness, or welfare, as wealth. So in the 33d verse: "Even as I please all men in all things, *not seeking my own profit*, but the profit of many, that they may be saved."

Therefore I say, that to make our own interest the supreme object of pursuit, is as contrary to the gospel as it is to the law.

5. It is contrary to conscience.

The universal conscience of mankind has decided that a supreme regard to our own happiness is not virtue. Men have always known that to serve God and benefit mankind is what is right, and to seek supremely their own personal interest is not right. They have always regarded it mean and contemptible for individuals to seek their own happiness as the supreme object, and consequently, we see how much pains men take to conceal their selfishness and to appear benevolent. It is impossible for any man, unless his conscience is strangely blunted by sin, or perverted by false instruction, not to see that it is sinful to regard his own happiness above other interests of more importance.

6. It is contrary to right reason.

Right reason teaches us to regard all things according to their real value. God does this, and we should do the same. God has given us reason for this very purpose, that we should weigh and compare the relative value of things. It is a mockery of reason, to deny that it teaches us to regard things according to their real value. And if so, then to aim at and prefer our own interest, as the supreme end, is contrary to reason.

7. It is contrary to common sense.

What has the common sense of mankind decided on this point? Look at the common sense of mankind in regard to what is called patriotism. No man was ever regarded as a true patriot, in fighting for his country, if his object was to subserve his own interest. Suppose it should appear that his object in fighting was to get himself crowned king; would anybody give him credit for patriotism? No. All men agree that it is patriotism when a man is disinterested, like Washington; and fights for his country, for his country's sake. The common sense of mankind has written reprobation on that spirit that seeks its own things, and prefers its own interest, to the greater interests of others. It is evident that all men so regard it. Otherwise, how is it that every one is anxious to appear disinterested?

8. It is contrary to the constitution of the mind.

I do not mean, by this, that it is impossible, by our very constitution, for us to seek our own happiness as the supreme object. But we are so constituted that if we do this, we never can attain it. As I have said in a former lecture, happiness is the gratification of desire. We must desire something, and gain the object we desire. Now, suppose a man to desire his own happiness, the object of his desire will always keep just so far before him, like his shadow, and the faster he pursues it, the faster it flies. Happiness is inseparably attached to the attainment of the object desired. Suppose I desire a thousand dollars. That is the thing on which my desire fastens, and when I get it that desire is gratified, and I am happy, so far as gratifying this desire goes to make me happy. But if I desire the thousand dollars for the purpose of getting a watch, a dress, and such like things, the desire is not gratified till I get those things. But now suppose the thing I desired was my own happiness. Getting the thousand dollars then does not make me happy, because that is not the thing my desire was fixed on. And so getting the watch, and the dress, and other things will not make me happy, for they do not gratify my desire. God has so constituted things, and given such laws to the mind, that man never can gain happiness by pursuing it. This very constitution plainly indicates the duty of disinterested benevolence. Indeed, He has made it impossible for them to be happy, but in proportion as they are disinterested.

Here are two men walking along the street together. They come across a man that has just been run over by a cart, and lies weltering in his gore. They take him up, and carry him to the surgeon, and relieve him. Now it is plain that their gratification is in proportion to the intensity of their desire for his relief. If one of them felt but little and cared but little about the sufferings of the poor man, he will be but little gratified. But if his desire to have the man relieved amounted to agony, his gratification would be accordingly. Now suppose a third individual that had no desire to relieve the distressed man; certainly relieving him could be no gratification to that person. He could pass right by him, and see him die. Then he is not gratified at all. Therefore, you see, happiness is just in proportion as the desires are gratified, by obtaining the things desired.

Here observe, that in order to make the happiness of gratified desire complete, the desire itself must be virtuous. Otherwise, if the desire is selfish, the gratification will be mingled with pain, from the conflict of the mind.

That all this is true, is a matter of consciousness, and is proved to us by the very highest kind of testimony we can have. And for any one to deny it, is to charge God foolishly, as if He had given us a constitution that would not allow us to be happy in obeying Him.

9. It is also inconsistent with our own happiness, to make our own interest the supreme object. This follows from what I have just said. Men may enjoy a certain kind of pleasure, but not true happiness. The pleasure which does not spring from the gratification of virtuous desire, is a deceptive delusion. The reason why all mankind do not find happiness, when they are all so anxious for it, is that they are seeking IT. If they would seek the glory of God and the good of the universe as their supreme end, IT would pursue them.

10. It is inconsistent with the public happiness. If each individual is to aim at his own happiness as his chief end, these interests will unavoidably clash and come into collision, and universal war and confusion will follow in the train of universal selfishness.

11. To maintain that a supreme regard to our own interest is true religion, is to contradict the experience of all real saints. I answer, that every real saint knows that his supreme happiness consists in going out of himself, and regarding the glory of God and the good of others. If he does not know this, he is no saint.

12. It is also inconsistent with the experience of all those who have had a selfish religion, and have found out their mistake and got true religion. This is a common occurrence. I suppose I have known hundreds of cases. Some members in this church have recently made this discovery. And they can all testify that they know now by experience that benevolence is true religion.

13. It is contrary to the experience of all the impenitent. Every impenitent sinner knows that he is aiming supremely at the promotion of his own interest, and he knows that he has not true religion. The very thing that his conscience condemns him for is this, that he is regarding his own interest instead of the glory of God.

Now just turn the leaf over, for a moment, and admit that a supreme regard for our own happiness is true religion; and then see what will follow.

1. Then it will follow that God is not holy. That is, if a supreme regard to our own interest, *because* it is our own, is true religion, then it will follow that God is not holy. God regards His own happiness, but it is because it is the greatest good, not because it is His own. But He is love, or benevolence; and if benevolence is not true religion, God's nature must be changed.

2. The law of God must be altered. If a supreme regard to our own happiness is religion, then the law should read, "Thou shalt love thyself with all thy heart and with all thy soul, and with all thy mind, and with all thy strength, and God and thy neighbor infinitely less than thyself."

3. The gospel must be reversed. Instead of saying, "Whether ye eat or drink, or whatsoever ye do, do all to the glory of God," it should read, "Do all for your own happiness." Instead of "He that will save his life shall lose it," we should find it saying, "He that is supremely anxious to save his own life shall save it; but he that is benevolent, and willing to lose his life for the good of others, shall lose it."

4. The consciences of men should be changed so as to testify in favor of selfishness, and condemn and reprobate everything like disinterested benevolence.

5. Right reason must be made not to weigh things according to their relative value, but to decide our own little interest to be of more value than the greatest interests of God and the universe.

6. Common sense will have to decide, that true patriotism consists in every man's seeking his own interest instead of the public good, and each one seeking to build himself up as high as he can.

7. The human constitution must be reversed. If supreme selfishness is virtue, the human constitution was made wrong. It is so made, that man can be happy only by being benevolent. And if this doctrine is true, that religion consists in seeking our own happiness as a supreme good, then the more religion a man has the more miserable he is.

8. And the whole framework of society will have to be changed. Now it is so, that the good of the community depends on the extent to which everyone regards the public interest. And if this doctrine holds, it must be changed, so that the public good will be best promoted when every man is scrambling for his own interest regardless of the interests of others.

9. The experience of the saints will have to be reversed. Instead of finding, as they now do, that the more benevolence they have, the more religion and the more happiness, they should testify that the more they aim at their own good, the more they enjoy of religion and the favor of God.

10. The impenitent should be found to testify that they are supremely happy in supreme selfishness, and that they find true happiness in it.

I will not pursue this proof any farther; it would look like trifling. If there is any such thing as proof to be had, it is fully proved, that to aim at our own happiness supremely, is inconsistent with true religion.

REMARKS.

I. We see why it is, that while all are pursuing happiness, so few find it.

The fact is plain. The reason is this; the greater part of mankind do not know in what true happiness consists, and they are seeking it in that which can never afford it. They do not find it because they are pursuing it. If they would turn round and pursue holiness, happiness would pursue them. If they would become disinterested, and lay themselves out to do good, they could not but be happy. If they choose happiness as an end, it flies before them. True happiness consists in the gratification of virtuous desires; and if they would set themselves to glorify God, and do good, they would find it. The only class of persons that never do find it, in this world, or the world to come, are those who seek it as an end.

II. The constitution of the human mind and of the universe, affords a beautiful illustration of the economy of God.

Suppose man could find happiness, only by pursuing his own happiness. Then each individual would have only the happiness that himself had gained, and all the happiness in the universe would be only the sum total of what individuals had gained, with the offset of all the pain and misery produced by conflicting interests. Now mark! God has so constituted things, that while each lays himself out to promote the happiness of others, his own happiness is secured and made complete. How vastly greater then is the amount of happiness in the universe, than it would have been, had selfishness been the law of Jehovah's kingdom. Because each one who obeys the law of God, fully secures his own happiness by his benevolence, and the happiness of the whole is increased by how much each receives from all others.

Many say, "Who will take care of my happiness if I do not? If I am to care only for my neighbor's interest, and neglect my own, none of us will be happy." That would be true, if you care for your neighbor's happiness was a detraction from your own. But if your happiness consists in doing good and promoting the happiness of others, the more you do for others, the more you promote your own happiness.

III. When I gave out the subject of this lecture, I avoided the use of the term, selfishness, lest it should be thought invidious. But I now affirm, that a supreme regard to our own interest is selfishness, and nothing else. It would be selfishness in God, if He regarded His own interest; supremely because it is His own. And it is selfishness in man. And whoever maintains that a supreme regard to our own interest is true religion, maintains that selfishness is true religion.

IV. If selfishness is virtue, then benevolence is sin. They are direct opposites and cannot both be virtue. For a man to set up his own interest over God's interest, giving it a preference, and placing it in opposition to God's interest is selfishness. And if this is virtue, then Jesus Christ, in seeking the good of mankind as He did, departed from the principles of virtue. Who will pretend this?

V. Those who regard their own interest as supreme, and yet think they have true religion, are deceived. I say it solemnly, because I believe it is true, and I would say it if it were the last word I was to speak before going to the judgment. Dear hearer, whoever you are, if you are doing this, you are not a Christian. Don't call this being censorious. I am not censorious. I would not denounce any one. But as God is true, and your soul is going to the judgment, you have not the religion of the Bible.

VI. Some will ask here, "What! are we to have no regard to our happiness, and if so, how are we to decide whether it is supreme or not?" I do not say that. I say, you may regard it according to its relative value. And now I ask, is there any real practical difficulty here? I appeal to your consciousness. You cannot but know, if you are honest, what it is that you regard supremely. Are these interests, your own interest on one side, and God's glory and the good of the universe on the other, so nearly balanced in your mind, that you cannot tell which you prefer? It is impossible! If you are not as conscious that you prefer the glory of God to your own interest, as you are that you exist, you may take it for granted that you are all wrong.

VII. You see why the enjoyment of so many professors of religion depends on their evidences. These persons are all the time hunting after evidence; and just in proportion as that varies, their enjoyments wax and wane. Now, mark! If they really regarded the glory of God and the good of mankind, their enjoyment would not depend on their evidences. Those who are purely selfish, may enjoy much in religion, but it is by anticipation. The idea of going to heaven is pleasing to them. But those who go out of themselves, and are purely benevolent, have a present heaven in their breasts.

VIII. You see, here, that all of you, who had no peace and joy in religion before you had a hope, are deceived. Perhaps I can give an outline of your experience. You were awakened, and were distressed, as you had reason to be, by the fear of going to hell. By and by, perhaps while you were engaged in prayer, or while some person was conversing with you, your distress left you. You thought your sins were pardoned. A gleam of joy shot through your mind, and warmed up your heart into a glow, that you took for evidence, and this again increased your joy. How very different is the experience of a true Christian! His peace does not depend on his hope; but true submission and benevolence produce peace and joy, independent of his hope.

Suppose the case of a man in prison, condemned to be hung the nest day. He is in great distress, walking his cell, and waiting for the day. By and by, a messenger comes with a pardon. He seizes the paper, turns it up to the dim light that comes through his grate, reads the word PARDON, and almost faints with emotion, and leaps for joy. He supposes the paper to be genuine. Now suppose it turns out that the paper is counterfeit. Suddenly his joy is all gone. So in the case of a deceived person. He was afraid of going to hell, and of course he rejoices if he believes he is pardoned. If the devil should tell him so, and he believed it, his joy would be just as great, while the belief lasts, as if it was a reality. True Christian joy does not depend on evidence. He submits himself into the hands of God with such confidence, and that very act gives him peace. He had a terrible conflict with God, but all at once he yields the controversy, and says, "God will do right, let God's will be done." Then he begins to pray, he is subdued, he melts down before God, and that very act affords sweet, calm, and heavenly joy. Perhaps he has not thought of a hope. Perhaps he may go for hours, or even for a day or two, full of joy in God, without thinking of his own salvation. You ask him if he has a hope, he never thought of that. His joy does not depend on believing that he is pardoned, but consists in *a state of mind*, acquiescing in the government of God. In such a state of mind, he could not but be happy.

Now let me ask which religion have you? If you exercise true religion, suppose God should put you into hell, and there let you exercise supreme love to God, and the same love to your neighbor as to yourself, that itself is a state of mind inconsistent with being miserable.

I wish this to be fully understood. These hope-seekers will be always disappointed. If you run after hope, you will never have a hope good for anything. But if you pursue holiness, hope, and peace, and joy, will come of course. Is your religion the love of holiness, the love of God and of souls? Or is it only a hope?

IX. You see why it is that anxious sinners do not find peace.

They are looking at their own guilt and danger. They are regarding God as an avenger, and shrinking from His terrors. This will render it impossible they should ever come at peace. While looking at the wrath of God, making them wither and tremble, they cannot love Him, they hide from Him. Anxious sinners, let me tell you a secret. If you keep looking at that feature of God's character, it will drive you to despair, and that is inconsistent with true submission. You should look at His whole character, and see the reasons why you should love Him, and throw yourself upon Him without reserve, and without distrust; and instead of shrinking from Him, come right to Him, and say, "O, Father in heaven, thou art not inexorable, thou art sovereign, but thou art good, I submit to thy government, and give myself to thee, with all I have and all I am, body and soul, for time and for eternity."

The subject for the next lecture will be, the distinction between legal submission and gospel submission, or between the religion of the law and the religion of faith. And here let me observe, that when I began to preach on the subject of selfishness in religion, I did not dream that it would be regarded by anyone as a controversial subject at all. I have no fondness for controversy, and I should as soon think of calling the doctrine of the existence of God a controversial subject, as this. The question is one of the greatest importance, and we ought to weigh the arguments, and decide according to the word of God. Soon we shall go together to the bar of God, and you must determine whether you will go there with selfishness in your hearts, or with that disinterested benevolence that seeketh not her own.—Will you now be honest? For as God is true, if you are seeking your own, you will soon be in hell, unless you repent. O be honest! and lay aside prejudice, and act for eternity.

LECTURE IV.

RELIGION OF THE LAW AND GOSPEL.

TEXT: —"What shall we say then? That the Gentiles, which followed not after righteousness, have attained to righteousness, even the righteousness which is of faith: but Israel, which followed after the law of righteousness, hath not attained to the law of righteousness. Wherefore? Because they sought it not by faith, but as it were by the works of the law. For they stumbled at that stumbling-stone; as it is written, Behold, I lay in Sion a stumbling-stone, and rock of offense: and whosoever believeth on him shall not be ashamed." — Rom. ix. 30-33.

In the Epistle to the Romans, the apostle pursues a systematic course of reasoning, to accomplish a particular design. In the beginning of it, he proves that not only the Gentiles, but the Jews also, were in a state of entire depravity; and that the Jews were not, as they vainly imagined, naturally holy. He then introduces the Moral Law, and by explaining it shows that by works of law no flesh could be saved. His next topic is Justification by Faith, in opposition to Justification by Law. Here I will observe, in passing, that it is my design to make this the subject of my next lecture. The next subject, with which he begins chap. 6, is to show that sanctification is by faith; or that all true religion, all the acceptable obedience there ever was in the world, is based on faith. In the eighth and ninth chapters, he introduces the subject of divine sovereignty; and in the last part of the ninth chapter, he sums up the whole matter, and asks, "What shall we say, then?" What shall we say of all this?—That the Gentiles, who never thought of the law, have become pious, and obtained the holiness which is by faith; but the Jews, attempting it by the law, have entirely failed. Wherefore? Because they made the fatal mistake of attempting to become pious by obeying the law, and have always come short, while the Gentiles have obtained true religion, by faith in Jesus Christ.—Jesus Christ is here called "that stumbling-stone," because the Jews were so opposed to Him. But whosoever believeth in Him shall not be confounded.

My design tonight is, to point out as distinctly as I can, the true distinction between the religion of law and the religion of faith. I shall proceed in the following order:

I. Show in what the distinction does not consist.

II. Show in what it does consist. And

III. Bring forward some specimens of both, to show more plainly in what they differ.

I. I am to show in what the distinction between the religion of law and the religion of faith does not consist.

1. The difference does not lie in the fact, that under the law men were justified by works, without faith. The method of salvation in both dispensations has been the same. Sinners were always justified by faith. The Jewish dispensation pointed to a Savior to come, and if men were saved at all, it was by faith in Christ. And sinners now are saved in the same way.

2. Not in the fact that the gospel has canceled or set aside the obligations of the moral law. It is true, it has set aside the claims of the ceremonial law, or law of Moses. The ceremonial law was nothing but a set of types pointing to the Savior, and was set aside, of course, when the great ante-type appeared. It is now generally admitted by all believers, that the gospel has not set aside the moral law. But that doctrine has been maintained in different ages of the church. Many have maintained that the gospel has set aside the moral law, so that believers are under no obligation to obey it. Such was the doctrine of the Nicolaitans, so severely reprobated by Christ. The Antinomians, in the days of the apostles and since, believed that they were without any obligation to obey the moral law; and held that Christ's righteousness was so imputed to believers, and that He had so fulfilled the law for them, that they were under no obligation to obey it themselves.

There have been many, in modern times, called Perfectionists, who held that they were not under obligation to obey the law. They suppose that Christ has delivered them from the law, and given them the Spirit, and that the leadings of the Spirit are now to be their rule of life, instead of the law of God. Where the Bible says, sin shall not have dominion over believers, these persons understand by it, that the same acts, which would be sin if done by an unconverted person, are not sin in them. The others, they say, are under the law, and so bound by its rules, but themselves are sanctified, and are in Christ, and if they break the law it is no sin.

But all such notions must be radically wrong. God has no right to give up the moral law. He cannot discharge us from the duty of love to God and love to man, for this is right in itself. And unless God will alter the whole moral constitution of the universe, so as to make that right which is wrong, He cannot give up the claims of the moral law. Besides, this doctrine represents Jesus Christ and the Holy Ghost as having taken up arms openly against the government of God.

3. The distinction between law religion and gospel religion does not consist in the fact that the gospel is any less strict in its claims, or allows any greater latitude of self-indulgence than the law. Not only does the gospel not cancel the obligations of the moral law, but it does in no degree abate them. Some people talk about gospel liberty; as though they had got a new rule of life, less strict, and allowing more liberty than the law. I admit that it has provided a new method of justification, but it everywhere insists that the rule of life is the same with the law. The very first sentence of the gospel, the command to repent, is in effect a re-enactment of the law, for it is a command to return to obedience. The idea that the liberty of the gospel differs from the liberty of the law, is erroneous.

4. Neither does the distinction consist in the fact that those called legalists, or who have a legal religion, do, either by profession or in fact, depend on their own works for justification. It is not often the case, at least in our day, that legalists do profess dependence on their own works, for there are few so ignorant as not to know that this is directly in the face of the gospel. Nor is it necessarily the case that they really depend on their own works. Often they really depend on Christ for salvation. But their dependence is false dependence, such as they have no right to have. They depend on Him, but they make it manifest that their faith, or dependence, is not that which actually "worketh by love," or that "purifieth the heart," or that "overcometh the world." It is a simple matter of fact, that the faith which they have does not do what the faith does which men must have in order to be saved, and so it is not the faith of the gospel. They have a *kind* of faith, but not *that* kind that makes men real Christians, and brings them under the terms of the gospel.

II. I am to mention some of the particulars in which these two kinds of religion differ.

There are several different classes of persons who manifestly have a legal religion. There are some who really profess to depend on their own works for salvation. Such were the Pharisees. The Hicksite Quakers formerly took this ground, and maintained that men were to be justified by works; setting aside entirely justification by faith. When I speak of works, I mean works of law. And here I want you to distinguish between works of law and works of faith. This is the grand distinction to be kept in view. It is between works produced by legal considerations, and those produced by faith. There are but two principles on which obedience to any government can turn: One is the principle of hope and fear, under the influence of conscience. Conscience points out what is right or wrong, and the individual is induced by hope and fear to obey. The other principle is confidence and love. You see this illustrated in families, where one child always obeys from hope and fear, and another from affectionate confidence. So in the government of God, the only thing that ever produced even the appearance of obedience, is one of these two principles.

There is a multitude of things that address our hopes and fears; such as character, interest, heaven and hell, &c. These may produce external obedience, or conformity to the law. But filial confidence leads men to obey God from love. This is the only obedience that is acceptable to God. God not only requires a certain course of conduct, but that this should spring from love. There never was and never can be, in the government of God, any acceptable obedience but the obedience of faith. Some suppose that faith will be done away in heaven. This is a strange notion! As if there were no occasion to trust God in heaven, or no reason to exercise confidence in Him. Here is the great distinction between the religion of law and gospel religion. Legal obedience is influenced by hope and fear, and is hypocritical, selfish, outward, constrained. Gospel obedience is from love, and is sincere, free, cheerful, true. There is a class of legalists, who depend on works of law for justification, who have merely deified what they call a principle of right, and have set themselves to do right; it is not out of respect to the law of God, or out of love to God, but just because it is right.

There is another distinction here. The religion of law is the religion of *purposes, or desires*, founded on legal considerations, and not the religion of *preference, or love to God. The individual intends to put* off his sins; he purposes to obey God and be religious; but his purpose does not grow out of love to God, but out of hope and fear. It is easy to see that a purpose, founded on such considerations, is very different from a purpose growing out of love. But the religion of the gospel is not a purpose merely, but an actual preference consisting in love.

Again, there is a class of legalists that depend on Christ, but their dependence is not gospel dependence, because the works which it produces are works of law; that is, from hope and fear, not from love. Gospel dependence may produce, perhaps, the very same outward works, but the motives are radically different. The legalist drags on a painful, irksome, moral, and perhaps, outwardly, religious life. The gospel believer has an affectionate confidence in God, which leads him to obey out of love. His obedience is prompted by his own feelings. Instead of being dragged to duty, he goes to it cheerfully, because he loves it, and doing it is a delight to his soul.

There is another point. The legalist expects to be justified by faith, but he has not learned that he must be sanctified by faith. I propose to examine this point another time, in full. Modern legalists do not expect to be justified by works; they know these are inadequate—they know that the way to be saved is by Christ. But they have no practical belief that justification by faith is only true, as sanctification by faith is true, and that men are justified by faith only, as they are first sanctified by faith. And therefore, while they expect to be justified by faith, they set themselves to perform works that are works of law.

Again: I wish you to observe that the two classes may agree in these points; the necessity of good works, and, theoretically, in what constitutes good works; that is, obedience springing from love to God. And further, they may agree in aiming to perform good works of this kind. But the difference lies here; in the different influences to which they look, to enable them to perform good works. The considerations by which they expect their minds to be affected, are different. They look to different sources for motives. And the true Christian alone succeeds in actually performing good works. The legalist, aiming to perform good works, influenced by hope and fear, and a selfish regard to his own interest, obeying the voice of conscience because he is afraid to do otherwise, falls entirely short of loving God with all his heart, and soul, and strength. The motives under which he acts have no tendency to bring him to the obedience of love. The true Christian, on the contrary, so appreciates God, so perceives and understands God's character, in Christ, as begets such an affectionate confidence in

God, that he finds it easy to obey from love. Instead of finding it, as a hymn has strangely represented,

Hard to obey, and harder still to love,"

he finds it no hardship at all. The commandments are not grievous. The yoke is easy, and the burden light. And he finds the ways of wisdom to be ways of pleasantness, and all her paths to be peace.

Is it so with most professors of religion? Is it so with YOU? Do you feel, in your religious duties constrained by love? Are you drawn by such strong cords of love, that it would give you more trouble to omit duty than to obey? Do your affections flow out in such a strong current to God, that you cannot but obey? How is it with those individuals who find it "hard to obey, and harder still to love?" What is the matter? Ask that wife who loves her husband, if she finds it hard to try to please her husband? Suppose she answers, in a solemn tone, "O yes, I find it hard to obey and harder still to love my husband," what would the husband think? What would anyone of you who are parents say, if you should hear one of your children complaining, "I find it harder to obey my father, and harder still to love?" The truth is, there is a radical defect in the religion of those people who love such expressions and live as if they were true. If any one of you find religion a painful thing, rely on it, you have the religion of the law. Did you ever find it a painful thing to do what you love to do? No. It is a pleasure to do it. The religion of the gospel is no labor to them that exercise it. It is the feeling of the heart. What would you do in heaven, if religion is such a painful thing here?—Suppose you were taken to heaven and obliged to grind out just so much religion every week, and month and year, to eternity. What sort of a heaven would it be to you? Would it be heaven, or would it be hell?—If you were required to have ten thousand times as much as you have here, and your whole life were to be filled up with this, and nothing else to do or enjoy but an eternal round of such duties, would not hell itself be a respite to you?

The difference, then, lies here. One class are striving to be religious from hope and fear, and under the influence of conscience which lashes them if they do not do their duty. The other class act from love to God, and the impulses of their own feelings, and know what the text means, which says, "I will put my law in their inward parts, and write it on their hearts, I will be their God, and they shall be my people."

III. I will give some specimens of these two classes, by way of illustration.

The first example I shall give is that of the apostle Paul, as he has recorded it in the 7th of Romans, where he exhibits the struggle to obey the law, under the influence of law alone. [Here Mr. Finney proceeded, at a considerable length, to comment on the 7th chapter of Romans, but as he has since concluded to give a separate lecture on that subject, these remarks are omitted here. He showed how Paul had struggled, and labored, under the motives of law, until he absolutely despaired of help from that quarter; and how, when the gospel was brought to view, the chain was broken, and he found it easy to obey. He then proceeded:]

You may see the same in the experience of almost any convicted sinner, after he has become truly converted. He was convicted, the law was brought home to his mind, he struggled to fulfill the law, he was in agony, and then he was filled with joy and glory. Why? He was agonized under the law, he had no rest and no satisfaction, he tried to please God by keeping the law, he went about in pain all the day, he read the Bible, he tried to pray; but the Spirit of God was upon him, showing him his sins, and he had no relief. The more he attempts to help himself the deeper he sinks in despair. All the while, his heart is cold and selfish. But now let another principle be introduced, and let him be influenced by love to God. The same Holy Spirit is upon him, showing him the same sins that grieved and distressed him so before. But now he goes on his knees, his tears flow like water as he confesses his guilt, and his heart melts in joyful relentings, such as cannot be described, but easily understood by them that have felt it. Now he engages in performing the same duties that he tried before. But, O, how changed! The Spirit of God has broken his chains, and now he loves God and is filled with joy and peace in believing.

The same thing is seen in many professors of religion, who find religion a painful thing. They have much conviction, and perhaps much of what they call religion, but their minds are chiefly filled with doubts and fears, doubts and fears, all the time. By and by, perhaps, that same professor will come out, all at once, a different character. His religion now is not all complaints and sighs, but the love of God fills his heart, and he goes cheerfully and happily to his duty; and his soul is so light and happy in God, that he floats in an ocean of love and joy, and the peace that fills him is like a river.

Here, then, is the difference between the slavery of law and the liberty of the gospel. The liberty of the gospel does not consist in being freed from doing what the law requires, but in a man's being in such a state of mind that doing it is itself a pleasure, instead of a burden. What is the difference between slavery and freedom? The slave serves because he is obliged to do so, the freeman serves from choice. The man who is under the bondage of law does duty because conscience thunders in his ears if he does not obey, and he hopes to go to heaven if he does. The man who is in the liberty of the gospel does the same things because he loves to do them. One is influenced by selfishness, the other by disinterested benevolence.

REMARKS.

I. You can easily see, that if we believe the words and actions of most professors of religion, they have made a mistake; and that they have the religion of law, and not gospel religion. They are not constrained by the love of Christ, but moved by hopes and fears, and by the commandments of God. They have gone no farther in religion than to be convicted sinners. Within the last year, I have witnessed the regeneration of so many professors of religion, that I am led to fear that great multitudes in the church are yet under the law; and although they profess to depend on Christ for salvation, their faith is not that which works by love.

II. Some persons are all faith, without works. These are Antinomians. Others are all works and no faith. These are Legalists. In all ages of the church, men have inclined first to one of these extremes, and then over to the other. Sometimes they are settled down on their lees, pretending to be all faith, and waiting God's time. Then they get roused up and dash on in works, without regard to the motive from which they act.

III. You see the true character of those professors of religion who are forever crying out "Legality!" as soon as they are pressed up to holiness. When I first began to preach, I found this spirit in many places; so that the moment Christians were urged up to duty, the cry would rise, This is legal preaching, do preach the gospel; salvation is by faith, not by duty; you ought to comfort saints, not to distress them. All this was nothing but rank Antinomianism.

On the other hand, the same class of churches now complain, if you preach faith to them, and show them what is the true nature of gospel faith. They now want to do something, and insist that no preaching is good that does not excite them, and stir them up to good works. They are all for doing, doing, doing, and will be dissatisfied with preaching that discriminates between true and false faith, and urges obedience of the heart, out of love to God. The Antinomians wait for God to produce right feelings in them. The Legalists undertake to get right feelings by going to work. It is true that going to work is the way, when the church feels right, to perpetuate and cherish right feelings. But it is not the way to get right feeling, in the first place, to dash right into the work, without any regard to the motives of the heart.

IV. Real Christians are a stumbling block to both parties; to those who wait God's time and do nothing, and to those who bustle about with no faith. The true Christian acts under such a love to God and to his fellow man, and he labors to pull sinners out of the fire with such earnestness, that the waiting party cry out, "O, he is getting up an excitement; he is going to work in his own strength; he don't believe in the necessity of divine influences; we ought to feel our dependence; let us wait God's time, and not try to get up a revival without God." So they sit down and fold their hands, and sing, "We feel our dependence, we feel our dependence; wait God's time; we don't trust in our own works." On the other hand, the legalists when once they get roused to bustle about, will not see but their religion is the same with the real Christian. They make as strenuous outward efforts, and suppose themselves to be actuated by the same spirit.

You will rarely see a revival, in which this does not show itself. If the body of the church are awakened to duty, and have the spirit of prayer and zeal for the conversion of sinners, there will be some who sit still and complain that the church are depending on their own strength, and others very busy and noisy, but without any feeling; while the third class are so full of love and compassion to sinners that they can hardly eat or sleep, and yet so humble and tender that you would imagine they felt themselves to be nothing. The legalist, with his dry zeal, makes a great noise, deceives himself, perhaps, and thinks he is acting just like a Christian. But mark! The true Christian is stirring and active in the service of Christ, but moves with the holy fire that burns within his own bosom. The legalist depends on some protracted meeting, or some other influence from without, to excite him to do his duty.

V. You see why the religion of some persons is so steady and uniform, and that of others, is so fitful and evanescent. You will find some individuals, who seem to be always engaged in religion.

Talk to them any time, on the subject, and their souls will kindle. Others are awake only now and then. Once in a while you may find them full of zeal. The truth is, when one has the anointing that abides, he has something that is durable. But if his religion is only that of the law, he will only have just so much of it as he has of conviction at the present moment, and his religion will be fitful and evanescent, of course.

VI. You see why some are so anxious to get to heaven, while others are so happy here. There are some, who have such a love for souls, and such a desire to have Christ's kingdom built upon earth, that they are perfectly happy here, and willing to live and labor for God, as long as He chooses to have them. Nay, if they were sent to hell, and permitted to labor there for souls, they would be happy. While others talk as if people were never to expect true enjoyment in this life; but when they get to heaven, they expect to be happy. One class have no enjoyment but in hope. The other has already the reality, the very substance of heaven begun in the soul.

Now, beloved, I have as particularly as I could in the time, pointed out to you the distinction between the religion of the law and the religion of the gospel. And now, what religion have you? True religion is always the same, and consists in disinterested love to God and man. Have you that kind of religion? Or have you the kind that consists, not in disinterested love, but in the pursuit of happiness as the great end. Which have you? The fruits of the Spirit are love, joy, peace.—There is no condemnation of such religion. But if any man have not the spirit of Christ, he is none of His.—Now, don't make a mistake here, and suffer yourselves to go down to hell with a lie in your right hand, because you have the religion of the law. The Jews failed here, while the Gentiles attained true holiness by the gospel. O, how many are deceived, and are acting under legal considerations, while they know nothing of the real religion of the gospel!

LECTURE V.

JUSTIFICATION BY FAITH.

TEXT:—"Knowing that a man is not justified by the works of the law, but by the faith of Jesus Christ, even we have believed in Jesus Christ, that we might be justified by the faith of Christ, and not by the works of the law: for by the works of the law shall no flesh be justified."

This last sentiment is expressed in the same terms, in the 3rd chapter of Romans. The subject of the present lecture, as I announced last week, is Justification by Faith. The order which I propose to pursue in the discussion is this:

I. Show what justification by law, or legal justification, is.

II. Show that by the deeds of the law no flesh can be justified.

III. Show what gospel justification is.

IV. Show what is the effect of gospel justification, or the state into which it brings a person that is justified.

V. Show that gospel justification is *by faith*.

VI. Answer some inquiries which arise in many minds on this subject.

I. I am to show what legal justification is.

1. In its general legal sense it means not guilty. To justify an individual in this sense, is to declare that he is not guilty of any breach of the law. It is affirming that he has committed no crime. It is pronouncing him innocent.

2. More technically, it is a form of pleading to a charge of crime, where the individual who is charged admits the fact, but brings forward an excuse, on which he claims that he had a right to do as he did, or that he is not blameworthy. Thus, if a person is charged with murder, the plea of justification admits that he killed the man, but alleges either that it was done in self-defense and he had a right to kill him, or that it was by unavoidable accident, and he could not help it. In either case, the plea of justification admits the fact, but denies the guilt, on the ground of a sufficient excuse.

II. I am to show that by the deeds of the law there shall no flesh be justified. And this is true under either form of justification.

1. Under the first, or general form of justification. In this case, the burden of proof is on the accuser, who is held to prove the facts

charged. And in this case, he only needs to prove that a crime has been committed once. If it is proved once, the individual is guilty. He cannot be justified, in this way, by the law. He is found guilty. It is not available for him to urge that he has done more good than hurt, or that he has kept God's law longer than he has broken it, but he must make it out that he has fulfilled every jot and tittle of the law. Who can be justified by the law in this way? No one.

2. Nor under the second, or technical form of justification. In this case, the burden of proof lies on him who makes the plea. When he pleads in justification he admits the fact alleged, and therefore he must make good his excuse, or fail. There are two points to be regarded. The thing pleaded as an excuse must be *true*, and it must be a good and sufficient *excuse* or justification, not a frivolous apology, or one that does not meet the case. If it is not true, or if it is insufficient, and especially if it reflects on the court or government, it is an infamous aggravation of his offense. You will see the bearing of this remark, by and by.

I will now mention some of the prominent reasons which sinners are in the habit of pleading as a justification, and will show what is the true nature and bearing of these excuses, and the light in which they stand before God. I have not time to name all these pleas, but will only refer to two of each of the classes I have described, those which are good if true, and those which are true but unavailing.

(1.) Sinners often plead their *sinful nature* as a justification.

This excuse is a good one, if it is true. If it is true, as they pretend, that God has given them a nature which is itself sinful, and the necessary actings of their nature are sin, it is a good excuse for sin, and in the face of heaven and earth, and at the day of judgment, will be a good plea in justification. God must annihilate the reason of all the rational universe, before they will ever blame you for sin if God made you sin, or if He gave you a nature that is itself sinful. How can your nature be sinful? What is sin? Sin is a transgression of the law. There is no other sin but this. Now, does the law say you must not have such a nature as you have? Nothing like it.

The fact is, this doctrine overlooks the distinction between sin and the occasion of sin. The bodily appetites and constitutional susceptibilities of body and mind, when strongly excited, become the occasions of sin. So it was with Adam. No one will say that Adam had a sinful nature. But he had, by his constitution, an appetite for food and a desire for knowledge. These were not sinful, but were as God made them, and were necessary to fit him to live in this world, as a subject of God's moral government. But being strongly excited, as you know, led to prohibited indulgence, and thus became the occasions of his sinning against God. They were innocent in themselves, but he yielded to them in a sinful manner, and that was his sin. When the sinner talks about his sinful nature as a justification, he confounds these innocent appetites and susceptibilities, with sin itself. By so doing, he in fact charges God foolishly, and accuses Him of giving him a sinful nature, when in fact his nature, in all its elements, is essential to moral agency, and God has made it as well as it could be made, and perfectly adapted to the circumstances in which he lives in this world. The truth is, man's nature is all right, and is as well fitted to love and obey God as to hate and disobey Him. Sinner! the day is not far distant, when it will be known whether this is a good excuse or not. Then you will see whether you can face your Maker down in this way; and when He charges you with sin, turn round and throw the blame back upon Him.

Do you inquire what influence Adam's sin has then had in producing the sin of his posterity? I answer, it has subjected them to *aggravated temptation*, but has by no means rendered their nature *in itself* sinful.

2. Another excuse coming under the same class, is *inability*. This also is a good excuse if it is true. If sinners are really unable to obey God, this is a good plea in justification. When you are charged with sin, in not obeying the laws of God, you have only to show, if you can, by good proof, that God has required what you were not able to perform, and the whole intelligent universe will resound with the verdict of *not guilty*. If you have not natural power to obey God, they must give this verdict, or cease to be reasonable beings. For it is a first law of reason, that no being is obliged to do what he has no power to do.

Suppose God should require you to undo something which you have done. This, everyone will see, is a natural impossibility. Now, are you to blame for not doing it? God requires repentance of past sins, and not that you should undo them. Now, suppose it was your duty, on the first of January, to warn a certain individual, who is now dead. Are you now under obligation to warn that individual? No. That is an impossibility. All that God can now require is, that you should repent. It never can be your duty, now, to warn that sinner. God may hold you responsible for not doing your duty to him when it was in your power. But it would be absurd to make it your duty to do what it is not in your power to do.

This plea being false, and throwing the blame of tyranny on God, is an infamous aggravation of the offense. If God requires you to do what you have no power to do, it is tyranny. And what God requires is on penalty of eternal death——He threatens an infinite penalty for not doing what you have no power to do, and so He is an infinite tyrant. This plea, then, charges God with infinite tyranny, and is not only insufficient for the sinner's justification, but is a horrible aggravation of his offense.

Let us vary the case a little. Suppose God requires you to repent for not doing what you never had natural ability to do. You must either repent, then, of not doing what you had no natural power to do, or you must go to hell. Now, you can neither repent of this, nor can He make you repent of it. What is repentance? It is to blame yourself and justify God. But if you had no power, you can do neither. It is a natural impossibility that a rational being should ever blame himself for not doing what he is conscious he had not power to do. Nor can you justify God. Until the laws of mind are reversed, the verdict of all intelligent beings must pronounce it infinite tyranny to require that which there is no power to perform.

Suppose God should call you to account, and require you to repent for not flying. By what process can He make you blame yourself for not flying, when you are conscious that you have no wings, and no power to fly? If He could cheat you into the belief that you had the power, and make you believe a lie, then you might repent. But what sort of a way is that for God to take with His creatures?

What do you mean, sinner, by bringing such an excuse? Do you mean to have it go, that you have never sinned? It is a strange contradiction you make, when you admit that you ought to repent, and in the next breath say you have no power to repent. You ought to take your ground, one way or the other. If you mean to rely on this excuse, come out with it in full, and take your ground before God's bar, and say, "Lord, I am not going to repent at all——I am not under any obligation to repent, for I have not power to obey thy law, and therefore I plead not guilty absolutely, for I have never sinned!"

In which of these ways can any one of you be justified? Will you, dare you take ground on this excuse, and throw back the blame upon God?

3. Another excuse which sinners offer for their continued impenitence is their *wicked heart.*

This excuse is true, but it is not sufficient. The first two that I mentioned, you recollect were good if they had been true, but they were false. This is true, but is no excuse. What is a wicked heart? It is not the bodily organ which we call the heart, but the affection of the soul, the wicked disposition, the wicked feelings, the actings of the mind. If these will justify you, they will justify the devil himself. Has he not as wicked a heart as you have? Suppose you had committed murder, and you should be put on trial and plead this plea. "It is true," you would say, "I killed the man, but then I have such a thirst for blood, and such a hatred of mankind, that I cannot help committing murder, whenever I have an opportunity." "Horrible!" the judge would exclaim, "Horrible! Let the gallows be set up immediately, and let this fellow be hung before I leave the bench; such a wretch ought not to live an hour. Such a plea! Why, that is the very reason he ought to be hung, if he has such a thirst for blood, that no man is safe." Such is the sinner's plea of a wicked heart in justification of sin. Out of thine own mouth will I condemn thee, thou wicked servant.

4. Another great excuse which people make, is *the conduct of Christians.*

Ask many a man among your neighbors why he is not religious, and he will point you at once to the conduct of Christians as his excuse. "These Christians," he will say, "are no better than anybody else; when I see them live as they profess, I shall think it time for me to attend to religion." Thus he is hiding behind the sins of Christians. He shows that he knows how Christians ought to live, and therefore he cannot plead that he has sinned through ignorance. But what does it amount to as a ground of justification? I admit the fact, that Christians behave very badly, and do much that is entirely contrary to their profession. But is that a good excuse for you? So far from it, this is itself one of the strongest reasons why you ought to be religious. You know so well how Christians ought to live, you are bound to show an example. If you had followed them ignorantly, because you did not know any better, and had fallen into sin in that way, it would be a different case. But the plea, as it stands, shows that you know they are wrong, which is the very reason why you ought to be right, and exert a better influence than they do. Instead of following them and doing wrong because they do, you ought to break off from them, and rebuke them, and pray for them, and try to lead them in a better way. This excuse, then, is true in fact, but unavailable in justification. You only make it an excuse for charging God foolishly, and instead of clearing you, it only adds to your dreadful, damning guilt. A fine plea this, to get behind some deacon, or some elder in the church, and there shoot your arrows of malice and caviling at God!

Who among you, then, can be justified by the law?—Who has kept it? Who has got a good excuse for breaking it? Who dare go to the bar of God on these pleas, and face his Maker with such apologies?

III. I am to show what Gospel Justification is.

First, Negatively.

1. Gospel Justification is not the imputed righteousness of Jesus Christ.

Under the gospel, sinners are not justified by having the obedience of Jesus Christ set down to their account, as if He had obeyed the law for them, or in their stead. It is not an uncommon mistake to suppose that when sinners are justified under the gospel they are accounted righteous in the eye of the law, by having the obedience or righteousness of Christ imputed to them. I have not time to go into an examination of this subject now. I can only say that this idea is absurd and impossible, for this reason, that Jesus Christ was bound to obey the law for himself, and could no more perform works of supererogation, or obey on our account, than anybody else. Was it not His duty to love the Lord his God, with all His heart and soul and mind and strength, and to love His neighbor as himself? Certainly; and if He had not done so, it would have been sin. The only work of supererogation He could perform was to submit to sufferings that were not deserved. This is called His obedience unto death, and this is set down to our account. But if His obedience of the law is set down to our account, why are we called on to repent and obey the law ourselves? Does God exact double service, yes, triple service, first to have the law obeyed by the surety for us, then that He must suffer the penalty for us, and then that we must repent and obey ourselves? No such thing is demanded. It is not required that the obedience of another should be imputed to us. All we owe is perpetual obedience to the law of benevolence. And for this there can be no substitute. If we fail of this we must endure the penalty, or receive a free pardon.

2. Justification by faith does not mean that faith is accepted as a substitute for personal holiness, or that by an arbitrary constitution, faith is imputed to us *instead* of personal obedience to the law.

Some suppose that justification is this, that the necessity of personal holiness is set aside, and that God arbitrarily dispenses with the requirement of the law, and imputes faith as a substitute. But this is not the way. Faith is accounted for just what it is, and not for something else that it is not. Abraham's faith was imputed unto him for righteousness, because it was itself an act of righteousness, and because it worked by love, and thus produced holiness. Justifying faith is holiness, so far as it goes, and produces holiness of heart and life, and is imputed to the believer as holiness, not instead of holiness.

3. Nor does justification by faith imply that a sinner is justified by faith without good works, or personal holiness.

Some suppose that justification by faith only, is without any regard to good works, or holiness. They have understood this from what Paul has said, where he insists so largely on justification by faith. But it should be borne in mind that Paul was combating the error of the Jews, who expected to be justified by obeying the law. In opposition to *this error*, Paul insists on it that justification is by faith, without works of *law*. He does not mean that good works are unnecessary to justification, but that works of law are not good works, because they spring from legal considerations, from hope and fear, and not from faith that works by love. But inasmuch as a false theory had crept into the church on the other side, James took up the matter, and showed them that they had misunderstood Paul. And to show this, he takes the case of Abraham. "Was not Abraham our father justified by works when he had offered Isaac his son upon the altar? Seest thou how faith wrought with his works, and by works was faith made perfect?—-And the scripture was fulfilled, which saith, Abraham believed God, and it was imputed unto him for righteousness: and he was called the Friend of God. Ye see then how that by works a man is justified, and not by faith only." This epistle was supposed to contradict Paul, and some of the ancient churches rejected it on that account. But they overlooked the fact that Paul was speaking of one kind of works, and James of another. Paul was speaking of works performed from legal motives. But he has everywhere insisted on good works springing from faith, or the righteousness of faith, as indispensable to salvation. All that he denies is, that works of law, or works grounded on legal motives, have anything to do in the matter of justification. And James teaches the same thing, when he teaches that men are justified, not by works nor by faith alone, but by faith together with the works of faith; or as Paul expresses it, faith that works by love. You will bear in mind that I am speaking of gospel justification, which is very different from legal justification.

Secondly, Positively.

4. Gospel justification, or justification by faith, consists in *pardon and acceptance with God.*

When we say that men are justified by faith and holiness, we do not mean that they are accepted on the ground of law, but that they are *treated as if* they were righteous, on account of their faith and works of faith. This is the method which God takes, in justifying a sinner. Not that faith is the foundation of justification. The foundation is in Christ. But this is the manner in which sinners are pardoned, and accepted, and justified, that if they repent, believe, and become holy, their past sins shall be forgiven, for the sake of Christ.

Here it will be seen how justification under the gospel differs from justification under the law. Legal justification is a declaration of actual innocence and freedom from blame. Gospel justification is pardon and acceptance, *as if* he was righteous, but on other grounds than his own obedience. When the apostle says, "By deeds of law shall no flesh be justified", he uses justification as a lawyer, in a strictly legal sense. But when he speaks of justification by faith, he speaks not of legal justification, but of a person's being *treated as if* he were righteous.

IV. I will now proceed to show the effect of this method of justification; or the state into which it brings those who are justified.

1. The first item to be observed is, that when an individual is pardoned, the penalty of the law is released. The first effect of a pardon is to arrest and set aside the execution of the penalty. It admits that the penalty was deserved, but sets it aside. Then, so far as punishment is concerned, the individual has no more to fear from the law, than if he had never transgressed. He is entirely released. Those, then, who are justified by true faith, as soon as they are pardoned, need no more be influenced by fear or punishment. The penalty is as effectually set aside, as if it had never been incurred.

2. The next effect of pardon is, to remove all the liabilities incurred in consequence of transgression, such as forfeiture of goods, or incapacity for being a witness, or holding any office under government. A real pardon removes all these, and restores the individual back to where he was before he transgressed. So, under the government of God, the pardoned sinner is restored to the favor of God. He is brought back into a new relation, and stands before God and is treated by Him, so far as the law is concerned, as if he were innocent. It does not suppose or declare him to be really innocent, but the pardon restores him to the same state as if he were.

3. Another operation of pardon under God's government is, that the individual is restored to sonship. In other words, it brings him into such a relation to God, that he is received and treated as really a child of God.

Suppose the son of a sovereign on the throne had committed murder, and was convicted and condemned to die. A pardon, then, would not only deliver him from death, but restore him to his place in the family. God's children have all gone astray, and entered into the service of the devil; but the moment a pardon issues to them, they are brought back; they receive a spirit of adoption, are sealed heirs of God, and restored to all the privileges of children of God.

4. Another thing effected by justification is to secure all needed grace to rescue themselves fully out of the snare of the devil, and all the innumerable entanglements in which they are involved by sin.

Beloved, if God were merely to pardon you, and then leave you to get out of sin as you could by yourselves, of what use would your pardon be to you? None in the world. If a child runs away from his father's house, and wanders in a forest, and falls into a deep pit, and the father finds him and undertakes to save him; if he merely pardons him for running away, it will be of no use, unless he lifts him up from the pit and leads him out of the forest. So in the scheme of redemption, whatever helps and aids you need, are all guaranteed, if you believe. If God undertakes to save you, he pledges all the light and grace and help that are necessary to break the chains of Satan and the entanglements of sin, and leads you back to your Father's house.

I know when individuals are first broken down under a sense of sin, and their hearts gush out with tenderness, they look over their past lives and feel condemned and see that it is all wrong, and then they break down at God's feet and give themselves away to Jesus

Christ; they rejoice greatly in the idea that they have done with sin. But in a little time they begin to feel the pressure of old habits and former influences, and they see so much to be done before they overcome them all, that they often get discouraged, and cry, "O, what shall I do, with so many enemies to meet, and so little strength of resolution or firmness of purpose to overcome them?" Let me tell you, beloved, that if God has undertaken to save you, you have only to keep near to Him, and He will carry you through. You need not fear your enemies. Though the heavens should thunder and the earth rock, and the elements melt, you need not tremble, nor fear for enemies without or enemies within. God is for you, and who can be against you? "Who is he that condemneth? It is Christ that died, yea, rather that is risen again, who is even at the right hand of God, who also maketh intercession for us."

5. Justification enlists all the divine attributes in your favor, as much as if you had never sinned.

See that holy angel, sent on an errand of love to some distant part of the universe. God's eye follows him, and if He sees him likely to be injured in any way, all the divine attributes are enlisted at once to protect and sustain him. Just as absolutely are they all pledged for you, if you are justified, to protect and support and save you. Notwithstanding you are not free from remaining sin, and are so totally unworthy of God's love, yet if you are truly justified, the only wise and eternal God is pledged for your salvation. And shall you tremble and be faint-hearted, with such support?

If a human government pardons a criminal, it is then pledged to protect him as a subject, as much as if he had never committed a crime. So it is when God justifies a sinner. The Apostle says, "Being justified by faith, we have peace with God." Henceforth, God is on his side, and pledged as his faithful and eternal Friend.

Gospel justification differs from legal justification, in this respect: If the law justifies an individual, it holds no longer than he remains innocent. As soon as he transgresses once, his former justification is of no more avail. But when the gospel justifies a sinner, it is not so; but "if any man sin, we have an Advocate with the Father, Jesus Christ the righteous." A new relation is now constituted, entirely peculiar. The sinner is now brought out from under the covenant of works, and placed under the covenant of grace. He no longer retains God's favor by the tenure of absolute and sinless obedience. If he sins, now, he is not thrust back again under the law, but receives the benefit of the new covenant. If he is justified by faith;

and so made a child of God, he receives the treatment of a child, and is corrected, and chastised, and humbled, and brought back again. "The gifts and calling of God are without repentance." The meaning of that is not, that God calls and saves the sinner without his repenting, but that God never changes His mind when once he undertakes the salvation of a soul.

I know this is thought by some to be very dangerous doctrine, to teach that believers are perpetually justified—because, say they, it will embolden men to sin. Indeed! To tell a man that has truly repented of sin, and heartily renounced sin, and sincerely desires to be free from sin, that God will help him and certainly give him the victory over sin, will embolden him to commit sin! Strange logic that! If this doctrine emboldens any man to commit sin, it only shows that he never did repent; that he never hated sin, and never loved God for His own sake, but only feigned repentance, and if he loved God it was only a selfish love, because he thought God was going to do him a favor. If he truly hated sin, the consideration that notwithstanding all his unworthiness God had received him as a child, and would give him a child's treatment, is the very thing to break him down and melt his heart in the most godly sorrow. O, how often has the child of God, melted in adoring wonder at the goodness of God, in using means to bring him back, instead of sending him to hell, as he deserved! What consideration is calculated to bring him lower in the dust, than the thought that notwithstanding all God had done for him, and the gracious help God was always ready to afford him, he should wander away again, when his name was written in the Lamb's book of life!

6. It secures the discipline of the covenant. God has pledged Himself that if any who belong to Christ go astray, He will use the discipline of the covenant, and bring them back. In the eighty-ninth psalm, God says, putting David for Christ, "If his children forsake my law, and walk not in my judgments; if they break my statutes, and keep not my commandments; then will I visit their transgression with the rod, and their iniquity with stripes. Nevertheless my loving kindness will I not utterly take from him, nor suffer my faithfulness to fail. My covenant will I not break, nor alter the thing that is gone out of my lips."

Thus you see that professors of religion may always expect to be more readily visited with God's judgments, if they get out of the way, than the impenitent. The sinner may grow fat, and live in riches, and have no bands in his death, all according to God's established principles of government. But let a child of God forsake his God, and go after riches or any other worldly object, and as certain as he is a child, God will smite him with His rod. And when he is smitten and brought back, he will say with the Psalmist, "It is good for me that I have been afflicted, that I might learn thy statutes. Before I was afflicted, I went astray, but now have I kept thy word." Perhaps some of you have known what it is to be afflicted in this way, and to feel that it was good.

7. Another effect of gospel justification is, to *insure sanctification.* It not only insures all the means of sanctification, but the actual accomplishment of the work, so that the individual who is truly converted, will surely persevere in obedience till he is fitted for heaven and actually saved.

V. I am to show that this is justification by *faith.*

Faith is the medium by which the blessing is conveyed to the believer. The proof of this is in the Bible. The text declares it expressly. "Knowing that a man is not justified by the works of the law, but by the faith of Jesus Christ, even we have believed in Jesus Christ, that we might be justified by the faith of Christ, and not by the works of the law: for by the works of the law shall no flesh he justified." The subject is too often treated of in the New Testament to be necessary to go into a labored proof. It is manifest, from the necessity of the case, that if men are saved at all, they must be justified in this way, and not by works of law, for "by the deeds of the law shall no flesh be justified."

VI. I will now answer several inquiries which may naturally arise in your minds, growing out of this subject.

1. "Why is justification said to be by *faith*, rather than by repentance, or love, or any other grace."

Answer. It is no where said that men are justified or saved *for* faith, as the ground of their pardon, but only that they are justified *by* faith, as the medium or instrument. If it is asked why faith is appointed as the instrument, rather than any other exercise of the mind, the answer is, because of the nature and effect of faith. No other exercise *could be* appointed. What is faith? It is that confidence in God which leads us to love and obey Him. We are therefore justified by faith *because we are sanctified by faith.* Faith is the appointed instrument of our justification, because it is the natural instrument of sanctification. It is the instrument of bringing us back to obedience, and therefore is designated as the means of obtaining the blessings of that return. It is not *imputed* to us, by an arbitrary act, FOR what it is not, but *for what it is*, as the foundation of all real obedience to God. This is the reason why faith is made the medium through which pardon comes. It is simply set down to us for what it really is; because it first leads us to obey God, from a principle of love to God. We are forgiven our sins *on account* of Christ. It is our duty to repent and obey God, and when we do so, this is imputed to us as what it is, holiness, or obedience to God. But for the forgiveness of our past sins, we must rely on Christ. And therefore justification is said to be by faith in Jesus Christ.

2. The second query is of great importance: "*What is* justifying faith? What must I believe, in order to be saved?"

Answer. (1) Negatively, justifying faith does not consist in believing that your sins are forgiven. If that was necessary, you would have to believe it *before* it was done, or to believe a lie. Remember, your sins are not forgiven *until* you believe. But if saving faith is believing that they are already forgiven, it is believing a thing before it takes place, which is absurd. You cannot believe your sins are forgiven, before you have evidence that they are forgiven; and you cannot have evidence that they are forgiven until it is true that they are forgiven, and they cannot be forgiven until you exercise saving faith. Therefore saving faith must be believing something else.

Nor (2) does saving faith consist in believing that you shall be saved at all. You have no right to believe that you shall be saved at all, until after you have exercised justifying or saving faith.

But (3) justifying faith consists in believing the atonement of Christ, or believing the record which God has given of his Son.

The correctness of this definition has been doubted by some; and I confess my own mind has undergone a change on this point. It is said that Abraham *believed God*, and it was imputed to him for righteousness. But what did Abraham believe? He believed that he should have a son. Was this all? By no means. But his faith included the *great blessing* that depended on that event, that the Messiah, the Savior of the world, should spring from him. This was the great subject of the Abrahamic covenant, and it depended on his having a son. Of course, Abraham's faith included the "Desire of all nations," and was faith in Christ. The apostle Paul has showed this, at full length, in the 3d chapter of Galatians, that the sum of the covenant was, "In thee shall all nations be blessed." In verse 16, he says, "Now to Abraham and his seed were the promises made. He saith not, And to seeds as of many; but as of one, And to thy seed, which is Christ."

It is said that in the 11th of Hebrews, the saints are not all spoken of as having believed in Christ. But if you examine carefully, you will find that in all cases, faith in Christ is either included in what they believed, or fairly implied by it. Take the case of Abel. "By faith Abel offered unto God a more excellent sacrifice than Cain, by which he obtained witness that he was righteous, God testifying of his gifts: and by it he being dead yet speaketh." Why was his sacrifice more excellent? Because, by offering the firstlings of his flock, he recognized the necessity of the atonement, and that "without the shedding of blood there is no remission." Cain was a proud infidel, and offered the fruits of the ground, as a mere thank offering, for the blessings of Providence, without any admission that he was a sinner, and needed an atonement, as the ground on which he could hope for pardon.

Some suppose that an individual might exercise justifying faith, while denying the divinity and atonement of Jesus Christ. I deny this. The whole sum and substance of revelation, like converging rays, all center on Jesus Christ, His divinity and atonement. All that the prophets and other writers of the Old Testament say about salvation comes to Him. The Old Testament and the New, all the types and shadows point to Him. All the Old Testament saints were saved by faith in Him. Their faith terminated in the coming Messiah, as that of the New Testament saints did in the Messiah already come. In the 15th chapter of 1 Corinthians, the apostle Paul shows what place *he* would assign to this doctrine: "For I delivered unto you first of all that which I also received, how that Christ died for our sins according to the scriptures; and that he was buried, and that he rose again the third day according to the scriptures." Mark that expression, "first of all." It proves that Paul preached that Christ died for sinners, as the "first" or primary doctrine of the gospel. And so you will find it, from one end of the Bible to the other, that the attention of men was directed to this new and living way, as the only way of salvation. This truth is the only truth that can sanctify men. They may believe a thousand other things, but this is the great source of sanctification, "God in Christ, reconciling the world unto himself." And this alone can therefore be justifying faith.

There may be many other acts of faith, that may be right and acceptable to God. But nothing is justifying faith, but believing the record that God has given of His Son. Simply believing what God has revealed on any point, is an act of faith; but justifying faith fastens on Christ, takes hold of His atonement, and embraces Him as the only ground of pardon and salvation. There may be faith in prayer, the faith that is in exercise in offering up prevailing prayer to God. But that is not properly justifying faith.

3. "When are men justified?"

This is also an inquiry often made. I answer—-Just as soon as they believe in Christ, with the faith which worketh by love. Sinner, you need not go home from this meeting under the wrath of Almighty God. You may be justified here, on the spot, now, if you will only believe in Christ. Your pardon is ready, made out and sealed with the broad seal of heaven; and the blank will be filled up, and the gracious pardon delivered, as soon as, by one act of faith, you receive Jesus Christ as He is offered in the gospel.

4. "How can I know whether I am in a state of justification or not?""

Answer. You can know it in no way, except by inference. God has not revealed it in the scriptures, that you, or any other individuals, are justified; but He has set down the characteristics of a justified person, and declared that all who have these characteristics *are justified*.

(1.) Have you the witness of the Spirit? All who are justified have this. They have intercourse with the Holy Ghost, He explains the Scriptures to them, and leads them to see their meaning, He leads them to the Son and to the Father, and reveals the Son in them, and reveals the Father. Have you this? If you have, you are justified. If not, you are yet in your sins.

(2.) Have you the fruits of the Spirit? They are love, joy, peace, and so on. These are matters of human consciousness; have you them? If so, you are justified.

(3.) Have you peace with God? The apostle says, "Being justified by faith, we have peace with God." Christ says to his disciples, "My peace I give unto you; not as the world giveth give I unto you." And again, "Come unto me, all ye that labor and are heavy laden, and I will give you rest." Do you find *rest* in Christ? Is your peace like a river, flowing gently through your soul, and filling you with calm and heavenly delight? Or do you feel a sense of condemnation before God?

Do you feel a sense of acceptance with God, of pardoned sin, of communion with God? This must be a matter of experience, if it exists. Don't imagine you *can be in* a justified state, and yet have no evidence of it. You may have great peace in reality, filling your soul, and yet not draw the inference that you are justified. I remember the time, when my mind was in a state of such sweet peace, that it seemed to me as if all nature was listening for God to speak; but yet I was not aware that this was the peace of God, or that it was evidence of my being in a justified state. I thought I had lost all my conviction, and actually undertook to bring back the sense of condemnation that I had before. I did not draw the inference that I was justified, till after the love of God was so shed abroad in my soul by the Holy Ghost, that I was compelled to cry out, "Lord, it is enough, I can bear no more." I do not believe it possible for the sense of condemnation to remain, where the act of pardon is already past.

(4.) Have you the spirit of adoption? If you are justified, you are also adopted, as one of God's dear children, and He has sent forth His Spirit into your heart, so that you naturally cry, "Abba, Father!" He seems to you just like a father, and you want to call him father. Do you know anything of this? It is one thing to *call* God your father in heaven, and another thing to *feel* towards Him as a father. This is one evidence of a justified state, when God gives the spirit of adoption.

REMARKS.

I. I would go around, to all my dear hearers tonight, and ask them one by one, "Are you in a state of justification? Do you honestly think you are justified?"

I have briefly run over the subject, and showed what justification is not, and what it is, how you can be saved, and the evidences of justification. Have you it? Would you dare to die now? Suppose the loud thunders of the last trumpet were now to shake the universe, and you should see the Son of God coming to judgment—are you ready? Could you look up calmly and say, "Father, this is a solemn sight, but Christ has died, and God has justified me, and who is he that shall condemn me?"

II. If you think you ever was justified, and yet have not at present the evidence of it, I want to make an inquiry. *Are you under the discipline of the covenant?*—If not, have you any reason to believe you ever were justified? God's covenant with you, if you belong to Christ, is this—"If they backslide, I will visit their iniquity with the rod, and chasten them with stripes." Do you feel the stripes? Is

God awakening your mind, and convicting your conscience, is He smiting you? If not, where are the evidences that He is dealing with you as a son? If you are not walking with God, and at the same time are not under chastisement, you cannot have any good reason to believe you are God's children.

III. Those of you who have evidence that you are justified, should maintain your relation to God, and live up to your real privileges. This is immensely important. There is no virtue in being distrustful and unbelieving. It is important to your growth in grace. One reason why many Christians do not grow in grace is, that they are afraid to claim the privileges of God's children which belong to them. Rely upon it, beloved, this is no virtuous humility, but criminal unbelief. If you have the evidence that you are justified, take the occasion from it to press forward to holiness of heart, and come to God with all the boldness that an angel would, and know how near you are to Him. It is your duty to do so. Why should you hold back? Why are you afraid to recognize the covenant of grace, in its full extent? Here are the provisions of your Father's house, all ready and free; and are you converted and justified, and restored to His favor, and yet afraid to sit down at your Father's table? Do not plead that you are so unworthy. This is nothing but self-righteousness and unbelief. True, you are so unworthy. But if you are justified, that is no longer a bar. It is now your duty to take hold of the promises as belonging to you. Take any promise you can find in the Bible, that is applicable, and go with it to your Father, and plead it before Him, believing. Do you think He will deny it? These exceeding great and precious promises were given you for this very purpose, that you may become a partaker of the divine nature. Why then should you doubt? Come along, beloved, come along up to the privileges that belong to you, and take hold of the love, and peace, and joy, offered to you in this holy gospel.

IV. If you are not in a state of justification, however much you have done, and prayed, and suffered, you are nothing. If you have not believed in Christ, if you have not received and trusted in Him, as He is set forth in the gospel, you are yet in a state of condemnation and wrath. You may have been, for weeks and months, and even for years, groaning with distress, but for all that, you are still in the gall of bitterness. Here you see the line drawn; the moment you pass this, you are in a state of justification.

Dear hearer, are you now in a state of wrath? Now believe in Christ. All your waiting and groaning will not bring you any nearer. Do you say you want more conviction? I tell you to come now to Christ. Do you say you must wait till you prayed more? What is the use of praying in unbelief? Will the prayers of a condemned rebel avail? Do you say you are so unworthy? But Christ died for just such as you. He comes right to you now, on your seat. Where do you sit? Where is that individual I am speaking to? Sinner, you need not wait. You need not go home in your sins, with that heavy load on your heart. Now is the day of salvation. Hear the word of God: "If thou believe in thine heart in the Lord Jesus Christ, and if thou confess with thy mouth that God raised him from the dead, thou shalt be saved."

Do you say, "What must I believe?" Believe just what God says of his Son; believe any of those great fundamental truths which God has revealed respecting the way of salvation, and rest your soul on it, and you shall be saved. Will you now trust Jesus Christ to dispose of you? Have you confidence enough in Christ to leave yourself with Him, to dispose of your body and your soul, for time and eternity? Can you say

"Here, Lord, I give myself away; 'Tis all that I can do?"

Perhaps you are trying to pray yourself out of your difficulties *before* coming to Christ. Sinner, it will do no good. Now, cast yourself down at His feet, and leave your soul in His hands. Say to Him, "Lord, I give myself to thee, with all my powers of body and of mind; use me and dispose of me, as thou wilt, for thine own glory; I know thou wilt do right, and that is all I desire." Will you do it?

LECTURE VI.

SANCTIFICATION BY FAITH.

TEXT:—"Do we then make void the law through faith? God forbid; yea, we establish the law."— Romans iii. 31.

The apostle had been proving that all mankind, both Jews and Gentiles, were in their sins, and refuting the doctrine so generally entertained by the Jews, that they were a holy people and saved by their works. He showed that justification can never be by works, but by faith. He then anticipates an objection, like this, "Are we to understand you as teaching that the law of God is abrogated and set aside by this plan of justification?" "By no means," says the apostle, "we rather establish the law." In treating of this subject, I design to pursue the following order:

I. Show that the gospel method of justification does not set aside or repeal the law.

II. That it rather establishes the law, by producing true obedience to it, and as the only means that does this.

The greatest objection to the doctrine of Justification by Faith has always been, that it is inconsistent with good morals, conniving at sin, and opening the flood-gates of iniquity. It has been said, that to maintain that men are not to depend on their own good behavior for salvation, but are to be saved by faith in another, is calculated to make men regardless of good morals, and to encourage them to live in sin, depending on Christ to justify them. By others, it has been maintained that the gospel does in fact release from obligation to obey the moral law, so that a more lax morality is permitted under the gospel than was allowed under the law.

I. I am to show that the gospel method of justification does not set aside the moral law.

1. It cannot be that this method of justification sets aside the moral law, because the gospel everywhere enforces obedience to the law, and lays down the same standard of holiness.

Jesus Christ adopted the very words of the moral law, "Thou shalt love the Lord thy God with all thy heart, and with all thy soul, and with all thy mind, and with all thy strength, and thy neighbor as thyself."

2. The conditions of the gospel are designed to sustain the moral law.

The gospel requires repentance, as the condition of salvation. What is repentance? The renunciation of sin. The man must repent of his breaches of the law of God, and return to obedience to the law. This is tantamount to a requirement of obedience.

3. The gospel maintains that the law is right.

If it did not maintain the law to its full extent, it might be said that Christ is the minister of sin.

4. By the gospel plan, the sanctions of the gospel are added to the sanctions of the law, to enforce obedience to the law.

The apostle says, "He that despised Moses' law, died without mercy under two or three witnesses: of how much sorer punishment, suppose ye, shall he be thought worthy, who hath trodden under foot the Son of God, and hath counted the blood of the covenant, wherewith he was sanctified, an unholy thing, and hath done despite unto the Spirit of grace?" Thus adding the awful sanctions of the gospel to those of the law, to enforce obedience to the precepts of the law.

II. I am to show that the doctrine of justification by faith produces sanctification, by producing the only true obedience to the law.

By this I mean, that when the mind understands this plan, and exercises faith in it, it naturally produces sanctification. Sanctification is holiness, and holiness is nothing but obedience to the law, consisting in love to God and love to man.

In support of the proposition that justification by faith produces true obedience to the law of God, my first position is, that sanctification never can be produced among selfish or wicked beings, by the law itself, separate from the considerations of the gospel, or the motives connected with justification by faith.

The motives of the law did not restrain those beings from committing sin, and it is absurd to suppose the same motives can *reclaim* them from sin, when they have fallen under the power of selfishness, and when sin is a confirmed by habit. The motives of the law lose a great part of their influence, when a being is once fallen. They even exert an opposite influence. The motives of the law, as viewed by a selfish mind, have a tendency to cause sin to abound. This is the experience of every sinner. When he sees the spirituality of the law, and does not see the motives of the gospel, it raises the pride of his heart, and confirms him in his rebellion. The case of the devil is an exhibition of what the law can do, with all its principles and sanctions, upon a wicked heart. He understands the law, sees its reasonableness, has experienced the blessedness of obedience, and knows full well that to return to obedience would restore his peace of mind. This he knows better than any sinner of our race, who never was holy, can know it, and yet it presents to his mind no such motives as reclaim him, but on the contrary, drive him to a returnless distance from obedience.

When obedience to the law is held forth to the sinner as the condition of life, immediately it sets him upon making self-righteous efforts. In almost every instance, the first effort of the awakened sinner is to obey the law. He thinks he must first make himself better, in some way, before he may embrace the gospel. He has no idea of the simplicity of the gospel plan of salvation by faith, offering eternal life as a mere gratuitous gift. Alarm the sinner with the penalty of the law, and he naturally, and by the very laws of his mind, sets himself to do better, to amend his life, and in some self-righteous manner obtain eternal life, under the influence of slavish fear. And the more the law presses him, the greater are his pharisaical efforts, while hope is left to him, that if he obeys he may be accepted. What else could you expect of him? He is purely selfish, and though he ought to submit at once to God, yet, as he does not understand the gospel terms of salvation, and his mind is of course first turned to the object of getting away from the danger of the penalty, he tries to get up to heaven some other way. I do not believe there is an instance in history, of a man who has submitted to God, until he has seen that salvation must be by faith, and that his own self-righteous strivings have no tendency to save him.

Again; if you undertake to produce holiness by legal motives, the very fear of failure has the effect to divert attention from the objects of love, from God and Christ. The sinner is all the while compassing Mount Sinai, and taking heed to his footsteps, to see how near he comes to obedience; and how can he get into the spirit of heaven?

Again; the penalty of the law has no tendency to produce love in the first instance. It may increase love in those who already have it, when they contemplate it as an exhibition of God's infinite holiness. The angels in heaven, and good men on earth, contemplate its propriety and fitness, and see in it the expression of the good will of God to His creatures, and it appears amiable and lovely, and increases their delight in God and their confidence towards Him. But it is right the reverse with the selfish man. He sees the penalty hanging over his own head, and no way of escape, and it is not in mind to become enamored with the Being that holds the thunderbolt over his devoted head. From the nature of mind, he will flee *from* Him, not *to* Him. It seems never to have been dreamed of, by the inspired writers, that the law could sanctify men. The law is given rather to slay than to make alive, to cut off men's self-righteous hopes forever, and compel them to flee to Christ.

Again; *Sinners*, under the naked law, and irrespective of the gospel—I say, *sinners*, naturally and necessarily, and of right, under such circumstances, view God as an irreconcilable enemy. They are wholly selfish; and apart from the considerations of the gospel, they view God just as the devil views Him. No motive in the law can be exhibited to a selfish mind that will beget love. Can the influence of penalty do it?

A strange plan of reformation this, to send men to hell to reform them! Let them go on in sin and rebellion to the end of life, and then be punished until he becomes holy. I wonder the devil has not become holy! He has suffered long enough, he has been in hell these thousands of years, and he is no better than he was. The reason is, there is no gospel there, and no Holy Spirit there to apply the truth, and the penalty only confirms his rebellion.

Again: The doctrine of justification by faith can relieve these difficulties. It can produce and it has produced real obedience to the precept of the law. Justification by faith does not set aside the law as a rule of duty, but only sets aside the penalty of the law. And the preaching of justification as a mere gratuity, bestowed on the simple act of faith, is the only way in which obedience to the law is ever brought about. This I shall now show from the following considerations:

1. It relieves the mind from the pressure of those considerations that naturally tend to confirm selfishness.

While the mind is looking only at the law, it only feels the influence of hope and fear, perpetuating purely selfish efforts. But justification by faith annihilates this spirit of bondage. The apostle says, "We have not received the spirit of bondage again to fear." This plan of salvation begets love and gratitude to God, and leads the soul to taste the sweets of holiness.

2. It relieves the mind also from the necessity of making its own salvation its supreme object.

The believer in the gospel plan of salvation finds salvation, full and complete, including both sanctification and eternal life, already prepared; and instead of being driven to the life of a Pharisee in religion, of laborious and exhausting effort, he receives it as a free gift, a mere gratuity, and is now left free to exercise disinterested benevolence, and to live and labor for the salvation of others, leaving his own soul unreservedly to Christ.

3. The fact that God has provided and given him salvation as a gratuity, is calculated to awaken in the believer a concern for others, when he sees them dying for the want of this salvation, that they may be brought to the knowledge of the truth and be saved. How far from every selfish motive are those influences. It exhibits God, not as the law exhibits Him, as an irreconcilable enemy, but as a grieved and offended *father*, willing to be reconciled, nay, very desirous that His subjects should become reconciled to Him and live. This is calculated to beget love. It exhibits God as making the greatest sacrifice to reconcile sinners to Himself; and from no other motive than a pure and disinterested regard to their happiness. Try this in your own family. The law represents God as armed with wrath, and determined to punish the sinner, without hope or help. The gospel represents Him as offended, indeed, but yet so anxious they should return to Him, that He has made the greatest conceivable sacrifices, out of pure disinterested love to His wandering children.

I once heard a father say, that he had tried in his family to imitate the government of God, and when his child did wrong he reasoned with him and showed him his faults; and when he was fully convinced and confounded and condemned, so that he had not a word to say, then the father asked him, Do you deserve to be punished? "Yes, sir." I know it, and now if I were to let you go, what influence would it have over the other children? Rather than do that, I will take the punishment myself. So he laid the ferule on himself, and it had the most astonishing effect on the mind of the child. He had never tried anything so perfectly subduing to the mind as this. And from the laws of mind, it must be so. It affects the mind in a manner entirely different from the naked law.

4. It brings the mind under an entire new set of influences, and leaves it free to weigh the reasons for holiness, and decide accordingly.

Under the law, none but motives of hope and fear can operate on the sinner's mind. But under the gospel, the influence of hope and fear are set aside, and a new set of considerations presented, with a view of God's entire character, in all the attractions He can command. It gives the most heart-breaking sin-subduing views of God. It presents Him to the senses in human nature. It exhibits His disinterestedness. The way Satan prevailed against our first parents was by leading them to doubt God's disinterestedness. The gospel demonstrates the truth, and corrects this lie. The law represents God as the inexorable enemy of the sinner as securing happiness to all who perfectly obey, but thundering down wrath on all who disobey. The gospel reveals new features in God's character, not known before. Doubtless the gospel increases the love of all holy beings, and gives greater joy to the angels in heaven, greatly increasing their love and confidence and admiration, when they see God's amazing pity and forbearance towards the guilty. The law drove the devils to hell, and it drove Adam and Eve from Paradise. But when the blessed spirits see the same holy God waiting on rebels, nay, opening His own bosom and giving His beloved Son for them, and taking such unwearied pains for thousands of years to save sinners, do you think it has no influence in strengthening the motives in their minds to obedience and love?

The devil, who is a purely selfish being, is always accusing others of being selfish. He accused Job of this, "Doth Job fear God for naught?" He accused God to our first parents, of being selfish, and that the only reason for His forbidding them to eat of the tree of knowledge was the fear that they might come to know as much as Himself. The gospel shows what God is. If He was selfish, He would not take such pains to save those whom He might with perfect ease crush to hell. Nothing is so calculated to make selfish persons ashamed of their selfishness, as to see disinterested benevolence in others. Hence the wicked are always trying to appear disinterested. Let the selfish individual, who has any heart, see true benevolence in others, and it is like coals of fire on his head. The wise man understood this, when he said, "If thine enemy hunger, feed him; and if he thirst, give him drink; for in so doing thou shalt heap coals of fire on his head." Nothing is so calculated to cut down an enemy, and win him over, and make him a friend.

This is what the gospel does to sinners. It shows them, that notwithstanding all that they have done to God, God still exercises towards them disinterested love. When he sees God stooping from heaven to save him, and understands that it is indeed TRUE, O, how it melts and breaks down the heart, strikes a death blow to selfishness, and wins him over to unbounded confidence and holy love. God has so constituted the mind that it must necessarily do homage to virtue. It must do this, as long as it retains the powers of moral agency. This is as true in hell as in heaven. The devil feels this. When an individual sees that God has no interested motives to condemn him, when he sees that God offers salvation as a mere gratuity, through faith, he cannot but feel admiration of God's benevolence. His selfishness is crushed, the law has done its work, he sees that all his selfish endeavors have done no good; and the next step is for his heart to go out in disinterested love.

Suppose a man was under sentence of death for rebellion, and had tried many expedients to recommend himself to the government, but failed, because they were all hollow hearted and selfish. He sees that the government understands his motives, and that he is not really reconciled. He knows himself that they were all hypocritical and selfish, moved by the hope of favor or the fear of wrath, and that the government is more and more incensed at his hypocrisy. Just now let a paper be brought to him from the government, offering him a free pardon on the simple condition that he would receive it as a mere gratuity, making no account of his own works—what influence will it have on his mind? The moment he finds the penalty set aside, and that he has no need to go to work by any self-righteous efforts, his mind is filled with admiration. Now, let it appear that the government has made the greatest sacrifices to procure this; his selfishness is slain, and he melts down like a child at his sovereign's feet, ready to obey the law because he loves his sovereign.

5. All true obedience turns on faith. It secures all the requisite influences to produce sanctification. It gives the doctrines of eternity access to the mind and a hold on the heart. In this world the motives of time are addressed to the senses. The motives that influence the spirits of the just in heaven do not reach us through the senses. But when faith is exercised, the wall is broken down, and the vast realities of eternity act on the mind here with the same kind of influence that they have in eternity. Mind is mind, everywhere. And were it not for the darkness of unbelief, men would live here just as they do in the eternal world. Sinners here would rage and blaspheme, just as they do in hell; and saints would love and obey and praise, just as they do in heaven. Now, faith makes all these things realities, it swings the mind loose from the clogs of the world, and he beholds God, and apprehends His law

and His love. In no other way *can* these motives take hold on the mind. What a mighty action must it have on the mind, when it takes hold of the love of Christ! What a life-giving power, when the pure motives of the gospel crowd into the mind and stir it up with energy divine! Every Christian knows, that in proportion to the strength of his faith, his mind is buoyant and active, and when his faith flags, his soul is dark and listless. It is faith alone that places the things of time and eternity in their true comparison, and sets down the things of time and sense at their real value. It breaks up the delusions of the mind, the soul shakes itself from its errors and clogs, and it rises up in communion with God.

REMARKS.

I. It is as unphilosophical as it is unscriptural to attempt to convert and sanctify the minds of sinners without the motives of the gospel.

You may press the sinner with the law, and make him see his own character, the greatness and justice of God, and his ruined condition. But hide the motives of the gospel from his mind, and it is all in vain.

II. It is absurd to think that the offers of the gospel are calculated to beget a selfish hope.

Some are afraid to throw out upon the sinner's mind all the character of God; and they try to make him submit to God, by casting him down in despair. This is not only against the gospel, but it is absurd in itself. It is absurd to think that, in order to destroy the selfishness of a sinner, you must hide from him the knowledge of how much God loves and pities him, and how great sacrifices He has made to save him.

III. So far is it from being true, that sinners are in danger of getting false hopes if they are allowed to know the real compassion of God, while you hide this, it is impossible to give him any other than a false hope. Withholding from the sinner who is writhing under conviction, the fact that God has provided salvation as a mere gratuity, is the very way to confirm his selfishness; and if he gets any hope, it must be a false one. To press him to submission by the law alone, is to set him to build a self-righteous foundation.

IV. So far as we can see, salvation by grace, not bestowed in any degree for our own works, is the only possible way of reclaiming selfish beings.

Suppose salvation was not altogether gratuitous, but that some degree of good works was taken into the account, and *for* those good works in part we were justified—just so far as this consideration is in the mind, just so far there is a stimulus to selfishness. You must bring the sinner to see that he is entirely dependent on free grace, and that a full and complete justification is bestowed, on the first act of faith, as a mere gratuity, and no part of it as an equivalent for anything he is to do. This alone dissolves the influence of selfishness, and secures holy action.

V. If all this is true, sinners should be put in the fullest possible possession, and in the speediest manner, of the whole plan of salvation.

They should be made to see the law, and their own guilt, and that they have no way to save themselves; and then, the more fully the whole length and breadth and height and depth of the love of God should be opened, the more effectually will you crush his selfishness, and subdue his soul in love to God. Do not be afraid, in conversing with sinners, to show the whole plan of salvation, and give the fullest possible exhibition of the infinite compassion of God. Show him that, notwithstanding his guilt, the Son of God is knocking at the door and beseeching him to be reconciled to God.

VI. You see why so many convicted sinners continue so long compassing Mount Sinai, with self-righteous efforts to save themselves by their own works.

How often you find sinners trying to get more feeling, or waiting till they have made more prayers and made greater efforts, and expecting to recommend themselves to God in this way. Why is all this? The sinner needs to be driven off from this, and made to see that he is all the while looking for salvation under the law. He must be made to see that all this is superseded by the gospel offering him all he wants as a mere gratuity. He must hear Jesus, saying, "Ye will not come *unto me* that ye may have life: O, no, you are willing to pray, and go to meeting, and read the Bible, or anything, but come unto me. Sinner, this is the road; I am the way, and the truth, and the life. No man cometh to the Father but by me. I am the resurrection and the life. I am the light of the world. Here, sinner, is what you want. Instead of trying your self-righteous prayers and efforts, here is what you are looking for, only believe and you shall be saved."

VII. You see why so many professors of religion are always in the dark.

They are looking at their sins, confining their observations to themselves, and losing sight of the fact, that there have only to take right hold of Jesus Christ and throw themselves upon Him, and all is well.

VIII. The law is useful to convict men; but, as a matter of fact, it never breaks the heart. The Gospel alone does that. The degree in which a convert is broken hearted, is in proportion to the degree of clearness with which he apprehends the gospel.

IX. Converts, if you call them so, who entertain a hope under legal preaching, may have an intellectual approbation of the law, and a sort of dry zeal, but never make mellow, broken hearted Christians. If they have not seen God in the attitude in which He is exhibited in the gospel, they are not such Christians as you will see sometimes, with the tear trembling in their eye, and their frames shaking with emotion, at the name of Jesus.

X. You see what needs to be done with sinners who are under conviction, and what with those professors who are in darkness. They must be led right to Christ, and made to take hold of the plan of salvation by faith. It is in vain to expect to do them good in any other way.

LECTURE VII.

LEGAL EXPERIENCE.

Text:— The 7th chapter of Romans.

I have more than once had occasion to refer to this chapter, and have read some portions of it and made remarks. But I have not been able to go into a consideration of it so fully as I wished, and therefore thought I would make it the subject of a separate lecture. In giving my views I shall pursue the following order:

I. Mention the different opinions that have prevailed in the church concerning this passage.

II. Show the importance of understanding this portion of scripture aright, or of knowing which of these prevailing opinions is the true one.

III. Lay down several facts and principles which have a bearing on the exposition of this passage.

IV. Refer to some rules of interpretation which ought always to be observed in interpreting either the scriptures or any other writing or testimony.

V. Give my own views of the real meaning of the passage, with the reasons.

I shall confine myself chiefly to the latter part of the chapter, as that has been chiefly the subject of dispute. You see from the manner in which I have laid out my work, that I design to simplify the subject as much as possible, so as to bring it within the compass of a single lecture. Otherwise I might make a volume; as much has been written to show the meaning of this chapter.

I. I am to show what are the principal opinions that have prevailed concerning the application of this chapter.

1. One opinion that has extensively prevailed and still prevails, is that the latter part of the chapter is an epitome of Christian experience.

It has been supposed to describe the situation and exercises of a Christian, and designed to exhibit the Christian warfare with indwelling sin. It is to be observed, however, that this is, comparatively, a modern opinion. No writer is known to have held this view of the chapter, for centuries after it was written. According to Professor Stuart, who has examined the subject more thoroughly than any other man in this country, Augustine was the first writer that exhibited this interpretation, and he resorted to it in his controversy with Pelagius.

2. The only other interpretation given is that which prevailed in the first centuries, and which is still generally adopted on the continent of Europe as well as by a considerable number of writers in England and in this country; that this passage describes the experience of a sinner under conviction, who was acting under the motives of the law, and not yet brought to the experience of the gospel. In this country, the most prevalent opinion is, that the 7th of Romans delineates the experience of a Christian.

II. I am to show the importance of a right understanding of this passage.

A right understanding of this passage must be fundamental. If this passage in fact describes a sinner under conviction, or a purely legal experience, and if a person supposing that it is a Christian experience finds his own experience to correspond with it, his mistake is a fatal one. It must be a fatal error, to rest in his experience as that of a real Christian, because it corresponds with the 7th of Romans, if Paul is in fact giving only the experience of a sinner under legal motives and considerations.

III. I will lay down some principles and facts, that have a bearing on the elucidation of this subject.

1. It is true, that mankind act, in all cases, and from the nature of mind must always act, as on the whole they feel to be preferable.

Or, in other words, the will governs the conduct. Men never act against their will. The will governs the motion of the limbs. Voluntary beings cannot act contrary to their will.

2. Men often *desire* what, on the whole, they do not *choose*.

The desires and the will are often opposed to each other. The conduct is governed by the choice, not by the desires. The desires may be inconsistent with the choice. You may *desire* to go to some other place tonight, and yet on the whole choose to remain here. Perhaps you desire very strongly to be somewhere else, and yet choose to remain in meeting. A man wishes to go a journey to some place. Perhaps he desires it strongly. It may be very important to his business or his ambition. But his family are sick, or some other object requires him to be at home, and on the whole he chooses to remain. In all cases, the conduct follows the actual choice.

3. Regeneration, or conversion, is a change in the choice.

It is a change in the supreme controlling choice of the mind. The regenerated or converted person prefers God's glory to everything else. He chooses it as the supreme object of affection. This is a change of heart. Before, he chose his own interest or happiness, as his supreme end. Now, he chooses God's service in preference to his own interest. When a person is truly born again, his choice is habitually right, and of course his conduct is in the main right.

The force of temptation may produce an occasional wrong choice, or even a succession of wrong choices, but his habitual course of action is right. The will, or choice, of a converted person is habitually right, and of course his conduct is so. If this is not true, I ask, in what does the converted differ from the unconverted person? If it is not the character of the converted person, that he habitually does the commandments of God, what is his character? But I presume this position will not be disputed by anyone who believes in the doctrine of regeneration.

4. Moral agents are so constituted, that they naturally and necessarily approve of what is right.

A moral agent is one who possesses understanding, will, and conscience. Conscience is the power of discerning the difference of moral objects. It will not be disputed that a moral agent can be led to see the difference between right and wrong, so that his moral nature shall approve of what is right. Otherwise, a sinner never can be brought under conviction. If he has not a moral nature, that can see and highly approve the law of God, and justify the penalty, he cannot be convicted. For this is conviction, to see the goodness of the law that he has broken and the justice of the penalty he has incurred. But in fact, there is not a moral agent, in heaven, earth, or hell, that cannot be made to see that the law of God is right, and whose conscience does not approve the law.

5. Men may not only approve the law, as right, but they may often, when it is viewed abstractly and without reference to its bearing on themselves, take real pleasure in contemplating on it.

This is one great source of self-deception. Men view the law of God in the abstract, and love it. When no selfish reason is present for opposing it, they take pleasure in viewing it. They approve of what is right, and condemn wickedness, in the abstract. All men do this, when no selfish reason is pressing on them. Whoever found a man so wicked, that he approved of evil in the abstract? Where was a moral being ever found that approved the character of the devil, or that approved of other wicked men, unconnected with himself?

How often do you hear wicked men express the greatest abhorrence and detestation of enormous wickedness in others. If their passions are in no way enlisted in favor of error or of wrong, men always stand up for what is right. And this merely constitutional approbation of what is right may amount even to delight, when they do not see the relations of right interfering in any manner with their own selfishness.

6. In this constitutional approbation of truth and the law of God, and the delight which naturally arises from it, *there is no virtue.*

It is only what belongs to man's moral nature. It arises naturally from the constitution of the mind. Mind is constitutionally capable of seeing the beauty of virtue. And so far from their being any virtue in it, it is in fact only a clearer proof of the strength of their depravity, that when they know the right, and see its excellence, they do not obey it. It is not then that impenitent sinners have in them something that is holy. But their wickedness is herein seen to be so much the greater. For the wickedness of sin is in proportion to the light that is enjoyed. And when we find that men may not only see the excellence of the law of God, but even strongly approve of it and take delight in it, and yet not obey it, it shows how desperately wicked they are, and makes sin appear exceeding sinful.

7. It is a common use of language for persons to say, "I would do so and so, but cannot," when they only mean to be understood as desiring it, but not as actually choosing to do it. And so to say, "I could not do so," when they only mean that they would not do it, and, they could if they would.

Not long since, I asked a minister to preach for me next Sabbath. He answered, "I can't." I found out afterwards that he could if he would. I asked a merchant to take a certain price for a piece of goods. He said, "I can't do it." What did he mean? That he had not power to accept of such a price? Not at all. He could if he would, but he did not choose to do it. You will see the bearing of these remarks, when I come to read the chapter. I proceed, now,

IV. To give several rules of interpretation, that are applicable to the interpretation not only of the Bible, but of all written instruments, and to all evidence whatever.

There are certain rules of evidence, which all men are bound to apply, in ascertaining the meaning of instruments and the testimony of witnesses, and of all writings.

1. We are always to put that construction on language which is required by the nature of the subject.

We are bound always to understand a person's language as it is applicable to the subject of discourse. Much of the language of common life may be tortured into anything, if you lose sight of the subject, and take the liberty to interpret it without reference to what they are speaking of. How much injury has been done, by interpreting separate passages and single expressions in the scriptures, in violation of this principle. It is chiefly by overlooking this simple rule, that the scriptures have been tortured into the support of errors and contradictions innumerable and absurd beyond all calculation. This rule is applicable to all statements. Courts of justice never would allow such perversions as have been committed upon the Bible.

2. If a person's language will admit, we are bound always to construe it so as to make him *consistent with himself.*

Unless you observe this rule, you can scarcely converse five minutes with any individual on any subject and not make him contradict himself. If you do not hold to this rule, how can one man ever communicate his ideas so that another man will understand him? How can a witness ever make known the facts to the jury, if his language is to be tortured at pleasure, without the restraints of this rule?

3. In interpreting a person's language, we are always to keep in view the point to which he is speaking.

We are to understand the scope of his argument, the object he has in view, and the point to which he is speaking. Otherwise we shall of course not understand his language. Suppose I were to take up a book, any book, and not keep my eye on the object the writer had in view in making it, and the point to which he is aiming, I never can understand that book. It is easy to see how endless errors have grown out of a practice of interpreting the scriptures in disregard of the first principles of interpretation.

4. When you understand the point to which a person is speaking, you are to understand him *as speaking to that point,* and not to put a construction on his language unconnected with his object, or inconsistent with it.

By losing sight of this rule, you may make nonsense of everything. You are bound always to interpret language in the light of the subject to which it is applied, or about which it is spoken.

V. Having laid down these rules and principles I proceed in the light of them to give my own view of the meaning of the passage, with the reasons for it. But first I will make a remark or two.

1st. REMARK. Whether the apostle was speaking of himself in this passage, or whether he is supposing a case, is not material to the right interpretation of the language.

It is supposed by many, that because he speaks in the first person, he is to be understood as referring to himself. But it is a common practice, when we are discussing general principles, or arguing a point, to suppose a case by way of illustration, or to establish a point. And it is very natural to state it in the first person, without at all intending to be understood, and in fact without ever being understood, as declaring an actual occurrence, or an experience of our own. The apostle Paul was here pursuing a close train of argument, and he introduces this simply by way of illustration. And it is no way material whether it is his own actual experience, or a case supposed.

If he is speaking of himself, or if he is speaking of another person, or if he is supposing a case, he does it with a design to show a general principle of conduct, and that all persons under like circumstances would do the same. Whether he is speaking of a Christian, or of an impenitent sinner, he lays down a general principle.

The apostle James, in the 3d chapter, speaks in the first person; even in administering reproof. "My brethren, be not many masters, knowing that we shall receive the greater condemnation. For in many things we offend all."

"Therewith bless we God, even the Father; and therewith curse we men, which are made after the similitude of God."

The apostle Paul often says "I," and uses the first person, when discussing and illustrating general principles: "All things are lawful unto me, but all things are not expedient: all things are lawful for me, but I will not be brought under the power of any:" And again, "Conscience, I say, not thine own, but of the other: for why is my liberty judged of another man's conscience? For if I by grace be a partaker, why am I evil spoken of for that for which I give thanks? For now we see through a glass, darkly; but then face to face: now I know in part; but then shall I know even as also I am known. And now abideth faith, hope, charity, these three; but the greatest of these is charity." So also, "For if I build again the things which I destroyed, I make myself a transgressor." In lst Corinthians iv. 6. he explains exactly how he uses illustrations, "And these things, brethren, I have in a figure transferred to myself, and to Apollos, for your sakes: that ye might learn in us not to think of men above that which is written, that no one of you be puffed up for one against another."

2nd. REMARK. Much of the language which the apostle uses here, is applicable to the case of a backslider, who has lost all but the form of religion. He has left his first love, and has in fact fallen under the influence of legal motives, of hope and fear, just like an impenitent sinner. If there be such a character as a real backslider, who has been a real convert, he is then actuated by the same motives as the sinner, and the same language may be equally applicable to both. And therefore the fact that some of the language before us is applicable to a Christian who has become a backslider, does not prove at all that the experience here described is Christian experience, but only that a backslider and a sinner are in many respects alike. I do not hesitate to say this much, at least; that no one who was conscious that he was actuated by love to God could ever have thought of applying this chapter to himself. If anyone is not in the exercise of love to God, this describes his character; and whether he is backslider or sinner, it is all the same thing.

3rd. REMARK. Some of the expressions here used by the apostle are supposed to describe the case of a believer who is not a habitual backslider, but who is overcome by temptation and passion for a time, and speaks of himself as if he were all wrong. A man is tempted, we are told, when he is drawn away by his own lusts, and enticed. And in that state, no doubt, he might find expressions here that would describe his own experience, while under such influence. But that proves nothing in regard to the design of the passage, for while he is in this state, he is so far under a certain influence, and the impenitent sinner is all the time under just such influence. The same language, therefore, may be applicable to both, without inconsistency.

But although some expressions may bear this plausible construction, yet a view of the whole passage makes it evident that it cannot be a delineation of Christian experience. My own opinion therefore is, that the apostle designed here to represent the experience of a sinner, not careless, but strongly convicted and yet not converted, The reasons are these:

1. Because the apostle is here manifestly *describing the habitual character* of some one; and this one who is wholly under the

dominion of the flesh. It is not as a whole a description of one who, under the power of present temptation, is acting inconsistently with his general character, but his general character is so. It is one who uniformly falls into sin, notwithstanding his approval of the law.

2. It would have been *entirely irrelevant to his purpose*, to state the experience of a Christian as an illustration of his argument. That was not what was needed. He was laboring to vindicate the law of God, in its influence on a carnal mind. In a previous chapter he had stated the fact, that justification was only by faith, and not by works of law. In this seventh chapter, he maintains not only that *justification* is by faith, but also that *sanctification* is only by faith. "Know ye not brethren, (for I speak to them that know the law) how that the law hath dominion over a man as long as he liveth? So then, if while her husband liveth, she be married to another man, she shall be called an adulteress: but if her husband be dead, she is free from that law; so that she is no adulteress, though she be married to another man." What is the use of all this? Why, this, "Wherefore, my brethren, ye also are become dead to the law by the body of Christ; that ye should be married to another, even to him who is raised from the dead, that we should bring forth fruit unto God." While you were under the law you were bound to obey the law, and hold to the terms of the law for justification. But now being made free from the law, as a rule of judgment, you are no longer influenced by legal considerations, of hope and fear, for Christ to whom you are married, has set aside the penalty, that by faith ye might be justified before God.

"For when we were in the flesh," that is, in an unconverted state, "the motions of sins, which were by the law, did work in our members to bring forth fruit unto death: But now we are delivered from the law, that being dead wherein we were held; that we should serve in newness of spirit, and not in the oldness of the letter." Here he is stating the real condition of a Christian, that he serves in newness of spirit and not in the oldness of the letter. He had found that the fruit of the law was only death, and by the gospel he had been brought into true subjection to Christ. What is the objection to this? "What shall we say then? Is the law sin? God forbid. Nay, I had not known sin, but by the law: for I had not known lust, except the law had said, Thou shalt not covet. And the commandment which was ordained to life, I found to be unto death." The law was enacted that people might live by it, if they would perfectly obey it; but when we were in the flesh, we found it unto death. "For sin, taking occasion by the commandment, deceived me, and by it slew me. Wherefore the law is holy, and the commandment holy, and just, and good." Now he brings up the objection again. How can anything that is good be made death unto you?—"Was, then, that which is good made death unto me?—God forbid. But sin, that it might appear sin, working death in me by that which is good; that sin by the commandment might be exceedingly sinful." And he vindicates the law, by showing that it is not the fault of the law, but the fault of sin, and that this very result shows at once the excellence of the law and the exceeding sinfulness of sin. Sin must be a horrible thing, if it can work such a perversion, as to take the good law of God and make it the means of death.

"For we know that the law is spiritual; but I am carnal, sold under sin." Here is the hinge, on which the whole questions turns. Now mark; *the apostle is here vindicating the law against the objection, that if the law is the means of death to sinners, it cannot be good.* Against this objection, he goes on to show, that all its action on the mind of the sinner proves it to be good. Keeping his eye on this point, he argues, that the law is good, and that the evil comes from the motions of sin in our members. Now he comes to that part which is supposed to delineate a Christian experience, and which is the subject of controversy. He begins by saying, "the law is spiritual but I am carnal." This word *carnal* he uses once and only once, in reference to Christians, and then it was in reference to persons who were in a very low state in religion. "For ye are yet carnal; for whereas there is among you envying, and strife, and divisions, are ye not carnal, and walk as men." These Christians had backslidden, and acted as if they were not converted persons, but were carnal. The term itself is generally used to signify the worst of sinners. Paul here defines it so; "*carnal, sold under sin.*" Could that be said of Paul himself, at the time he wrote this epistle? Was that his own experience? Was he sold under sin?" Was that true of the great apostle? No, but he was vindicating the law, and he uses an illustration, by supposing a case. He goes on, "For that which I do, I allow not; for what I would, that I do not; but what I hate, that do I."

Here you see the application of the principles I have laid down. In the interpretation of this word "would," we are not to understand it of the choice or will, but only a desire. Otherwise the apostle contradicts a plain matter of fact, which everybody knows to be true, that the will governs the conduct. Professor Stuart has very properly rendered the word *desire*; what I desire, I do not, but what I disapprove, that I do. Then comes the conclusion, "If, then, I do that which I would not, I consent unto the law, that it is good." If I do that which I disapprove, if I disapprove of my own conduct, if I condemn myself, I thereby bear testimony that the law is good. Now, keep your eye on the object the apostle has in view, and read the next verse, "Now then it is no more that I do it, but sin that dwelleth in me." Here he, as it were, divides himself against himself, or speaks of himself as possessing two natures, or, as some of the heathen philosophers taught, as having two souls, one which approves the good and another which loves and chooses evil. "For I know that in me (that is, in my flesh) dwelleth no good thing: for to will is present with me; but how to perform that which is good I find not." Here "to will" means to approve, for if men really *will* to do a thing, they do it. This everybody knows. Where the language will admit, we are bound to interpret it so as to make it consistent with known facts. If you understand "to will" literally, you involve the apostle in the absurdity of saying that he willed what he did not do, and so acted contrary to his own will, which contradicts a notorious fact. The meaning must be desire. Then it coincides with the experience of every convicted sinner. He knows what he ought to do, and he strongly approves it, but he is not ready to do it. Suppose I were to call on you to do some act. Suppose, for instance, I were to call on those of you who are impenitent, to come forward and take that seat, that we might see who you are, and pray for you, and should show you your sins and that it is your duty to submit to God, some of you would exclaim, "I know it is my duty, and I greatly desire to do it, but I cannot." What do you mean by it? Why, simply, that on the whole, the balance of your will is on the other side.

In the 20th verse he repeats what he had said before, "Now if I do that I would not, it is no more I that do it, but sin that dwelleth in me." Is that the habitual character and experience of a Christian? I admit that a Christian may fall so low that this language may apply to him; but if this is his *general* character, how does it differ from that of an impenitent sinner? If this is the habitual character of a Christian, there is not a word of truth in the scripture representations, that the saints are those who really obey God; for here is one called a Christian of whom it is said expressly that he never does obey.

"I find then a law, that when I would do good, evil is present within me." Here he speaks of the action of the carnal propensities, as being so constant and so prevalent that he calls it a "law." "For I delight in the law of God after the inward man." Here is the great stumbling-block. Can it be said of an impenitent sinner that he "delights" in the law of God? I answer, yes. I know the expression is a strong one, but the apostle was using strong language all along, on both sides. It is no stronger language than the prophet Isaiah uses in chapter lviii. He was describing as wicked and rebellious a generation as ever lived. He says, "Cry aloud, spare not; lift up thy voice like a trumpet, and show my people their transgression, and the house of Jacob their sins." Yet he goes on to say of this very people, "Yet they seek me daily, and delight to know my ways, as a nation that did righteousness, and forsook not the ordinance of their God; they ask of me the ordinances of justice; they TAKE DELIGHT in approaching to God." Here is one instance of impenitent sinners manifestly delighting in approaching to God. So in Ezekiel xxxiii. 32. "And lo, thou *art* unto them as a very lovely song of one that hath a pleasant voice, and can play well on an instrument: for they hear thy words, but they do them not." The prophet had been telling how wicked they were. "And they come unto thee as the people cometh, and they sit before thee *as* my people, and they hear thy words, but they will not do them: for with their mouth they show much love, but their heart goeth after their covetousness." Here were impenitent sinners, plainly enough, yet they loved to hear the eloquent prophet. How often do ungodly sinners delight in eloquent preaching or powerful reasoning, by some able minister! It is to them an intellectual feast. And sometimes they are so pleased with it, as really to think they love the word of God. This is consistent with entire depravity of heart and enmity against the true character of God. Nay, it sets their depravity in a stronger light, because they know and approve the right, and yet do the wrong.

So, notwithstanding this delight in the law, he says, "But I see another law in my members, warring against the law of my mind, and bringing me into captivity to the law of sin which is in my members. O wretched man that I am! who shall deliver me from the body of this death?" Here the words, "I thank God, through Jesus Christ our Lord," are plainly a parenthesis, and a brake in upon the train of thought. Then he sums up the whole matter, "So then, with the mind I myself serve the law of God, but with the flesh the law of sin."

It is as if he had said, My better self, my unbiased judgment, my conscience, approves the law of God; but the law in my members, my passions, have such a control over me that I still disobey. Remember, the apostle was describing the habitual character of one who was wholly under the dominion of sin. It was irrelevant to his purpose to adduce the experience of a Christian. He was vindicating the law, and therefore it was necessary for him to take the case of one who was under the law. If it is Christian experience, he was reasoning against himself, for if it is Christian experience, this would prove, not only that the law is inefficacious for the subduing of passion and the sanctification of men, but that the gospel also is inefficacious. Christians are under grace, and it is irrelevant, in vindicating the law, to adduce the experience of those who are not under the law, but under grace.

Another conclusive reason is, that he here actually states the case of a believer, as entirely different. In verses 4 and 6, he speaks of those who are not under law and not in the flesh, that is, not carnal, but delivered from the law, and actually *serving*, or obeying God, in spirit.

Then, in the beginning of the 8th chapter, he goes on to say, "There is therefore now no condemnation to them which are in Christ Jesus, who walk not after the flesh, but after the Spirit. For the law of the Spirit of life in Christ Jesus, hath made me free from the law of sin and death." He had alluded to this in the parenthesis above, "I thank God," &c. "For what the law could not do, in that it was weak through the flesh, God sending his own Son in the flesh, and for sin, condemned sin in the flesh: that the righteousness of the law might be fulfilled in us, who walk not after the flesh, but after the Spirit." Who is this, of whom he is now speaking? If the person in the last chapter was one who had a Christian experience, whose experience is this? Here is something entirely different. The other was wholly under the power of sin, and under the law, and while he knew his duty, never did it. Here we find one for whom what the law could not do, through the power of passion, the gospel has done, so that the righteousness of the law is fulfilled, or what the law requires is obeyed. "For they that are after the flesh, do mind the things of the flesh; but they that are after the Spirit, the things of the Spirit. For to be carnally minded is death; but to be spiritually minded is life and peace: because the carnal mind is enmity to God: for it is not subject to the law of God, neither indeed can be. So then they that are in the flesh cannot please God." There it is. Those whom he had described in the 7th chapter, as being carnal, cannot please God. "But ye are not in the flesh, but in the Spirit, if so be that the Spirit of God dwell in you. Now, if any man have not the Spirit of Christ, he is none of his. And if Christ be in you, the body is dead because of sin; but the Spirit is life because of righteousness." But here is an individual whose body is dead. Before, the body had the control, and dragged him away from duty and from salvation; but now the power of passion is subdued.

Now I will give you the sum of the whole matter:

(1.) The strength of the apostle's language cannot decide this question, for he uses strong language on both sides. If it is objected that the individual he is describing is said to "delight in the law," he is also said to be "carnal, sold under sin." When a writer uses strong language, it must be so understood as not to make it irrelevant or inconsistent.

(2.) Whether he spoke of himself, or of some other person, or merely supposed a case by way of illustration, is wholly immaterial to the question.

(3.) It is plain that the point he wished to illustrate was the vindication of the law of God, as to its influence on a carnal mind.

(4.) The point required by way of illustration, the case of a convicted sinner, who saw the excellence of the law, but in whom the passions had the ascendency.

(5.) If this is spoken of Christian experience, it is not only irrelevant, but proves the reverse of what he intended. He intended to show that the law, though good, could not break the power of passion. But if this is Christian experience, then it proves that the gospel, instead of the law, cannot subdue passion and sanctify men.

(6.) The contrast between the state described in the 7th chapter, and that described in the 8th chapter, proves that the experience of the former was not that of a Christian.

REMARKS.

I. Those who find their own experience written in the 7th chapter of Romans, are not converted persons. If that is their habitual character, they are not regenerated; they are under conviction, but not Christians.

II. You see the great importance of using the law in dealing with sinners, to make them prize the gospel, to lead them to justify God and condemn themselves. Sinners are never made truly to repent but as they are convicted by the law.

III. At the same time, you see the entire insufficiency of the law to convert men. The case of the devil illustrates the highest efficacy of the law, in this respect.

IV. You see the danger of mistaking mere desires, for piety. Desire, that does not result in right choice, has nothing good in it. The devil may have such desires. The wickedest men on earth may desire religion, and no doubt often do desire it, when they see that it is necessary to their salvation, or to control their passions.

V. Christ and the gospel present the only motives that can sanctify the mind. The law only convicts and condemns.

VI. Those who are truly converted and brought into the liberty of the gospel, do find deliverance from the bondage of their own corruptions.

They do find the power of the body over the mind broken. They may have conflicts and trials, many and severe; but as an habitual thing, they are delivered from the thraldom of passion, and get the victory over sin, and find it easy to serve God. His commandments are not grievous to them. His yoke is easy, and His burden light.

VII. The true convert finds peace with God. He feels that he has it. He enjoys it. He has a sense of pardoned sin, and of victory over corruption.

VIII. You see, from this subject, the true position of a vast many church members. They are all the while struggling under the law. They approve of the law, both in its precept and its penalty, they feel condemned, and desire relief. But still they are unhappy. They have no spirit of prayer, no communion with God, no evidence of adoption. They only refer to the 7th of Romans as their evidence. Such a one will say, "There is my experience exactly." Let me tell you, that if this is your experience, you are yet in the gall of bitterness and the bonds of iniquity. You feel that you are in the bonds of guilt, and you are overcome by iniquity, and surely you know that it is bitter as gall. Now, don't cheat your soul by supposing that with such an experience as this, you can go and sit down by the side of the apostle Paul. You are yet carnal, sold under sin, and unless you embrace the gospel, you will be damned.

LECTURE VIII.

CHRISTIAN PERFECTION.

TEXT:—"Be ye therefore perfect, even as your Father which is in heaven is perfect."

Matthew v. 48.

In the 43rd verse, the Savior says, "Ye have heard that it hath been said, Thou shalt love thy neighbor, and hate thine enemy; but I say unto you, Love your enemies, bless them that curse you, do good to them that hate you, and pray for them which despitefully use you and persecute you; that ye may be the children of your Father which is in heaven: for he maketh his sun to rise on the evil and on the good, and sendeth rain on the just and on the unjust. For if ye love them which love you, what reward have ye? do not even the publicans the same? And if ye salute your brethren only, what do ye more than others? do not even the publicans so? Be ye therefore perfect, even as your Father which is in heaven is perfect."

In discoursing on the subject of Christian Perfection, it is my design to pursue this order:

I. I shall show what is not to be understood by the requirement, "Be ye therefore perfect;" or, what Christian Perfection is not.

II. Show what is the perfection here required.

III. That this perfection is a duty.

IV. That it is attainable; and,

V. Answer some of the objections which are commonly argued against the doctrine of Christian Perfection.

I. I am to show you what Christian Perfection is not.

1. It is not required that we should have the same natural perfections that God has.

God has two kinds of perfections, natural and moral. His natural perfections constitute His nature, essence, of constitution. They are His eternity, immutability, omnipotence, etc. These are called natural perfections, because they have no moral character. They are not voluntary. God has not given them to Himself, because He did not create himself, but existed from eternity, with all these natural attributes in full possession. All these God possesses in an infinite degree. These natural perfections are not the perfection here required. The attributes of our nature were created in us, and we are not required to produce any new natural attributes, nor would it be possible. We are not required to possess any of them in the degree that God possesses them.

2. The perfection required in the text is not perfection of knowledge, even according to our limited faculties.

3. Christian Perfection, as here required, is not freedom from temptation, either from our constitution or from things that are about us. The mind may be ever so sorely tried with the animal appetites, and yet not sin. The apostle James says, "Every man is tempted, when he is drawn away of his own lust, and enticed." The sin is not in the temptations, but in yielding to them. A person may be tempted by Satan, as well as by the appetites, or by the world, and yet not have sin. All sin consists in voluntary consenting to the desires.

4. Neither does Christian perfection imply a freedom from what ought to be understood by the Christian warfare.

5. The perfection required is not the *infinite* moral perfection which God has; because man, being a finite creature, is not capable of infinite affections. God being infinite in Himself, for Him to be perfect is to be infinitely perfect. But this is not required of us.

II. I am to show what Christian perfection is; or what is the duty actually required in the text.

It is perfect obedience to the law of God. The law of God requires perfect, disinterested, impartial benevolence, love to God and love to our neighbor. It requires that we should be actuated by the same feeling, and to act on the same principles that God acts upon; to leave self out of the question as uniformly as He does, to be as much separated from selfishness as He is; in a word, to be in our measure as perfect as God is. Christianity requires that we should do neither more nor less than the law of God prescribes. Nothing short of this is Christian perfection. This is being, morally, just as perfect as God. Everything is here included, to feel as He feels, to love what He loves, and hate what He hates, and for the same reasons that He loves and hates.

God regards every being in the universe according to its real value. He regards His own interests according to their real value in the scale of being, and no more. He exercises the same love towards Himself that He requires of us, and for the same reason. He loves himself supremely, both with the love of benevolence and the love of complacency, because He is supremely excellent. And He requires us to love Him just so, to love Him as perfectly as He loves Himself. He loves Himself with the love of benevolence, or regards His own interest, and glory, and happiness, as the supreme good, because *it is* the supreme good. And He requires us to love Him in the same way. He loves Himself with infinite complacency, because He knows that He is infinitely worthy and excellent, and He requires the same of us. He also loves His neighbor as Himself, not in the same degree that He loves Himself, but in the same proportion, according to their real value. From the highest angel to the smallest worm, He regards their happiness with perfect love, according to their worth. It is His duty to conform to these principles, as much as it is our duty. He can no more depart from this rule than we can, without committing sin; and for Him to do it would be as much worse than for us to do it, as He is greater than we. God is infinitely obligated to do this. His very nature, not depending on His own volition, but uncreated, binds Him to this. And He has created us moral beings in His own image, capable of conforming to the same rule with Himself. This rule requires us to have the same character with Him, to love as impartially, with as perfect love—to seek the good of others with as single an eye as He does. This, and nothing less than this, is Christian Perfection.

III. I am to show that Christian Perfection is a duty.

1. This is evident from the fact that God requires it, both under the law and under the gospel.

The command in the text, "Be ye perfect, even as your Father which is in heaven is perfect," is given under the gospel. Christ here commands the very same thing that the law requires. Some suppose that much less is required of us under the gospel, than was required under the law. It is true that the gospel does not require perfection, as the condition of salvation. But no part of the obligation of the law is discharged. The gospel holds those who are under it to the same holiness as those under the law.

2. I argue that Christian Perfection is a duty, because God has no right to require anything less.

God cannot discharge us from the obligation to be perfect, as I have defined perfection. If He were to attempt it, He would just so far give a license to sin. He has no right to give any such license. While we are moral beings, there is no power in the universe that can discharge us from the obligation to be perfect. Can God discharge us from the obligation to love Him with all our heart and soul and mind and strength? That would be saying that God does not deserve such love. And if He cannot discharge us from the whole law, He cannot discharge from any part of it, for the same reason.

3. Should anyone contend that the gospel requires less holiness than the law, I would ask him to say just how much less it requires.

If we are allowed to stop short of perfect obedience, where shall we stop? How perfect are we required to be? Where will you find a rule in the Bible, to determine how much less holy you are allowed to be under the gospel, than you would be under the law? Shall we say each one must judge for himself? Then I ask, if you think it is your duty to be any more perfect than you are now? Probably all would say, Yes. Can you lay down any point at which, when you have arrived, you can say, "Now I am perfect enough; it is true, I have some sin left, but I have gone as far as it is my duty to go in this world?" Where do you get your authority for any such notion? No; the truth is, that all who are truly pious, the more pious they are, the more strongly they feel the obligation to be perfect, as God is perfect.

IV. I will now show that Christian Perfection is attainable, or practicable, in this life.

1. It may be fairly inferred that Christian Perfection is attainable, from the fact that it is commanded.

Does God command us to be perfect as He is perfect, and still shall we say it is an impossibility? Are we not always to infer, when God commands a thing, that there is a natural possibility of doing that which He commands? I recollect hearing an individual say, he would preach to sinners that they ought to repent, because God commands it; but he would not preach that they *could* repent, because God has nowhere said that they can. What consummate trifling! Suppose a man were to say he would preach to citizens, that they ought to obey the laws of the country because the government had enacted them, but he would not tell them that they could obey, because it is nowhere in the statute book enacted that they have the ability. It is always to be understood, when God requires anything of men, that they possess the requisite faculties to do it. Otherwise God requires of us impossibilities, on pain of death, and sends sinners to hell for not doing what they were in no sense able to do.

2. That there is natural ability to be perfect is a simple matter of fact.

There can be no question of this. What is perfection. It is to love the Lord our God with all our heart and soul and mind and strength and to love our neighbor as ourselves. That is, it requires us not to exert the powers of somebody else, but our own powers. The law itself goes no farther than to require the right use of the powers you possess. So that it is a simple matter of fact that you possess natural ability, or power, to be just as perfect as God requires.

Objection. Here some may object, that if there is a natural ability to be perfect, there is a moral inability, which comes to the same thing, for inability is inability, call it what you will, and if we have moral inability, we are as really unable as if our inability was natural.

Answer 1. There is no more moral inability to be perfectly holy, than there is to be holy at all. So far as moral ability is concerned, you can as well be perfectly holy as you can be holy at all. The true distinction between natural ability and moral ability, is this: Natural ability relates to the powers and faculties of the mind; Moral ability only to the will. Moral inability is nothing else than unwillingness to do a thing. So it is explained by President Edwards, in his Treatise on the Will, and by other writers on the subject. When you ask whether you have moral ability to be perfect, if you mean by it, whether you are willing to be perfect, I answer, No. If you were willing to be perfect, you would be perfect; for the perfection required is only a perfect conformity of the will to God's law, or willing right. If you ask then, Are we able to will right? I answer, the question implies a contradiction, in supposing that there can be such a thing as a moral agent unable to choose, or will. President Edwards says expressly, in his chapter on Moral Inability, as you may see, if you will read it, that strictly speaking, there is no such thing as Moral Inability. When we speak of inability to do a thing, if we mean to be understood, of a real inability, it implies a willingness to do it, but a want of power. To say, therefore, we are unable to will, is absurd. It is saying we will and yet are unable to will, at the same time.

Answer 2. But I admit and believe, that there is desperate unwillingness in the case. And if this is what you mean by Moral Inability, it is true. There is a pertinacious unwillingness in sinners to become Christians, and in Christians to become perfect, or to come up to the full perfection required both by the law and gospel. Sinners may strongly wish to become Christians, and Christians may strongly wish or desire to be rid of all their sins, and may pray for it, even with agony. They may think they are willing to be perfect, but they deceive themselves. They may feel, in regard to their sins taken all together, or in the abstract, as if they are willing to renounce them all. But take them up in the detail, one by one, and there are many sins they are unwilling to give up. They wrestle against sin in general, but cling to it in the detail.

I have known cases of this kind where individuals will break down in such a manner that they think they never will sin again; and then perhaps in one hour, something will come up that they are ready to fight for the indulgence, and need to be broken down again and again. Christians actually need to be hunted from one sin after another, in this way, before they are *willing* to give them up, and after all, are *unwilling* to give up all sins. When they are truly willing to give up all sin, when they have no will of their own, but merge their own will entirely in the will of God, then their bonds are broken. When they will yield absolutely to God's will, then they are filled with all the fullness of God.

After all, the true point of inquiry is this: Have I any right to expect to be perfect in this world? Is there any reason for me to believe that I can be so completely subdued, that my soul shall burn with a steady flame, and I shall love God wholly, up to what the law requires? That it is a real duty, no one can deny. But the great query is, Is it attainable?

I answer, Yes, I believe it is.

Here let me observe, that so much has been said within a few years about Christian Perfection, and individuals who have entertained the doctrine of Perfection have run into so many wild notions, that it seems as if the devil had anticipated the movements of the church, and created such a state of feeling, that the moment the doctrine of the Bible respecting the sanctification is crowded on the church, one and another cries out, "Why, this is Perfectionism." But I will say, notwithstanding the errors into which some of those called Perfectionists have fallen, there is such a thing held forth in the Bible as Christian Perfection, and that the Bible doctrine on the subject is what nobody need to fear, but what everybody needs to know. I disclaim, entirely, the charge of maintaining the peculiarities, whatever they be, of modern Perfectionists. I have read their publications, and have had much knowledge of them as individuals, and I cannot assent to many of their views. But the doctrine that Christian Perfection is a duty, is one which I have always maintained, and I have been more convinced of it within a few months, that *it is attainable in this life*. Many doubt this, but I am persuaded it is true, on various grounds.

1. God wills it.

The first doubt which will arise in many minds, is this; "Does God really *will* my sanctification in this world?" I answer: He says He does. The law of God is itself as strong an expression as He can give of His will on the subject, and it is backed up by an infinite sanction. The gospel is but a republication of the same will, in another form. How can God express His will more strongly on this point than He has in the text? "Be ye therefore perfect, even as your Father which is in heaven is perfect." In the Thessalonians iv. 3, we are told expressly, "For this is the will of God, even your sanctification." If you examine the Bible carefully, from one end to the other, you will find that it is everywhere just as plainly taught that God wills the sanctification of Christians in this world, as it is that He wills sinners should repent in this world. And if we go by the Bible, we might just as readily question whether He wills that men should repent, as whether He wills that Christians should be holy. Why should He not reasonably expect it? He requires it. What does He require? When He requires men to repent, He requires that they should love God with all the heart, soul, mind, and strength. What reason have we to believe that He wills they should repent at all, or love Him at all, which is not a reason for believing that He wills they should love Him perfectly? Strange logic, indeed! to teach that He wills it in one case, because He requires it, and not admit the same inference in the other. No man can show, from the Bible, that God does not require perfect sanctification in this world, nor that He does not will it, nor that it is not just as attainable as any degree of sanctification.

I have turned over the Bible with special reference to this point, and thought I would note down on my card, where I have the plan of my discourse, the passages that teach this doctrine. But I found they were altogether too numerous to do it, and that if I collected them all, I should do nothing else this evening, but stand and read passages of scripture. If you have never looked into the Bible with this view, you will be astonished to see how many more passages there are that speak of deliverance from the commission of sin, than there are that speak of deliverance from the punishment of sin. The passages that speak only of deliverance from punishment, are as nothing, in comparison of the others.

2. *All the promises and prophecies of God*, that respect the sanctification of believers in this world, are to be understood of course, *of their perfect sanctification.*

What is sanctification, but holiness? When a prophecy speaks of the sanctification of the church, are we to understand that it is to be sanctified only partially? When God *requires* holiness, are we to understand *that* of partial holiness? Surely not. By what principle, then, will you understand it of partial holiness when He *promises* holiness. We have been so long in the way of understanding the scriptures with reference to the existing state of things, that we lose sight of the real meaning. But if we look only at the language of the Bible, I defy any man to prove that the promises and prophecies of holiness mean anything short of perfect sanctification, unless the requirements of both the law and gospel are to be understood of partial obedience which is absurd.

3. Perfect sanctification is *the great blessing* promised, throughout the Bible.

The apostle says we have exceeding great and precious promises, and what are they, and what is their use? "Whereby are given unto us exceeding great and precious promises, that by these *ye might be partakers of the divine nature*, HAVING ESCAPED THE CORRUPTION that is in the world through lust." 2 Peter i. 4. If that is not perfect sanctification, I beg to know what is. It is a plain declaration that these "exceeding great and precious promises" are given for this object, that by believing and appropriating and using them, we might become partakers of the divine nature. And if we will use them for the purposes for which they were put in the Bible, we may become perfectly holy.

Let us look at some of these promises in particular. I will begin with the promise of the Abrahamic covenant. The promise is that his posterity should possess the land of Canaan, and that through him, by the Messiah, all nations should be blessed. The seal of the covenant, circumcision, which everyone knows is a type of holiness, shows us what was the principal blessing intended. It was HOLINESS. So the apostle tells us, in another place, Jesus Christ was given, that He might sanctify unto Himself a peculiar people.

All the purifications and other ceremonies of the Moasic ritual signified the same thing; as they are all pointed forward to a Savior to come. Those ordinances of purifying the body were set forth, everyone of them, with reference to the purifying of the mind, or holiness.

Under the gospel, the same thing is signified by baptism; the washing of the body representing the sanctification of the mind.

In Ezekiel xxxvi. 25, this blessing is expressly promised, as the great blessing of the gospel: "Then will I sprinkle clean water upon you, and ye shall be clean: from all your filthiness, and from all your idols, will I cleanse you. A new heart also will I give you, and a new spirit will I put within you: and I will take away the stony heart out of your flesh, and I will give you a heart of flesh. And I will put my spirit within you: and cause you to walk in my statutes, and you shall keep my judgments, and do them."

So it is in Jeremiah xxxiii. 8: "And I will cleanse them from all their iniquity, whereby they have sinned against me; and I will pardon all their iniquities, whereby they have sinned, and whereby they have transgressed against me." But it would take up too much time to quote all the passages in the Old Testament prophecies, that represent holiness to be the great blessing of the covenant. I desire you all to search the Bible for yourselves, and you will be astonished to find how uniformly the blessing of sanctification is held up as the principal blessing promised to the world through the Messiah.

Why, who can doubt that the great object of the Messiah's coming was to sanctify His people? Just after the fall it was predicted that Satan would bruise His heel, but that He should bruise Satan's head. And the apostle John tells us that "For this purpose the Son of God was manifested, that he might destroy the works of the devil." He has undertaken to put Satan under His feet. His object is to win us back to our allegiance to God, to sanctify us, to purify our minds. As it is said in Zecheriah xiii. 1, "In that day there shall be a fountain opened to the house of David and to the inhabitants of Jerusalem for sin and for uncleanness."

And Daniel says, "Seventy weeks are determined upon thy people and upon thy holy city, to finish the transgression, and to make an end of sins, and to make reconciliation for iniquity, and to bring in everlasting righteousness, and to seal up the vision and prophecy, and to anoint the Most Holy." But it is in vain to name the multitude of these texts. The Old Testament is full of it.

In the New Testament, the first account we have of the Savior, tells us, that he was called "JESUS, for he shall save his people from their sins." So it is said, "He was manifested to take away our sins," and " to destroy the works of the devil." In Titus ii. 13, the apostle Paul speaks of the grace of God, or the gospel, as teaching us to deny ungodliness. "Looking for that blessed hope, and the glorious appearing of the great God, and our Savior Jesus Christ, who gave himself for us, that he might redeem us from all iniquity, and purify unto himself a peculiar people, zealous of good works." And in Ephesians v. 25, we learn that "Christ loved the church, and gave himself for it; that he might sanctify and cleanse it with the washing of water by the word, that he might present it to himself a glorious church, not having spot or wrinkle or any such thing; but that it should be holy and without blemish." I only quote these few passages by way of illustration, to show that the object for which Christ came is to sanctify the church to such a degree that it should be absolutely "holy and without blemish." So in Romans xi. 26, "And so all Israel shall be saved: as it is written, There shall come out of Sion the Deliverer, and shall turn away ungodliness from Jacob; For this is my covenant unto them, when I shall take away their sins." And in 1 John i. 9, it is said, "If we confess our sins, he is faithful and just to forgive us our sins, and to cleanse us from all unrighteousness." What is it to "cleanse us from ALL unrighteousness," if it is not perfect sanctification? I presume all of you who are here tonight, if there is such a thing promised in the Bible as perfect sanctification, wish to know it. Now what do you think? In 1 Thessalonians v. 23, the apostle Paul prays a very remarkable prayer: "And the very God of peace sanctify you wholly; and I pray God your whole spirit, and soul, and body, be preserved blameless unto the coming of our Lord Jesus Christ." What is that? "Sanctify you wholly." Does that mean perfect sanctification? You may think it does not mean perfect sanctification in this world. But the apostle says not only that your whole soul and spirit, but that your "body be preserved blameless." Could an inspired apostle make such a prayer, if he did not believe the blessing prayed for to be possible? But he goes on to say, in the very next verse, "Faithful is he that calleth you, who also WILL DO IT." Is that true, or is it false?

4. The perfect sanctification of believers is the very *object for which the Holy Spirit is promised.*

To quote the passages that show this, would take up too much time. The whole tenor of scripture respecting the Holy Spirit proves it. The whole array of gospel means through which the Holy Spirit works, is aimed at this, and adopted to the end of sanctifying the church. All the commands to be holy, all the promises, all the prophecies, all the ordinances, all the providences, the blessings and the judgments, all the duties of religion, are means which the Holy Ghost is to employ for sanctifying the church.

5. If it is not a practicable duty to be perfectly holy in this world, then it will follow that the devil has so completely accomplished his design in corrupting mankind, that Jesus Christ is at fault, and has *no way to sanctify His people but by taking them out of the world.*

Is it possible that Satan has so got the advantage of God, that God's kingdom cannot be re-established in this world, and that the Almighty has no way but to back out, and to take His saints to heaven, before He can make them holy? Is God's kingdom to be only partially established, and is it to be always so, that the best saints shall one-half of their time be serving the devil? Must the people of God always go drooping and driveling along in religion, and live in sin, until they get to heaven? What is that stone cut out of a mountain without hands, that is to fill the earth, if it does not show that there is yet to be a universal triumph of the love of God in the world?

6. If perfect sanctification is not attainable in this world, it must be, either from a want of motives in the gospel, or a want of sufficient power in the Spirit of God.

It is said that in another life we may be like God, for we shall see Him as He is. But why not here, if we have that faith which is the "substance of things hoped for, and the evidence of things not seen?" There is a promise to those who "hunger and thirst after righteousness" that "they shall be filled." What is it to be "filled" with righteousness, but to be perfectly holy? And are we never to be filled with righteousness till we die? Are we to go through life hungry and thirsty and unsatisfied? So the Bible has been understood, but it does not read so.

OBJECTIONS.

1. "The power of habit is so great, that we ought not to expect to be perfectly sanctified in this life."

Answer. If the power of habit can be so far encroached upon that an impenitent sinner can be converted, why can it not be absolutely broken, so that a converted person may be wholly sanctified? The *greatest* difficulty, surely, is when selfishness has the entire control of the mind, and when the habits of sin are wholly unbroken. This obstacle is so great, in all cases, that no power but that of the Holy Ghost can overcome it, and so great in many instances, that God Himself cannot, consistently with His wisdom, use the means necessary to convert the soul. But is it possible to suppose, that after

He has begun to overcome it, after He has broken the power of selfishness and the obstinacy of habit, and actually converted the individual, that after this God has not resources sufficient to sanctify the soul altogether?

2. "*Many physical difficulties* have been created by a life of sin, that cannot be overcome or removed by moral means."

This is a common objection. Men feel that they have fastened upon themselves appetites and physical influences, which they do not believe it possible to overcome by moral means. The apostle Paul, in the 7th of Romans, describes a man in great conflict with the body. But in the next chapter he speaks of one who had gotten the victory over the flesh. "And if Christ be in you, the body is dead because of sin; but the spirit is life because of righteousness. But if the Spirit of Him that raised up Jesus from the dead dwell in you, He that raised up Christ from the dead shall also quicken your mortal bodies by His Spirit that dwelleth in you." This quickening of the body is not spoken of the *resurrection* of the body, but of the influence of the Spirit of God upon the body—the sanctification of the body.

You will ask, "Does the Spirit of God produce a physical change in the body?" I will illustrate it by the case of the drunkard. The drunkard has brought upon himself a diseased state of the body, an unnatural thirst, which is insatiable, and so strong that it seems impossible he should be reclaimed. But very likely you know cases in which they have been reclaimed, and have entirely overcome this physical appetite. I have heard of cases, where drunkards have been made to see the *sin* of drunkenness in such a strong light, that they abhorred strong drink, and forever renounced it, with such a loathing that they never had the least desire for strong drink again.

I once knew an individual who was a slave to the use of tobacco. At length he became convinced that it was a sin for him to use it, and the struggle against it finally drove him to God in such an agony of prayer, that he got the victory at once over the appetite, and never had the least desire for it again. I am not now giving you philosophy, but FACTS. I have heard of individuals over whom a life of sin had given to certain appetites a perfect mastery, but in time of revival they have been subdued into perfect quiescence, and these appetites have ever after been as dead as if they had no body. I suppose the fact is, that the mind may be so occupied and absorbed with greater things, as not to give a thought to the things that would revive the vicious appetite. If a drunkard goes by a grocery, or sees people drinking, and allows his mind to run upon it, the appetite will be awakened. The wise man, therefore, tells him to "Look not upon the wine when it is red." But there is no doubt that any appetite of the body may be subdued, if a sufficient impression is made upon the mind to break it up. I believe every real Christian will be ready to admit that this is possible, from his own experience. Have you not, beloved, known times when one great absorbing topic has so filled your mind, and controlled your soul, that the appetites of the body remained, for the time, perfectly neutralized? Now, suppose this state of mind to continue, to become constant; would not all these physical difficulties be overcome, which you speak of as standing in the way of perfect sanctification?

3. "The Bible is against this doctrine, where it says, there is not a just man on the earth, that liveth and sinneth not."

Answer. Suppose the Bible does say that there *is not* one on earth, it does not say there *cannot be* one. Or, it may have been true at that time, or under that dispensation, that there was not one man in the world who was perfectly sanctified; and yet it may not follow that at this time, or under the gospel dispensation, there is no one who lives without sin. "For the law made nothing perfect, but the bringing in of a better hope did." Hebrews 7. 9. i.e. The gospel did.

4. "The apostles admit that they were not perfect."

Answer. I know the apostle Paul says, in one place, "Not as though I had already attained, either were already perfect." But it is not said that he continued so till his death, or that he never did attain to perfect sanctification, and the manner in which he speaks in the remainder of the verse, looks as if he expected to become so: "But I follow after, if that I may apprehend that for which also I am apprehended of Christ Jesus." Nor does it appear to me to be true that in this passage referred to, he is speaking of perfect sanctification, but rather of perfect knowledge.

And the apostle John speaks of himself as if he loved God perfectly. But whatever may be the truth, as to the actual character of the apostles, it does not follow, because they were not perfect that no others can be. They clearly declare it to be a duty, and that they were aiming at it, just as if they expected to attain it in this life. And they command us to do the same.

5. "But is it not presumption for us to think we can be better than the apostles and primitive Christians?"

Answer. What is the presumption in the case? Is it not a fact that we have far greater advantages for religious experience, than the primitive churches. The benefit of their experience, the complete scriptures, the state of the world, the near approach of the millennium, all give us the advantage over the primitive believers. Are we to suppose the church is always to stand in regard to religious experience, and never to go ahead in anything? What scripture is there for this? Why should not the church be always growing better? It seems to be the prevailing idea that the church is to be always looking back to the primitive saints as the standard. I suppose the reverse of this is a duty, and that we ought to be always aiming at a much higher standard than theirs. I believe the church must go far ahead of the primitive Christians, before the millennium can come. I leave out of view the apostles, because it does not clearly appear but what they become fully sanctified.

6. "But so many profess to be perfect, who are not so, that I cannot believe in perfection in this life."

Answer. How many people profess to be rich, who are not;. Will you therefore say, you cannot believe anybody is rich? Fine logic!

7. "So many who profess perfection have run into error and fanaticism, that I am afraid to think of it."

Answer. I find in history, that a sect of Perfectionists has grown out of every great and general revival that ever took place. And this is exactly one of the devil's masterpieces, to counteract the effects of a revival. He knows that if the church were brought to the proper standard of holiness, it would be a speedy death blow to his power on earth, and he takes this course to defeat the efforts of the church for elevating the standard of piety, by frightening Christians from marching right up to the point, and aiming at living perfectly conformed to the will of God. And so successful has he been, that the moment you begin to crowd the church up to be holy, and give up all their sins, somebody will cry out, "Why, this leads to Perfectionism;" and thus give it a bad name and put it down.

8. "But do you really think anybody ever has been perfectly holy in this world?"

Answer. I have reason to believe there have been many. It is highly probable that Enoch and Elijah were free from sin, before they were taken out of the world. And in different ages of the church there have been numbers of Christians who were intelligent and upright, and had nothing that could be said against them, who have testified that they themselves lived free from sin. I know it is said, in reply, that they must have been proud, and that no man would say he was free from sin for any other motive but pride. But I ask, why may not a man say he is free from sin, if it is so, without being proud, as well as he can say he is converted without being proud? Will not the saints say it in heaven, to the praise of the grace of God, which has thus crowned His glorious work? And why may they not say it now, from the same motive? I do not myself profess now to have attained perfect sanctification, but if I had attained it, if I felt that God had really given me the victory over the world, the flesh and the devil, and made me free from sin, would I keep it a secret, locked up in my own breast, and let my brethren stumble on in ignorance of what the grace of God can do? Never. I would tell them, that they might expect complete deliverance, if they would only lay hold on the arm of help which Christ reaches forth, to save His people from their sins.

I have heard people talk like this, that if a Christian really was perfect, he would be the last person that would tell of it. But would you say of a person who professed conversion, "If he was really converted, he would be the last person to tell of it?" On the contrary, is it not the first impulse of a converted heart to say, "Come and hear, all ye that fear God, and I will declare what He hath done for my soul!" Why then should not the same desire exist in one who feels that he has obtained sanctification? Why all these suspicions, and refusing to credit evidence? If anyone gives evidence of great piety, if his life is irreproachable, and his spirit not to be complained of, if he shows the very spirit of the Son of God, and if such a person testifies that after great struggles and agonizing prayer God has given him the victory, and his soul is set at liberty by the power of divine grace; why are we not bound to receive his testimony, just as much, as when he says he is converted. We always take such testimony, so far. And now, when he says he has gone farther, and got the victory over all sin, and that Christ has actually fulfilled His promise in this respect, why should we not credit this also?

I have recently read Mr. Wesley's "Plain Account of Christian Perfection," a book I never saw until lately. I find some expressions in it to which I should object, but I believe it is rather the expression than the sentiments. And I think, with this abatement, it is an admirable book, and I wish every member of this church would read it. An edition is in the press, in this city. I would also recommend the memoir of James Brainerd Taylor, and I wish every

Christian would get it, and study it. I have read the most of it three times within a few months. From many things in that book, it is plain that he believed in the doctrine that Christian perfection is a duty, and that it is attainable by believers in this life. There is nothing published which shows that he professed to have attained it, but it is manifest that he believed it to be attainable. But I have been told that much which is found in his diary on this subject, as well as some things in his letters, were suppressed by his biographer, as not fitted for the eye of the church in her present state. I believe if the whole could come to light, that it would be seen that he was a firm believer in this doctrine. These books should be read and pondered by the church.

I have now in my mind an individual, who was a member of the church, but very worldly, and when a revival came he opposed it, at first; but afterwards he was awakened, and after an awful conflict, he broke down, and has ever since lived a life of the most devoted piety, laboring and praying incessantly, like his blessed Master, to promote the kingdom of God. I have never heard this man say he thought he was perfect, but I have often heard him speak of the duty and practicability of being perfectly sanctified. And if there is a man in the world who is so, I believe he is one.

People have the strangest notions on this subject. Sometimes you will hear them argue against Christian Perfection on this ground, that a man who was perfectly holy could not live, could not exist in this world. I believe I have talked just so myself, in time past. I know I have talked like a fool on the subject. Why, a saint who was perfect would be more alive than ever, to the good of his fellow men. Could not Jesus Christ live on earth? He was perfectly holy. It is thought that if a person was perfectly sanctified, and loved God perfectly, he would be in such a state of *excitement*, that he could not remain in the body, could neither eat nor sleep, nor attend to the ordinary duties of life. But there is no evidence of this. The Lord Jesus Christ was a man, subject to all the temptations of other men, He also loved the Lord his God with all His heart and soul and strength. And yet it does not appear that He was in such a state of excitement that He could not both eat and sleep, and work at His trade as a carpenter, and maintain perfect health of body and perfect composure of mind. And why needs a saint that is perfectly sanctified, to be carried away with uncontrollable excitement, or killed with intense emotion, any more than Jesus Christ? There is no need of it, and Christian Perfection implies no such thing.

REMARKS.

We can see now the reasons why there is no more perfection in the world.

1. Christians do not believe that it is the will of God, or that God is willing they should be perfectly sanctified in this world.

They know He commands them to be perfect, as He is perfect, but they think that He is secretly unwilling, and does not really wish them to be so; "Otherwise," say they, "why does He not do more for us, to make us perfect?" No doubt, God prefers their remaining as they are, to using any other means or system of influences to make them otherwise; because He sees that it would be a greater evil to introduce a new system of means than to let them remain as they are. Where one of the evils is unavoidable, He chooses the least of the two evils, and who can doubt that He prefers their being perfect in *the circumstances in which they are*, to their sinning in these circumstances. Sinners reason just as these professors reason. They say, "I don't believe He wills my repentance; if He did, He would make me repent." Sinner, God may prefer your continued impenitence, and your damnation, to using any other influences than He does use to make you repent. But for you to infer from this, that He does not wish you to yield to the influences He does use, is strange logic! Suppose your servant should reason so, and say, "I don't believe my master means I should obey him, because he don't stand by me all day, to keep me at work." Is that a just conclusion? Very likely, the master's time is so valuable, that it would be a greater evil to his business, than for that servant to stand still all day.

So it is in the government of God. If God were to bring all the power of His government to bear on one individual, He might save that individual, while at the same time, it would so materially derange His government, that it would be a vastly greater evil than for that individual to go to hell. In the same way, in the case of a Christian, God has furnished him with all the means of sanctification, and required him to be perfect, and now he turns round and says, "God does not really prefer my being perfect; if He did, He would make me so." This is just the argument of the impenitent sinner, and no better in one case than the other. The plain truth is, God does desire, of both, that in the circumstances in which they are placed, they should do just what He commands them to do.

2. They do not expect it themselves.

The great part of the church do not really expect to be any more pious than they are.

3. Much of the time, they do not even desire perfect sanctification.

4. They are satisfied with their hunger and thirst after righteousness, and do not expect to be filled.

Here let me say, that hunger and thirst after holiness IS NOT HOLINESS. The desire of a thing is not the thing desired. If they hunger and thirst after holiness, they ought to give God no rest, till He comes up to His promise, that they shall be filled with holiness, or made perfectly holy.

5. They overlook the great design of the gospel.

Too long has the church been in the habit of thinking that the great design of the gospel is, to save men from the punishment of sin, whereas its real design and object is to deliver men FROM SIN. But Christians have taken the other ground, and think of nothing but that they are to go on in sin, and all they hope for is to be forgiven, and when they die made holy in heaven. Oh, if they only realized that the whole framework of the gospel is designed to break the power of sin, and fill men on earth with all the fullness of God, how soon there would be one steady blaze of love in the hearts of God's people all over the world!

6. The promises are not understood, and not appropriated by faith.

If the church would read the Bible, and lay hold of every promise there, they would find them exceeding great and precious. But now the church loses its inheritance, and remains ignorant of the extent of the blessings she may receive. Had I time tonight, I could lead you to some promises which, if you would only get hold of and appropriate, you would know what I mean.

7. They seek it by the law, and not by faith.

How many are seeking sanctification by their own resolutions and works, their fastings and prayers, their endeavors and activity, instead of taking right hold of Christ, by faith, for sanctification, as they do for justification. It is all *work*, work, WORK, when it should be by faith in "Christ Jesus, who of God is made unto us wisdom, and righteousness, and SANCTIFICATION, and redemption." When they go and take right hold of the strength of God, they will be sanctified. Faith will bring Christ right into the soul, and fill it with the same spirit that breathes through Himself. These dead works are nothing. It is faith that must sanctify, it is faith that purifies the heart; that faith which is the substance of things hoped for, takes hold of Christ and brings Him into the soul, to dwell there the hope of glory; that the life which we live here should be by the faith of the Son of God. It is from not knowing, or not regarding this, that there is so little holiness in the church.

And finally,

8. From the want of the right kind of dependence.

Instead of taking scriptural views of their dependencies and seeing where their strength is, and realizing how willing God is to give His Holy Spirit to them that ask, now and continually, and thus taking hold and holding on by the arm of God, they sit down, in unbelief and sin, to wait God's time, and call this depending on God. Alas how little is felt, after all this talk about dependence on the Holy Spirit, how little is really felt of it, and how little is there of the giving up of the whole soul to His control and guidance, with faith in His power to enlighten, to lead, to sanctify, to kindle the affections, and fill the soul continually with all the fullness of God!

LECTURE IX.

CHRISTIAN PERFECTION.

TEXT:—"Be ye therefore perfect, even as your Father which is in heaven is perfect."

Matthew v. 48.

In speaking from these words, two weeks ago, I pursued the following order.

I. I showed what is implied in being perfect.
II. What Christian perfection is.
III. That it is a duty.
IV. That it is attainable in this life.
V. Answered some objections, and then gave some reasons why so many persons are not perfect.

Tonight my object is to mention some additional causes which prevent the great body of Christians from attaining perfect sanctification. As a matter of fact, we know that the church is not sanctified, and we ought to know the reasons. If the defect is in God, we ought to know it. If He has not provided a sufficient revelation, or if the power of the Holy Spirit is not adequate to sanctify His people in this world, we ought to understand it, so as not to perplex ourselves with idle endeavors after what is unattainable. And if the fault is in us, we ought to know it, and the true reasons ought to be understood, lest by any means we should charge God foolishly, even in thought, by imagining that He has required of us that which He has furnished us no adequate means of attaining.

I. The first general reason which I shall mention, for persons not being sanctified, is that they seek sanctification *by works*, and not *by faith*.

The religion of works assumes a great variety of forms; and it is interesting to see the ever-varying, shifting forms it takes:

1. One form is where men are aiming to live so as to render their damnation unjust. It matters not, in this case, whether they deem themselves Christians or not, if they are in fact trying to live so as to render it unjust for God to send them to hell. This was the religion of the ancient Pharisees. And there are not a few, in the present day,

whose religion is purely of this character. You will often find them out of the church, and perhaps ready to confess that they have never been born again. But yet they speak of their own works in a way that makes it manifest that they think themselves quite too good to be damned.

2. Another form of the religion of works is, where persons are not aiming so much to render it unjust in God to damn them, but are seeking by their works to recommend themselves to the mercy of God. They know they deserve to be damned, and will forever deserve it. But they also know that God is merciful; and they think that if they live honest lives, and do many kind things to the poor, it will so recommend them to the general mercy of God, that He will not impute their iniquities to them, but will forgive their sins and save them. This is the religion of most modern moralists. Living under the gospel, they know they cannot be saved by their works, and yet they think that if they go to meeting, and help support the minister, and do this and that and the other kinds of good works, it will recommend them to God's mercy sufficiently for salvation. So far as I understand the system of religion held by modern Unitarians, this must be their system. Whether they understand it so, or admit it to be so, or not, as far as I can see, it comes to this. They set aside the atonement of Christ, and do not expect to be saved by the righteousness of Jesus Christ; and I know not on what they do depend, but this. They seem to have a kind of sentimental religion, and on this, with their morality and their liberality, they depend to recommend them to the mercy of God. On this ground they expect to receive the forgiveness of their sins, and to be saved.

3. Another form of the religion of works is, where persons are endeavoring to *prepare themselves to accept of Christ.*

They understand that salvation is only through Jesus Christ. They know that they cannot be saved by works, nor by the general mercy of God, without an atonement, and that the only way to be saved is by faith in Christ. But they have heard the relations of the experience of others, who went through a long process of distress before they submitted to Christ and found peace in believing. And they think a certain preparatory process is necessary, and that they must make a great many prayers and run hither and thither to attend meetings, and lie awake many nights, and suffer so much distress, and perhaps fall into despair, and then they shall be in a situation to accept of Christ. This is the situation of many convicted sinners. When they are awakened, and get so far as to find that they cannot be saved by their own works, then they set themselves to prepare to receive Christ. Perhaps some of you, who are here tonight, are in just this case. You dare not come to Christ just as you are, when you have made so few prayers, and attended so few meetings, and felt so little distress, and done so little and been so little engaged. And so, instead of going right to Christ for all you need, as a poor lost sinner, throwing yourself unreservedly into His hands, you set yourself to lash your mind into more conviction and distress, in order to prepare you to accept of Christ. Such cases are just about as common as convicted sinners are. How many there are, who abound in such works, and seem determined they will not fall down at once at the feet of Christ. It is not necessary to go into an argument here, to show that they are growing no better by all this process. There is no love to God in it, and no faith, and no religion. It is all mere mockery of God, and hypocrisy, and sin. There may be a great deal of feeling, but it is of no use; it brings them in fact no nearer to Christ; and after all, they have to do the very thing at last, which they might have done just as well at first.

Now suppose an individual should take it into his head that this is the way to become holy. Every Christian can see that it is very absurd, and that however he may multiply such works, he is not beginning to approach to holiness. The first act of holiness is to believe, to take hold of Christ by faith. And if a Christian, who is awakened to feel the need of sanctification, undertakes to go through a preparatory process of self-created distress, before he applies to Christ, it is just as absurd as for an awakened sinner to do it.

4. Another form of the religion of works is, where individuals *perform works to beget faith and love.*

The last mentioned class was where individuals are preparing to come to Christ. Here we suppose them to have come to Christ, and that they have accepted Him, and are real Christians; but having backslidden they set themselves to perform many works to beget faith and love, or to beget and perfect a right state of feeling. This is one of the most common and most subtle forms in which the religion of works shows itself at the present day.

Now this is very absurd. It is an attempt to produce holiness by sin. For if the feelings are not right, the act is sin. If the act does not proceed from faith and love, whatever they may do is sin. How idle, to think that a person, by multiplying sins, can beget holiness! And yet it is perfectly common for persons to think they can beget holiness by a course of conduct that is purely sinful. For certainly, any act that does not spring from love already existing, is sinful. The individual acts not from the impulse of faith that works by love and purifies the heart, but he acts without faith and love, with a design to beget those affections by such acts as these.

It is true, when faith and love exist, and are *the propelling motive* to action, the carrying of them out in action has a tendency to increase them. This arises from the known laws of mind, by which every power and every faculty gains strength by exercise. But the case supposed is where individuals have left their first love, if ever they had any, and then set themselves, without faith or love, to bustle about and warn sinners, or the like, under the idea that this is the way to wake up, or to become holy, or to get into the state of feeling that God requires. It is really most unphilosophical and absurd, and ruinous, to think of waking up faith in the soul, where it does not exist, by performing outward acts from some other motive. It is mocking God, to pretend, by doing things from wrong motives, to produce a holy frame of mind. By and by, I shall show where the deception lies, and how it comes to pass that any persons should ever dream of such a way of becoming sanctified. The fact is too plain to be proved, that pretending to serve God in such a way, so far from having any tendency to produce a right spirit, is in fact grieving the Holy Ghost, and insulting God.

So far as the philosophy of the thing is concerned, it is just like the conduct of convicted sinners. But there is one difference: the sinner, in spite of all his wickedness, may by and by learn his own helplessness, and actually renounce all his own works, and feel that his continued refusal to come to Christ, so far from being a preparation for coming, is only heaping up so many sins against God. But it is otherwise with those who think themselves to be already Christians, as I will explain by and by.

It is often remarked, by careful observers in religion, that many persons who abound in religious acts, are often the most hardened, and the farthest removed from spiritual feeling. If performing religious duties was the way to produce religious feeling, we should expect that ministers, and leaders in the church, would be always the most spiritual. But the fact is, that where faith and love are not in exercise, in proportion as persons abound in outward acts without the inward life, they become hardened and cold, and full of iniquity. They may have been converted but have backslidden, and so long as they are seeking sanctification in this way, by multiplying their religious duties, running round to protracted meetings, or warning sinners, without any spiritual life, they will never find it, but will in fact become more hardened and stupid. Or if they get into an excitement in this way, it is a spurious superficial state of mind that has nothing holy in it.

II. Another reason why so many persons are not sanctified is this: *They do not receive Christ in all His relations, as He is offered in the gospel.*

Most people are entirely mistaken here, and they will never go ahead in sanctification, until they learn that there is a radical error in the manner in which they attempt to attain it. Take a case: Suppose an individual who is convinced of sin. He sees that God might in justice send him to hell, and that he has no way in which he can make satisfaction. Now tell him of Christ's atonement, show him how Christ died to make satisfaction, so that God can be just and yet the justifier of them that believe in Jesus, he sees it to be right and sufficient, and exactly what he needs, and he throws himself upon Christ, in faith, for justification. He accepts Him as his justification, and that is as far as he understands the gospel. He believes, and is justified, and feels the pardon of his sins. Now, here is the very attitude in which most convicted sinners stop. They take up with Christ in the character in which, as sinners, they most feel the need of a Savior, as the propitiation of their sins, to make atonement and procure forgiveness, and there they stop. And after that, it is often exceedingly difficult to get their attention to what Christ offers beyond. Say what you will in regard to Christ as the believer's wisdom and righteousness and his sanctification, and all his relations as a Savior from sin—they do not feel their need of Him sufficiently to make them really throw themselves upon Him in these relations. The converted person feels at peace with God, joy and gratitude fill his heart, he rejoices in having found a Savior that can stand between him and his Judge, he may have really submitted, and for a time, he follows on in the way of obedience to God's commandments. But, by and by, he finds the workings of sin in his members, unsubdued pride, his old temper breaking forth, and a multitude of enemies assaulting his soul, from within and without, and he is not prepared to meet them.

Hitherto, he has taken up Christ and regarded Him, mainly, in one of His relations, that of a Savior to save him from hell. If I am not mistaken, the great mass of professing Christians lose sight, almost altogether, of many of the most interesting relations which Christ sustains to believers. Now, when the convert finds himself thus brought under the power of temptation, and drawn into sin, he needs to receive Christ in a new relation, to know more of the extent of His provision, to make a fresh application to Him, and give a new impulse to his mind to resist temptation. This is not fully apprehended by many Christians. They never really view Christ, under his name Jesus, because he saves His people *from their sins*. They need to receive him AS A KING, to take the throne in their hearts, and rule over them with absolute and perfect control, bringing every faculty and every thought into subjection. The reason why the convert thus falls under the power of temptation, is that he has not submitted his own will to Christ, as a king, in *everything*, as perfectly as he ought, but is, after all, exercising his own self-will in some particulars.

Again: There are a multitude of what are called sins of ignorance, which need not be. Christians complain that they cannot understand the Bible, and there are many things concerning which they are always in doubt. Now, what they need is, to receive Christ as wisdom, to accept Him in His relation as the source of light and knowledge. Who of you now attach a full and definite idea to the text which says, "We are in Christ Jesus, who of God is made unto us wisdom, and righteousness, and sanctification, and redemption?" What do you understand by it? It does not say He is a justifier, and a teacher, and a sanctifier, and a redeemer; but that He is wisdom, and righteousness, and sanctification, and redemption. What does that mean? Until Christians shall find out by experience, and know what that scripture meaneth, how can the church be sanctified? The church is now just like a branch plucked off from a vine; "Except ye abide in me, ye cannot bear fruit." Suppose a branch had power voluntarily to separate itself from the vine, and then should undertake to bring forth fruit, what would you think? So with the church; until Christians will go to the Eternal Source of sanctification, and wisdom, and redemption, it will never become holy. If they would become, by faith, absolutely united with Him, in all those offices and relations in which He is offered, they would know what sanctification is.

I may, at some other time, take this text as the foundation of a separate discourse, and discuss these points, one by one, and show what this means. I will only say, at present, as much as this: that it means just what it says, and there is no need of explaining it away, as has too commonly been done. And when the church shall once take hold of Christ, in ALL His relations, as here set forth, they will know what it is, and will see that He is the light and the life of the world. To be sanctified by Him, they must so embrace Him, as to receive from Him those supplies of grace and knowledge, which alone can purify the soul and give the complete victory over sin and Satan.

I will mention some reasons why Christians do not receive Christ in all his relations.

(1.) They may not have those particular convictions, that are calculated to make them deeply feel the necessity of a Savior in those relations.

If an individual is not deeply convicted of his own depravity, and has not learned intimately his own sinfulness, and if he does not know experimentally, as a matter of fact, that he needs help to overcome the power of sin, he will never receive Jesus Christ into his soul AS A KING. When men undertake to help themselves out of sin, and feel strong in their own strength to cope with their spiritual enemies, they never receive Christ fully, nor rely on Him solely to save them from sin. But when they have tried to keep themselves by their own watchfulness and prayers, and binding themselves by resolution and oaths to obey God, and find that, after all, if left to themselves, there is nothing in them but depravity, then they feel their own helplessness, and begin to inquire what they shall do? The Bible teaches all this plainly enough, and if people would believe the Bible, converts would know their own helplessness, and their need of a Savior to save from sin, at the outset. But, as a matter of fact, they do not receive nor believe the Bible on this subject, until they have set themselves to work out a righteousness of their own, and thus have found out by experiment that they are nothing without Christ. And therefore they do not receive Him in this relation, till after they have spent, it may be, years, in these vain and self-righteous endeavors to do the work of sanctification themselves. Having begun in the Spirit they are trying to be made perfect by the flesh.

(2.) Others, when they see their own condition, do not receive Christ as a Savior from sin, because they are, after all unwilling to abandon all sin.

They know that if they give themselves up entirely to Christ, all sin must be abandoned; and they have some idol which they are unwilling to give up.

(3.) Sometimes, when persons are deeply convinced, and anxious to know what they shall do to get rid of sin, they do not apply to Christ in faith, because they do not know what they have a right to expect from Him.

There are many who seem to suppose they are under a fatal necessity to sin, and that there is no help for it, but they must drag along this load of sin till their death. They do not absolutely charge God foolishly, and say in words that He has made no provision for such a case as this. But they seem to suppose that Christ's atonement being so great as to cover all sins, and God's mercy being so great, if they do go on in sin all their days, as they expect they shall, He will forgive all at last, and it will be just about as well in the end, as if they had been really sanctified. They do not see that the gospel has made provision sufficient to rid us forever of the commission of all sin. They look at it as merely a system of pardon, leaving the sinner to drag along his load of sin to the very gate of heaven; instead of a system to break up the very power of sin in the mind. The consequence is, they make very little account of the promises. O, how little use do Christians make of those exceeding great and precious promises, in the Bible, which were given expressly for this purpose, that we might become partakers of the divine nature! Here God has suited His promises to our exigencies, for this end, and we have only to draw upon Him for all that we want, and we shall have whatever we need for our sanctification. Hear the Savior say, "What things soever ye desire when ye pray, BELIEVE that ye receive them and ye shall have them."

The fact is, Christians do not really believe much that is in the Bible. Now, suppose you were to meet God, and you knew it was God himself, speaking to you, and He should reach out a book in His hand, and tell you to take that book, and that the book contains exceeding great and precious promises, of all that you need, or ever can need, to resist temptation, to overcome sin, and to make you perfectly holy, and fit you for heaven; and then He tells you that whenever you are in want of anything for this end, you need only take the appropriate promise, and present it to Him at any time, and He will do it. Now, if you were to receive such a book, directly from the hand of God, and knew that God had written it for you, with His own hand, would you not believe it?

And would you not read it a great deal more than you now read the Bible? How eager you would be to know all that was in it? And how ready to apply the promises in time of need! You would want to get it all by heart, and often repeat it all through, that you might keep your mind familiar with its contents, and be always ready to apply the promises you read! Now, the truth is, the Bible is that book. It is written just so, and filled with just such promises; so that the Christian, by laying hold of the right promise, and pleading it, can always find all that he needs for his spiritual benefit.

Christ is a complete Savior. All the promises of God are in him *Yea*, and in him *Amen*, to the glory of God the Father. That is, God has promised in the second person of the Trinity, in the person of Jesus Christ, and made them all certain through Him. Now, the thing which is needed is, that Christians should understand these promises, and believe them, and in every circumstance of need apply them, for sanctification. Suppose they lack wisdom. Let them go to God, and plead the promise. Suppose they cannot understand the scriptures, or the path of duty is not plain. The promise is plain enough, take that. Whatever they lack of wisdom, righteousness, sanctification, and redemption, only let them go to God in faith, and take hold of the promise, and if He does not prove false, they will assuredly receive all that they need.

4.) Another reason why many do not receive Christ in all His relations is, that they are too proud to relinquish all self-dependence or reliance on their own wisdom and their own will.

How great a thing it is, for the proud heart of man to give up its own wisdom, and knowledge, and will, and everything, to God. I have found this the greatest of all difficulties. Doubtless all find it so. The common plea is, "Our reason was given us, to be exercised in religion, but what is the use, if we may not rely on it, or follow it?" But there is one important discrimination to be made, which many overlook. Our reason was given us to use in religion; but it is not in the proper province of reason to ask whether what God says is reasonable, but to show us the infinite reasonableness of believing that ALL which God says must be true, whether we in our ignorance and blindness can see the reasonableness of it or not. And if we go beyond this, we go beyond the proper province of reason. But how unwilling the proud heart of man is to lay aside all its own vain wisdom, and become like a little child, under the teaching of God! The apostle says, "If any man think that he knoweth anything, he knoweth nothing yet as he ought to know." There is a vast meaning in this. He that does not receive Christ alone as his wisdom, knows nothing in religion to any purpose. If he is not taught by Jesus Christ, he has not learned the first lesson of Christianity. So again, "No man knoweth the Father but the Son, and he to whomsoever the Son revealeth him." The individual who has learned this lesson, feels that he has not one iota of knowledge in religion, that is of any value, only as he is taught by Jesus Christ. For it is written, "And they shall all be taught of God."

REMARKS.

I. You see what kind of preaching the church now needs.

The church needs to be searched thoroughly, shown their great defects, and brought under conviction, and then pointed to where their great strength lies. With their everlasting parade of dead works, they need to be shown how poor they are. "Thou sayest I am rich, and increased with goods, and have need of nothing, and knowest not that thou art wretched, and miserable, and poor, and blind, and naked." Until Christians are shown their poverty, and the infinite emptiness and abominable wickedness of their dead works, and then shown just where their help is, and that it is by FAITH ALONE they can never be sanctified, the church will go farther and farther from God, till it will have only the form of godliness, denying the power thereof.

II. When you see the Christian character defective in any particular, you may always know that the individual needs to receive Christ more fully in the very relation that is calculated to supply this defect.

The defect, whatever it be, in the character of any believer, will never be remedied, until he sees the relation of Christ to that part of his character, so as by faith to take hold of Christ and bring Him in to remedy that defect. Suppose a person is naturally penurious and selfish, and reluctant to act in a disinterested manner; he will never remedy that defect, until he receives Christ as his pattern, and the selfishness is driven out of his heart by imbuing his very soul with the infinite benevolence of the Savior. So it is with regard to any other defect; he will never conquer it, until you make him see that the infinite fullness of Christ is answerable to that very want.

III. You see the necessity there is that ministers should be persons of deep experience in religion.

It is easy for even a carnal mind to preach so as to bring sinners under conviction. But until the tone of sanctification is greatly raised among ministers, it is not to be expected that the piety of the church will be greatly elevated. Those Christians who have experience of these things should therefore be much in prayer for ministers, that the sons of Levi may be purified, that the leaders of Israel may take hold of Christ for the sanctification of their own hearts, and then they will know what to say to the church on the subject of holiness.

IV. Many seek sanctification by works, who do not know that they are seeking in this way.

They profess that they are seeking sanctification only by faith. They tell you they know very well that it is in vain to seek it in their own strength. But yet the results show how conclusively, that they are seeking by works, and not by faith. It is of the last importance that you should know, whether you are seeking sanctification by works, or by faith, for all seeking of it by works is absurd, and never will lead to any good results. How will you know?

Take again the case of a convicted sinner. Sinner, how are you seeking salvation? The sinner replies, "By faith, of course; everybody knows that no sinner can be saved by works." I say, No, you are seeking salvation by works. How shall I show it to him? Sinner, do you believe in Christ? "I do." But does He give you peace with God? "O no, not yet, but I am trying to get more conviction, and to pray more, and be more earnest in seeking, and I hope He will give me peace if I persevere." Now, every Christian sees, at a glance, that with all his pretensions to the contrary, this man is seeking salvation by works. And the way to prove it to him is exceedingly simple. It is evident he is seeking by works, because he is relying on certain preparatory steps and processes to be gone through, *before* he exercises saving faith. He is not ready now to accept of Christ, he is conscious he is not, but thinks he must bring himself into a different state of mind as a preparation, and it is at this he is aiming. That is works. No matter what the state of mind is, that he aims at as preparatory to coming to Christ; if it is anything that must precede faith, or any preparatory process for faith, and he is trying *without faith* to get into a proper state of mind to have faith, it is all the religion of works.

Now, how common is just such a state of mind among those Christians who profess to be seeking sanctification. You say, you must mortify sin, but the way you go about it is by a self-righteous preparation, seeking to recommend yourselves to Christ as worthy to receive the blessing, instead of coming right to Christ, as an unworthy and ruined beggar, to receive at once, by faith, the very blessing you need. No efforts of your own are going to make you any better. Like a person in a horrible pit of miry clay, every struggle of your own sinks you deeper in the clay. You have no need of any such thing, and all your endeavors, instead of bringing you any nearer to Christ, are only sinking you down in the filth, farther and farther from God. It is not even the beginning of help.

The sinner, by his preparatory seeking, gains no advantage. There he lies, dead in trespasses and sins, as far removed from spiritual life, or holiness, as ever a dead corpse was from natural life; until at length, ceasing from his own dead works, he comes to the conviction that there is nothing he can do for himself but to go NOW, *just as he is*, and submit to Christ. As long as he thinks there is something he must do first, he never feels that now is God's time of salvation. And as long as the Christian is seeking sanctification in the way of works, he never feels that now is God's time to give him the victory over sin.

V. Multitudes deceive themselves in this matter, by the manner in which they have seen certain old-fashioned, Antinomian churches roused up, who were dragging along in death.

Where such a church has been found, that had been fed on dry doctrine till they were about as stupid as the seats they sat on, the first thing has been to rouse them up to do something, and that very fact perhaps would bring such a church under conviction, and lead them to repentance. It is not because there is any religion in these *doings* of professors in such a state; but it shows them their deficiencies, and their unfitness to be members of the church, and awakens their consciences. So it is, sometimes, when a careless sinner has been set to praying. Everybody knows there is no piety in such prayers, but it calls his attention to the subject of religion, and gives the Holy Spirit an opportunity to bring the truth full upon his conscience. But if you take a man who has been in the habit of praying from his childhood, and whose formal prayers have made him as cold as a stone, praying will never bring that man under conviction, till you show him what is the true character of his prayers, and STOP his ungodly and heaven-daring praying.

In many cases, where a church has sunk down in stupidity, the most effectual way to rouse them has been found to be, setting them to warning sinners of their danger. This would get the attention of the church to the subject of religion, and perhaps bring many of them to repentance. Hence many have formed a general rule, that the way for a church to wake up, always is, to go to work, and warn sinners. They do not discriminate, here, between the habits of different churches, and the different treatment they consequently require. Whereas, if you take what is called a "working church," where they have been in the habit of enjoying revivals and holding protracted meetings, you will find there is no difficulty in rousing up the church to act, and bustle about, and make a noise. But as a general rule, unless there is great wisdom and faithfulness in dealing with the church, every succeeding revival will make their religion more and more superficial; and their minds will be more hardened instead of being convicted, by their efforts. Tell such a church they are self-righteous, and that there is no Holy Ghost in their bustling, and they will be affronted and stare at you, "Why, don't you know that the way to wake up in religion is to go to work in religion?" Whereas, the very fact that activity has become a habit with them, shows that they require a different course. They need first to be thoroughly probed and searched, and made sensible of their deficiencies, and brought humble and believing to the foot of the cross, for sanctification.

When I was an evangelist, I labored in a church that had enjoyed many revivals, and it was the easiest thing in the world to get the church to go out and bring in sinners to the meetings; and the impenitent would come in and hear, but there was no deep feeling, and no faith in the church. The minister saw that this way of proceeding was ruining the church, and that each successive revival, brought about in this manner, made the converts more and more superficial, and unless we came to a stand, and got more sanctification in the church, we should defeat our object. We began to preach with that view, and the church members writhed under it. The preaching ran so directly across all their former notions, about the way to promote religion, that some of them were quite angry. They would run about and talk but would do nothing else. But after a terrible state of things many of them broke down, and became as humble and as teachable as little children.

Now there are multitudes in the churches who insist upon it that the way to get sanctification is to go to work, and they think that, by dint of mere friction, they can produce the warm love of God in their hearts. This is all wrong. Mere driving about and bustle and noise will never produce sanctification. And least of all, when persons have been accustomed to this course.

VI. You that are in the habit of performing many religious duties, and yet fall short of holiness, can see what is the matter.

The truth is, you have gone to *work* to wake up, instead of at once throwing yourself on the Lord Jesus Christ for sanctification, and then going to work to serve Him. You have gone to work *for your life* instead of working *from* a principle of life within, impelling you to the work of the Lord. You have undertaken to get holiness by a lengthened process, like that of the convicted sinner, who is *preparing* to come to Christ. But the misfortune is, that you have not half the perseverance of the sinner. The sinner is driven by the fear of going to hell, and he exerts himself in the way of works till his strength is all exhausted, and all his self-righteousness is worked up, and then, feeling that he is helpless and undone, he throws himself into the arms of Christ. But you have not so much perseverance, because you have not so much fear. You think you are a Christian, and that however you may come short of sanctification, yet you are safe from hell, and can go to heaven without it. And so you will not persevere and put forth your efforts for holiness by works, till you have used up all your self-righteousness, and are driven to Christ as your only hope for sanctification. This is the reason why convicted Christians so generally fall short of that submission to Christ for holiness, which the convicted sinner exercises for forgiveness.

You say to the sinner, who is seeking salvation by works, "Why don't you yield up all your self-righteous efforts, and come right to Christ for salvation? He is ready to receive you NOW!" And why don't *you* do so too? When will you learn the first lesson in religion, that *you* have no help in yourselves, and that all *your* exertions without Christ, for sanctification, are just as vain as it is for the wretch who is in the horrible pit and miry clay, by his own struggling to get himself out.

VII. The growth of works in the church is no certain sign of growth in holiness.

If the church grows in holiness, it will grow in works. But it does not follow, that growth in works always proves growth in holiness. It may be that works of religion may greatly increase, while the power of religion is actually and rapidly declining. It often happens in a church, that when a revival begins to lose its power, the church may be willing to do even more than ever, in works, but it will not arrest the decline, unless they get broken down before God.

I see I must take up this subject again. O, that I could convince the whole church that they need no other help but Christ, and that they would come at once to Christ for all they want, and receive Him as their wisdom, and righteousness, and sanctification, and redemption. How soon would all their wants be supplied, from His infinite fullness.

LECTURE X.

WAY OF SALVATION.

TEXT:—"Sirs, what must I do to be saved? And they said, Believe on the Lord Jesus Christ. Who of God is made unto us wisdom, and righteousness, and sanctification, and redemption."
Acts xvi.30, 31, with 1 Cor. 1. 30.

There can be no objection to putting these texts together in this manner as only a clause in the first of them is omitted, which is not essential to the sense, and which is irrelevant to my present purpose.

In the passage first quoted, the apostle tells the inquiring jailer, who wished to know what he must do to be saved, "Believe on the Lord Jesus Christ and thou shalt be saved." And in the other he adds the explanatory remark, telling what a Savior Jesus Christ is, "Who of God is made unto us wisdom, and righteousness, and sanctification, and redemption." The following is the order in which I design to discuss the subject tonight:

I. Show what salvation is.
II. Show the way of salvation.

I. What is salvation?

Salvation includes several things; sanctification, justification, and eternal life and glory. The two prime ideas, are sanctification and justification. Sanctification is the purifying of the mind, or making it holy. Justification relates to the manner in which we are accepted and treated by God.

II. The way of salvation.

1. It is by faith, in opposition to works.

Here I design to take a brief view of the gospel plan of salvation, and exhibit it especially in contrast with the original plan on which it was proposed to save mankind.

Originally, the human race was put on the foundation of law for salvation; so that, if saved at all, they were to be saved on the ground of perfect and eternal obedience to the law of God. Adam was the natural head of the race. It has been supposed by many, that there was a covenant made with Adam such as this, that if he continued to obey the law for a limited period, all his posterity should be confirmed in holiness and happiness forever. What the reason is for this belief, I am unable to ascertain; I am not aware that the doctrine is taught in the Bible. And if it is true, the condition of mankind now, does not differ materially from what it was at first. If the salvation of the race originally turned wholly on the obedience of one man, I do not see how it could be called a covenant of *works* so far as the race is concerned. For if their weal or woe was suspended on the conduct of one head, it was a covenant of grace to them, in the same manner, that the present system is a covenant of grace. For according to that view, all that related to works depended on one man, just as it does under the gospel; and the rest of the race had no more to do with works, than they have now, but all that related to works was done by the representative. Now, I have supposed, and there is nothing in the Bible to the contrary, that if Adam had continued in obedience forever, his posterity would have stood forever on the same ground, and must have obeyed the law themselves forever in order to be saved. It may have been, that if he had obeyed always, the natural influence of his example would have brought about such a state of things, that as a matter of fact all his posterity would have continued in holiness. But the salvation of each individual would still have depended on his own works. But if the works of the first father were to be so set to the account of the race, that on account of his obedience they were to be secured in holiness and happiness forever, I do not see wherein it differs materially from the covenant of grace, or the gospel.

As a matter of fact, Adam was the natural head of the human race, and his sin has involved them in its consequences, but not on the principle that his sin is literally accounted their sin. The truth is simply this; that from the relation in which he stood as their natural head, as a matter of fact his sin has resulted in the sin and ruin of his posterity. I suppose that mankind were originally all under a covenant of works, and that Adam was not so their head or representative, that his obedience or disobedience involved them irresistibly in sin and condemnation, irrespective of their own acts. As a fact it resulted so, that "by one man's disobedience many were made sinners;" as the apostle tells us in the 5th of Romans. So that, when Adam had fallen, there was not the least hope, by the law, of saving any of mankind. Then was revealed THE PLAN, which had been provided in the counsels of eternity, on foresight of this event, for saving mankind by a proceeding of mere grace. Salvation was now placed on an entire new foundation, by a Covenant of Redemption. You will find this covenant in the 89th Psalm, and other places in the Old Testament. This, you will observe, is a covenant between the Father and the Son, regarding the salvation of mankind, and is the foundation of another covenant, the covenant of grace. In the covenant of redemption, man is no party at all, but merely the subject of the covenant; the parties being God the Father and the Son. In this covenant, the Son is made the head or representative of His people. Adam was the *natural* head of the human family, and Christ is the *covenant* head of His church.

On this covenant of redemption was founded the covenant of grace. In the covenant of redemption, the Son stipulated with the Father, to work out an atonement; and the Father stipulated that He should have a seed, or people, gathered out of the human race. The covenant of grace was made with men and was revealed to Adam, after the fall, and more fully revealed to Abraham. Of this covenant, Jesus Christ was to be the Mediator, or He that should administer it. It was a covenant of grace, in opposition to the original covenant of works, under which Adam and his posterity were placed at the beginning; and salvation was now to be by faith, instead of works, because the obedience and death of Jesus Christ were to be regarded as the reason why any individual was to be saved, and not each one's personal obedience. Not that His obedience was, strictly speaking, performed for us. As a man, He was under the necessity of obeying, for Himself; because He had not put Himself under the law, and if He did not obey it He became personally a transgressor. And yet there is a sense in which it may be said that His obedience is reckoned to our account. His obedience has so highly honored the law, and His death has so fully satisfied the demands of public justice, that *grace* (not justice,) has reckoned His righteousness to us. If He had obeyed the law strictly *for us*, and had owed no obedience for Himself, but was at liberty to obey only for us, then I cannot see why *justice* should not have accounted His obedience to us, and we could have *obtained* salvation on the score of right, instead of *asking* it on the score of grace or favor. But it is only in this sense accounted ours, that He, being God and man, having voluntarily assumed our nature, and then voluntarily laying down His life to make atonement, casts such a glory on the law of God, that grace is willing to consider His obedience in such a sense ours, as, on His account, to treat us as if we were righteous.

Christ is also the covenant head of those that believe. He is not the natural head, as Adam was, but our *covenant* relation to Him is such, that whatever is given to Him is given to us. Whatever He is, both in His divine and human nature; whatever He has done, either as God or man, is given to us by covenant, or promise, and is absolutely ours. I want you should understand this. The church, as a body, has never yet understood the fullness and richness of this covenant, and that all there is in Christ is made over to us in the covenant of grace.

And here let me say, that we receive this grace by faith. It is not by works, by anything we do, more or less, previous to the exercise of faith, that we become interested in this righteousness. But as soon as we exercise faith, all that Christ has done, all there is of Christ, all that is contained in the covenant of grace, becomes ours by faith. Hence it is, that the inspired writers make so much of faith. Faith is the voluntary compliance, on our part, with the condition of the covenant. It is the eye that discerns, the hand that takes hold, the medium by which we become possessed of the blessings of the covenant. By the act of faith, the soul becomes actually possessed of all that is embraced is that act of faith. If there is not enough received to break the bonds of sin and set the soul at once at liberty, it is because the act has not embraced enough of what Christ is, and what He has done.

I have read the verse from Corinthians, for the purpose of remarking on some of the fundamental things contained in this covenant of grace. "Of him are ye in Christ Jesus, who of God is made unto us wisdom, and righteousness, and sanctification, and redemption." When Christ is received and believed on, He is made to us what is meant by these several particulars. But what is meant? How and in what sense is Christ our wisdom and righteousness, and sanctification, and redemption? I will dwell a few moments on each.

This is a very peculiar verse, and my mind has long dwelt on it with great anxiety to know its exact and full meaning. I have prayed over it as much as over any passage in the Bible, that I might be enlightened to understand its real import. I have long been in the habit, when my mind fastened on any passage that I did not understand, to pray over it till I felt satisfied. I have never dared to preach on this verse, because I never felt fully satisfied that I understood it. I think I understand it now. At all events, I am willing to give my opinion on it. And if I have any right knowledge respecting its meaning, I am sure I have received it from the Spirit of God.

1. In what sense is Christ our *wisdom?*

He is often called "the Wisdom of God." And in the Book of Proverbs He is called Wisdom. But how is He made to us wisdom.

One idea contained in it is, that we have absolutely all the benefits of His wisdom; and if we exercise the faith we ought, we are just as certain to be directed by it, and it is in all respects just as well for us, as if we had the same wisdom, originally, of our own. Else it cannot be true that He is made unto us wisdom. As He is the infinite source of wisdom, how can it be said that He is made unto us wisdom, unless we are partakers of His wisdom, and have it guaranteed to us; so that, at any time, if we trust in Him, we may have it as certainly, and in any degree we need, to guide us as infallibly, as if we had it originally ourselves? This is what we need from the gospel, and what the gospel must furnish, to be suited to our necessities. And the man who has not learned this, has not known anything as he ought. If he thinks his own theorizing and speculating are going to bring him to any right knowledge on the subject of religion, he knows nothing at all, as yet. His carnal, earthly heart, can no more study out the realities of religion so as to get any available knowledge of them than the heart of a beast. "What man knoweth the things of a man, save the spirit of a man which is in him? Even so the things of God knoweth no man, but the Spirit of God." What can we know, without experience, of the character or Spirit of God? Do you say, "We can reason about God." What if we do reason? What can reason do here? Suppose here was a mind that was all pure intellect, and had no other powers, and I should undertake to teach that pure intellect what it was to love. I could lecture on it, and instruct that pure intellect in the words, so that it could reason and philosophize about love, and yet anybody can see that it is impossible to put that pure intellect in possession of the idea of what love is, unless it not only has power to exercise love, but has actually exercised it! It is just as if I should talk about colors to a man born blind. He hears the word, but what idea can he attach to it, unless he has seen? It is impossible to get the idea home to his mind, of the difference of colors. The term is a mere word.

Just so it is in religion. One whose mind has not experienced it, may reason upon it. He may demonstrate the perfections of God, as he would demonstrate a proposition in Euclid. But that which is the spirit and life of the gospel, can no more be carried to the mind by mere words, without experience, than love to a pure intellect, or colors to a man born blind. You may so far give him the letter, as to crush him down to hell with conviction; but to give the spiritual meaning of things, without the Spirit of God, is as absurd as to lecture a blind man about colors.

These two things, then are contained in the idea of wisdom.

1. As Christ is our representative, we are interested in all His wisdom, and all the wisdom He has is exercised for us. His infinite wisdom is actually employed for our benefit. And, 2. That His wisdom, just as much as is needed, is guaranteed to be always ready to be imparted to us, whenever we exercise faith in Him for wisdom. From His infinite fullness, in this respect, we may receive all we need. And if we do not receive from Him the wisdom which we need, in any and every case, it is because we do not exercise faith.

2. He is made unto us righteousness. What is the meaning of this?

Here my mind has long labored to understand the distinction which the apostle intended to make between righteousness and sanctification. Righteousness means holiness, or obedience to law; and sanctification means the same.

My present view of the distinction aimed at is, that by His being made unto us righteousness, the apostle meant to be understood, that Christ is our *outward* righteousness; or, that His obedience is, under the covenant of grace, accounted to us. Not in the sense that on the footing of justice he obeyed *for us*, and God accounts us just, because our substitute has obeyed; but that we are so interested in His obedience, that *as a matter of grace*, we are treated as if we had ourselves obeyed.

You are aware there is a view of this subject, which is maintained by some, different from this;—that the righteousness of Christ is so imputed to us, that we are considered as having been always holy. It was at one time extensively maintained that righteousness was so imputed to us, that we had a right to demand salvation, on the score of justice. My view of the matter is entirely different. It is, that Christ's righteousness becomes ours by *gift*. God has so united us to Christ, as on His account to treat us with favor. It is just like a case, where a father had done some signal service to his country, and the government thinks it proper to reward such signal service with signal reward; and not only is the individual himself rewarded, but all his family receive favors on his account, because they are the children of a father who had greatly benefited their country. Human governments do this, and the ground of it is very plain. It is just so in the divine government. Christ's disciples are in such a sense considered one with Him, and God is so highly delighted with the single service He has done the kingdom, from the circumstances under which He became a Savior, that God accounts His righteousness to them as if it were their own; or in other words, treats them just as He would treat Christ Himself. As the government of the country, under certain circumstances, treats the son of a father who had greatly benefited the country, just as they would treat the father, and bestow on him the same favors. You will bear in mind, that I am now speaking of what I called the *outward* righteousness; I mean, the reason out of the individual, why God accepts and saves them that believe in Christ. And this reason includes both the obedience of Christ to the law, and His obedience unto death, or suffering upon the cross to make atonement.

3. In what sense is Christ made unto us *sanctification?*

Sanctification is inward purity. And the meaning is, that He is our inward purity. The control which Christ Himself exercises over us, His Spirit working in us, to will and to do, His shedding His love abroad in our hearts, so controlling us that we are ourselves, through the faith which is of the operation of God, made actually holy.

I wish you to get the exact idea here. When it is said that Christ is our sanctification, or our holiness, it is meant that He is the author of our holiness. He is not only the procuring cause, by His atonement and intercession, but by His direct intercourse with the soul He himself produces holiness. He is not the remote but the immediate cause of our being sanctified. He works our works in us, not by suspending our own agency, but He so controls our minds, by the influences of His Spirit in us, in a way perfectly consistent with our freedom, as to sanctify us. And this, also, is received *by faith*. It is by faith that Christ is received and enthroned as KING in our hearts; when the mind, from confidence in Christ, just yields itself up to Him, to be led by His Spirit, and guided and controlled by His hand. The act of the mind, that thus throws the soul into the hand of Christ for sanctification, is faith. Nothing is wanting, but for the mind to break off from any confidence in itself, and to give itself up to Him, to be led and controlled by Him, absolutely:

just as the child puts out its little hand to its father, to have him lead it anywhere he pleases. If the child is distrustful, or not willing to be led, or if it has confidence in its own wisdom and strength, it will break away and try to run alone. But if all that self-confidence fails, it will cease from its own efforts, and come and give itself up to its father again, to be led entirely at his will. I suppose this is similar to the act of faith, by which an individual gives his mind up to be led and controlled by Christ. He ceases from his own efforts to guide and control and sanctify himself; and just gives himself up, as yielding as air, and leaves himself in the hands of Christ as his sanctification.

4. It is said Christ is made of God unto us *redemption*. What are we to understand by that?

Here the apostle plainly refers to the Jewish practice of redeeming estates, or redeeming relatives that had been sold for debt. When an estate had been sold out of the family, or an individual had been deprived of liberty for debt, they could be redeemed, by paying the price of redemption. There are very frequent allusions in the Bible to this practice of redemption. And where Christ is spoken of as our redemption, I suppose it means just what it says. While we are in our sins, under the law, we are sold as slaves, in the hand of public justice, bound over to death, and have no possible way to redeem ourselves from the curse of the law. Now, Christ makes Himself the price of our redemption. In other words, He is our redemption money; He buys us out from under the law, by paying Himself as a ransom. Christ hath redeemed us from the curse of the law, being made a curse for us; and thus, also, redeems us from the power of sin. But I must leave this train of thought, and return to a consideration of the plan of salvation.

Under this covenant of grace, our own works, or anything that we do, or can do, as *works of law*, have no more to do with our salvation, than if we had never existed. I wish your minds to separate entirely between salvation by works, and salvation by grace. Our salvation by grace is founded on a reason entirely separate from and out of ourselves. Before, it depended on ourselves. Now we *receive* salvation, as a free gift, *solely* on account of Jesus Christ. He is the sole author, ground, and reason of our salvation. Whether we love God or do not love God, so far as it is a *ground* of our salvation, is of no account. The whole is entirely a matter of grace, through Jesus Christ. You will not understand me as saying that there is no necessity for love to God or good works. I know that "without holiness no man shall see the Lord." But the necessity of holiness is not at all on this ground. Our own holiness does not enter at all into the ground or reason for our acceptance and salvation. We are not going to be indebted to Christ for awhile, until we are sanctified, and all the rest of the time stand in our own righteousness. But however perfect and holy we may become, in this life, or to all eternity, Jesus Christ will forever be the sole reason in the universe why we are not in hell. Because, however holy we may become, it will be forever true that we *have sinned*, and in the eye of justice, nothing in us, short of our eternal damnation can satisfy the law. But now, Jesus Christ has undertaken to help, and He forever remains the sole ground of our salvation.

According to this plan, we have the benefit of His obedience to the law, just as if He had obeyed it for us. Not that He did obey for us, in distinction from himself, but we have the benefits of His obedience, by the gift of grace, the same as if He had done so.

I meant to dwell on the idea of Christ as our *Light*, and our *Life*, and our *Strength*. But I find there is not time tonight. I wish to touch a little on this question, "*How does faith put us in possession* of Christ, in all these relations?"

Faith in Christ puts us in possession of Christ, as the sum and substance of the blessings of the gospel. Christ was the very blessing promised in the Abrahamic covenant. And throughout the scriptures, He is held forth as the sum and substance of all God's favors to man.—He is the Bread of Life, the Water of Life, our Strength, our All. The gospel has taxed all the powers of language to describe the vast variety of His relations, and to show that faith is to put believers in possession of Jesus Christ, in all these relations.

The manner in which Faith puts the mind in possession of all these blessings is this: It annihilates all those things that stand in the way of our intercourse with Christ. He says, "Behold, I stand at the door, and knock; if any man hear my voice, and open the door, I will come in to him, and will sup with him, and he with me." Here is a door, an obstacle to our intercourse with Christ, something that stands in the way. Take the particular of wisdom. Why do we not receive Christ as our wisdom? Because we depend on our own wisdom, and think we have ourselves some available knowledge of the things of God, and as long as we depend on this, we keep the door shut. That is the door. Now, let us just throw this all away, and give up all wisdom of our own, and see how infinitely empty we are of any available knowledge, as much so as a beast that perisheth, as to the way of salvation, until Christ shall teach us. Until we feel this, there is a door between us and Christ. We have something of our own instead of coming and throwing ourselves perfectly into the hands of Christ, we just come to Him to help out our own wisdom.

How does faith put us in possession of the Righteousness of Christ? This is the way. Until our mind takes hold on the righteousness of Christ, we are alive to our own righteousness. We are naturally engaged in working out a righteousness of our own, and until we cease entirely from our own works, by absolutely throwing ourselves on Christ for righteousness, we do not come to Christ. Christ will not patch up our own righteousness, to make it answer the purpose. If we depend on our prayers, our tears, our charities, or anything we have done, or expect to do, He will not receive us. We must have none of this. But the moment an individual takes hold on Christ, he receives and appropriates all Christ's righteousness as his own; as a perfect and unchangeable reason for his acceptance with God, by grace.

It is just so, with regard to Sanctification and Redemption. I cannot dwell on them so particularly as I wished. Until an individual receives Christ, he does not cease from his own works. The moment he does that, by this very act he throws the entire responsibility upon Christ. The moment the mind does fairly yield itself up to Christ, the responsibility comes upon Him, just as the person who undertakes to conduct a blind man is responsible for his safe conduct. The believer by the act of faith pledges Christ for his obedience and sanctification. By giving himself up to Christ, all the veracity of the Godhead are put at stake, that he shall be led right or made holy.

And with regard to Redemption, as long as the sinner supposes that his own sufferings, his prayers or tears, or mental agony, are of any avail, he will never receive Christ. But as soon as he receives Christ, he sinks down as lost and condemned, as in fact a dead person, unless redeemed by Christ.

REMARKS.

I. There is no such thing as spiritual life in us, or anything acceptable to God, until we actually believe in Christ.

The very act of believing, receives Christ as just that influence which alone can wake up the mind to spiritual life.

II. We are nothing, as Christians, any farther than we believe in Christ.

III. Many seem to be waiting to do something first, before they receive Christ.

Some wait to become more dead to the world. Some to get a broken heart. Some to get their doubts cleared up, before they come to Christ. THIS IS A GRAND MISTAKE. It is expecting to do that first, before faith, which is only the result of faith. Your heart will not be broken, your doubts will not be cleared up, you will never die to the world, until you believe. The moment you grasp the things of Christ, your mind will see, as in the light of eternity, the emptiness of the world, of reputation, riches, honor and pleasure. To expect this *first*, preparatory to the exercise of faith, is beginning at the wrong end. It is seeking that as a preparation for faith, which is always the result of faith.

IV. Perfect faith will produce perfect love.

When the mind duly recognizes Christ, and receives Him, in His various relations; when the faith is unwavering and the views clear, there will be nothing left in the mind contrary to the law of God.

V. Abiding faith would produce abiding love.

Faith increasing, would produce increasing love. And here you ought to observe, that love may be perfect at all times, and yet be in different degrees at different times. An individual may love God perfectly and eternally, and yet his love may increase in vigor to all eternity, as I suppose it will. As the saints in glory see more and more of God's excellencies, they will love Him more and more, and yet will have perfect love all the time. That is, there will be nothing inconsistent with love in the mind, while the degrees of love will be different as their views of the character of God unfold. As God opens to their view the wonders of His glorious benevolence, they will have their souls thrilled with new love to God. In this life, the exercises of love vary greatly in degree. Sometimes God unfolds to His saints the wonders of His government, and gives them such views as well-nigh prostrate the body, and then love is greatly raised in degree. And yet the love may have been perfect before; that is, the love of God was supreme and single, without any mixture of inconsistent affections. And it is not unreasonable to suppose, that it will be so to all eternity; that *occasions* will occur in which the love of the saints will be brought into more lively exercise by new unfoldings of God's glory. As God develops to them wonder after wonder, their love will be increased indefinitely, and they will have continually enlarged accessions of its strength and fervor, to all eternity.

I designed to mention some things on the subject of instantaneous and progressive sanctification. But there is not time tonight, and they must be postponed.

VI. You see, beloved, from this subject, *the way* in which you can be made holy, and *when* you can be sanctified.

Whenever you come to Christ, and receive Him for all that He is, and accept a whole salvation by grace, you will have all that Christ is to you, wisdom, and righteousness, and sanctification, and redemption. There is nothing but unbelief to hinder you from *now* enjoying it all. You need not wait for any preparation. There is no preparation that is of any avail. You must RECEIVE a whole salvation, as a FREE GIFT. When will you thus lay hold on Christ? When will you believe? Faith, true faith, *always* works by love, and purifies the heart, and overcomes the world. Whenever you find any difficulty in your way, you may know what is the matter. It is a want of faith. No matter what may befall you outwardly: if you find yourself thrown back in religion, or your mind thrown all into confusion, unbelief is the cause, and faith the remedy. If you lay hold on Christ, and keep hold, all the devils in hell can never drive you away from God, or put out your light. But if you let unbelief prevail, you may go on in this miserable, halting way, talking about sanctification, using words without knowledge, and dishonoring God, till you die.

LECTURE XI.

NECESSITY OF DIVINE TEACHING.

"Nevertheless I tell you the truth—it is expedient for you that I go away—for if I go not away, the Comforter will not come unto you—but if I depart, I will send him unto you. And when he is come, he will reprove the world of sin, and of righteousness, and of judgment. Of sin, because they believe not on me—of righteousness, because I go to my Father, and ye see me no more—of judgment, because the prince of this world is judged. I have yet many things to say unto you, but ye cannot bear them now. Howbeit when he, the Spirit of truth is come, he will guide you into all truth—for he shall not speak of himself; but whatsoever he shall hear, that shall he speak: and he will show you things to come."—John xvi 7-13.

The doctrine of the necessity of Divine Influence, to enlighten and sanctify the minds of men, is very abundantly taught in the Bible, and is generally maintained, as a matter of opinion at least, in all orthodox churches. But, as a matter of fact, there seems to be very little available knowledge of the gospel among mankind; so little that it exerts comparatively little influence. The great ends of the gospel have hardly begun to be realized, in the production of holiness on the earth. It is a grand question, whether we do need Divine Influence to attain the ends of the gospel; and if we do need it, then in what degree do we need it, and why? If our minds are unsettled on this question, we shall be unsettled on all the subjects that practically concern our sanctification.

In discoursing on this subject tonight, I design to pursue the following order:

I. Inquire how far the reason of man, unaided by Divine illumination, is capable of understanding the things of religion.

II. Show wherein the reason of man is defective, in regard to the capacity of gaining any available knowledge of the gospel.

III. That the Spirit of God alone can supply the Illumination that is needed.

IV. That every one may have the influence of the Spirit, according to his necessities.

V. The reasons why any individual fails to receive this divine aid to the extent of his necessities.

VI. That men are responsible for the light which they might have, as well as for that which they actually enjoy.

I. I shall inquire how far the reason of man, unaided by Divine illumination, is capable of apprehending the things of religion.

1. The mind of man is capable of understanding the historical facts of religion; just as it comprehends any other historical facts.

2. It is capable of understanding the doctrinal propositions of the gospel.

That is, it can understand those abstractions which make up the skeleton of the gospel; such as the being and character of God, the divine authority and inspiration of the scriptures, and other fundamental doctrines which make up the framework of the gospel. That is, it can understand them as propositions, and see the evidence that supports them as true, just as it can any other propositions in science. For instance, to enter a little into detail:

A man, by his reason, may understand the law of God. He can understand that it requires him to exercise perfect love, towards God and all other beings. He can see the ground of his obligation to do this, because he is a moral being. He knows by experience what love is, for he has exercised love towards different objects. And he can, therefore, form or comprehend the idea of love, so far as to see the reasonableness of the requirement. He can understand the foundation and the force of moral obligation, and see, in some measure, the extent of his obligation to love God.

So, likewise, he can see that he is a sinner, and that he cannot be saved by his own works. He has broken the law, so that the law can never justify him. He can see, that if he is ever saved, he must be justified through mere mercy, by an act of pardon.

I might go through the whole circle of theology, and show that the human understanding is capable of knowing it, in the abstract, as a system of propositions, to be received and believed, on evidence, like any other science. I do not mean to be understood, as saying, that unaided reason can attain any *available* knowledge of the things of religion, or any such knowledge as will be effectual to produce a sanctifying change.

II. I am to show *wherein* our knowledge of the things of religion is necessarily defective, without the aids of the Holy Spirit.

In other words, I am to show what our knowledge of the gospel lacks, to make it available to salvation.

And here it is needful to distinguish between knowledge which *might* be available, to one that was himself *disposed* to love and obey God; and what will be available, in fact, to a *sinner*, who is wholly indisposed to holiness. It is easy to see, that one who is disposed to do right would be influenced to duty by a far less amount of illumination, or a far less clear and vivid view of motives, than one who is disposed to do wrong. What we are now inquiring after respects the matter of fact, in this world. Whether the knowledge attainable by our present faculties would be available to influence us to do right, were there no sin in the world, is more than I can say. As a matter of fact, the knowledge which Adam had when in a state of innocency *did not* avail to influence him to do right. But we are now speaking of things as they are in this world, and to show what is the reason that men, as *sinners*, can have no available knowledge of divine things; no *such* knowledge as will, as a matter of fact, influence them to love and serve God.

Knowledge, to avail anything towards effecting its object, must be such as will influence the mind. The *will* must be controlled. And to do this, the mind must have such a view of things as to excite *emotion*, corresponding to the object in view. Mere intellect never will move the soul to act. A pure scientific abstraction of the intellect, that does not touch the feelings, or excite any emotion, is wholly unavailable to move the will. It is so everywhere. It would be so in heaven. You must bring the mind under a degree of excitement, to influence the will in any case. And in the case of sinners, to influence sinners to love and obey God, you must have a great degree of light, such as will powerfully excite the mind, and produce strong emotions. The reasons for obedience must be made to appear with great strength and vividness, so as to subdue their rebellious hearts and bring them voluntarily to obey God. This is available knowledge. This men never have, and never can have, without the Spirit of God. If men were disposed to do right, I know not how far their knowledge, attainable by unaided reason, might avail. But, as they are universally and totally indisposed, this knowledge will never do it. I will mention some of the reasons:

1. All the knowledge we can have here of spiritual things, is by analogy, or comparison.

Our minds are here shut up in the body, and derive all our ideas from external objects, through the senses. Now, we never can of ourselves obtain knowledge of spiritual or eternal things in this way sufficient to rightly influence our wills. Our bodily powers were not created for this. All the ideas we can have of the spiritual world is by analogy, or comparing them with the things around us. It is easily seen that all ideas conveyed to our minds in this way, must be extremely imperfect, and that we do not, after all, get the true idea in our minds. The Jewish types were probably the most forcible means which God could then use, for giving to the Jews a correct idea of the gospel. Considering how the eastern nations were accustomed, by their education, to the use of figures, and parables, and types, probably the system of types was the most impressive and happy mode that could be devised to gain a more ready access for the truth to their minds, and give them a more full idea of the plan of redemption than could be communicated in any other way. And yet it is manifest that the ideas which were communicated in this way were extremely imperfect; and that, without divine illumination to make them see the reality more fully than they could by unaided reason, they never would have got any available knowledge in this way.

So words are merely signs of *ideas*. They are not the ideas, but the representatives of ideas. It is often very difficult, and sometimes impossible to convey ideas by words. Take a little child, and attempt to talk with him, and how difficult it is, on many subjects, to get your ideas into his little mind. He must have some experience of the things you are trying to teach, before you can convey ideas to him by words.

Suppose this congregation were all blind, and had never seen colors. Then suppose that on that wall hung a most grand and beautiful painting, and that I was a perfect master of the subject, and should undertake to describe it to you. No language that I could use would give you such an idea of the painting, as to enable you to form a picture of it in your minds.—Where, on any subject, we are obliged, from the nature of the case, to use figurative language, analogies, and resemblances, the knowledge we communicate is necessarily defective and inadequate. Who of you have not heard descriptions of persons and places, till you thought you had an accurate knowledge of them; but when you come to see them you find you had no true idea of the reality?

Suppose an individual were to visit this world, from another planet, where all things are constituted on the most opposite principles from those which are adopted here. Suppose him to remain here long enough to learn our language, and that then he should undertake to give us a description of the world he had left. We should understand it according to our ideas and experience. Now, if the analogy between the two worlds is very imperfect, it is plain that our knowledge of things there, from his description, must be imperfect in proportion. So, when we find in the Bible descriptions of heaven and hell, or anything in the invisible world, it is plain that from mere words we can get no true ideas at all adequate to the reality.

2. The *wickedness of our hearts* is so great, as to pervert our judgment, and shut out from our minds much that we might understand of the things of religion.

When a man's mind is so perverted on any subject, that he will not take up the evidence concerning it, he cannot, of course, come at the knowledge of the truth on that subject. This is our case in regard to religion. Perverseness of heart so shuts out the light, that the intellect does not, and from the nature of things *cannot*, get even the ideas it might otherwise gain, respecting divine things.

3. Prejudice is a great obstacle to the reception of correct knowledge concerning religion.

Take the case of the disciples of Christ. They had strong Jewish prejudices respecting the plan of salvation—so strong that all the instructions of Christ himself could not make them understand the truth. After teaching them personally, for three years, with all the talent, and simplicity, and skill He was master of, He could never get their minds in possession of the first principles of the gospel. Up to His very death, He could not make them see that He should die, and rise from the dead. Therefore He says in his last conversation—"If I go not away, the Comforter will not come unto you; but if I depart, I will send him unto you." This was the very design of His going away from them, that the Spirit of Truth might come, and put them in possession of *the things* which He meant by the words He had used in teaching them.

The general truth is this; that without divine illumination, men can understand from the Bible enough to convict and condemn them, but not enough to sanctify and save them.

Some may ask, What, then, is the use of revelation?

It is of much use. The Bible is as plain as it can be. Who doubts that our Lord Jesus Christ gave instructions to His disciples, as plainly as He could? See the pains which He took to illustrate His teaching; how simple His language; how He brings it down to the weakest comprehension, as a parent would to a little child. And yet it remains true, that without divine illumination, the unaided reason of man never did, and never will attain any available knowledge of the gospel. The difficulty lies in the subject. The Bible contains the gospel, as plain as it can be made. That is, it contains the signs of the ideas, as far as language can represent the things of religion. No language but figurative language can be used for this purpose. And this will forever be inadequate to put our minds in real possession of the things themselves. The difficulty is in our ignorance and sin, and in the nature of the subject. This is the reason why we need divine illumination, to get any available knowledge of the gospel.

III. **The Spirit of God alone, can give us this illumination.**

The Bible says, "No man can say that Jesus Christ is Lord, but by the Holy Ghost." Now the abstract proposition of the Deity of Christ, can be proved, as a matter of science, so as to gain the assent of any unbiased mind to the truth, that Jesus is Lord. But nothing short of the Holy Ghost can so put the mind in possession of the idea of Christ, as God, as to fix the soul in the belief of the fact, and make it available to sanctify the heart.

Again, it is said that "No man can come to me, except the Father which hath sent me draw him; and I will raise him up at the last day. It is written in the prophets, And they shall be all taught of God. Every man, therefore, that hath heard, and hath learned of the Father, cometh unto me." Here it is evident that the drawing spoken of, is teaching by the Holy Spirit. They must be taught of God, and learn of the Father, before they can ever have such a knowledge of the things of religion as actually to come to Christ.

Christ says, "It is expedient for you that I go away; for if I go not away, the Comforter will not come unto you." The word *Paracletos*, here translated Comforter, properly means a Helper or Teacher. "When he is come, he will reprove the world of sin, and of righteousness, and of judgment: Of sin, because they believe not on me; of righteousness, because I go to my Father, and ye see me no more; of judgment, because the prince of this world is judged. I have yet many things to say unto you, but ye cannot bear them now. Howbeit, when he, the Spirit of Truth, is come, he will guide you into all truth; for he shall not speak of himself; but whatsoever he shall hear, that shall he speak: and he will show you things to come."

So in the fourteenth chapter the Savior says, "I will pray the Father, and he shall give you another Comforter, that he may abide with you forever; even the Spirit of Truth; whom the world cannot receive, because it seeth him not, neither knoweth him; but ye know him, for he dwelleth with you, and shall be in you." And again, in the 26th verse, "But the comforter, which is the Holy Ghost, whom the Father will send in my name, he shall teach you all things, and bring all things to your remembrance, whatsoever I have said unto you." Here you see the office of the Spirit of God is, to instruct mankind in regard to the things of religion.

Now, it is manifest that *none but* the Spirit of God can supply this defect, from a single consideration—That all teaching by words, whether by Jesus Christ, or by apostles, or by any inspired or uninspired teacher, coming merely through the senses, can never put the mind in possession of the idea of spiritual things. The kind of teaching that we need is this; we want someone to teach us the things of religion, who is not obliged to depend on words, or to reach our minds through the medium of the senses. We want some way in which the *ideas themselves can* be brought to our minds, and not merely the signs of the ideas. We want a teacher who can directly approach the mind itself, and not through the senses; and who can exhibit the ideas of religion, without being obliged to use words. This the Spirit of God can do.

The manner in which the Spirit of God does this, is what we can never know in this world. But the fact is undeniable, that He can reach the mind without the use of words, and can put our minds in possession of the ideas themselves, of which the types, or figures, or words, of the human teacher, are only the signs or imperfect representatives. The human teacher can only use words to our senses, and finds it impossible to possess us of the ideas of that which we have never experienced. But the Spirit of God, having direct access to the mind, can, through the outward sign, possess us of the actual idea of things. What Christian does not know this, as a matter of fact? What Christian does not know, from his own experience, that the Spirit of God does lead him instantly to see that in a passage of scripture, which all his study, and effort of mind to know the meaning of could never have given him in the world?

Take the case again, of a painting on the wall there, and suppose that all the congregation were blind, and I was trying to describe to them this painting. Now suppose, while I was laboring to make them understand the various distinctions and combinations of colors, and they are bending their minds to understand it, all at once their eyes are opened! You can then see for yourselves the very things which I was vainly trying to bring to your minds by words. Now, the office of the Spirit of God, and what He alone can do, is to open the spiritual eye, and bring the things which we try to describe by analogy and signs, in all their living reality, before the mind, so as to put the mind in complete possession of the thing as it is.

It is evident, too, that no one but the Spirit of God so knows the things of God as to be able to give us the idea of those things correctly. "What man knoweth the things of a man, save the spirit of man that is in him?" What can a beast know of the things of a man, of a man's character, designs, etc.? I can speak to your consciousness—being a man, and knowing the things of a man. But I cannot speak these things to the consciousness of a beast, neither can a beast speak of these things, because he has not the spirit of a man in him, and cannot know them. In like manner the Bible says, "The things of God knoweth no man, but the Spirit of God." The Spirit of God, knowing from consciousness the things of God, possesses a different kind of knowledge of these things from what other beings can possess; and therefore, can give us the kind of instruction that we need, and such as no other being can give.

IV. The needed influences of the Spirit of God may be possessed by all men, freely, and under the gospel.

A few passages from the Bible will show this:

Jesus Christ says God is more willing to give His Holy Spirit to them that ask Him, than parents are to give their children bread. "Ask, and it shall be given you; seek, and ye shall find; knock, and it shall be opened unto you." "And all things whatsoever ye shall ask in prayer, believing, ye shall receive." "Therefore, I say unto you, What things soever ye desire when ye pray, believe that ye receive them, and ye shall have them." James says, "If any of you lack wisdom, let him ask of God, that giveth to all men liberally, and upbraideth not; AND IT SHALL BE GIVEN HIM." If it be true, that God has made these unlimited promises, that ALL MEN, who will ask of Him, may have divine illumination as much as they will ask for, then it is true that all men may have as much of divine illumination as they need.

V. I will show the reasons why any do not have as much divine illumination as they need.

1. They do not ask for it in any such manner or degree as they need it.

2. They ask amiss, or from selfish motives.

The apostle James says, "Ye ask and receive not, because ye ask amiss, that ye may consume it on your lusts." When an individual has a selfish motive for asking, or some other reason, than a desire to glorify God, he need not expect to receive divine illumination. If his object in asking for the Holy Ghost, is that he may always be happy in religion, or that he may be very wise in the scriptures, or be looked upon as an eminent Christian, or have his experience spoken of as remarkable, or any other selfish view, that is a good reason why he should not receive even what he asks.

3. They do not use the proper means to attain what they ask.

Suppose a person neglects his Bible, and yet asks God to give him a knowledge of the things of religion. That is tempting God. The manner in which God gives knowledge is through the Bible, and preaching, and the other appointed means of instruction. If a person will not use these means, when they are in his power, however much he may pray, he need not expect divine instruction. "Faith cometh by hearing and hearing by the word of God."

There is an important difference to be observed, between the cases of those who possess these means, and those who do not. I suppose that a person may learn the gospel, and receive all the illumination he needs, under any circumstances of privation of means. As if he was on a desolate island, he might receive direct illumination from the Spirit of God. And so he might, in any other circumstances, where he absolutely *could not* have access to any means of instruction. Some very remarkable cases of this kind have occurred within a few years. I have known one case, which I looked upon at the time as miraculous, and for that reason have seldom mentioned it, feeling that even the church were not prepared to receive it. When I was an evangelist, I labored once in a revival, in a neighborhood where there were many Germans. They had received but little instruction, and many of them could not read. But when the gospel was preached among them, the Spirit of God was poured out, and a most powerful revival followed. In the midst of the harvest, if a meeting, was appointed at any place, the whole neighborhood would come together, and fill the house, and hang upon the preacher's lips, while he tried to possess their minds with the truths of the gospel. One poor German woman naturally intelligent, but who could not read, in relating her experience in one of these meetings, told this fact which was certified to by her neighbors. With many tears and a heart full of joy, she said, "When I loved God, I longed to read the Bible, and I prayed to Jesus Christ, I said and felt, O Jesus! thou canst teach me to read thy Holy Bible, and the Lord taught me to read. There was a Bible in the house, and when I had prayed, I thought I could read the Bible, and I got the book, and opened it, and the words were just what I had heard people read. I said, O Lord Jesus Christ, thou *canst* teach me to read," and I believed He could, and I thought I did read, but I went and asked the school-madam if I read, and she said I read it right, and the Lord has taught me to read my Bible, blessed be His name for it." I do not know but the school-madam to whom she referred was in the house and heard her relation. At all events, she was a woman of good character among her neighbors, and some of the most respectable of them afterwards told me, they did not doubt the truth of what she said. I have no doubt it was true.

At the time, I thought it was a miracle; but since the facts which have been developed within a few years, respecting the indestructibleness of the memory, I have thought this case might be explained in that way; and that she had probably been told the names of letters and their powers when young, and now the Spirit of God, in answer to her prayer, had quickened her mind, and brought it all to her remembrance, so that she could read the Bible.

Some of you will recollect the facts which were stated here, one evening, by President Mahan, which show that every impression which is made on the mind of man, remains there forever indelible. One case that he mentioned was that of an old lady, who when she was young, had read some lines of poetry, relating a little story; and afterwards, when old, she wished to tell the story to some children, to whom she thought it would be useful, and to her surprise the whole of the lines came up fresh in her memory, and she repeated them *verbatim*, although she had never committed them to memory at all, but only read them when she was young. Another was the case of an ignorant servant girl. She had once lived with a learned minister, who was accustomed to read aloud the Hebrew Bible, in his study, which was in hearing of the place where this girl did her work. Of course she understood nothing of the words, but only heard the sounds. Long afterwards when she was on her death-bed, she astonished the bystanders by reciting whole chapters of Hebrew and Chaldaic. The neighbors at first thought it was a miracle, but at length learned the explanation. It is plain from this, that even unintelligible sound may be so impressed on the memory, as afterwards to recur with entire distinctness. I suppose that was probably the case with this poor German woman, and that the Spirit of God, in answer to her fervent prayer, so refreshed her memory as to recall the sounds and forms of letters, she had been told when a child, and thus enable her at once to read the Bible.

I say, therefore, that while those who do not possess any outward means of instruction may obtain directly from the Spirit of God whatever degree or kind of illumination they need in the things of religion; those who possess or can obtain the outward means, and do not use them, tempt God, when they pray for divine illumination and neglect the use of means for obtaining knowledge. To those who have the opportunity, "faith cometh by hearing, and hearing by the word of God." If any man keeps away from the means within his reach, he can expect illumination in no other way. Whereas, if he is shut out from the use of means, as God is true to His promises, we must believe that he can be illuminated without means, to any extent that he needs.

4. Another reason why many do not receive that illumination from the Spirit of God which they need is, because *they grieve the Spirit*, in many ways.

They live in such a manner, as to grieve, or offend the Holy Spirit, so that He cannot consistently grant them His illuminating grace.

5. Another reason is, that they *depend on instructions and means*, as available without divine influence.

How many rely on the instructions they receive from ministers, or commentaries, or books, or their own powers of inquiry; not feeling that all these things, without the Spirit of God, will only kill, but can never make alive—can only damn, but never save. It seems as though the whole church was in error on this point; depending on means for divine knowledge, without feeling that NO MEANS are available, without the Spirit of God. Oh! if the church felt this—if they really felt that all the means in creation are unavailing without the teaching of the Holy Ghost, how they would pray, and cleanse their hands, and humble their hearts, until the Comforter would descend to teach them all things that they need to know of religion.

6. *Self-confidence* is another reason why so little is experienced of divine illumination.

So long as professing Christians place confidence in learning, or criticism, or their natural ingenuity, to learn the things of religion, rely on it, they are not likely to enjoy much of the illumination of the Spirit of God.

VI. I am to show that men are responsible for what they might have of divine illumination.

This is a universal truth, and is acknowledged by all mankind, that a man is just as responsible for what light he might have, as for that he actually has. The common law, which is the voice of common reason, adopts it as a maxim that no man who breaks the law is to be excused for ignorance of the law, because all are held bound to know what the law is. So it is with your children, in a case where they might know your will, you consider them so much the more blameworthy, if they offend. So it is in religion: where men have both the outward means of instruction, and the inward teachings of the Holy Spirit, absolutely within their reach, if they sin in ignorance, they are not only without excuse on that score, but their ignorance is itself a crime, and is an aggravation of their guilt. And all men are plainly without excuse for not possessing all the knowledge which would be available for their perfect and immediate sanctification.

REMARKS.

I. You see what is the effect of all other instructions on a congregation where no divine influence is enjoyed.

It may convince the church of duty, but will never produce sanctification. It may harden the heart, but will never change it. Without divine influence, it is but a savor of death unto death.

II. You see that it is important to use all the appropriate means of religious instruction in our power, as the medium through which the Spirit of God conveys divine illumination to the mind.

There is no reason why we should not use the means in our power, and apply our natural faculties to acquire knowledge of religion, as faithfully as if we could understand the whole subject without divine influence. And if we do not use means, when within our power, we have no reason to expect divine aid. When we help ourselves, God helps us. When we use our natural faculties to understand these things, we may expect God will enlighten us. To turn our eyes away from the light, and then pray that we may be made to see, is to tempt God.

III. They are blind leaders of the blind, who attempt to teach the things of religion without being themselves taught of God.

No degree of learning, or power of discrimination as to the didactics of theology, will ever make a man a successful teacher of religion, unless he enjoys the illuminating powers of the Holy Ghost. He is blind if he supposes he understands the Bible without this, and if he undertakes to teach religion, he deceives himself, and all who depend on him, and both will fall into the ditch together.

IV. If an individual teaches the gospel with the Holy Ghost sent down from heaven, he will be understood.

He may understand the gospel himself, and yet not make his hearers understand it, because the Holy Ghost is not sent on them as well as himself. But if the Spirit of God is on them, precisely in proportion as he himself understands the real meaning of the gospel, he will make his hearers understand it.

V. In preaching the gospel, ministers should never use texts, the meaning of which they have not been taught by the Spirit of God.

They should not attempt to explain passages of which they are not confident they have been taught the meaning by the Holy Spirit. It is presumption. And they need not do it, for they may always have the teachings of the Spirit, by asking. God is more ready to bestow divine illumination than an earthly parent is to give bread to his child; and if they ask, as a child, when he is hungry, asks his mother for a piece of bread, they may always receive all the light they need. This is applicable both to preachers and to teachers in Sabbath schools and Bible classes. If any of them attempt to teach the scriptures without being themselves taught, they are no more fit to teach without divine teaching, than the most ignorant person in the streets is fit to teach astronomy. I fear both minister and teachers generally, have understood very little of their *need* of this divine teaching, and have felt very little of the necessity of praying over their sermons and bible lessons, till they felt confident that the Spirit of God has possessed their minds with the true idea of the word of God. If this was done as it ought to be, their instructions would be far more effectual than we now see them.

Do you, who are teachers of Bible and Sabbath school classes in this church, believe this? Are you in the habit, conscientiously and uniformly, of seeking the true idea of every lesson on your knees? Or do you go to some commentary and then come and peddle out your dry stuff to your classes, that you get out of the commentaries and books, without any of the Holy Ghost in your teaching? If you do this, let me tell you, that you had better be doing something else. What would you say of a minister, if you knew he never prayed over his texts? You might as well have Balaam's ass for a minister, and even the dumb beast in such a case might speak with man's voice and rebuke the madness of such a man. He could give just as much available instruction to reach the deep fountains of the heart, as such a preacher. Well, now, this is just as important for a Sunday school teacher as for a minister. If you do not pray over your lesson, until you feel that God has taught you the idea contained in it, BEWARE! How dare you go and teach that for religion, which you do not honestly suppose you have been taught of God?

VI. It is a vast error in theological students, when they study to get the views of all the great teachers, the tomes of the fathers and doctors, and everybody's opinion as to what the Bible means, *but the opinion of the Holy Ghost.*

With hearts as cold as marble, instead of going right to the source of light, they go and gather up the husks of learning, and peddle it out among the churches as religious instruction. Horrible! While they do thus, we never shall have an efficient ministry. It is right they should get all the help they can from learning, to understand the word of God. But they ought never to rest in anything they get from book learning, until they are satisfied that God has put them in possession of the very idea which HE would have them receive.

I have tried hard to make this impression, and I believe I have succeeded in some degree, on the theological students under my care. And if I had done it more, I have no doubt I might have succeeded better. And I can say, that when I studied theology, I spent many hours on my knees, and perhaps I might say weeks, often with the Bible before me, laboring and praying to come at the very mind of the Spirit. I do not say this boastingly, but as a matter of fact, to show that the sentiment here advanced is no novel opinion with me. And I have always got my texts and sermons on my knees. And yet I am conscious that I have gained very little knowledge in religion, compared with what I might have had, if I had taken right hold of the source of Light, as I ought to have done.

VII. How little knowledge have the great body of the church, respecting the word of God!

Put them, for instance, to read the epistles, and other parts, and probably they will not have knowledge enough to give an opinion as to the real meaning of one-tenth of the Bible. No wonder the church is not sanctified! They need MORE TRUTH. Our Savior says, "Sanctify them *through thy truth.*" This grand means of sanctification must be more richly enjoyed before the church will know what entire sanctification means. The church do not understand the Bible. And the reason is, THEY HAVE NOT GONE TO THE AUTHOR to explain it. Although they have this blessed privilege every day, and just as often as they choose, of carrying the book right to the Author for His explanation; yet how little, how very little, do the church know of the Bible, which they are conscious they have been taught to know by the Holy Ghost! Read the text again, read other similar passages, and then say if Christians are not exceedingly to blame for not understanding the Bible.

VIII. You see the necessity that we should all give ourselves up to the study of the Bible, under divine teaching.

I have recently recommended several books to you to read, such as Wesley's Thoughts on Christian Perfection, the Memoirs of Brainerd Taylor, Payson, Mrs. Rogers, and others. I have found that, in a certain state of mind, such books are useful to read. But I never pretend to make but ONE BOOK my study. I read them occasionally, but have little time or inclination to read other books much while I have so much to learn of my Bible. I find it like a deep mine, the more I work it, the richer it grows. We must read that more than any or all other books. We must pause and pray over it, verse after verse, and compare part with part, dwell on it, digest it, and get it into our minds, till we feel that the Spirit of God has filled us with the spirit of holiness.

Will you do it? Will you lay your hearts open to God, and not give Him rest, till He has filled you with divine knowledge? Will you SEARCH the scriptures? I have often been asked by young converts, and young men preparing for the ministry, what they should read. READ THE BIBLE. I would give the same answer five hundred times, over and above all other things, study the Bible. It is a sad fact, that most young men, when they enter the ministry often know less of the Bible than of any other book they study. Alas! alas! O, if they had the spirit of James Brainerd Taylor, his love for the scriptures, his prayer for divine teaching, we should no longer hear the groans of the churches over the barrenness of so many young preachers, who come out of our seminaries full of book-learning, and almost destitute of the Holy Ghost.

LECTURE XII.

LOVE THE WHOLE OF RELIGION.

TEXT:—"Love worketh no ill to his neighbor; therefore love is the fulfilling of the law".—Romans xiii. 10

In speaking from these words, I design,
I. To make some remarks on the nature of love.
II. To show that love is the whole of religion.
III. Some things that are not essential to perfect love.
IV. Some things that are essential.
V. Some of the effects of perfect love.

I. I am to make some remarks on the nature of love.

1. The first remark I have to make is, that there are various forms under which love may exist.

The two principal forms, so far as religion is concerned, are benevolence and complacency. Benevolence is an *affection of* the mind, or an act of the will. It is willing good, or a desire to promote the happiness of its object. Complacency is esteem, or approbation of the character of its object. Benevolence should be exercised towards all beings, irrespective of their moral character. Complacency is due only to the good and holy.

2. Love may exist either as an affection or as an emotion.

When love is an affection, it is voluntary, or consists in the act of the will. When it is an emotion, it is involuntary. What we call feelings, or emotions, are involuntary. They are not directly dependent on the will, or controlled by a direct act of will. The virtue of love is mostly when it is in the form of an affection. The happiness of love is mostly when it is in the form of an emotion. If the affection of love be very strong, it produces a high degree of happiness, but the emotion of holy love is happiness itself.

I said that the emotion of love is involuntary. I do not mean that the will has nothing to do with it, but that it is not the result of a mere or direct act of the will. No man can exercise the emotion of love by merely willing it. And the emotion may often exist in spite of the will. Individuals often feel emotions rising in their minds, which they know to be improper, and try by direct effort of will to banish them from their minds; and finding that impossible, therefore conclude that they have no control of these emotions. But they may always be controlled by the will in an indirect way. The mind can bring up any class of emotions it chooses, by directing the attention sufficiently to the proper object. They will be certain to rise in proportion as the attention is fixed, provided the will is right in regard to the object of attention. So of those emotions which are improper or disagreeable; the mind may be rid of them, by turning the attention entirely away from the object, and not suffering the thoughts to dwell on it.

3. Ordinarily, the *emotions* of love towards God are experienced when we exercise love towards Him in the form of *affection*.

But this is not always the case. We may exercise good will towards any object, and yet at times feel no sensible emotions of love. It is not certain that even the Lord Jesus Christ exercised love towards God, in the form of emotion, at all times. So far as our acquaintance with the nature of the mind goes, we know that a person may exercise affection, and be guided and be governed by it, constantly, in all his actions, without any felt emotion of love towards its object at the time. Thus a husband and father may be engaged in laboring for the benefit of his family, and his very life controlled by affection for them, while his thoughts are not so engaged upon them as to make him feel any sensible emotions of love to them at the time. The things about which he is engaged may take up his mind so much, that he has scarcely a thought of them, and so he may have no felt emotion towards them, and yet he is all the time guided and governed by affection for them. Observe, here, that I use the term, affection, in the sense of President Edwards, as explained by him in his celebrated Treatise on the Will. An affection in his treatise is an act of the will or a volition.

4. Love to our neighbor naturally implies the existence of love to God, and love to God naturally implies love to our neighbor.

The same is declared in the 8th verse, "Owe no man anything, but to love one another: for he that loveth another hath fulfilled the law. For this, Thou shalt not commit adultery, Thou shalt not kill, Thou shalt not steal, Thou shalt not bear false witness, Thou shalt not covet; and if there be any other commandment, it is briefly comprehended in this saying, namely, Thou shalt love thy neighbor as thyself." Here it is taken for granted that love to our neighbor implies the existence of love to God, otherwise it could not be said that "he that loveth *another* hath fulfilled the law." The apostle James recognizes the same principle, when he says, "If ye fulfill the royal law according to the scripture, Thou shalt love thy neighbor as thyself, ye do well." Here love to our neighbor is spoken of as constituting obedience to the whole law. Benevolence, that is, good will to our neighbor, naturally implies love to God. It is love to the happiness of being. So the love of complacency towards holy beings naturally implies love to God, as a being of infinite holiness.

II. I am to show that love is the whole of religion.

In other words, all that is required of man by God consists in love, in various modifications and results. Love is the sum total of all.

1. The first proof I shall offer is, that the sentiment is taught in the text, and many other passages of scripture.

The scriptures fully teach, that love is the sum total of all the requirements, both of the law and gospel. Our Savior declares that the great command, Thou shalt love the Lord thy God with all thy heart, soul, mind and strength, and thy neighbor as thyself, is the sum total of all the law and the prophets, or implies and includes all that the whole scriptures, the law and the gospel require.

2. God is love, and to love is to be like God, and to be perfect in love is to be perfect as God is perfect.

All God's moral attributes consist in love, acting under certain circumstances and for certain ends. God's justice in punishing the wicked, His anger at sin, and the like, are only exercises of His love to the general happiness of His kingdom. So it is in man. All that is good in man is some modification of love. Hatred to sin, is only love to virtue acting itself out in opposing whatever is opposed to virtue. So true faith implies and includes love, and faith which has no love in it, or that does not work by love, is no part of religion. The faith that belongs to religion is an affectionate confidence in God. There is a kind of faith in God, which has no love in it. The devil has that kind of faith. The convicted sinner has it. But there is no religion in it. Faith might rise even to the faith of miracles, and yet if there is no love in it, it amounts to nothing. The apostle Paul, in the 13th chapter of 1 Corinthians, says, "Though I have the gift of prophecy, and understand all mysteries, and all knowledge; and though I have all faith, so that I could remove mountains, and have not charity, I am nothing."

Just so it is with repentance. The repentance that does not include love is not "repentance *towards* God." True repentance implies obedience to the law of love, and consequent opposition to sin.

III. I will mention some things that are not essential to perfect love.

1. The *highest degree of emotion* is not essential to perfect love.

It is manifest that the Lord Jesus Christ very seldom had the highest degree of emotion of love, and yet He always had perfect love. He generally manifested very little emotion, or excitement. Excitement is always proportioned to the strength of the emotions as it consists in them. The Savior seemed generally remarkably calm. Sometimes His indignation was strong, or His grief for the hardness of men's hearts; and sometimes we read that He rejoiced in spirit. But He was commonly calm, and manifested no high degree of emotion. And it is plainly not essential to perfect love, that the *emotion* of love should exist in a high degree.

2. Perfect love does not exclude the idea of increase in love, or growth in grace.

I suppose the growth of the mind in knowledge, to all eternity, naturally implies growth in love to all eternity. The Lord Jesus Christ, in His human nature, grew in stature, and in favor with God and man. Doubtless, as a child, He grew in knowledge, and as He grew in knowledge, He grew in love *towards* God, as well as in favor *with* God. His love was perfect when He was a child, but it was greater when He became a man. As a human being, He probably always continued to increase in love to God, as long as He lived. From the nature of mind, we see that it may be so with all the saints in glory, that their love will increase to all eternity, and yet it is always perfect love.

3. It is not essential to perfect love, that love should always be exercised towards all individuals alike.

We cannot think of all individuals at once. You cannot even think of every individual of your acquaintance at once. The degree of love towards an individual depends on the fact that the individual is present to the thoughts.

4. It is not essential to perfect love, that there should be the same degree of the spirit of prayer for every individual, or for the same individual at all times.

The spirit of prayer is not always essential to pure and perfect love. The saints in heaven have pure and perfect love for all beings, yet we know not that they have the spirit of prayer for any. You may love any individual with a very strong degree of love, and yet not have the spirit of prayer for that individual. That is, the Spirit of God may not lead you to pray for the salvation of that individual. You do not pray for the wicked in hell. The spirit of prayer depends on the influences of the Holy Ghost, leading the mind to pray for things agreeable to the will of God. You cannot pray in the Spirit, with the same degree of fervor and faith for all mankind. Jesus Christ said expressly, He did not pray for all mankind: "I pray not for the world." Here has been a great mistake in regard to the spirit of prayer. Some suppose that Christians have not done all their duty, if they have not prayed in faith for every individual, as long as there is a sinner on earth. Then Jesus Christ never did all His duty, for He never did this. God has never told us He will save all mankind, and never gave us any reason to believe He will do it. How then can we pray in faith for the salvation of all? What has that faith to rest on?

5. Perfect love is not inconsistent with those feelings of languor or constitutional debility, which are the necessary consequence of exhaustion or ill health.

We are so constituted, that excitement naturally and necessarily exhausts our powers. But love may be perfect, notwithstanding. Though one may feel more like lying down and sleeping, than he does like praying, yet his love may be perfect The Lord Jesus Christ often felt this weariness and exhaustion, when the spirit was still willing, but the flesh was weak.

IV. What is essential to perfect love.

I. It implies that there is nothing in the mind inconsistent with love.

No hatred, malice, wrath, envy, or any other malignant emotions that are inconsistent with pure and perfect love.

2. That there is nothing in the life inconsistent with love.

All the actions, words, and thoughts, continually under the entire and perfect control of love.

3. That the love to God is supreme.

The love to God is completely supreme, and so entirely above all other objects, that nothing else is loved in comparison with God.

4. That love to God is disinterested.

God is loved for what He is; not for His relation to us, but for the excellence of His character.

5. That love to our neighbor should be equal, i.e. that his interest and happiness should be regarded by us of equal value with our own, and he and his interests are to be treated accordingly by us.

V. I am to mention some of the effects of perfect love.

1. One effect of perfect love to God and man will certainly be, delight in self-denial for the sake of promoting the interests of God's kingdom and the salvation of sinners.

See affectionate parents, how they delight in self-denial for the sake of promoting the happiness of their children. There is a father; he gives himself up to exhausting labor, day by day, and from year to year, through the whole of a long life, rising early, and eating the bread of carefulness continually, to promote the welfare of his family. And he counts all this self-denial and toil not a grief or a burden, but a delight, because of the love he bears to his family. See that mother; she wishes to educate her son at college, and now, instead of finding it painful it is a joy to her to sit up late and labor incessantly to help him. That is because she really loves her son. Such parents rejoice more in conferring gifts on their children, than they would in enjoying the same things themselves. What parent does not enjoy a piece of fruit more in giving it to his little child, than in eating it himself? The Lord Jesus Christ enjoyed more solid satisfaction in working out salvation for mankind, than any of His saints can never enjoy in receiving favors at His hands. He testified that it is more blessed to give than to receive. This was the joy set before Him for which he endured the cross and despised the shame. His love was so great for mankind, that it constrained Him to undertake this work, and sustained Him triumphantly through it. The apostle Paul did not count it a grief and a hardship to be hunted from place to place, imprisoned, scourged, stoned, and counted the offscouring of all things, for the sake of spreading the gospel and saving souls. It was his joy. The love of Christ so constrained him, he had such a desire to do good, that it was his highest delight to lay himself on that altar as a sacrifice to the cause. Other individuals have had the same mind with the apostle. They have been known who would be willing to live a thousand years, or to the end of time, if they could be employed in doing good, in promoting the kingdom of God, and saving the souls of men, and willing to forego even sleep and food to benefit objects they so greatly love.

2. It delivers the soul from the power of legal motives.

Perfect love leads a person to obey God, not because he fears the wrath of God, or hopes to be rewarded for doing this or that, but because he loves God and loves to do the will of God. There are two extremes on this subject. One class make virtue to consist in doing right, simply because it is right, without any reference to the will of God, or any influence from God. Another class make virtue to consist in acting from love to the employment, but without reference to God's authority, as a Ruler and Law-giver. Both of these are in error. To do a thing simply because he thinks it right, and not out of love to God is not virtue. Neither is it virtue to do a thing because he loves to do it, with no regard to God's will. A woman might do certain things *because* she knew it would please her husband, but if she did the same thing merely because she loved to do it, and with no regard to her husband, it would be no virtue as it respects her husband. If a person loves God, as soon as he knows what is God's will, he will do it *because it is* God's will. Perfect love will lead to universal obedience, to do God's will in all things, because it is the will of God.

3. The individual who exercises perfect love will be dead to the world.

I mean by this, that he will be cut loose from the influence of worldly considerations. Perfect love will so annihilate selfishness, that he will have no will but the will of God, and no interest but God's glory. He will not be influenced by public sentiment, or what this and that man will say or think. See that woman, what she will do from natural affection to her husband? She is willing to cut loose from all her friends, as much as if she was dead to them, and not pay the least regard to what they say, and leave all the riches, and honors, and delights they can offer, to join the individual whom she loves, and live with him in poverty, in disgrace, and in exile. Her affection is so great, that she does it joyfully, and is ready to go from a palace, to any cottage or cave in earth, and be perfectly happy. And all that her friends can say against the man of her affection has not the least influence on her mind, only to make her cling the more closely to him. This one ALL-ABSORBING affection has actually killed all the influences that used to act on her. To attempt to influence her by such things is in vain. There is only one avenue of approach to her mind; only one class of motives move her, and that is through the object of her affection.

So far as the philosophy of mind is concerned, the perfect love of God operates in the same way. The mind that is filled with perfect love, it is impossible to divert from God, while love continues in exercise. Take away his worldly possessions, his friends, his good name, his children, send him to prison, beat him with stripes, bind him to the stake, fill his flesh full of pine knots and set them on fire; and then leave him his God, and he is happy. His strong affection can make him insensible to all things else. He is as if he were dead to all the world but his God. Cases have been known of martyrs who, while their bodies were frying at the stake, were so perfectly happy in God, as to lose their sense of pain. Put such a one in hell, in the lake of fire and brimstone, and as long as he enjoys God, and the love of God fills his soul, he is happy.

Who has not witnessed or heard of cases of affection, approaching in degree to what I have described, where a person is in fact dead to all other things, and lives only for the loved object. How often do you see fond parents, who live for an only child, and when that child dies, wish themselves dead. Sometimes a husband and wife have such an absorbing affection for each other, that they live for nothing else; and if the husband dies, the wife pines away and dies also. The soul-absorbing object for which she lived is gone, and why should she live any longer? So, when an individual is filled with the perfect love of God, he wishes to live only to love and serve God; he is dead to the world, dead to his own reputation, and has no desire to live for any other reason, here, or in heaven, or anywhere else in the universe, but to glorify God. He is willing to live, here or anywhere else, and suffer and labor a thousand years, or to all eternity, if it will glorify God.

I recollect hearing a friend say, often, "I don't know that I have one thought of living a single moment for any other purpose than to glorify God, any more than I should think of leaping right into hell." This was said soberly and deliberately, and the whole life of that individual corresponded with the declaration. He was intelligent, sober-minded, and honest, and I have no doubt expressed what had been the fullest conviction of his mind for years. What was this but perfect love? What more does any angel in heaven do than this? His love may be greater in degree, because his strength is greater. But the highest angel could not love more perfectly than to be able to say in sincerity, "I should as soon think of leaping into hell, as of living one moment for any other object but to glorify God." What could Jesus Christ himself say more than that?

4. It is hardly necessary to say that perfect joy and peace are the natural results of perfect love.

But I wish to turn your attention here to what the apostle says in the 13th chapter of 1 Corinthians, speaking of charity, or love. You will observe that the word here translated *charity* is the same that is in other places rendered *love*. It means love. "Though I speak with the tongues of men and of angels, and have not charity, I am become as sounding brass, or a tinkling cymbal. And though I have the gift of prophecy, and understand all mysteries, and all knowledge; and though I have all faith so that I could remove mountains, and have not charity, I am nothing." He might have even the faith of miracles, so strong that he could move mountains from their everlasting foundations, and yet have no love. "And though I bestow all my goods to feed the poor, and though I give my body to be burned, and have not charity, it profiteth me nothing." You see how far he supposes a man may go without love. "Charity suffereth long." Long-suffering is meekness under opposition or injury. This is one of the effects of love, to bear great provocations, and not retaliate or revile again. Love "is kind," or affectionate in all intercourse with others, never harsh or rude, or needlessly giving pain to any. Love "envieth not," never dislikes others because they are more thought of or noticed, more honored or useful, or make greater attainments in knowledge, happiness or piety. "Is not puffed up" with pride, but always humble and modest. "Doth not behave itself unseemly," but naturally begets a pleasant and courteous deportment towards all. However unacquainted the individual may be with the ways of society, who is actuated by perfect love, he always appears well, it is natural to him to be so kind and gentle and courteous. "Seeketh not her own," or has no selfishness. "Is not easily provoked." This is always the effect of love. See that mother, how long she bears with her children, because she loves them.

If you see an individual that is testy, or crusty, easily flying into a passion when anything goes wrong—he is by no means perfect in love, if he has any love. To be easily provoked is always a sign of pride. If a person is full of love, it is impossible to make him exercise *sinful* anger while love continues. He exercises such indignation as God exercises, and as holy angels feel, at what is base and wrong, but he will not be provoked by it. "Thinketh no evil." Show me a man that is always suspicious of the motives of others, and forever putting the worst construction on the words and actions of his fellow men, and I will show you one who has the devil in him, not the Holy Ghost. He has that in his own mind which makes him think evil of others. If an individual is honest and simple-hearted himself, he will be the last to think evil of others. He will not be always smelling heresy or mischief in others. On the contrary, such persons are often liable to be imposed on by designing men, not from any want of good sense, but from the effect of love. They do not suspect evil, where the exterior appears fair, nor without the strongest proof.

Love "rejoiceth not in iniquity, but rejoiceth in the truth." See a man who exults at his neighbor's fall, or cries out, "I told you so;" and I tell you, that man is far enough from being perfect in love. "Beareth all things," all provocations and injuries, without revenge, "Believeth all things," instead of being hard to be convinced of what is in favor of others, is always ready to believe good wherever there is the least evidence of it. "Hopeth all things;" even where there is reason to suspect evil, as long as there is room for hope, by putting the best construction upon the thing which it will bear. Where you see an individual that has not this Spirit, rest assured, he is by no means perfect in love. Nay, he has no love at all.

I might pursue this course of thought farther, but have not time. "Love worketh no ill to his neighbor." Mark that, NO ILL! Perfect love never overreaches, nor defrauds, nor oppresses, nor does any ill to a neighbor. Would a man under the influence of perfect love, sell his neighbor rum? Never. Would a man that loved God with all his heart, perfectly, hold his neighbor as a slave? "Love worketh *no ill* to his neighbor;" Slavery denies him the wages that he has earned, and perhaps sells him, and tears him away from his family, deprives him of the Bible, and endeavors as far as possible to make him a brute. There cannot be greater falsehood and hypocrisy, than for a man who will do that, to pretend that he loves God. Now that light is shed upon this subject, and the attention of men turned upon it. Will a man hate his own flesh? How can he love God that hates or injures his neighbor?

I designed to remark on one other effect of perfect love. It uniformly shows itself in great efforts for the sanctification of the church and the salvation of souls. Where a person is negligent or deficient in either of these, he is by no means perfect in love, whatever may be his pretensions.

REMARKS.

I. You see why it is true, what the apostle James says, "If any man among you seem to be religious, and bridleth not his tongue, but deceiveth his own heart, this man's religion is vain.

The man that professes to be religious, and yet allows himself to speak against his neighbor with an unbridled tongue, to injure his neighbor, deceives himself, if he thinks he loves his neighbor as himself. Strange love!

II. There may be much light in the mind, concerning religion, without love.

You often see individuals, who understand a great deal, intellectually, about religion, and can spread it out before others, while it is plain they are not actuated by the spirit of love. They have not the law of kindness on their lips.

III. Those individuals who have much religious knowledge and zeal, without love, are most unlovely and dangerous persons.

They are always censorious, proud, heady, high-minded. They may make a strong impression, but do not produce true religion. They zealously affect you, but not well.

IV. The drift of a man's zeal will determine the character of his religion.

It will show whether the light in his mind is accompanied with love. If it is, his zeal will not be sectarian in its character. Show me a man full of jealously towards all that do not belong to his sect or party, and there is a man far enough from perfect love.

True love is never denunciatory or harsh. If it has occasion to speak of the faults of others, it does it in kindness, and with sorrow. Perfect love *cannot* speak in a rough or abusive manner, either to or of others. It will not lay great stress on the mere circumstantials of religion, nor be sticklish for particular measures or forms. Many will contend fiercely either for or against certain things, as for or against new measures; but if they were full of love they would not do it. The zeal that is governed by perfect love will not spend itself in contending for or against any forms in religion, nor attack minor errors and evils. Love leads to laying stress on the fundamentals in religion. It cleaves to warm-hearted Christians, no matter of what denomination they may be, and loves them, and delights to associate with them.

This zeal is never disputatious, or full of controversy. Find a man who loves to attend ecclesiastical meetings, and enters into all the janglings of the day, and that man is not full of love. To a mind filled with holy love, it is exceedingly painful to go to such meetings, and see ministers dividing into parties, and maneuvering, and caucussing, and pettifogging, and striving for the mastery. Find an individual who loves controversy in the newspapers, he is not full of love. If he was, he would rather be abused, and reviled, and slandered, either in person or by the papers, than turn aside to defend himself or to reply. He would never return railing for railing, but contrariwise blessing. And as much as possible, he would live peaceably with all men.

V. How much that is called religion has no love.

How much of what passes for works of religion, is constrained by outward causes and influences, and not by the inward power of love. It ought to be better understood than it is, that unless love is the mainspring, no matter what the outward action may be, whether praying, praising, giving, or anything else, there is no religion in it.—How much excitement that passes for religion, has no love. How much zeal has no religion in it. See that man always full of bitter zeal, and if reproved for it, flying to the example of Paul, when he said, "Thou child of the devil." If he was under the influence of perfect love, he would see that his circumstances are so different as not to justify the exercise of such a spirit.

VI. Those religious excitements which do not consist in the spirit of love, are not revivals of religion.

Perhaps the church may be much excited, and bustle about with a great show of zeal, and boisterous noise, but no tenderness of spirit. Perhaps those who go about may show a spirit of insolence, and rudeness, and pick a quarrel with every family they visit. I once knew a young man who acknowledged that he *aimed* at making people angry, and the reason he assigned was, that it often brought them under conviction, and so issued in conversion. And so it might if he should go in and utter horrid blasphemies in their presence, until they were frightened into a consideration of their own character. But who would defend such a conduct on the ground that such was now and then the result? And if this is the character of the excitement, it may be a revival of wrath, and malice, and all uncharitableness, but it is not a revival of religion. I do not mean that when some or many are "filled with wrath," it is certain evidence that there is no revival of religion. But that when the excitement has this prevailing character, it is not a true revival of religion. Some among them may have the spirit of love, but certainly those who are filled with a bitter disputatious zeal are not truly religious. Religion may be in some individuals revived, but in the main, in such cases, it is a revival of irreligion.

VII. When persons profess to be converted, if love is not the ruling feature in their character, they are not truly converted.

However well they may appear in other respects, no matter how clear their views, or how deep their feelings, if they have not the spirit of love to God, and love to man, they are deceived. Let no such converts be trusted.

VIII. See what the world will be, when mankind are universally actuated by a spirit of love.

We learn that the time will come, when there shall be nothing to hurt or destroy, and when the Spirit of love will universally prevail. What a change in society! What a change in all the methods of doing business, and in all the intercourse of mankind, when each shall love his neighbor as himself, and seek the good of others as his own. Could one of the saints that live now revisit the earth at that day, he would not know the world in which he lived, everything will be so altered. "Is it possible," he would exclaim, "that this is the earth; the same earth that used to be so full of jangling, and oppression, and fraud?"

IX. The thing on which the Lord Jesus Christ is bent, is to bring all mankind under the influence of love.

Is it not a worthy object? He came to destroy the works of the devil. And this is the way to do it. Suppose the world was full of such men as Jesus Christ was in His human nature. Compare it with what it is now. Would not such a change be worthy of the Son of God? What a glorious end, to fill the earth with love!

X. It is easy to see what makes heaven.

It is love—perfect love. And it is easy to see what makes heaven begun on earth, in those who are full of love. How sweet their temper, what delightful companions, how blessed to live near them, to associate with them, so full of candor, so kind, so gentle, so careful to avoid offense, so divinely amiable in all things!

And is this to be attained by men? Can we love God, here in this world, with all the heart, and soul, and strength, and mind? Is it our privilege and our duty to have the Spirit of Christ; and shall we exhibit the spirit of the devil? Beloved, let our hearts be set on perfect love, and let us give God no rest till we feel our hearts full of love, and till all our thoughts and all our lives are full of love to God and love to man. O, when will the church come up to this ground? Only let the church be full of love, and she will be fair as the moon, clear as the sun, and terrible to all wickedness, in high places and low places, as an army with banners.

LECTURE XIII.

REST OF THE SAINTS.

TEXT:—"For we which have believed do enter into rest."
Heb. iv. 3.

The following is the course of thought to which I wish to direct your attention this evening:
I. I shall endeavor to show what *is not the rest* here spoken of.
II. Show *what* it is.
III. Show *when* we are to enter into this rest.
IV. Show *how* to come into possession of this rest.
V. Show that all sin consists in or is caused by unbelief.

I. I will endeavor to show what is not the rest spoken of in the text.
1. It is evidently not a *state of inactivity* in religion, that is spoken of in the text under the name of *rest*.
The apostle who wrote this was very far from being himself inactive in religion, or from encouraging it in others. Those of whom he spoke, including himself, where he says, "WE who haved believed, do enter into rest," would know at once that it was not true, that they had entered into the rest of supineness.
2. Neither are we to understand that the *perfect rest of heaven*, is the rest here spoken of.
He speaks of it a as a present state, "we DO enter," which was not consistent with the idea that heaven is the rest here spoken of. The perfect rest of heaven includes an absolute freedom form all pains, trials, sufferings and temptations of this life.—The rest of the believer here, may be of the *same nature*, substantially, with the rest in heaven. It is that rest begun on earth. But it is not made perfect. It differs in some respects, because it does not imply a deliverance from all trials, pains, sickness, and death. The apostles and primitive Christians had not escaped these trials, but still suffered their full share of them.

II. I will show what we are to understand by the rest here spoken of.
1. It is rest from controversy with God.

In this sense of cessation from controversy, the word rest, is often used in the Bible. In the context, it is said the children of Israel rested, when they were freed from their enemies. It is cessation from strife or war. Those who enter into this rest cease from their warfare with God, from their struggle against the truth, their war with their own conscience. The reproaches of conscience, that kept them in agitation, the slavish fears of the wrath of God under which men exert themselves as slaves in building up their own works, all are done away. They rest.

2. It implies *cessation from our own works.*

(1.) Cessation from works performed *for* ourselves.

Much of the apparent religion there is in the world is made up of works done by people which are their own, in this sense. They are working for their own lives—that is, they have this end in view, and are working *for* themselves, as absolutely as the man who is laboring for his bread. If the object of what you do in religion be, that *you* may be saved, it matters not whether it is from temporal or eternal ruin, it is for yourself, and you have not ceased from you own works, but are still multiplying works of your own. Now, the rest spoken of in the text, is entire cessation from all this kind of works.—The apostle, in verse 10th, affirms this: "He that is entered into his rest, hath ceased from his own works." And in the text, he says, "We that believe do enter," or have entered, "into rest." It is plain that this rest is ceasing from our own works. Not ceasing from all kinds of works, for that is true neither of the saints on earth nor of saints in heaven. We have no reason to believe that any saint or angel, or that God Himself, or any holy being is ever inactive. But we cease to perform works with any such design as merely to save our own souls. It is ceasing to work for ourselves, that we may work for God. We are performing our own works, just as long as the supreme object of our works is to be saved. But if the question of our own salvation is thrown entirely on Jesus Christ, and our works are performed out of love to God, they are not our own works.

(2.) In entering into this rest, we cease from all works performed *from* ourselves, as well as works performed *for* ourselves.

Works are *from* ourselves, when they result from the simple, natural principles of human nature, such as conscience, hope, fear, &c., without the influences of the Holy Ghost. Such works are universally and wholly sinful. They are the efforts of selfishness, under the direction of mere natural principles.—His conscience convicts him, hope and fear come in aid, and under this influence, the carnal, selfish mind acts. Such acts cannot but be wholly sinful. It is nothing but selfishness.—Multiply the forms of selfishness by selfishness forever, and it will never come to love. Where there is nothing but natural conscience pointing out the guilt and danger, and the constitutional susceptibilities of hope and fear leading to do something, it comes to nothing but the natural workings of an unsanctified mind. Such works are always the works of the flesh, and not the works of the Spirit. To enter into rest is to cease from all these, and no more to perform works *from* ourselves than *for* ourselves. Who does not know what a painful time those have, who set about religion from themselves; painfully grinding out about so much religion a month, constrained by hope and fear, and lashed up to the work by conscience, but without the least impulse from that divine principle of the love of God shed abroad in the heart by the Holy Ghost? All such works are just as much from themselves, as any work of any devil is. No matter what kind of works are performed, if the love of God is not the mainspring and life and heart of them, they are our own works, and there is no such thing as rest in them. We must cease from them, because they set aside the gospel. The individual, who is actuated by these principles, sets aside the gospel, in whole or in part. If he is actuated *only* by these considerations, he sets aside the gospel entirely. And just so far as he is influenced by them, he refuses to receive Christ as his Savior in that relation. Christ is offered as a complete Savior, as our Wisdom, Righteousness, Sanctification, and Redemption. And just so far as any one is making efforts to dispense with a Savior in any of these particulars, he is setting aside the gospel for so much.

(3.) To enter into rest implies that we cease from doing anything for ourselves.

We are not so much as to eat or drink for ourselves; "Whether, therefore, ye eat or drink, or whatsoever ye do, do all to the glory of God." The man who has entered into this rest, has ceased from doing it. God requires it, and he that has entered into rest has ceased to have any interest of his own. He has wholly merged his own interest in that of Christ. He has given himself so perfectly to Christ, that he has no work of his own to do. There is no reason why he should go about any work of his own. He knows he might as well sit still till he is in hell, as attempt anything of his own, as to any possibility of saving himself by any exertions of his own. When a man fully understands this, he ceases from making any efforts in this way. See the convicted sinner, how he will strain himself, and put forth all his efforts to help himself, until he learns that he is nothing; and then he ceases from all this, and throws himself helpless and lost, into the hands of Christ. Until he feels that he is in himself without strength, or help, or hope, for salvation or anything that tends to it, he will never think of the simplicity of the gospel. No man applies to Christ for righteousness and strength, until he has used up his own, and feels that he is helpless and undone. Then he can understand the simplicity of the gospel plan, which consists in RECEIVING salvation, by faith, as a free gift. When he has done all that he could, in his own way, and finds that he as grown no better, that he is no nearer salvation, but rather grown worse, that sin is multiplied upon sin, and darkness heaped upon darkness, until he is crushed down with utter helplessness, then he ceases, and gives all up into the hand of Christ. See that sinner, trying to get into a agony of conviction, or trying to understand religion, and finding all dark as Egypt, and cannot see what it is that he must do. O, says he, what must I do? I am willing to do anything. I can't tell why I don't submit, I know not how to do anything more; what am I to do, or *how shall* I find out what is the difficulty? When he is fully convinced, then he turns his eyes to the Savior, and there he finds all he needs, Wisdom, Righteousness, Sanctification, and Redemption. Christ the Life of the world, the Light of the World, the Bread of Life, and he needs nothing of all these but what is in Christ, that all he wants, and all he can ask, is in Christ, and to be received by faith; then he ceases from his own works, and throws himself at once and entirely upon Christ for salvation.

(4.) To cease from our own works is to cease attempting to do anything in our own strength.

Everyone who has entered into rest knows, that whatever he does in his own strength, will be an abomination to God. Unless Christ lives in him, unless God worketh in him, to will and to do, of His good pleasure, nothing is ever done acceptably to God. To set himself to do anything in his own strength, independent of the Spirit of God, is forever an utter abomination to God. He who has not learned this, has not ceased from his own works, and has not accepted the Savior. The apostle says we are not able of ourselves to think anything, as of ourselves. The depth of degradation to which sin has reduced us, is not understood until this is known and felt.

3. To enter into rest also includes the idea of throwing our burdens upon the Lord Jesus Christ.

He invites us to throw all our burdens and cares on Him. "Come unto me, all ye that labor and are heavy laden, and I will give you rest." "Casting all your cares upon him, for he careth for you." These words mean just as they say. Whether your burden is temporal or spiritual, whether your care is for the soul or body, throw it all upon the Lord. See that little child, going along with his father; the father is carrying something that is heavy, and the child takes hold with its little hand to help, but what can he do towards carrying such a load? Many Christians make themselves a great deal of trouble, by trying to help the Lord Jesus Christ in His work. They weary and worry themselves with one thing and another, as if everything hung on their shoulders. Now, the Lord Jesus Christ is as much pledged to the believer for ALL that concerns him, as He is for his justification; and just as absolutely bound for his temporal as for his eternal interests. There is nothing that concerns the Christian, which he is not to cast on the Lord Jesus Christ. I do not mean to be understood, that the Christian has no agency in the matter. Here is a man who has cast his family upon Jesus Christ; but he has not done it in any such manner, that he is not to do anything for his family. But he has so cast himself upon God, for direction, for light, for strength, for success, that he has yielded himself up absolutely to God, to guide and to sustain him; and Christ is pledged to see to it, that everything is done right.

4. To enter into rest is to make the Lord Jesus Christ our Wisdom, our Righteousness, our Sanctification, and our Redemption; and to receive Him in all His offices, as a full and perfect substitute for all our own deficiencies.

We lack all these things, absolutely, and are to receive Him as a full and perfect substitute, to fill the vacancy, and supply all our needs. It is to cease expecting or hoping or attempting anything of ourselves, to fill the vacancy; and receiving Christ as all.

5. Entering into this rest implies the yielding up or our powers so perfectly to His control, that henceforth all our works shall be His works.

I hope you will not understand anything from this language, more mystical than the Bible. It is a maxim of the Common Law, that what a man does by another, he does by himself. Suppose I hire a man to commit murder; the deed is as absolutely my own as if I had done it with my own hand. The crime is not in the hand which struck the blow, any more than it is in the sword, that stabs the victim. The crime is in my mind. If I use another's hand, if my mind, as the moving cause, influenced him, it is my act still. Suppose that I had taken his hand by force, and used it to shoot my neighbor, would not that be my act? Certainly, but it was in my mind, and it is just as much my act, if I influenced his mind to do it. Now apply this principle to the doctrine, that the individual who has entered into rest has so yielded himself up to Christ's control, that all his works are the works of Jesus Christ. The apostle Paul says, "I labored more abundantly than they all; yet not I, but the grace of God in me." And he frequently insists upon it, that it was not himself that did the works, but Christ in him. Do not misunderstand it now. It is no said, and is not to be so understood, that the believer acts upon compulsion, or that Christ acts in him without his own will, but that Christ by His spirit dwelling in him, influences and leads his mind that he acts voluntarily in such a way as to please God. When one ceases from his own works, he so perfectly gives up his own interest and his own will, and places himself so perfectly under the dominion and guidance of the Holy Spirit, that whatever he does is done by the impulse of the Spirit of Christ. The Apostle describes it exactly, when he says, "Work out your own salvation, with fear and trembling, for it is God that worketh in you, to will and to do of his good pleasure." God influences the will, not by force but by love, to do just what will please Him. If it was done by force, we should be no longer free agents. But it is love that so sweetly influences the will, and brings it entirely under the control of the Lord Jesus Christ.

It is not that our agency is suspended, but is employed by the Lord Jesus Christ. Our hands, our feet, our powers of body and mind, are all employed to work for Him. He does not suspend the laws of our constitution, but so directs our agency, that the love of Christ so constrains us, that we will and do of His good pleasure.

Thus you see, that all works that are really good in man, are, in an important sense, Christ's works. This is affirmed in the Bible, over and over again, that our good works are not from ourselves, nor in any way by our own agency without God, but God directs our agency, and influences our wills, to do his will, and we do it. They are in one sense our works, because we do them by our voluntary agency. Yet, in another sense they are His works, because He is the moving cause of all.

6. Entering into this rest implies, that insomuch as we yield our agency to Christ, insomuch we cease from sin.

If we are directed by the Lord Jesus Christ, He will not direct us to sin. Just as far as we give ourselves up to God we cease from sin. If we are controlled by Him so that He works in us, it is to will and to do of His good pleasure. And just so far as we do this, so far we cease from sin. I need not spend time to prove this.

III. I am to inquire *when* they that believe do enter into rest. It is in this life.

1. This appears from the text and context. The apostle in connection with the text, was reasoning with the Jews. He warns them to beware, lest they fail of entering into the true rest, which was typified by their fathers' entering into the land of Canaan. The Jews supposed *that* was the true rest. But the apostle argues with them, to show that there was a higher rest, of which the rest of temporal Canaan was only a type, and into which the Jews might have entered but for their unbelief. If Joshua had given them the real rest, he would not have spoken of another day. Yet another day is spoken of. Even so late as David's day, it is spoken of in the Psalms as yet to come: "To-day, after so long a time; as it is said, Today if ye will hear his voice, harden not your hearts. For if Jesus (that is Joshua) had given them rest, then would he not afterwards have spoken of another day. There remaineth therefore a rest to the people of God." He therefore argues, that the rest in Canaan was not the real rest which was promised, but was typical of the true rest. What then was the true rest? It was the rest of repose of faith in Christ or the gospel state, a cessation from our own works. And believers enter into that state by faith.

I know it is generally supposed that the rest here spoken of is the heavenly rest, beyond this life. But it is manifestly a rest that commences here. "We which believe DO enter into rest." It begins here, but extends into eternity. It is the same in kind, but made there more perfect in degree, embracing freedom from the sorrows and trials to which all believers are subject in this life. But it is the same in kind, the rest of faith, the Sabbath-keeping of the soul when it ceases from its own works, and casts itself wholly upon the Savior.

2. It is manifest that this rest must commence in this world, if *faith* puts us in possession of it. This is the very point that the apostle was arguing, that faith is essential to taking possession of it. They "could not enter in because of unbelief." "Beware, lest ye fail of entering in after the same example of unbelief." He warns them not to indulge in unbelief, because by faith they may take

immediate possession of the rest. If this rest by faith ever commences at all, it must be in this world.

3. The nature of the case proves this. Nothing short of this taking possession of rest is fully embracing Jesus Christ. It is a spiritual rest from the conflict with God, from the stings of conscience, and from efforts to help ourselves by any workings of our own mind. Nothing short of this is getting clear away from the law, or entering fully into the gospel.

IV. I am to show *how* we are to enter into this rest.

From what has already been said, you will understand that we take possession of it by faith.

The text, with the context, shows this. You will recollect also what the Lord Jesus Christ says, Matthew xi. 28,29—"Come unto me, all ye that labor and are heavy laden, and I will give you rest. Take my yoke upon you, and learn of me; for I am meek and lowly in heart; and ye shall find rest unto your souls." Here this same rest is spoken of, and we are told that if we will only come to Christ, we may find it. If we will take His easy yoke, which is love, and trust Him to bear all our burdens, we shall find rest. The Psalmist speaks of the same rest—"Return unto thy rest, O my soul." What Christian does not know what it is to have the soul rest in Christ, to hang upon His arm, and find rest from all the cares and perplexities and sorrows of life?

Again—It is evident that faith in Christ, from its own nature, brings the soul into the very state of rest which I have described. How instantly faith breaks up slavish fear, and brings the soul into the liberty of the gospel! How it sets us free from selfishness, and all those influences we formerly acted under! By faith we confide all to Christ, to lead us, and sanctify us, and justify us. And we may be just as certain to be led and to be sanctified, as we are to be justified, if we only exercise faith and leave ourselves in the hands of Christ *for all.* As a simple matter of fact, such faith brings the soul into a state of rest. The soul sees that there is not need of its own selfish efforts, and no hope from them if they were needed. In itself, it is so far gone in sin that it is as hopeless as if it had been in hell a thousand years. Take the best Christian on earth, and let the Lord Jesus Christ leave his soul, and where is he? Well he pray, or do anything good, or acceptable to God, without Christ! Never. The greatest saint on earth will go right off into sin in a moment, if abandoned by Jesus Christ. But faith throws all upon Christ, and that is rest.

Again: Faith makes us cease from all works *for* ourselves. By faith we see, that we have no more need of doing works for ourselves, than the child needs to work for his daily bread, whose father is worth millions. He may work, from love to his father, or from love to the employment, but not from any necessity to labor for his daily bread. The soul that truly understands the gospel, sees perfectly well that there is no need of mingling his own righteousness with the righteousness of Christ, or his own wisdom with the wisdom of Christ, or His own sufferings with the sufferings of Christ. If there was any need of this, there would be just so much temptation to selfishness, and to working from legal motives. But there is none.

Again: By faith the soul ceases from all works performed *from* itself. Faith brings a new principle into action, entirely above all considerations addressed to the natural principles, of hope and fear and conscience. Faith brings the mind under the influence of love. It takes the soul out from the influences of conscience, lashing it up to duty, and brings it under the influence of the same holy, heavenly principles, that influenced Christ himself.

Again: Faith brings the mind into rest, inasmuch as it brings it to cease from all efforts merely for its own salvation, and puts the whole being in to the hands of Christ.

Faith is confidence. It is yielding up all our powers and interests to Christ, in confidence, to be led, and sanctified, and saved by Him.

It annihilates selfishness, and thus leaves no motives for our own works.

In short: Faith is an absolute resting of the soul in Christ, for all that it needs, or can need. It is trusting Him for everything. For instance—Here is a little child, wholly dependent on its father. Now, if the little child did not trust its father, it must be constantly miserable. It is absolutely dependent on its father, for house and home, food and raiment, and everything under the sun. Yet that little child feels no uneasiness, because it confides in its father. It rests in him, and gives itself no uneasiness, but that he will provide all that it needs. It is just as cheerful and happy, all the day long, as if it had all things in itself, because it has such confidence. Now the soul of the believer rests in Christ, just as the infant does on the arms of its mother. The penitent sinner, like a condemned wretch, hangs all on Christ, without the least help or hope, only as they come from Christ alone, and as Christ does all that is needed.

If faith does consist in thus trusting absolutely in Christ, then it is manifest, that this rest is taken possession of, when we believe; and that it must be in this life, if faith is to be exercised in this life.

V. I am to show that unbelief is the cause of all the sin there is the world.

I do not mean to imply, by this, that unbelief is not itself a sin; but to say, that it is the fountain, out of which flows all other sin. Unbelief is distrust of God, or want of confidence. It is manifest that it was this want of confidence which constituted Adam's real crime. It was not the mere eating of the fruit, but the distrust which led to the outward act, that constituted the real crime, for which he was cast out of Paradise. That unbelief is the cause of all sin, is manifest from the following considerations:

The moment an individual wants faith, and is left to the simple influence of natural principles and appetites, he is left just like a beast, and the things that address his mind through the senses, alone influence him. The motives that influence the mind when it acts right, are discerned by faith. Where there is no faith, there are no motives before the mind, but such as are confined to this world. The soul is then left to its mere constitutional propensities, and gives itself up to the minding of the flesh. This is the natural and inevitable result of unbelief. The eye is shut to eternal things, and there is nothing before the mind, calculated to beget any other action but that which is selfish. It is therefore left to grovel in the dust, and can never rise above its own interest and appetites. It is a natural impossibility that the effect should not be so; for how can the mind act without motives? But the motives of eternity are seen only by faith. The mere mental and bodily appetites that terminate on this world, can never raise the mind above the things of this world, and the result is only sin, sin, sin, the minding of the flesh forever. The very moment Adam distrusted God, he was given up to follow his appetites. And it is so with all other minds.

Suppose a child loses all confidence in his father. He can henceforth render no hearty obedience. It is a natural impossibility. If he pretends to obey, it is only from selfishness, and not from the heart; for the mainspring and essence of all real hearty obedience is gone. It would be so in heaven, it is so in hell. Without faith it is impossible to please God. It is a natural impossibility to obey God in such a manner as to be accepted of Him, without faith. Thus unbelief is shown to be the fountain of all the sin in earth and hell, and the soul that is destitute of faith, is just left to work out its own damnation.

REMARKS.

I. The rest which those who believe do enter into here on earth, is of the same nature with the heavenly rest.

The heavenly rest will be more complete; for it will be a rest from all the sorrows and trials to which even a perfect human soul is liable here. Even Christ himself experienced these trials and sorrows and temptations. But the soul that believes, rests as absolutely in Him here, as in heaven.

II. We see why faith is said to be *the substance* of things hoped for.

Faith is the very thing that makes heaven; and therefor it is the substance of heaven, and will be to all eternity.

III. We see what it is to be led by the Spirit of God.

It is to yield up all our powers and faculties to His control, so as to be influenced by the Spirit in all that we do.

IV. We see that perfect faith would produce perfect love, or perfect sanctification.

A perfect yielding up of ourselves, and continuing to trust all that we have and are to Christ, would make us perfectly holy.

V. We see that just as far as any individual is not sanctified, it is because his faith is weak.

When the Lord Jesus Christ was on earth, if his disciples fell into sin, he always reproached them with a want of faith: "O ye of little faith." A man that believes in Christ has no more right to expect to sin, than he has a right to expect to be damned. You may startle at this, but it is true.

You are to receive Christ as your sanctification, just as absolutely as for your justification. Now you are bound to expect to be damned, unless you receive Christ as your justification. But if you receive Him as such, you have then no reason and no right to expect to be damned. Now, He is just as absolutely your sanctification, as your justification. If you depend upon Him for sanctification, He will no more let you sin, than He will let you go to hell. And it is as unreasonable, and unscriptural and wicked, to expect one as the other. And nothing but unbelief, in any instance, is the cause of your sin. Some of you have read the life of Mrs. Hester Ann Rogers, and recollect how habitual it was with her, when any temptation assailed her, instantly to throw herself upon Christ. And she testifies, that in every instance He sustained her.

Take the case of Peter. When the disciples saw Christ walking upon the water, after their affright was over, Peter requested to be permitted to come to Him on the water, and Christ told him to come; which was a promise on the part of Christ, that if he attempted it, he should be sustained. But for this promise, his attempt would have been tempting God. But with this promise, he had no reason and no right to doubt. He made the attempt, and while he believed, the energy of Christ bore him up, as if he had been walking upon the ground. But as soon as he began to doubt, he began to sink. Just so it is with the soul; as soon as it begins to doubt the willingness and the power of Christ to sustain it in a state of perfect love, it begins to sink. Take Christ at His word, make Him responsible, and rely on Him, and heaven and earth will sooner fail then He will allow such a soul to fall into sin. Say, with Mrs. Rogers, when Satan comes with a temptation, "Lord Jesus, here is a temptation to sin, see thou to that."

VI. You see why the self-denying labors of saints are consistent with being in a state of rest.

These self-denying labors are all constrained by love, and have nothing in them that is compulsory or hard. Inward love draws them to duty. So far is it from being true, that the self-denying labors of Christians are hard work, that it would be vastly more painful to them not to do it. Their love for souls is such, that if they were forbidden to do anything for them, they would be in agony. In fact, a state of inaction would be inconsistent with this rest. How could it be rest, for one whose heart was burning and bursting with love to God and to souls, to sit still and do nothing for them. But it is perfect rest for the soul to go out in prayer and effort for their salvation. Such a soul cannot rest, while God is dishonored and souls destroyed, and nothing done for their rescue. But when all his powers are used for the Lord Jesus Christ, this is true rest. Such is the rest enjoyed by angels, who cease not day nor night, and who are all ministering spirits, to minister to the heirs of salvation.

The apostle says, "Take heed, therefore, lest a promise being left of entering into rest, any of you should come short of it." And "Let us labor therefore, to enter into rest. Do any of you know what it is to come to Christ, and rest in Him? Have you found rest, from all your own efforts to save yourselves, from the thunders of Sinai, and the stings of conscience? Can you rest sweetly in Jesus, and find in Him everything essential to sanctification and eternal salvation? Have you found actual salvation in Him? If you have, then you have entered into rest. If you haven't found this, it is because you are still laboring to perform your own works.

CHAPTER XIV.

CHRIST THE HUSBAND OF THE CHURCH.

TEXT:—"Wherefore, my brethren, ye also are become dead to the law by the body of Christ; that ye should be married to another, even to him who is raised from the dead, that we should bring forth fruit unto God."—Romans vii 4

In the discussion of this subject, the following is the order in which I shall direct your thoughts:
I. Show that the marriage state is abundantly set forth in the Bible, as describing the relation between Christ and the church.
II. Show what is implied in this relation.
III. The reason for the existence of this relation.
IV. Show the great guilt of the church, in conducting towards Christ as she does.
V. The forbearance of Christ towards the church.

I. I am to show that the marriage state is abundantly set forth in the Bible, as describing the relation between Christ and the church.

Christ is often spoken of as the husband of the church. "Thy Maker is thy husband, the Lord of Hosts is his name." "Turn, O backsliding children, saith the Lord, for I am married unto you." The church is spoken of as the bride, the Lamb's wife. "The Spirit and the Bride say, Come." That is, Christ and the church say, "Come." In 2 Corinthians xi. 2, the apostle Paul says, "For I am jealous over you with godly jealously: for I have espoused you to one husband, that I may present you as a chaste virgin to Christ." I can merely refer to these passages. You that are acquainted with your Bibles, will not need that I should take up time to show that this relation is often adverted to in the Bible, in a great variety of forms.

II. I am to show what is implied in this relation.
1. The wife gives up her own name, and assumes that of her husband.

This is universally true in the marriage state. And the church assumes the name of Christ, and when united with Him is baptized into His name.

2. The wife's separate interest is merged in that of her husband.

A married woman has no separate interest, and no right to have any. So the church has no right to have a separate interest from the Lord Jesus Christ. If a wife has property, it goes to her husband. If it is real estate, the life interest passes to him, and if it is personal estate, the whole merges in him.

The reputation of the wife is wholly united to that of her husband, so that his reputation is hers, and her reputation is his. What affects her character, affects his; and what affects his character, affects hers. Their reputation is one, their interests are one. So with the church, whatever concerns the church is just as much the interest of Christ, as if it was personally His own matter. As the husband of the church, He is just as much pledged to do everything that is needful to promote the interest of the church, as the husband is pledged to promote the welfare of his wife. As a faithful husband gives up his time, his labor, his talents, to promote the interest and happiness of his wife; so Jesus Christ gives Himself up to promote the welfare of His church. He is as jealous of the reputation of His church, as ever a husband was of the reputation of his wife. Never was a human being so pledged, so devoted to the interest of his wife, or felt so keenly an injury, as Jesus Christ feels when His church has her reputation or her feelings injured. He declares that it were better a man had a mill stone hanged about his neck, and he were cast into the depths of the sea, than that he should offend one of these little ones that believe in Him.

3. The relation between husband and wife is such, that if anything is the matter with one, the other is full of sympathy.

So Christ feels for all the sufferings of the church, and the church feels for all the sufferings of Christ. When a believer has any realizing view of the sufferings of Christ, there is nothing in the universe so affects and dissolves the mind with sorrow. Never did a wife feel such distress, such broken-hearted grief, if she has occasioned suffering or death to her husband, as the Christian feels when he views his sins as the occasion of the death of Jesus Christ. Let me ask some of these married women present, how you would feel, if your husband, to redeem you from merited ignominy and death, had volunteered the greatest suffering and pain, and even death for you? When you saw his face, how would it affect you? To be reminded of it by any circumstance, how would it melt you down in broken-hearted grief? Now, have you never understood that your sins caused the death of Christ, and that He died for you just as absolutely, as if you had been the only sinner in all God's world? He suffered pain and contempt and death for you. He loved His church, and gave Himself for it. It is called the church of God, which He purchased with His own blood.

4. *The wife pledges herself to yield her will to the will of her husband, and to yield obedience to his will.*

She has no separate interest, and ought to have no separate will. The Bible enjoins this, and makes it a Christian duty for the wife to conform in all things to the will of her husband. The will of the husband becomes to the faithful wife the mainspring of her activity. Her entire life is only carrying out the will of her husband. The relation of the church to Christ is precisely the same. The church is governed by Christ's will.—When believers exercise faith, they are so, absolutely, and the will of Christ becomes the moving cause of all their conduct.

5. *The wife recognizes her husband as her head.*

The Bible declares that he is so. In like manner, as from the head proceed those influences that govern the body, so from Christ proceed those influences that govern the church.

6. *The wife looks to her husband as her support, her protector and her guide.*

Every believer places himself as absolutely under the protection of Christ, as a married woman is under the protection of her husband. The woman naturally looks to her husband to preserve her from injury, from insult, and from want. She hangs her happiness on him, and expects he will protect her; and he is bound to do it.

So Christ is pledged to protect His church from every foe. How often have the powers of hell tried to put down the church, but her husband has never abandoned her. No weapon formed against the church has ever been allowed to prosper, or ever shall. Never will the Lord Jesus Christ so far forget His relation to the church, as to have His bride unprotected. No. Let all earth and all hell conspire against the church, and just as certain as Christ has power to do it, His church is safe. And every individual believer is just as safe, as if he were the only believer on earth, and has Christ as truly pledged for his preservation. The devil can no more put down a single believer, to final destruction, than he can put down God Almighty. He may murder them, but that is no injury. Overcoming a believer by taking his life, affords Satan no triumph. He put Christ to death, but what did he gain by it? The grave had no power over

Him, to retain Him. So with a believer; neither the grave nor hell has any more power to injure one of Christ's little ones, that believe in Him, than they have to injure Christ Himself. He says, "Because I live, ye shall live also." And, "He that believeth in me, though he were dead, yet shall he live; and whosoever liveth, and believeth in me, shall never die."—There is no power in the universe, that can prevail against a single believer, to destroy him. Jesus Christ is the Head of the church, and Head over all things to the church, and the church is safe.

7. The legal existence of the wife is so merged in that of her husband, that she is not known in law as a separate person.

If any actions or civil liability come against the wife, the husband is responsible. If the wife has committed a trespass, the husband is answerable. It is his business to guide and govern her, and her business to obey; and if he does not restrain her from breaking the laws, he is responsible. And if the wife does not obey her husband, she has it in her power to bring him into great trouble, disgrace, and expense. In like manner, Jesus Christ is Lord over His church, and if He does not actually restrain His church from sin, He has it to answer for, and is brought into great trouble and reproach by the misconduct of His people. By human laws, the husband is not liable for capital crimes committed by the wife, but the law so far recognizes her separate existence, as to punish her. But Christ has assumed the responsibility for His church, of *all* her conduct. He took the place of His people, when they were convicted of capital crimes, and sentenced to eternal damnation. This is answering in good earnest. And now it is His business to take care of the church, and control her, and keep her from sin; and for every sin of every member, Jesus Christ is responsible, and must answer. And He does answer for them. He has made an atonement to cover all this, and ever liveth to make intercession for His people. So that He holds himself responsible before God for all the conduct of His church. Every believer is so a part of Jesus Christ, and so perfectly united to Him, that whatever any of them may be guilty of, Jesus Christ takes upon Himself to answer for. This is abundantly taught in the Bible.

What an amazing relation! Christ has here assumed the responsibility, not only for the civil conduct of his church, but even for the capital crime of rebellion against God. There is a sense, therefore, in which the church is lost in Christ, and has no separate existence known in law. God has so given up the church to Christ, by the covenant of grace, that strictly speaking, the church is not known in law. I do not mean that crimes, committed by believers against the moral law, are not sin, but that the law cannot get hold of them, for condemnation. There is now no condemnation to them that are *in* Christ Jesus. The penalty of the law is forever remitted. The crimes of the believer are not taken into account so as to bring him under condemnation; no, in no case whatever. Whatever is to be done falls upon Christ. He has assumed the responsibility of bringing them off from under the power of sin, as well as from under the law, and stands pledged to give them all the assistance they need to gain a complete victory.

III. I am to explain the reason why this relation is constituted between Christ and His church.

1. The first reason is assigned in the text, "that we should bring forth fruit unto God." A principal design of the institution of marriage is the propagation of the species. So it is in regard to the church. Through the instrumentality of the church, children are to be born to Christ, and He is to see His seed, and to see of the travail of His soul, and be satisfied, by converts multiplied as the drops of morning dew. It is not only through the travail of the Redeemer's soul, but through the travail of the church, that believers are born unto Jesus Christ. As soon as Zion travailed, she brought forth children.

2. Another object of the marriage institution is the protection and support of those who are naturally helpless and dependent. If the law of power prevailed in society, everybody knows that females, being the weaker sex, would be universally enslaved. And the design of the institution of marriage is to secure protection and support to those who are so much more frail, that by the law of force they would be continually enslaved. So Jesus Christ upholds His church, and affords her all the protection against her enemies, and all the powers of hell, that she needs.

3. The mutual happiness of the parties is another end of the marriage institution.

The same is true of the relation between Christ and His church. Perhaps you will think it strange, if I tell you that the happiness of Christ is increased by the love of the church. But what does the Bible say? "Who, for the joy set before him, endured the cross, despising the shame." What was the joy set before him, if the love of the church was not a part of it? It would be very strange to hear of a husband contributing to the happiness of his wife, that should not enjoy it himself. Jesus Christ enjoys the happiness of His church as much more, as He loves His church better than any husbands love their wives.

4. The alleviation of mutual sufferings and sorrows is one end of marriage.

Sharing each other's sorrow is a great alleviation. Who does not know this? In like manner do Christ and His church share each other's sorrows. The apostle Paul says he was always bearing about in his body the dying of the Lord Jesus; "For as the sufferings of Christ abound in us, so our consolation also aboundeth by Christ." And he declared that one end of all his toils and self-denials was that he might know the fellowship of Christ's sufferings." And he rejoiced in all his sufferings, that he might fill up that which was behind of the afflictions of Christ. The church feels, keenly, every reproach cast upon Christ, and Christ feels keenly every injury inflicted on the church.

5. The principal reason for this union of Christ with His church, is that he may sanctify the church.

Read what is said in Ephesians v. 22-27. "Wives, submit yourselves unto your own husbands, as unto the Lord. For the husband is the head of the wife, even as Christ is the head of the church; and he is the Savior of the body. Therefore as the church is subject unto Christ, so let the wives be to their own husbands in everything. Husbands, love your wives, even as Christ also loved the church, and gave himself for it; that he might sanctify and cleanse it with the washing of water by the word. That he might present it to himself a glorious church, not having spot or wrinkle, or any such thing; but that it should be holy and without blemish."

Here then is set forth the great design of Christ in marrying the church. It is that He might sanctify it, and cleanse it, or that it should be perfectly holy and without blemish. John, in the Revelation informs us that he saw those who had washed their robes and made them white in the blood of the Lamb. See how beautifully the Bride, the Lamb's wife, is described in the 21st chapter, coming down from God out of heaven, prepared as a bride adorned for her husband.

IV. I will make a few remarks on the wickedness of the church, in conducting towards Christ as she does.

1. Vast multitudes of those who profess to be a part of the church, the bride of Christ, really set up a separate interest.

They have pretended to merge their self-interest in the interest of Christ, but manifestly keep up a separate interest. And if you attempt to make them act on the principle that they have no separate interest, they will plainly show, that they have no such design. What would you think of a wife, keeping up a separate interest from her husband? You would say it was plain that she did not love her husband, as she ought.

2. The church is not satisfied with Christ's love.

Everybody knows what an abominable thing it is for a wife, not to be satisfied with the love of her husband, but continually seeking other lovers, and always associating with other men. Yet, how plain it is that the church is not satisfied with the love of Christ, but is always seeking after other lovers. What are we to think of those members of the church, who are not satisfied with the love of Christ for happiness, but must have the riches and pleasures and honors of the world to make them happy?

Still more horrible would be the conduct of a wife, who should select her lovers from the enemies of her husband, and should bring them home with her, and make them her chosen friends. Yet how many who profess to belong to Christ go away, and give their affections to Christ's enemies. Some will even marry those whom they know to be haters of God and religion. Horrible! Is that the way a bride should do?

3. Everyone knows that it is a disgraceful thing for the wife to play the harlot.

Yet God often speaks of His church as going astray and committing spiritual whoredom. And it is true. He does not make this charge, as a man makes it against his wife, when he is determined to leave her and cast her off. But he makes it with grief and tenderness, and accompanies it with the moving expostulations, and the most melting entreaties that she would return.

4. What would you think of a married woman, who should expect, at the very time of her marriage, that she should get tired of her husband, and leave him and play the harlot?

Yet, how many there are, professors of religion, who when they made a profession had no more expectation of living without sin, than they expected to have wings and fly. They have come into His house, and pledged themselves to live entirely for Him, and married Him in this public manner, covenanting to forsake all sin, and to live alone for Christ, and be satisfied with His love, and have no other lovers; and yet all the while they are doing it, they expect in their minds that they shall scatter their ways to strangers upon every high hill, and commit sin and dishonor Christ.

5. What are we to think of a woman, who at the very time of her marriage, expected to continue in her course of adultery as long as she lives, in spite of all the commands and expostulations of her husband?

Then what are we to think of professors of religion, who deliberately expect to commit spiritual adultery, and continue in it as long as they live?

6. But the most abominable part of such a wife's wickedness is, when she turns round and charges the blame of her conduct upon her faithful husband.

Now the church does this. Notwithstanding Christ has done all that He could do, short of absolute force, to keep His church from sinning, yet the church charges her sin upon Him, as if He had laid her under an absolute necessity of sinning, by not making any adequate provision for preserving His people against temptation. And they are horrified now at the very name of Christian Perfection, as if it was really dishonoring Christ to believe that He is able to keep His people from committing sin and falling into the snare of the devil. And so it has been, for hundreds of years, that with the greater part of the church it has not been orthodox to teach that Jesus Christ really has made such provision that His people may live free from sin. And it is really considered a wonder, that anybody should teach that the bride of the Lord Jesus Christ is expected to do as she pretends to do. Has He married a bride, and made no provision adequate to protect her against the arts and seductions of the devil? Well done! That must be the ridicule of hell.

7. Suppose a wife should refuse to obey her husband and then make him responsible for her conduct.

Yet the church refuses to obey Jesus Christ, and then makes Him answer for her sins. This is the great difficulty with the church, that she is continually bringing in her Head for her delinquencies.

8. The church is continually dishonoring Christ.

The reputation of husband and wife is one. Whatever dishonors one, dishonors the other. Now, the church, instead of avoiding every appearance of evil, is continually causing the enemies of God to blaspheme by her conduct.

V. I will say a few words on the forbearance of Christ towards the church.

What other husband, in such circumstances, would suffer the connection to remain, and bear what Christ bears? Yet He still offers to be reconciled, and lays himself out to regain the affections of His bride. Sometimes a husband really loses his affection towards his wife, and treats her so like a brute that, although she once loved him, she loves him no more. But where can anything be found in the character and conduct of Christ, to justify the treatment He receives? He has laid himself out to the utmost, to engross the affections of the church. What could He have done more? Where can any fault or any deficiency be found in Him. And even after all that the church has done against Him, What is He doing now? Suppose a husband should for years follow his wandering, guilty wife, from city to city, beseeching and entreating her, with tears, to return to his house and be reconciled; and after all, she should persist in going after her lovers, and yet he continues to cry after her and beg her to come back and live with him, and he will forgive and love her still. Is there any such forbearance and condescension known among men?

REMARKS.

I. Christians ought to understand the bearing of their sins.

Your sins dishonor Christ, and grieve Christ, and injure Christ, and then you make Christ responsible for them. You sustain such a relation to Him, and you ought to know what is the effect of your sin. How does a wife feel, when she has disgraced her husband? How blushes cover her face, and tears fill her eyes! When her guilty offended husband comes into her presence, how she falls down at his feet, with a full heart, and confesses her fault, and pours her penitential tears into his bosom. She is grieved and humbled, and though she loves him, his very presence is a grief, until she breaks down before him, and feels that he has forgiven her.

Now how can a Christian fail to recognize this; and when he is betrayed into sin and has injured Christ, how can he sleep? How can you help realizing that your sins take hold of Jesus Christ, and injure him, in all these tender relations?

II. One great difficulty of Christians is their expecting to live in sin, and this expectation insures their continuance in sin.

If an individual expects to live in sin, he in fact means to live in sin, and of course he will live in sin. It is very much to be feared, that many professors of religion never really meant to live without sin. The apostle insists that believers should reckon themselves dead to sin, that they should henceforth have no more to do with it than if they were dead, and no more expect to sin than a dead man should expect to walk. They should throw themselves upon Christ, and receive Him in all His relations, and expect to be preserved and sanctified and saved by Him. If they would do this, do you not suppose they would be kept from sin? Just as certainly as they believe in Christ for it. To believe in Christ that He will keep them, insures the result that He will. And the reason why they do not receive preserving grace at all times, as they need and all they need, is that they do not expect it, and do not trust in Christ to preserve them in perfect love. The man tries to preserve himself. Instead of throwing himself upon Christ, he throws himself upon his own resources, and then in his weakness expects to sin, and of course he does sin. If he knew his own entire emptiness, and would throw himself upon Christ as absolutely, and rest on Christ as confidently, for sanctification, as for justification, the one is just as certain as the other.

No one that trusted in God for anything He has promised, ever failed to receive according to his faith, the very thing for which he trusted. If you trust in God for what He has not promised, that is tempting God. If Peter had not been called by Christ to come to him on the water, it would have been tempting God for him to get down out of the ship into the water, and he would have lost his life for his presumption and folly. But as soon as Christ told him to come, it was merely an act of sound and rational faith for him to do it. It was a pledge on the part of Christ, that he should be sustained; and so he was sustained, as long as he had faith. Now, if the Bible has promised that those who receive Christ as their sanctification shall be sanctified, then you who believe in Him for this end have just as much reason to expect it, as Peter had to expect he should walk on the waves. It is true, we do not expect a miracle to be wrought to sustain the believer, as it was to sustain Peter. But it is promised that he shall be sustained, and if miracles were necessary, no doubt they would be performed, for God would move the universe, and turn the course of nature upside down, sooner than one of His promises should fail, to them that put their trust in Him. If God is pledged to anything, a person that venture, on that pledge will find it redeemed, just as certainly as God possesses almighty power. Has God promised sanctification to them that trust Him for it? If He has not, then to go to Him in faith for preservation from temptation and sin is tempting God. It is fanaticism. If God has left us to the dire necessity of getting along with our own watchfulness and our own firmness and strength, we must submit to it, and do the best we can. But if He has made any promises, He will redeem them to the uttermost, though all earth and all hell should oppose. And so it is in regard to the mistakes and errors which Christians fall into. If there is no promise that they shall be guided just so far as they need, and led into the truth, and in the way of duty and of peace; then for a Christian to look to God for knowledge, and wisdom, and guidance, and direction, without any promises, is tempting God. But if there are promises on this subject, depend on it, they will be fulfilled to the very last mite to the believer who trusts in them; and exercising confidence in such promises is only a sober and rational faith in the word of God.

I believe the great difficulty of the church on the subject of Christian perfection lies here, that she has not fully understood how the Lord Jesus Christ is wholly pledged in all these relations, and that the church has just as much reason and is just as much bound to trust in Him for sanctification as for justification. What saith the scripture? "Who of God is made unto us wisdom, and Righteousness, and Sanctification, and Redemption." How came the idea to be taken up in the church, that Jesus Christ is our Redemption, and has made Himself responsible for the meanest individual who throws himself on Him for justification shall infallibly obtain it? This has been universally admitted in the church, in all ages. But it is no more plainly or more abundantly taught, than it is, that Jesus Christ is promised and pledged for Wisdom and for Sanctification to all that receive Him in these relations. Has He promised that if any man lack wisdom, he may ask of God, and if he asks in faith, God will give it to him? What then?—Is there then no such thing as being preserved by Christ from falling into this and that delusion and error? God has made this broad promise, and Christ is as much pledged for our wisdom and our sanctification, if we only trust in Him, as He is for our justification. If the church would only renounce any expectation from herself, and die as absolutely to her own wisdom and strength, as she does to her own righteousness, or the expectation of being saved by her own works, Jesus Christ is as much pledged for one as for the other. The only reason why the church does not realize the same results, is that Christ is trusted for justification, and as for wisdom and sanctification He is not trusted.

The truth is, the great body of believers, having begun in the Spirit, are now trying to be made perfect by the flesh. We have thrown ourselves on Christ for justification, and then have been attempting to sanctify ourselves. If it is true, as the apostle affirms, that Christ is to the church both wisdom and sanctification, what excuse have Christians for not being sanctified?

III. If individuals do not as much expect to live without sin against Christ, as they expect to live without open sins against men, such as murder or adultery, it must be for one of three reasons:

1. Either we love our fellow men better than we do Christ, and so are less willing to do them an injury.

2. Or we are restrained by a regard to our own reputation; and this proves that we love reputation more than Christ.

3. Or we think we can preserve ourselves better from these disgraceful crimes than we can from less heinous sins.

Suppose I were to ask any of you, if you expect to commit murder, or adultery? Horrible! you say. But why not? Are you so virtuous that you can resist any temptation which the devil can offer? If you say so, you do not know yourself. If you have real power to keep yourself, so as to abstain from openly disgraceful sins, in your own strength, you have power to abstain from all sins. But if your only reliance is on Jesus Christ to keep you from committing murder and adultery, how is it, that you should get the idea, that He is not equally able to keep you from all sin? O, if believers would only throw themselves wholly on Christ, and make Him responsible, by placing themselves entirely at His control, they would know His power to save, and would live without sin.

IV. What a horrible reproach is the church to Jesus Christ.

V. You see why it is that converts are what they are.

Degenerate plants of a strange vine, sure enough! The church is in such a state, that it is no wonder those who are brought in, with few exceptions, prove a disgrace to religion. How can it be otherwise? How can the church, living in such a manner, bring forth offspring that shall do honor to Christ? The church does not, and individual believers do not, in general, receive Christ in all His offices, as He is offered in the Bible. If they did, it would be impossible they should live like such loathsome harlots.

www.ingramcontent.com/pod-product-compliance
Lightning Source LLC
Chambersburg PA
CBHW060816190426
43197CB00038B/1692